# Writing Matters

## PROCESS AND PRACTICE

# D. J. Henry

Daytona State College

**Longman**

New York   San Francisco   Boston
London   Toronto   Sydney   Tokyo   Singapore   Madrid
Mexico City   Munich   Paris   Cape Town   Hong Kong   Montreal

Adapted from D.J. Henry, *Writing for Life*

**Longman Publishers**
**Acquisitions Editor:** Matthew Wright
**Development Editor:** Katharine Glynn
**Marketing Manager:** Thomas DeMarco
**Senior Supplements Editor:** Donna Campion
**Production Manager:** Ellen MacElree
**Project Coordination:** Nesbitt Graphics, Inc.
**Cover Design Manager:** Wendy Ann Fredericks
**Cover Designer:** Dorling Kindersley
**Cover Photos:** *from left to right:* Image
  Source/Corbis; Stock Take/Alamy; Image
  Source Black/Alamy; and Think Stock
  Images/Jupiter Images.
**Image Permission Coordinator:** Joanne Dippel
**Manufacturing Manager:** Mary Fischer
**Printer and Binder:** Courier Kendallville
**Cover Printer:** Coral Graphic Services

**DK Education**
**Managing Art Editor:** Anthony Limerick
**Designers:** Ann Cannings and
  Ian Midson
**Design Director:** Stuart Jackman
**Publisher:** Sophie Mitchell

For permission to use copyrighted material, grateful acknowledgment is made to the copyright holders on page 435, which is hereby made part of this copyright page.

Cataloging-in-Publication Data on file at the Library of Congress

Please visit our website at http://www.ablongman.com/studyskills

ISBN 13: 978-0-205-63308-1
ISBN 10:  0-205-63308-0

1 2 3 4 5 6 7 8 9—CRK—11 10 09 08

**Longman**
is an imprint of

http://www.ablongman.com

# Dedication

*To my foremost teacher, my mom, Mary Maxine Powell*

Script in your head - roteiro
hours roaming the neighorhood - Naguear.
grasp grammar rules. agarrar, perceber.
gut - peito - coragem

# Brief Contents

# Detailed Contents

## Getting Ready to Write

## Using Patterns of Organization to Develop Paragraphs

## Part 1

## Part 2

# Writing an Essay

# Mastering Grammar, Punctuation, and Mechanics with MyWritingLab

**Part**

**3**

**Part**

**4**

# Part 5 Reading Selections

**Part**

# 5

# Preface

Writing requires confidence and courage. Every word that flows from mind to paper reveals something about who we are in that moment—our depth of thought, our mastery of language, our ability to connect to others. Our students have a gut-level understanding of the risks posed by writing, particularly in the writing classroom where assignments can seem artificial, and grades, editing marks, and high-stakes exit exams often infuse the writing experience with great anxiety. In a few short weeks, students need to master text structure, improve vocabulary, comprehend writing situations, develop a writing process, grasp grammar rules, change life-long habits, and find their voices.

As their guides and mentors, we writing teachers need a systematic curriculum that engages students with high-interest activities that cultivate success and that fosters deep growth as quickly as possible. *Writing Matters* offers a consistent approach that addresses the complex needs of the developing writer and communicates the power and importance of writing in everyday, college, and work situations. *Writing Matters* guides students step by step through writing instruction while showing them how to take responsibility for their learning.

*Writing Matters* is the culmination of over two decades of experience and education. In 1984, when I first volunteered to serve as a reader for Florida's College Level Academic Skills Test (CLAST), a state-wide exam, I had no idea what invaluable lessons I would learn about writing, the teaching of writing, and the assessment of writing. My motivation was to learn what I could about the test to better prepare my students. During the early years of my twenty-plus-year involvement with state-wide assessment, I began experimenting with portfolio assessment. Analyzing and using the scoring rubric dramatically improved my own abilities to write well, and I was eager for my students to experience the same kind of radical improvements in their own writing. Consequently, I began to write rubrics and create reflective questions that helped students to self-assess and take control of their learning. I quickly learned that they faced barriers that went beyond writing concepts and skills, so my lessons, rubrics, and reflective questions expanded to include learning styles, behavioral patterns, and habitual attitudes. Their improvement was amazing and encouraging!

My experiences with the CLAST exam and then later with the Florida Basic Skills Exit Exam, along with my growing understanding of authentic assessment, prepared me for my work with two key federally funded Title III grants at Daytona Beach Community College.

The first grant established the college's developmental program that included reading, writing, math, and student success. I acted as the portfolio consultant and facilitated the development of a comprehensive classroom portfolio assessment system for each of the four disciplines. Together, my colleagues and I learned about how to use writing to learn; we raised our awareness about various learning styles and pedagogical approaches; and we deepened our understanding of the connection between reading, writing, and learning in various disciplines. During the second grant, I served as Curriculum Revision Director. My role was to research best practices; offer instruction to professors about reading and writing in their content areas; and facilitate the revision of curriculum to incorporate meaningful, realistic reading and writing assignments in content areas. I learned much about what is expected of our students once they exit our developmental programs. These important lessons are the foundations of *Writing Matters*. I love to write and I love to teach, but, most of all, I love to see students succeed. The following series of purpose statements best summarizes my mission in *Writing Matters*.

- *Writing Matters is a highly motivational book geared to actively engage students and inspire their confidence in their own success.*

- *Writing Matters empowers students to identify and overcome barriers and to take responsibility for their learning.*

- *Writing Matters establishes, illustrates, and reinforces the connection between effort and improvement.*

- *Writing Matters fosters understanding and nurtures growth.*

- *Writing Matters clearly explains, demonstrates, and reinforces writing concepts, skills, and applications.*

- *Writing Matters illustrates the power of writing in life.*

On a final and most important note, if I could speak directly to every student who holds this book, I would offer the following encouragement. Writing well is a learned behavior, and you can learn most anything you put your mind to. Always remember, every minute you spend learning to write is an investment in yourself and your future. You're worth the effort. A great writer named Emerson once said, "Look to yourself and do good because you are good." Emerson expresses great faith in and respect for our individual abilities. I share his faith and have great confidence in *your ability* to master writing for life. You *can* do it—*writing matters!*

Sincere wishes for your success,
D. J. Henry

MyWritingLab has helped students all over the country move on to college courses. MyWritingLab can help you become a better writer and help you get a better grade.

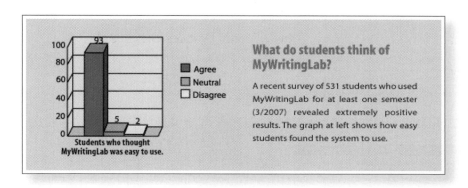

### What do students think of MyWritingLab?

A recent survey of 531 students who used MyWritingLab for at least one semester (3/2007) revealed extremely positive results. The graph at left shows how easy students found the system to use.

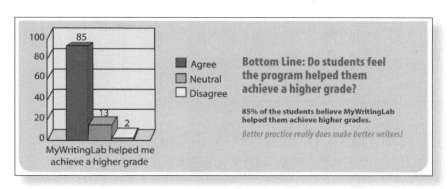

### Bottom Line: Do students feel the program helped them achieve a higher grade?

85% of the students believe MyWritingLab helped them achieve higher grades.

*Better practice really does make better writers!*

**www.mywritinglab.com**

# REGISTER ...

It is easy to get started! Simply follow these easy steps to get into your MyWritingLab course.

1  **Find Your Access Code** (it is either packaged with your textbook, or you purchased it separately). You will need this access code and your CLASS ID to log into your MyWritingLab course. Your instructor has your CLASS ID number, so make sure you have that before logging in.

2  Click on "Students" in the Register or Buy Access box. Here you will be prompted to enter your access code, enter your e-mail address, and choose your own Login Name and Password. **Once you register, you can click on "Returning users" and use your new login name and password every time you go back into your course in MyWritingLab.**

After logging in, you will see all the ways MyWritingLab can help you become a better writer.

**www.mywritinglab.com**

# HOME PAGE ...

Here is your MyWritingLab Home Page. You get a bird's eye view of where you are in your course every time you log in.

Your Course box shows you your class details.
Your Study Plan box shows what you last completed and what is next on your To Do list.
Your Gradebook box shows you a snapshot of how you are doing in the class.
Your Other Resources box supplies you with amazing tools such as:

- Pearson Tutor Services – click here and see how you can get help on your papers by qualified tutors ... before handing them in!

- Research Navigator – click here and see how this resembles your library with access to online journals to research paper assignments.

- Study Skills Website – click here for extra help that includes tips and quizzes on how to improve your study skills.

Now, let's start practicing to become better writers. Click on the View Study Plan button in the Study Plan tab. Your Study Plan is where you will do all your course work.

**www.mywritinglab.com**

# STUDY PLAN ...

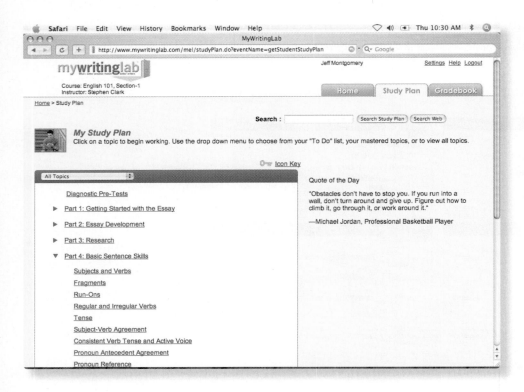

MyWritingLab provides you with a simple To Do list of the main writing skills that you need to master to be prepared for Freshman Composition. Start from the top of the list and work your way down. You may start with the Diagnostic Pre-Tests if your instructor has selected this option for you.

# DIAGNOSTIC PRE-TESTS ...

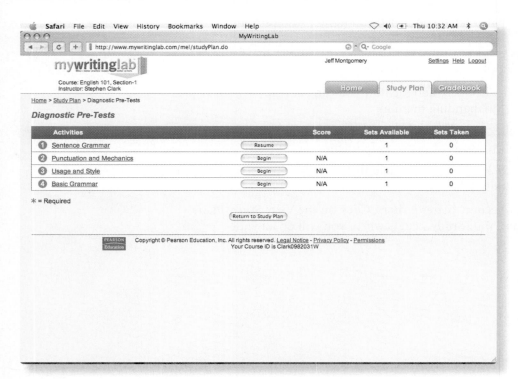

MyWritingLab's Diagnostic Pre-Tests are divided into four parts and cover all the major grammar, punctuation and usage topics. After you complete these diagnostic tests, MyWritingLab will generate a personalized Study Plan for you, showing all the topics you have mastered and listing all the topics yet unmastered.

**www.mywritinglab.com**

# DIAGNOSTIC PRE-TESTS …

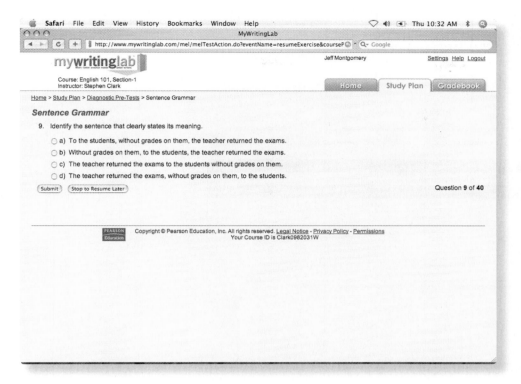

The Diagnostic Pre-Tests contain exercises on Sentence Grammar, Punctuation and Mechanics, Usage and Style, and Basic Grammar. You can achieve mastery of a topic based on your score in the Diagnostic Pre-Test.

After completing the Diagnostic Pre-Test you can return to your Study Plan to practice the topics you have yet to master.

**www.mywritinglab.com**

# WATCH, RECALL, APPLY, WRITE ...

Here is an example of a MyWritinglab Activity set that you will see once you enter into a topic on your To Do list. Take the time to briefly read the introductory paragraph and then watch the animated tutorial in the Review Materials section of the screen.

The tutorial provides you with a helpful review. Now you are ready to start the exercises. There are three types of exercises:

- Recall – activities that help you *recall* the rules of grammar that you learned about in the animated tutorial

- Apply – activities that help you *apply* these rules to brief paragraphs

- Write – activities that ask you to demonstrate these rules of grammar in your own writing

**www.mywritinglab.com**

# WATCH, RECALL, APPLY, WRITE …

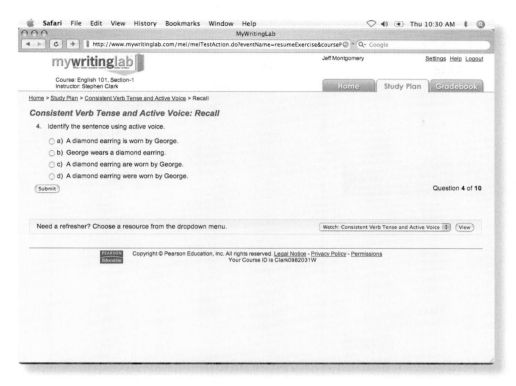

Recall questions help you recall the rules of grammar and writing. They are multiple-choice questions, usually with four possible answers. You get feedback after each question, so you can learn as you go!

There are many sets available for lots of practice. As soon as you are finished with a set of activities, you will receive a score sheet with helpful feedback, including the correct answers. This score sheet will be kept in your own gradebook, so you can always go back and review.

**www.mywritinglab.com**

# WATCH, RECALL, APPLY, WRITE ...

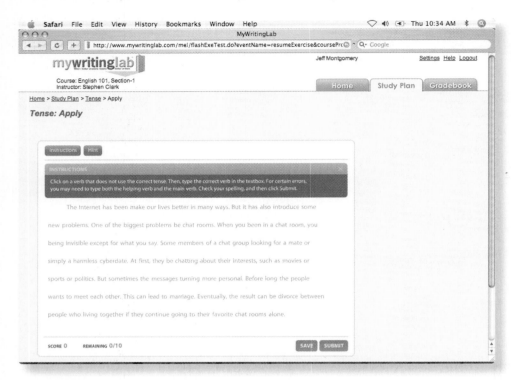

Apply exercises help you *apply* writing and grammar rules to brief paragraphs or essays. Sometimes these are multiple choice questions, and other times you will be asked to identify and correct mistakes in existing paragraphs and essays.

# WATCH, RECALL, APPLY, WRITE ...

Students just like you are finding MyWritingLab's Recall, Apply and Write exercises useful in their learning.

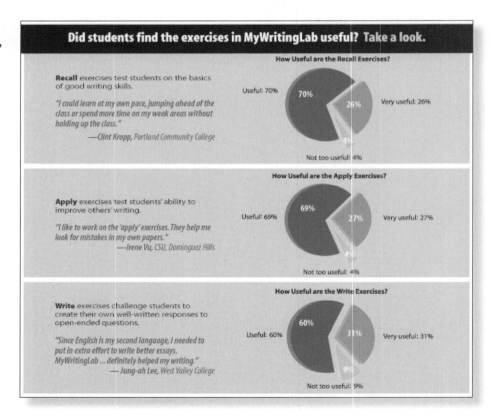

**Did students find the exercises in MyWritingLab useful?** Take a look.

**Recall** exercises test students on the basics of good writing skills.

*"I could learn at my own pace, jumping ahead of the class or spend more time on my weak areas without holding up the class."*
—Clint Kropp, Portland Community College

**How Useful are the Recall Exercises?**
Useful: 70% — 70%
Very useful: 26% — 26%
Not too useful: 4% — 4%

**Apply** exercises test students' ability to improve others' writing.

*"I like to work on the 'apply' exercises. They help me look for mistakes in my own papers."*
—Irene Vu, CSU, Dominguez Hills

**How Useful are the Apply Exercises?**
Useful: 69% — 69%
Very useful: 27% — 27%
Not too useful: 4% — 4%

**Write** exercises challenge students to create their own well-written responses to open-ended questions.

*"Since English is my second language, I needed to put in extra effort to write better essays. MyWritingLab ... definitely helped my writing."*
— Jung-ah Lee, West Valley College

**How Useful are the Write Exercises?**
Useful: 60% — 60%
Very useful: 31% — 31%
Not too useful: 9% — 9%

**www.mywritinglab.com**

# GRADEBOOK ...

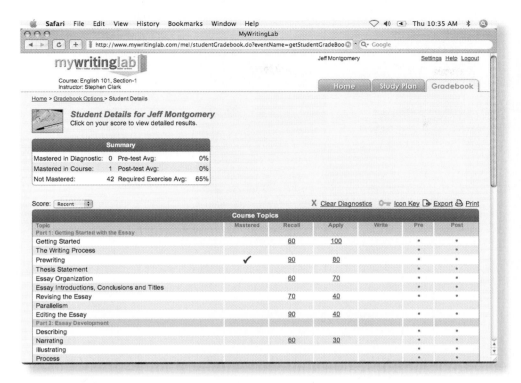

Let's look at how your own on-line gradebook will help you track your progress.

From the home page, click on the "Gradebook" tab and the "Student Detail" report

Here you are able to see how you are doing in each area. If you feel you need to go back and review, simply click on any score and your score sheet will appear.

You also have a Diagnostic Detail report so you can go back and review your diagnostic pretest and see how much MyWritingLab has helped you improve!

**www.mywritinglab.com**

# HERE TO HELP YOU …

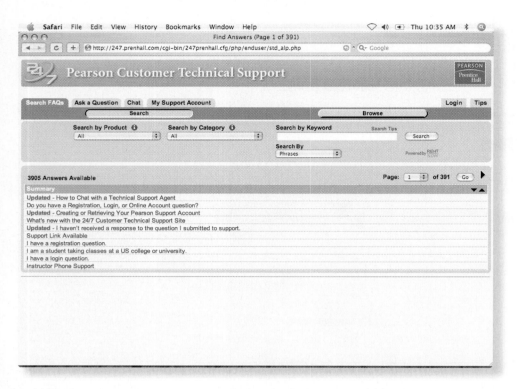

Our goal is to provide answers to your MyWritingLab questions as quickly as possible and deliver the highest level of support. By visiting www.mywritinglab.com/help.html, many questions can be resolved in just a few minutes or less. Here you will find help on:

- System Requirements
- How to Register for MyWritingLab
- How to Use MyWritingLab

**Contact Support.** We also invite you to contact Pearson Product Support (above). You can contact our Support Representatives online at http://247.pearsoned.com. Here you can:

- Search Frequently Asked Questions about MyWritingLab
- E-mail a Question to our Support Team
- Chat with a Support Representative

**www.mywritinglab.com**

# Getting Ready to Write

# 1

## Chapter Preview

- What's the Point of Preparing to Learn about Writing?

- Making a Point about Preparing to Learn about Writing: One Student Writer's Response

- Preparing Yourself to Learn about Writing

# Prepare to Learn about Writing

In countless situations in life, preparation is essential to success. Even a trip to the grocery store requires some planning in order to get all the items needed to feed a family and run a household in the most economical way. A careful shopper may create a menu, check the pantry and make a list of what is needed, read the ads for sale items, or clip coupons. Think of another situation or task that requires preparation. What kind of preparation might be needed to successfully complete the task?

Writing is an essential life skill, and learning to write well allows you to express yourself, influence others, succeed in college, and compete in the job market. By starting your academic career with this writing course, you are preparing for success. You are laying a sturdy foundation for writing for life. If you are like many others, you may have a few qualms about writing, but take heart! With the right attitude and a study plan, you *can* learn to write well. Get ready to learn about writing!

# What's the Point of Preparing to Learn about Writing?

Like any other worthwhile endeavor, learning requires preparation. Preparation usually involves setting a goal, adopting an attitude for success, setting aside time to accomplish the task, gathering tools or supplies, and planning a course of action.

**PHOTOGRAPHIC ORGANIZER: PREPARING TO LEARN**

The following pictures represent one student's effort to prepare to learn about writing. Write a caption for each photograph that identifies her efforts to prepare to learn.

*WRITING FROM LIFE*

*Practice 1*

What is this?

This is a Dictionary book

What is this?

Those are notebook, pencil, and rule.

What is this?

This is someone Typing in computer.

What is this?

This is a group of student discussing some subject

What's the point?

# Making a Point about Preparing to Learn about Writing: One Student Writer's Response

The following paragraph records one student's efforts to prepare to learn about writing. As you read the paragraph, underline specific steps he took that you might use as well.

## Prepared to Learn

(1) I began preparing to learn about writing even before the class began. (2) My first step was choosing a teacher. (3) I had heard that Professor Rickles was an excellent teacher, and RateMyProfessor.com verified what I had heard. (4) On the first day of class, he handed out his course syllabus which listed the books and materials I needed; later that day, I bought everything he required, and I brought everything I needed with me to every class. (5) Right away, Professor Rickles put us in small groups so we could get to know each other by working together. (6) I found three people who wanted to learn as much as I did so we formed a study group. (7) We helped each other a lot throughout the whole semester. (8) If one of us was sick, we made sure he or she got the notes and assignment for that day, and we read each other's papers to make sure they made sense and didn't have any careless errors. (9) I also used a daily planner to record assignments and set aside time to study and write. (10) I arrived a few minutes early when possible, so that when class began, I was prepared to get to work. (11) I have to admit I had to work on my attitude. (12) I was so shy and afraid of sounding silly that asking questions in class was really hard, so for a while, I stayed after class to ask my questions, but eventually, I gained enough confidence to ask them during class. (13) I also had to learn how to deal with Professor Rickles' comments on my papers. (14) I worked so hard on each essay, yet for a long time, my papers came back to me with grades and <u>edits</u> that showed I still needed to improve. (15) It took a while for my hard work to pay off, but I was determined to succeed. (16) I am proud to say, all my preparation and hard work paid off. (16) Not only did I earn an "A," but I also improved my ability to write.

# Preparing Yourself to Learn about Writing

As you prepare to learn about writing, take some time to evaluate yourself as a student writer. Think about your attitude, how you can become an active learner, your relationship with your teacher, your study plan, and how you will track your growing writing abilities. The more you think and the more you prepare, the more likely you are to learn about writing and to become an effective writer.

## The Attitude of Learning

*noteiro.*

### Use Positive Self-Talk

Many people have negative thoughts going through their minds that constantly repeat "I can't" phrases: "I can't write…… I can't spell…… I can't understand…… I just can't do it. Never have; never will!" Often these negative attitudes are the result of a prior negative event. A basic step to success is changing that script in your head. You have an amazing ability to learn, so tell yourself that you *can*. Replace "I can't" thoughts with "I can." Then, take steps to prove that you can. For example, instead of believing "I just can't spell," think, "I can use a spell checker," or "I can make a list of words I often misspell and memorize their correct spellings." Success begins in your mind!

### Be an Active Learner

Come to class. Be on time. Sit where you can see—and be seen. Take notes. Ask questions. Do your work—on time! Make connections between assignments. Apply what you learn. Seek help. Find a study partner. Take responsibility for your own learning. The more you do, the more you learn!

### Trust Your Teacher

One of the toughest tasks in a writing class is getting and accepting feedback on your writing. Many of us take the teacher's feedback as a personal rejection. Some of us become defensive. Teachers have the hard job of pointing out our errors so that we can correct them. Think of feedback as a service to you. You wouldn't want to go to a job interview with spinach in your teeth or walk into a restaurant with your zipper down, would you? Likewise, you don't want your writing to present your second best self to your reader. So accept feedback as helpful advice. Take note of those errors, study the rules, and revise your work. Turn feedback into an opportunity to learn!

## THE ATTITUDE OF LEARNING

Read the following reflection written by a student that records how she feels about writing and why. On a separate sheet of paper, write a letter to her, giving her advice to help her overcome her anxiety.

To this day, the very thought of writing an essay and turning it in for a grade makes my hands sweat and my stomach churn. I have pretty painful memories of writing classes. For example, in one class, I always sat at the back of the class. One day the teacher gave my paper back by handing it to the person in the front of the row to pass back. Every one in my row got to see the large red "D" at the top of my paper and all the red marks pointing out each one of my errors. I always thought that teacher had it in for me! I never could bring myself to read the comments, and I was too embarrassed to ask questions. It didn't seem to matter, anyway because I just can't write. Besides, I never really had time to write.

## THE ATTITUDE OF LEARNING

Reflect upon your own attitude and needs. Write your response to the following questions.

**A.** Explore your own feelings about writing: What have been your prior writing experiences? Were they positive or negative? Why? What are your feelings about writing?

---

---

**B.** In what areas of writing do you know you need to improve? Coming up with a topic? Generating details? Organizing ideas? Word choice? Spelling? Punctuation? Others?

# Create a Study Plan

A vital part of preparing to learn about writing is creating a study plan.

## Gather Your Tools

Foster success by preparing a place without distractions so you can study. Equip that space with all the tools you will need ahead of time to study. Both writers and students in general need the following: reference materials such as your textbook, a dictionary, a thesaurus, magazines, newspapers, and other reading materials of interest to you; pens (blue or black ink), pencils, and paper; a stapler and 3-hole punch. Optional items include a computer and a printer. In addition, you need a 3-ring binder to house the teacher's syllabus, handouts, assignments, class notes, textbook notes, and lab work. Be sure that you bring your textbook, binder, pens, and pencils to class every day.

## Set Goals

Students who set goals reduce stress, improve concentration, and increase self-confidence. Use the following guidelines to set effective goals. Aim high: Demand your best effort. Be realistic: Strive for balance to avoid burn out. Write goals down: Recording goals makes them clear and important. Be specific: Instead of writing, "Stop procrastinating," write, "Study English on Monday, Tuesday, and Wednesday evenings between 7 and 9 o'clock." Be positive: Instead of writing, "Don't make stupid comma errors," write, "Use commas properly." Set priorities: Rank goals based on need so you can pace your work. Set daily goals based on larger goals: Break a larger goal such as "Understand how to use semicolons" into a series of steps such as "Study the rule, take notes, and do the exercises; then proofread my paper for proper use of semicolons."

## Take Action

Turn your goals into action steps by setting up a time schedule for your study. The following study plan is easy to use, flexible, and will help you set long-term, intermediate, and short-term goals.

| SAMPLE STUDY PLAN | |
|---|---|
| Long-Term Schedule: | Record ongoing weekly commitments such as job hours, class meetings, church, and so on, for the entire semester. |
| Intermediate Schedule: | Make a short list of the events taking place and the tasks to be completed in your class (or classes) this week. Make a fresh list each week, as these activities will change from week to week: Writing assignment Tuesday; Math quiz Tuesday; Chapter 3 in English by Wednesday; Chapter 7 in math by Friday. |
| Short-Term Schedule: | On an index card every morning (or the night before), list your daily schedule. Be specific! Then, carry this card with you and cross off each goal as you accomplish it. Monday: 9:00–9:30 Revise writing assignment; 12:00–12:30 Review math for quiz; 3:30 Return books to library; 7:00–9:00 Read first 30 pages of Chapter 3 for English. |

Practice 4

**CREATE A STUDY PLAN**

Rewrite the following goals so that they are more specific. Be sure to use positive statements. Share your answers with your class or in a small group.

**1.** GOAL: *Get an education.*

REWRITE OF GOAL:

**2.** GOAL: *Pass the class.*

REWRITE OF GOAL:

**3.** GOAL: *Manage my time.*

REWRITE OF GOAL:

**CREATE A STUDY PLAN**

Evaluate your level of preparation for learning about writing.

**1.** Describe your study space and the tools you use to study. In what ways could you improve your study space?

------------------------------------------------

------------------------------------------------

------------------------------------------------

------------------------------------------------

------------------------------------------------

**2.** Rate your readiness to learn about writing. Describe your plan or set up a study plan that includes long-term, intermediate, and short-term goals.

------------------------------------------------

------------------------------------------------

------------------------------------------------

------------------------------------------------

------------------------------------------------

------------------------------------------------

# Create a Portfolio of Your Work

To ensure that you learn about writing and to develop writing skills, you need to track your strengths, your needs, and your growth. A portfolio enables you to organize your work and think about what you are learning.

## What Is a Portfolio?

A portfolio is a collection of all the work you do as a writer organized in a notebook or in an electronic folder. Your portfolio shows your hard work and your growth because its contents document how much time and effort you put into thinking about your writing. A portfolio allows you to assess your own strengths, needs, and goals. A portfolio requires that you use critical thinking skills to become a better writer.

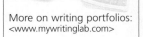

More on writing portfolios:
<www.mywritinglab.com>

## What Should I Include in My Portfolio?

Your portfolio may include class notes and activities, textbook notes and exercises, grammar tests, lab activities, reflective journal entries, prewrites, drafts, revisions, edited drafts, and polished copies of your writing. By collecting and organizing your work, you are better able to reflect upon your strengths and needs. As a result, you are able to set specific goals as a writer. For example, you may find that as a writer you need to better manage your time, so your portfolio may include a study plan that includes learning goals and a study schedule. The practices you have already completed for this chapter are excellent portfolio entries. Throughout this book, you will find many activities, practices, and workshops designed to help you think about your writing. All are excellent entries for your portfolio.

## What Is a Reflective Journal Entry?

A reflective journal entry is an informal piece of writing in which you analyze some aspect of your work as a student writer. For example, you may write a journal entry that lists and responds to the feedback that your teacher gave on a piece of your writing. In each of the chapters about writing paragraphs, you will read a writer's journal that records this kind of thinking.

# Reflective Journals

## Critical Thinking Questions

To deepen your critical thinking about the feedback, your reflective journal entry also answers the following questions:

☐ What steps did I take to write this piece? Did I prewrite, write, revise, and proofread? Do I need to spend more time on any one step?

☐ Which of my errors are proofreading errors? What steps will I take to catch these proofreading errors on my next piece of writing?

☐ Which of these errors results from the need to study a certain rule? Where in my textbook is this rule found? How much time do I need to learn this rule? How will I study this rule (take notes, complete exercises)?

By writing reflective journal entries, you can track and overcome your writing barriers.

## What Is the Best Way to Set Up My Portfolio?

Many students purchase a 3-ring binder large enough to hold their entire semester's work, and tabbed dividers to section off different types of study and writing tasks for class, lab, and homework. Be sure to date and label all work.

All work that is turned in for feedback should include the following information: At the top of the first page and flush with the left margin, place your name, your professor's name, the course name or number (include the section number if the course has multiple sections), and the date you're turning in the paper, each on a separate line with double-spacing throughout.

Iama Writer

Dr. Richards

ENC 001: Section 32

September 24, 2007

All independent work that is created for your notebook or portfolio should be labeled with the date and by the type of work:

*Oct. 9, 2007*

*Reflective Journal Entry for Narrative Paragraph*

*Oct. 10, 2007*

*Comma Splices, Chapter 21, pp. 422–437*

*Oct. 12, 2007*

*The Process Paragraph, Class notes*

The point of labeling is to help you see and discuss your strengths and needs as they occur in real time.

Practice 6

## CRITICAL THINKING

Rate yourself as a critical thinker on a scale of 1 through 6. 1 equals weak; 4 equals average; 6 equals excellent. Explain why and give examples.

CRITICAL THINKING RATING: ...............

REASONS AND EXAMPLES: ........................................................................................

........................................................................................

........................................................................................

........................................................................................

........................................................................................

........................................................................................

........................................................................................

........................................................................................

Practice 7

## THE PORTFOLIO

Write an email to a classmate who missed class. Explain the portfolio process.  Explain how portfolio assessment will improve critical thinking.

........................................................................................

........................................................................................

........................................................................................

........................................................................................

........................................................................................

........................................................................................

........................................................................................

........................................................................................

Academic Learning Log

**QUESTIONS FOR PREPARING TO LEARN**

To test and track your understanding of what you have studied, answer the following questions.

**1.** What are some of the materials and supplies needed by a writing student?

----------------------------------

----------------------------------

----------------------------------

**2.** What are the three attitudes of learning discussed in this chapter?

----------------------------------

----------------------------------

----------------------------------

**3.** What three general steps can you take to create a study plan?

----------------------------------

----------------------------------

----------------------------------

----------------------------------

**4.** What is a portfolio?

----------------------------------

----------------------------------

**5.** What is included in a portfolio?

----------------------------------

----------------------------------

**6.** What is a reflective journal entry?

----------------------------------

----------------------------------

----------------------------------

# 2

# Thinking Through the Writing Process

## The writing process has four stages: prewriting, drafting, revising, and proofreading.

Writing develops, records, and communicates your thoughts to other people. Careful writers rely on the writing process to discover, organize, and record information in response to a specific writing situation.

# What's the Point of the Writing Process?

The following photographs document some of the situations in which we use writing in our everyday, college, and working lives. Write a caption for each picture that includes a reason for writing well in that situation. Then, state the point of writing well.

PHOTOGRAPHIC ORGANIZER: REASONS TO WRITE

*Practice 1*

WRITING FROM LIFE

--------------------------------

--------------------------------

**What's the point of writing well?**

--------------------------------

--------------------------------

## My First Thoughts: A Prewriting Activity

PREWRITING

Set a time limit, such as five minutes, and jot down in your notebook your thoughts about the importance of writing. Do not let your pen or pencil stop, even if you must repeat ideas, keep writing until the time limit is up.

# Making a Point about the Writing Process: One Student Writer's Response

The following paragraph is one writer's response to the question "What's the point of writing?"

> Writing can increase our academic, personal, and economic power. Of course, writing is necessary to succeed in college, yet writing is also important outside the classroom. For example, if I have strong writing skills, I am much more likely to get a job, promotions, and higher pay. In addition, writing allows me to express myself in everyday life. For example, I am really worried about forest fires started by careless campers. A well-written letter to the editor might make just one person think about campfire safety. And a thank you note allows me to express my appreciation for someone who has supported me; it's a way of giving back. Really, writing is thinking on paper. Writing allows me to think, remember, organize, record, learn, and share ideas.

# Understanding the Point: Assessing the Writing Situation

When you write, you develop a point about a topic to fulfill a purpose for a specific audience. To develop your point, you need to think about two aspects of writing: the writing situation and the writing process.

A piece of writing develops in response to a specific **writing situation** that is composed of the **topic** (your subject), the **purpose** for writing (your goal), and the **audience** (your reader).

**TOPIC**
**What you write**

**AUDIENCE**
**Who reads what you write**

**PURPOSE**
**Why you write**

## The Topic: What You Write

When writing about situations in our personal lives, we may choose to compose a letter of complaint to a business or an email to a friend. Often in these circumstances, the topic of our writing naturally emerges from our need to communicate. However, when writing for college, many of us face writer's block in our search for a topic. You can break through writer's block by building a topic bank for college writing.

Use the following thinking guide to generate a bank of topics.

---

# The Writing Situation Step by Step:

## Topic

Build a bank of topics by listing ideas in a special section in your notebook. Use the following prompts to create several lists:

☐ The major topics of importance in a specific course (such as biology, psychology, history)

☐ Interesting or important current events

    ☐ Topics most covered in magazines and newspapers

    ☐ Controversial topics from television (such as news and talk shows)

    ☐ Topics about which you want to learn more

    ☐ Topics about which you feel deeply

    ☐ Hobbies and personal interests

☐ Share your lists with your classmates; use discussion to generate more ideas.

☐ Review and expand your list on a regular basis.

---

As you continue to build your bank of general topics, read, read, and read some more. Read newspapers, magazines, and textbooks for additional topics. Many textbooks provide writing topics at the end of sections or chapters; in addition, headings and subheadings of chapters or sections are excellent sources of topics for your writing.

**TOPICS**

Rank the following topics **1** through **5** to reflect your interest in each one, with **1** representing the least interesting topic and **5** representing the most interesting topic. Then, write a few sentences that explain the reasons for your ranking.

...... The United States' invasion of Iraq

...... The effect of hurricanes or other natural disasters

...... The differences between men and women

...... The benefits of technology

...... Important lessons learned in life

-------------------------------------------------------------------

-------------------------------------------------------------------

-------------------------------------------------------------------

*Practice 3*

More help with topics for writing: <www.mywritinglab.com>

## TOPICS

Skim a newspaper, a magazine, and a textbook and write a list of five topics from each one. Then, share your list with your class or in a small group.

TOPICS FROM A NEWSPAPER: ...............................................................................................

...................................................................................................................................................

TOPICS FROM A MAGAZINE: ...............................................................................................

...................................................................................................................................................

TOPICS FROM A TEXTBOOK: ...............................................................................................

...................................................................................................................................................

# The Purpose: Why You Write

Good writing focuses on a goal or purpose. Your writing will flow much more easily when you write with purpose. The following chart presents four basic purposes for writing.

| | |
|---|---|
| **Informative**<br>When writing informatively, your purpose is to share, explain, or demonstrate information.<br><br>**EXAMPLE:**<br>An **informative essay** that explains the steps of photosynthesis to your reader; a paragraph that answers an exam question about the major causes of stress. | **Persuasive**<br>When writing persuasively, your purpose is to change your reader's opinion or call your reader to take action. <br><br>**EXAMPLE:**<br>An **argumentative essay** that convinces your reader to begin a physical fitness program; a letter to the editor that argues in favor of a law that requires the use of seatbelts. |
| **Expressive**<br>When writing expressively, your purpose is to share with the reader your personal opinions, feelings, or reactions to a topic.<br><br>**EXAMPLE:**<br>An **expressive piece**–a poem, short story, or personal essay, for example–that expresses your anger about 9/11. | **Reflective**<br>When writing reflectively, your purpose is to record your understanding about what you have experienced or learned. <br><br>**EXAMPLE:**<br>An **informal essay** that explores what you think is significant about a current event; a journal entry that discusses the strengths of a paper written by you or a peer. |

Use the following thinking guide to identify your purpose in writing.

# The Writing Situation Step by Step:

## Purpose

☐ Annotate the lists of topics in your topic bank to indicate possible purposes for each topic: Beside each topic write I for informative, P for persuasive, E for expressive, or R for reflective.

☐ Generate four sets of topics based on different purposes for writing, using "The Writing Situation: Step by Step: Topic" box on page 17 to guide your thinking.

☐ Select one topic for each of the four purposes and complete the following statements:

   ☐ This topic will inform the reader about...

   ☐ This topic will persuade the reader to...

   ☐ This topic will express...

   ☐ This topic will reflect upon...

---

**PURPOSE**

*Practice 4*

State the purpose of each of the following topic sentences. Discuss with your class or in a small group how a writer's purposes may be combined in certain situations.

**1**. My experience and education make me an excellent candidate for this job.

.................................................................................................

**2**. Adult stem cell research should be funded by the government.

.................................................................................................

**3**. The gentle breeze, the lapping water, and the dappled shade soothes the human soul.

.................................................................................................

**4**. Eating disorders fall into several categories based on their symptoms.

.................................................................................................

**5**. Based on my unit exam, I need to review the following topics.

.................................................................................................

Practice 5

### PURPOSE

For each of the following topics, write a sentence that states a purpose you may have for writing about this subject. Discuss your answers with your class or in a small group.

**1**. Drug testing

---

**2**. Relaxation techniques

---

**3**. Job hunting

---

**4**. Global warming

---

More help with
purposes for writing:
<www.mywritinglab.com>

## The Audience: Who Reads Your Writing

When we take part in a conversation, we know exactly to whom we are speaking, and we adjust our tone, word choice, and examples to match the situation. For example, contrast how you talk with a friend to how you talk with the dean of your college. Audience has the same impact in the writing situation.

Assume that you have chosen to write about the topic of marijuana. What main points do you want each of the following audiences to consider about this drug? Use the blanks below each picture to record your ideas.

Use the following thinking guide to identify your audience.

# The Writing Situation Step by Step:

## Audience

- [ ] Choose a specific topic and purpose for writing.
- [ ] List the traits of your audience that are relevant to your topic and purpose:
    - [ ] Age
    - [ ] Gender
    - [ ] Education level
- [ ] If you are writing for a general audience of mixed traits, identify the main traits most relevant to your topic and purpose.
- [ ] Identify three or four points about the topic of most interest to a specific audience.
- [ ] Choose several key words to describe your topic and hook the interest of a specific audience. Use a thesaurus to find the words best suited for your audience.

Practice 6

AUDIENCE

Based on your first thoughts about the audiences represented by the four pictures on pages 20–21, write a brief response to the following questions. Then, discuss your answers with your class or in a small group.

- What are the most important traits of each audience represented by the pictures?
- Did your main points differ based on the audience? Why or why not?
- Will your word choice or examples differ based on the audience?
- Why or why not?

Practice 7

AUDIENCE

Each of the following four pieces of writing appeals to one of the audiences depicted by the photos on pages 20–21. Write the letter of the piece of writing in the picture of its audience.

A. Scientists funded by the National Institute on Drug Abuse (NIDA), a federal government agency, have found that the damage to the brain's thinking abilities that results from smoking marijuana can last up to 28 days after an individual last smoked the drug.

B. Marijuana use today starts at a younger age—and more potent forms of the drug are available to you. Marijuana use is a serious threat—do not use it!

C. Under the influence of marijuana, you can forget your best friend's phone number, watch your grade point average drop like a stone, or get into a car accident.

D. Welcome to the Mothers Against Drugs speaker series. During today's speaker panel, we'll investigate the fascinating facts about marijuana. You may have heard it called pot, weed, grass, ganja, or skunk, but marijuana by any other name is still a drug that affects the brain.

B

C

D

A

When student writers are asked "Who is your audience?" most reply, "The teacher." Of course, the teacher is your immediate audience, and you must carefully consider his or her expectations. However, many teachers understand the value of writing to a real-life audience. College is preparing you for success in life. You are learning to write for life.

*Practice 8*

### TOPIC AND AUDIENCE

The following writing prompts apply an academic topic to real audience.

Write the name of the college course(s) for each prompt and describe the traits of each audience. Discuss your answers with your class or in a small group. Talk about how each audience affects the writer's choice of words and details.

**1**. Write a letter to the editor of a newspaper that compares the war in Iraq to the Vietnam War.

COURSE(S): .......................................................................................................

AUDIENCE: ..........................................................................................................

.............................................................................................................................

.............................................................................................................................

**2**. Write a report for the school board that explains the benefits of smaller class sizes.

COURSE(S): .......................................................................................................

AUDIENCE: ..........................................................................................................

.............................................................................................................................

.............................................................................................................................

**3**. Write an email to a classmate explaining the five steps for problem solving.

COURSE(S): .......................................................................................................

AUDIENCE: ..........................................................................................................

.............................................................................................................................

**4**. Write a memo to a new, young employee at a fast food restaurant that explains how the cost of his insurance is based on his age.

COURSE(S): .......................................................................................................

AUDIENCE: ..........................................................................................................

.............................................................................................................................

More help with audience:
<www.mywritinglab.com>

# Understanding the Point: Using the Writing Process

Writing is a process that comprises a series of phases or steps. The process approach focuses on the writer, the way writing is produced, and how the writer can improve his or her personal writing process. The process approach is recursive; the writer may loop or combine any of the stages at any point during the writing process. The key outcome at the end of the process is a published piece of writing. Throughout each stage, think about the relationships among your topic, purpose, and audience.

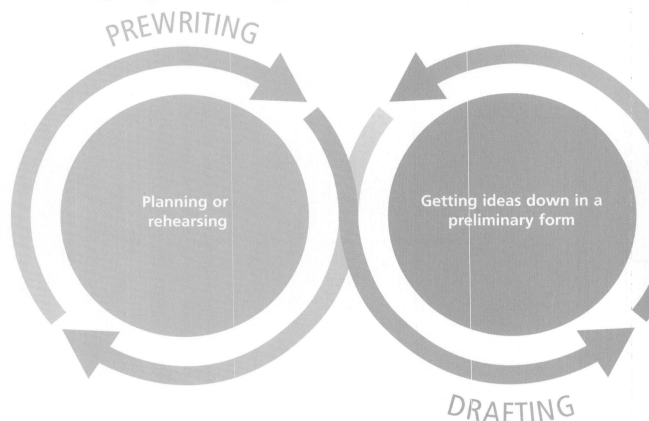

PREWRITING

Planning or rehearsing

Getting ideas down in a preliminary form

DRAFTING

## PREWRITING

During the prewriting stage, you create a plan for your piece of writing.

This phase of writing is made up of the following steps:

- Decide on a topic.
- Determine your purpose for writing.
- Gather information.
- Generate details by using clusters, lists, and freewrites.
- Organize details into an outline.

The rest of this chapter covers specific prewriting techniques.

## DRAFTING

During the drafting stage, you create a draft of your writing.

This phase may include the following steps:

- Decide on audience.
- Choose format (such as an essay or a letter).
- Create introduction, body, and conclusion for longer pieces.

Chapters 3-12 guide you through the entire writing process as you learn how to write paragraphs.

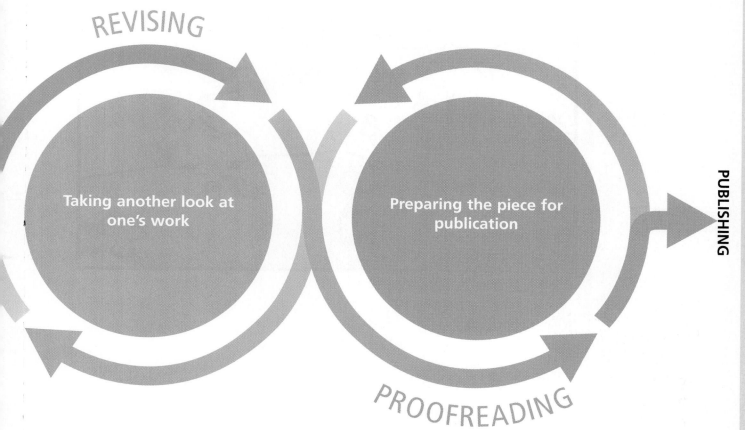

REVISING

Taking another look at one's work

Preparing the piece for publication

**PUBLISHING**

PROOFREADING

## REVISING

During the revision phase, you fine tune the ideas in your essay. After you have written a draft, allow some time to pass so that you can see your writing with fresh eyes.

This phase includes the following steps:
- Delete details that are not relevant.
- Add details to ideas that need more support.
- Reorder ideas for clarity.
- Insert transitions between details for a smooth flow of ideas.
- Replace vague or weak words with vivid, strong words.
- Write a new draft if necessary.

Part 5 covers specific skills to consider while revising.

## PROOFREADING

During the editing phase of the writing process, you polish your draft so your reader will not be distracted or confused by careless errors.

This phase includes correcting errors such as:

- fragments
- run-ons
- shift in tenses
- spelling
- punctuation

Part 6 covers the skills to consider during editing.

# Prewriting

Carefully examine the cartoon. Then, in the space provided, write a few sentences explaining your understanding of what prewriting is.

© 2004 David Farley.

What is prewriting?

Prewriting is when we put some ideas, information, thought together what ever we want to write about.

In general, writing occurs long before you pick up your pen or your fingers touch the keyboard. **Prewriting** includes reading, listening, discussing, and thinking about your topic before you write a rough draft, capturing your prewriting thinking on paper. It allows you to explore ideas and plan your strategies without worrying about polishing them.

Have you ever stared at a blank piece of paper with a blank mind, unable to think of how to start a writing task? Or, have you ever had so many ideas that they jumble up in chaos so that you can't even begin to write? Finding those first few words to put on paper can grind a writer's thinking process to a complete halt.

If you face these problems, take heart, you are not alone! Even the best writers face writer's block now and then. Although no cure-all for writer's block exists, prewriting fuels thinking, triggers the writing process, and fires past the block. Experienced writers have learned to spend time thinking about what they are going to write before they begin drafting.

> **Prewriting** is the act of generating, exploring, developing, and roughly organizing ideas. Prewriting can help you choose a topic, narrow a topic, and put details related to a topic in logical order.

The rest of this section guides you through six prewriting techniques:

- Asking Questions:
  The Reporter's Questions
  The Reflective Questions

- Freewriting
- Keeping a Journal
- Listing
- Concept Mapping
- Outlining

As you write for life, try out each one. Combine a few to stretch your thinking. Experiment with all of them. Discover which one(s) best suit you as a writer or in a particular writing situation.

## Asking Questions

Asking questions helps you identify a topic and develop details about it based on thoughtful insights. Asking and answering questions helps you discover both what you already know and what you need to learn about the topic. Your goal as a writer is to share a point or main idea about a topic. Usually, a main idea or point is made up of the topic and the writer's opinion about the topic. Two types of questions enable you to explore topics and your opinions about those topics: the reporter's questions and reflective questions.

### THE REPORTER'S QUESTIONS

To describe a newsworthy event, effective reporters gather the facts by asking six basic questions:

- Who?
- What?
- When?
- Where?
- Why?
- How?

At first, the answers to these questions may help you identify and narrow a topic that grabs your interest; once you have narrowed your topic, these questions also yield many details of support for your topic.

*Practice 9*

## TOPIC AND AUDIENCE

Assume that you are reporting on the power of propaganda. Discuss the following advertisement for Trim Spa, a weight-loss product, featuring Anna Nicole Smith as a powerful example of propaganda. Use the reporter's questions to brainstorm your first thoughts.

Who is the intended audience of the poster?

.................................................

.................................................

.................................................

.................................................

.................................................

Why is Smith effective in this advertisement?

.................................................

.................................................

How are women portrayed in this ad?

.................................................

.................................................

.................................................

.................................................

## THE REFLECTIVE QUESTIONS

Reflective questions also help you discover your purpose for writing by revealing your attitude toward a topic. By using these questions to reflect, identify, and add your opinion about a topic to your writing, you can also narrow a writing topic that is too general. For example, although the topic in Practice 9 was the power of propaganda, not everyone believes that propaganda is a positive force. For the purposes of narrowing this particular general topic—the power of propaganda—the following questions might help you identify your opinions about it:

- Why do some believe propaganda is negative?
- Why do some believe propaganda is transforming?
- In what ways do I agree or disagree with these opinions?
- How can I best express my point about the power of propaganda to someone with whom I disagree?

Answering these questions before writing will also guide you to make logical decisions about which details to select and highlight when you do begin to write.

When you are ready to explore ideas about a topic on paper, the following thinking guide can help you use questions as a prewriting technique.

# The Writing Process Step by Step:

## Prewriting by Asking Questions

Use the reporter's questions to identify a topic, purpose, and audience.

☐ What?

☐ Why?

☐ Who?

Use the reporter's questions to generate details about the topic.

☐ When?

☐ Where?

☐ How?

Use reflective questions to identify attitudes and generate additional details about the topic.

☐ What is my attitude or feelings about this topic?

☐ What is my audience's attitude or feelings about this topic?

☐ Why is this topic important?

☐ How will my audience respond to my point?

☐ How can I make this topic interesting and relevant to my audience?

---

**QUESTIONING**

Assume you are reporting on the 9/11 attack on the World Trade Center. Using the box "The Writing Process Step by Step: Prewriting by Asking Questions," write a list of questions to identify your point and generate details. Share your ideas with the class or in a small group.

_Practice 10_

More help with prewriting: <www.mywritinglab.com>

---

**QUESTIONING**

Ask questions to brainstorm your first thoughts about one of the following topics:

• Road Rage

• Graffiti

• Drug Abuse

• Positive Thinking

• Workplace Stress

_Practice 11_

## Freewriting

During **freewriting**, you record your thoughts as they stream through your head. The key to this brainstorming strategy, like all prewriting activities, is to turn off the critic inside your head. At this point, no thought is wrong, off base, or silly. The idea is to warm up your thinking muscles, flex your creativity, and set your ideas free. Use the following thinking guide to use freewriting as a prewriting technique.

# The Writing Process Step by Step:

## Prewriting by Freewriting

☐ Set a time limit, such as ten minutes, and write whatever comes to mind as fast as you can without stopping at all.

☐ If you get stuck, write the same word or phrase until a new idea comes along; do not stop writing. Do not worry about wording, organization, or grammar; later in the writing process, you will organize and polish your ideas—tell that critic inside your head to pipe down for now.

☐ When the time limit is up, read what you wrote and underline interesting ideas.

☐ Use one of the ideas you underlined as a starting point for a focused freewrite. A **focused freewrite** occurs when you freewrite about a specific topic you have chosen or been assigned.

Practice 12

**FREEWRITING**

Read the following two freewrites. Discuss with your class or in a small group how ideas develop using freewriting and focused freewriting. What are the advantages of freewriting? What are the disadvantages?

Well it is time for another writing assignment, and the teacher said we could choose our own topic, but I don't know what to write I always have a hard time coming up with topics writing is so hard I know I am a terrible at this but I need to find a topic not write about not finding a topic let's see what can I write about? It is so cold in here I can't think think think think think think well wats going on in the news oh, what about all the missing and abused children and the how child molesters are everywhere. Things seem to be getting worse all the time. Pretty depressing. I think things ar worse now than when I was growing up. My hometown was so safe no one locked their doors they didn't have too. We spent hours roaming the neighborhood on our bicycles, swimming in Lake Martha, enjoying being a kid. Now small towns seem as dangerous as crime ridden big cities.

**Focused Freewrite**

We spent hours roaming the neighborhood on our bicycles, swimming in Lake Martha, enjoying being a kid. There were about 20 of us kids pretty close in age who lived in my neighborhood, so we always had someone to play with or fight with, and we did both passionately. Our neighborhood was surrounded by orange groves, so we all learned at a pretty young age how to throw and dodge rotten oranges in our on-going orange wars. My brother earned the reputation of the best warrior. He could throw an orange further and straighter than any one any time. The best wars ended with a bike race to Lake Martha to rinse off the sticky juices and dirt that clung to us. I can still hear the ice cream truck's merry music and feel the hot sand beneath my feet as we dashed from the waters edge to catch the ice cream man as he rounded the corner during his afternoon route. Life seemed so simple, so safe, so fun.

More help with prewriting:
<www.mywritinglab.com>

**FOCUSED FREEWRITING**

**Step 1**: Choose one of the following topics and freewrite for five minutes. Feel free to ask and answer questions before you begin freewriting.

- Peer Pressure

- Useful Technology

- Eating Disorders

- A Role Model

**Step 2**: Read your freewrite and highlight ideas. Write a focused freewrite for an additional five minutes using the idea(s) you highlighted.

## Keeping a Journal

Many people keep a **journal** to record how they feel about the events of their daily lives, current events, or life in general. A journal allows the writer to explore experiences in a personal way and store them in a private place. Some writers use a spiral notebook; others use a diary or a pre-made journal. The point is to create a specific place where you can record and review your private thoughts and personal experiences. Journal entries are often freewrites with the main purpose of getting ideas onto paper, but they may take on different creative forms, such as a letter or a poem. Many writers use journals as a place to practice their writing and experiment with language. The key to keeping a journal is to write on a regular basis. Writing and reflecting on what you have written on a consistent basis leads to a deeper understanding of yourself and your world—and improves your writing!

Use the following thinking guide to use journaling as a prewriting technique.

# The Writing Process Step by Step:

## Prewriting by Journaling

☐ Create a section in your notebook for journal entries or buy a spiral notebook, diary, or pre-made journal that you will use only for journal writing.

☐ Commit to writing in your journal on a regular basis for the next two weeks. Select a time of day that you can write in your journal, such as during your lunch break or at the end of your day. Set a time limit for each journal entry such as fifteen minutes.

☐ Ask and answer reflective questions and the reporter's questions to stimulate your thinking.

Use the following topics to get started:

☐ Record events, images, or scenes of interest to you; write as many details as you can.

☐ Record a favorite memory; explore why that memory is so important.

☐ Write a brief autobiography.

☐ Recount a news event and your reactions to it.

☐ Write a letter to yourself or someone else, giving advice about a particular matter.

☐ Vent about something that really bothers you.

☐ Reread a previously written journal and develop an idea in greater detail.

*Practice 14*

**JOURNALING**

Read the following journal entry. Identify the academic courses that are relevant to the personal experiences recorded in the journal. Discuss with your class or in a small group the ways in which the ideas in the journal entry might be developed for an essay in each course.

April 20: 8:00 p.m.: Well, here I am again, eating once more out of stress. Today was incredibly stressful. For some reason I have a hard time communicating with my boss, so once again she scheduled me to work when I needed to be off for a doctor's appointment. I have been gaining weight like crazy, but I absolutely crave carbohydrates. And on days like this, a warm bowl of macaroni and cheese soothes my soul. My mom thinks I might have a thyroid problem which is making me gain weight, but I think it's just from eating too much, and too much stress. I wish I had more time. I would love to go to the beach tonight and observe the turtle nests. I wonder why they always come to this beach to nest. The county has made all the businesses along the beach dim their lights so the turtles won't be disturbed. I wonder why the light is such a problem.

Academic topics related to journal entry:

----------------------------------------

----------------------------------------

----------------------------------------

More help with prewriting:
<www.mywritinglab.com>

## Listing

A common way to brainstorm ideas is to **create a list**. If you have a free choice of topics, then create a topic bank: List ideas about which you want to learn more or topics about which you already know something and enjoy discussing. To create a list of topics for an academic course, look at the table of contents, the index, and the glossary of your textbook. Use these resources to create a list of topics based on what you will be studying throughout the semester. If you already have a topic, then create a list of everything that comes to mind as you think about your topic. Write your list as quickly as you can. Just as in freewriting, quiet your inner critic. Once you make a thorough list, then you can organize your ideas.

Use the following thinking guide to use listing as a prewriting technique.

# The Writing Process Step by Step:

## Prewriting by Listing

☐ Write a topic at the top of your page.

☐ List ideas as quickly as possible in the order that they occur to you.

☐ Use words or short phrases.

☐ List all ideas that occur to you; reject nothing.

☐ If you run out of ideas, choose one idea you have already recorded and begin a new list about that idea.

☐ Review your list and group ideas into logical relationships.

☐ Label each group of ideas as possible points of development for a piece of writing.

Practice 15

### LISTING: PREWRITING FOR AN ACADEMIC COURSE

The following lists are based on the table of contents of two textbooks. Identify the academic courses to which each list is related. Then, brainstorm a list of additional writing topics based on an idea from each list.

COURSES: _____     COURSES: _____

_____                _____

**List 1**
Mass Media and Politics
The Power of the Media
Sources of the Media
People in Politics
Stars of the News Broadcasts
Bias in the Media
Freedom versus Fairness

**List 2**
Basics of Good Health
Managing Mental Health
Coping with Stress
Eating Smart
Maintaining Proper Weight
Keeping Fit
Controllable Health Risks

**New Lists of Additional Ideas**       **New Lists of Additional Ideas**

**LISTING: PREWRITING FOR BUSINESS WRITING**

Assume you have just been given two weeks notice because your company is downsizing and eliminating your job. To locate job opportunities, take the following steps:

**Step 1**: Go to the classified section of your local newspaper and make a list of available jobs in your area.

_____

_____

_____

**Step 2**: Choose one of the advertised positions and list the skills needed to compete for the job.

_____

_____

_____

**Step 3**: List the skills you already possess that qualify you for the job.

_____

_____

_____

**Step 4**: List the skills you need to acquire to qualify for the job.

_____

_____

_____

**Step 5**: Repeat steps 2 through 4 for each of the jobs you listed in Step 1.

_____

_____

_____

More help with prewriting:
<www.mywritinglab.com>

## Concept Mapping

**Concept mapping**, also known as **clustering** or **webbing**, creates a visual picture of the relationships among the ideas you generate. Think of what you already know about a map. Someone can tell you how to get somewhere, but it is much easier to understand the directions when you can see how each road connects to other roads by studying a map. Likewise, a concept map shows how a topic connects to supporting details—how each idea connects to another idea, how the main idea connects to supporting details. Sometimes, as you use a concept map, the idea that first occurred to you might be a great example for a supporting detail. Rarely do ideas occur to us in a logical order. Concept mapping helps a writer figure out the logical order of ideas. Chapters 4 through 12 will show you how to adapt concept maps to specific writing situations and thought patterns.

Use the following thinking guide to use concept mapping as a prewriting technique.

# The Writing Process Step by Step:

## Prewriting by Concept Mapping

- ☐ Draw a circle in the middle of your page and write your topic in the circle.

- ☐ Write a word that relates to the topic, circle the word, and connect it to the topic circle with a line.

- ☐ Repeat this process so that a set of major supports radiate out from the topic circle.

- ☐ Write a word that relates to one of the major supports, circle it, and connect it to that major support circle.

- ☐ Repeat this process for each of the major supports to create clusters of minor supports.

*Practice 17*

**MAPPING**

The writer of the following paragraph used a concept map to brainstorm ideas. Read the paragraph. Then, recreate her concept map by filling in the appropriate blanks with ideas from her paragraph. Discuss how the concept map differs from her final draft.

According to *Merriam-Webster's Collegiate Dictionary*, a role model is "a person whose behavior in a particular role is imitated by others." In other words, a role model is anyone who has influence over us. A role model can be anyone including celebrities, such as actors, athletes, or politicians or plain folks, such as teachers, parents, and friends. Role models can be positive or negative. For example, a positive role model possesses several traits. A positive role model reflects an ideal, such as courage or honesty, has an upstanding reputation, and uses his or her influence for the greater good. In contrast, a negative role model negates an ideal by being cowardly or dishonest, has a damaged reputation, and uses his or her influence for selfish gain. Still, ideals such as courage, cowardice, honesty, and dishonesty are often a matter of opinion. For example, many thought Tom Cruise acted as a strong role model when he spoke out against the psychiatric profession. He claimed that vitamins and exercise, not therapy and drugs, are the best treatments for postpartum depression. He even condemned Brooke Shields as a role model for relying on drug therapy for her postpartum depression. However, many others saw his criticism as an unfair attack that damaged his reputation in their eyes. In the end, a role model actually reflects our own values.

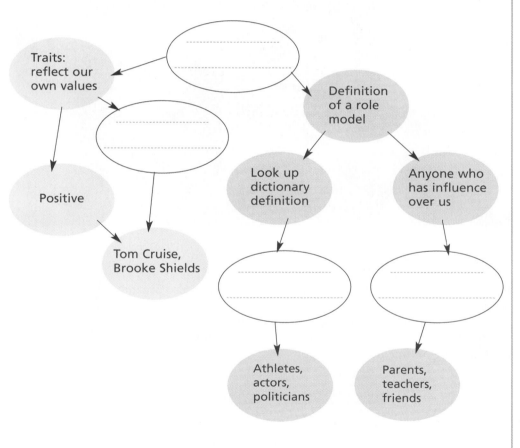

*Practice 17*

Practice 18

**MAPPING**

Using your own sheet of paper, create a concept map to brainstorm ideas for one of the following topics. Use circles and arrows to show your flow of ideas. Or feel free to use ideas generated in a freewrite during Practices 11 and 13.

- Road Rage
- Graffiti
- Positive Thinking
- Workplace Stress
- Gang Violence
- Legalizing Marijuana
- Eating Disorders
- A Role Model

More practice with prewriting:
<www.mywritinglab.com>

## Outlining: A Writing Plan

In addition to brainstorming first thoughts, a prewrite also organizes ideas into a writing plan. A concept map is one way to create a writing plan because it shows the flow of ideas among the topic, major details, and minor details. An outline is another way to create a writing plan. An **outline** lists ideas in blocks of thought, as shown in the following outline for a paragraph.

*Main Idea Statement: Topic Sentence*

    *A. Major supporting detail*
        *1. Minor detail*
        *2. Minor detail*

    *B. Major supporting detail*
        *1. Minor detail*
        *2. Minor detail*

    *C. Major supporting detail*
        *1. Minor detail*
        *2. Minor detail*

Use the following thinking guide to use outlining as a prewriting technique.

# The Writing Process Step by Step:

## Prewriting by Outlining

☐ Create an outline from other prewriting activities such as freewrites, lists, and concept maps.

☐ List and identify each item with Roman numerals, capitalized letters, Arabic numerals, and lowercase letters, in that order, to show the flow of ideas, as illustrated below:

I. Main Idea

    A. Major supporting detail

        1. Minor supporting detail

        2. Minor supporting detail

☐ Place a period after each numeral or letter.

☐ Capitalize each item.

☐ For topic outlines, state each item with a word or phrase.

☐ For sentence outlines, state each item as a complete thought.

---

**OUTLINING**

The following reflection and concept map was created by a student during the prewriting phase of an assignment. Complete the outline with ideas from the concept map.

**Laura's First Thoughts:**

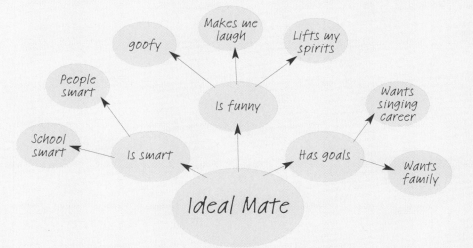

I am going to write about the topic "My Ideal Mate," and my classmates are my audience. I am going to focus my topic by discussing three traits of an ideal mate and how my boyfriend is a perfect example of an ideal mate. My purpose is to let the reader know what a great boyfriend I have.

Main Idea Statement: My boyfriend Kelly is my ideal mate.

Practice 19

**A.** ...................................................................................

    **1.** He excelled in high school and college.

    **2.** ...............................................................................

**B.** Kelly is funny.

    **1.** ...............................................................................

    **2.** He keeps me laughing.

    **3.** ...............................................................................

**C.** ...................................................................................

    **1.** He is working towards a singing career.

    **2.** ...............................................................................

Practice 20

### CREATING A WRITING PLAN

Choose your own topic or select one of the following topics. Identify your audience and purpose. Then, generate major and supporting details using the outline.
Use the reporter's questions *who? what? when? where? how?* and *why?*
to produce details.

- A place everyone should visit at least once
- A famous person who is an excellent role model for youth

TOPIC: ....................................................................................

AUDIENCE: ..............................................................................

PURPOSE: ...............................................................................

........................................................................................

........................................................................................

........................................................................................

TOPIC SENTENCE: ....................................................................

........................................................................................

........................................................................................

More practice with prewriting: <www.mywritinglab.com>

A. _____

   1. _____

   2. _____

B. _____

   1. _____

   2. _____

C. _____

   1. _____

   2. _____

*Practice 20*

# Drafting

The **drafting** stage of the writing process may include several tasks depending on the writing situation. An essay or letter may require the drafting of an introduction, a main idea, supporting details, and conclusion. A stand-alone paragraph may require only a main idea and supporting details.

> **Drafting** is putting your ideas into sentences and paragraphs.

## Compose a Main Idea

For more information on thesis statements, introductions, and conclusions, see Chapters 13 and 14.

The **main idea statement** for an essay is called a **thesis statement**. The main idea statement for a paragraph is called a **topic sentence**. In general, the main idea sentence presents a topic and the point you are making about the topic, as in the following example:

*TOPIC*

Hip-Hop music  has four unique elements including rapping or
MCing, DJing, breakdancing, and graffiti.

———— *WRITER'S POINT* ————

The writer's point focuses the topic "Hip-Hop music" into the narrowed subject "four unique elements of Hip-Hop music." With this statement, the writer narrowed the subject by stating the opinion "unique" and focusing on the details that will be discussed: "four unique elements."

Use the following thinking guide to draft a piece of writing.

# The Writing Process Step by Step:

## Drafting

☐ Write your main idea in a complete sentence.

☐ As you write a thesis statement or topic sentence, assert a point rather than announce your topic. Avoid the following announcements:

- "I am going to write about…"
- "My paragraph (or essay) is about…"
- "My topic is…."

☐ As you write your first draft, do not worry about issues such as spelling and grammar.

☐ Generate major and minor details to support your main idea.

☐ As you write, include new ideas as they occur to you without self-criticism or editing yourself before you have a complete draft; this first draft does not need to be perfect. You will use the revision process to evaluate details for logic and relevance once your draft is complete.

☐ Use the first draft to discover how your ideas flow and fit together.

☐ Resolve to write multiple drafts to produce your best work.

*Practice 21*

### STATING THE MAIN IDEA

Complete the following set of exercises about main idea statements. Discuss your work with your class or in a small group.

**A.** Read the following main idea statements. Underline the subject once and underline the writer's point twice.

**1.** Space exploration benefits society in three ways.

**2.** Three specific exercises reduce the effects of stress.

**3.** Misusing over-the-counter drugs can be just as dangerous as using illegal drugs.

**4.** Eating disorders harm the body, mind, and spirit.

**B.** Revise the following main idea statements so they are more effectively expressed. Identify the hint you used to revise each one.

**5.** I am going to write about how the automobile costs too much, pollutes the environment, and traps us in isolation.

---

---

**Hint:** ____

More help with drafting:
<www.mywritinglab.com>

**6.** The annoying and rude manners of people while talking on cell phones in public places.

Hint:

**7.** Minimum wage is a controversial issue.

Hint:

## Write a Draft of Your Paragraph

Writing a draft of a paragraph or essay is the result of careful thought based on prewriting activities. Creating a first or rough draft allows you to get a working copy of your ideas that can be improved upon during the revision process.

**COMPOSE A TOPIC SENTENCE AND A DRAFT**

**Step 1.** Choose a topic from a previous practice exercise, and compose a main idea statement. (Remember that your **main idea statement** is also called a **topic sentence** if you are writing a paragraph. If you are writing an essay, your main idea statement is also called a **thesis statement**.)

**Step 2.** Write a draft using your own paper.

AUDIENCE AND PURPOSE:

TOPIC:

WRITER'S POINT:

MAIN IDEA STATEMENT (topic sentence or thesis statement):

# Revising

Now that you have gotten your ideas on paper, you can review your work to make sure your paragraph offers a focused, unified, well-supported, and coherent chunk of information. As you revise your draft, review and apply what you have learned.

> **Revising** is re-seeing your work through the eyes of your reader. Revising is reworking your draft for clarity, logic, interest, and credibility.

Use the following thinking guide to revise a piece of writing.

# The Writing Process Step by Step:

## Revising

☐ Read your draft out loud (either on your own or to a peer). This is an easy way to identify parts of your draft that may be unclear or awkward.

☐ Make sure your main idea is stated clearly in a topic sentence or thesis statement.

☐ Make sure that the details in the body of your paragraph or essay fully support your topic sentence or thesis statement.

☐ Make sure every sentence in a paragraph relates to your main idea so that a reader can easily follow the logic of your ideas.

☐ Move information as needed into the most logical order.

☐ Add transitions as needed to clarify the relationship between ideas.

☐ Add details and examples as needed to strengthen or clarify the main idea and supporting points.

☐ Replace vague words and details with vivid and precise expressions.

☐ Delete irrelevant details.

☐ If your paragraph or essay draft seems to end abruptly, add a concluding sentence (or paragraph, if you are writing an essay) restating and summing up your main points.

**REVISING**

Read Laura's first draft of her paragraph "My Ideal Mate." Then, complete the activity that follows. Share your work and thoughts with a small group of your peers.

### My Ideal Mate

(1) My ideal mate is a man who is intelligent, funny, and goal oriented. (2) Kelly, my current boyfriend, has all of these wonderful traits. (3) Kelly has to be one of the smartest people I know. (4) He excelled academically in high school and college. (5) He is not only book smart but is street smart also. (6) He knows exactly how to keep the people he loves protected and safe from this cruel world. (7) Kelly has to be the funniest person I know. (8) If we didn't have fun and goof around, our relationship would be boring. (9) He can be serious when necessary, and like everyone, has his dark days. (10) Whenever I am down about something, he is the one to make me overcome the sadness and laugh. (11) The most important trait of all though is that Kelly is goal oriented; he knows what he wants out of life. (12) He has a plan to succeed. (13) Not too many guys know what they want. (14) Kelly wants to become a professional musician, have a family, and earn enough money to support his family. (15) All of these traits make Kelly my ideal mate. —Laura Bender, English Student

More help with revising:
<www.mywritinglab.com>

1. Locate the topic sentence by underlining the topic once and the writer's point about that topic twice.
2. Cross out any details that are not related to the topic sentence.
3. Circle any ideas that need more examples to fully support the main idea.
4. Choose three words to revise; cross out the words you chose and above them, write stronger, more vivid words. Use a thesaurus.
5. Insert the following transitions where they best show the logical flow of ideas: First, In addition, Finally.

**REVISING**

Review a draft you have written. Annotate or mark your paragraph with the changes you need to make, and write a journal entry about your revision. Do you need to brainstorm more details for certain ideas? Identify those ideas and describe or explain the kinds of details you need. Do you need to use a thesaurus to improve word choice? List and discuss the words that need to be replaced. Based on your review, revise to create a new draft of your work.

# Proofreading

Once you have revised your paragraph, take time to carefully proofread your work. Publishing a clean, error-free draft proves you are committed to excellence and that you take pride in your work. Many student writers struggle with common errors, and every writer has her or his own pattern or habit of careless errors. To create a polished draft, a writer masters the rules of writing and edits to eliminate careless errors.

> **Proofreading** is preparing your work for publication.
> Proofreading is correcting errors in punctuation, capitalization, mechanics, grammar, and spelling.

Use the following thinking guide to proofread a piece of writing.

# The Writing Process Step by Step:

## Proofreading

- [ ] Allow some time to pass between revising and proofreading.
- [ ] Read your work one sentence at a time from the *end* to the *beginning*. Reading your work from the end to the beginning allows you to focus on each sentence.
- [ ] Read again from the beginning with a cover that you slide down the page as you read so you focus on one sentence at a time.
- [ ] Use a highlighter to mark mistakes.
- [ ] Proofread more than once; focus on one type of error at a time.
- [ ] Proofread for the types of errors you commonly make.
- [ ] Use word processing spell checkers carefully (they don't know the difference between words such as there, their, or there).
- [ ] Use a dictionary to double check your spelling.
- [ ] Have someone else read over your work.

**Practice 25**

**PROOFREADING**

The following draft by a student writer reveals her struggle with two common errors: pronoun agreement and subject-verb agreement. The box below sums up the rules for pronoun agreement and subject-verb agreement and includes a few sentence examples that are correct. Read the rules and examples in the box, and then use them as a guide to correct the same kind of errors in pronoun agreement and subject-verb agreement in the student's draft.

### Pronoun Agreement

If a noun is singular (*I, you, he, she,* or *it*), then the pronoun that refers to the noun must be singular. If a noun is plural (*we, you, they*), then the pronoun that refers to the noun must be plural.

## Subject-Verb Agreement

If a subject of a sentence is singular, then the verb and object of the verb must be singular. If the subject of a sentence is plural, then the verb and object of the verb must be plural.

More help with proofreading: <www.mywritinglab.com>

**Student draft**

### The Bride to Be

(1) In a traditional wedding, the center of attention revolves around the bride. (2) Although brides vary in temperament and style, most often they fall into three common types: bridezilla, coldarella, and bellaella brides. (3) First, the bridezilla is the typically testy, irritated and acerbic bride. (4) The best known trait of a bridezilla is the tendency to have high voltage temper tantrums. (5) For example, they cannot settle a single, simple issue without blowing off the handle and making something out of nothing. (6) The second type of bride, coldarella, is also known as a runaway bride. (7) Though she may come across as calm and understanding, deep down they are repressing all their bottled tension. (8) A runaway bride often smiles until the day she skips town and leaves the man of her dreams waiting at the altar. (9) The third and best bride is the bellaella bride, the beautiful bride. (10) Her inner beauty makes them the most delightful ones to be around. (11) She loves the intrinsic details and although she wants everything to be perfect, they don't fuss if it is not. (12) This bride is gentle, easy going, and understanding. (13) She doesn't fret over unexpected circumstances. (14) This bride is the bride to be and the bride to marry!

*Practice 25*

Academic Learning Log

To test and track your understanding of what you have studied, answer the following questions.

1. A piece of writing develops in response to a specific situation that is composed of the

   ............................, the ............................ for writing, and the ............................ .

2. The four basic purposes for writing are ............................,

   ............................, ............................, and ............................ .

3. The four phases of the writing process are ............................,

   ............................, ............................, and ............................ .

4. The writing process is ............................: any step can be repeated as necessary.

5. Several prewriting techniques are ............................, ............................,

   ............................, ............................, and ............................ .

6. Drafting is putting your ideas into ............................ and ............................ .

7. Revising is ............................ your work through the eyes of your reader.

8. Revising is reworking your draft for ............................, ............................,

   ............................, and ............................ .

9. Proofreading is preparing your work for ............................ .

10. Proofreading is correcting errors in ............................, ............................,

    ............................, ............................, and ............................ .

# Using Thought Patterns to Develop Paragraphs

# 3

## Understanding the Paragraph

## A paragraph is a well-planned sequence of sentences coupled together.

All of us have had some experience reading, writing, or studying paragraphs. What do you already know about paragraphs? What are the traits of a paragraph?

A paragraph allows a writer to express clearly and powerfully one main idea about a narrowed subject. A well-written paragraph can express a valid consumer complaint, a compelling reason to be hired, a sincere apology to a loved one, or a concept tested by a written exam in a college course.

# What Is the Point of a Paragraph?

A paragraph is a well-thought-out chunk of information. A writer narrows a topic into a focused main idea, selects enough relevant details to support the main idea, and organizes these supporting details in a logical flow of information.

## Three Levels of Information in a Paragraph

The following flow chart shows the three levels of information within a paragraph.

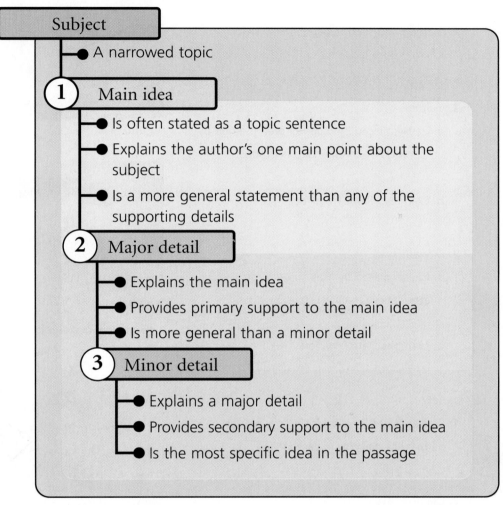

**Subject**
- A narrowed topic

**1 Main idea**
- Is often stated as a topic sentence
- Explains the author's one main point about the subject
- Is a more general statement than any of the supporting details

**2 Major detail**
- Explains the main idea
- Provides primary support to the main idea
- Is more general than a minor detail

**3 Minor detail**
- Explains a major detail
- Provides secondary support to the main idea
- Is the most specific idea in the passage

**PHOTOGRAPHIC ORGANIZER: LEVELS OF INFORMATION**

Study the following outline based on an article that was published in the journal *Dermatology Nursing* about types of tattoos. In the blanks, identify each piece of information as the narrowed topic, main idea, major supporting detail, or minor supporting detail.

Four Types of Tattoos .........................................

There are four major types of tattoos: traumatic, amateur, professional, and cosmetic.

.........................................

**A.** Traumatic .........................................

    **1.** Cause: accidental embedding of colored material, which leaves pigment after

       healing .........................................

*WRITING FROM LIFE*

*Practice 1*

**2.** Examples: motorcycle rash, "graphite tattoo" from a puncture injury with a pencil

...........................................

**B.** Amateur ...........................................

**1.** Cause: placed by the person being tattooed or by a friend with little experience

...........................................

**2.** Example: boyfriend's name; gang tattoo

...........................................

**C.** Professional ...........................................

**1.** Cultural ...........................................

**a.** Cause: placed by time-honored method by members of certain cultural groups

...........................................

**b.** Example:  Samoan tattoos

...........................................

**2.** Modern ...........................................

**a.** Cause: placed by "tattoo gun" by experienced, paid artists

...........................................

**b.** Example:  Tattoo parlors

...........................................

**D.** Cosmetic ...........................................

**1.** Cause: placed by a cosmetic specialist as permanent makeup or camouflage

...........................................

**2.** Example: eyeliner ...........................................

▲ **Cultural**

▲ **Permanent makeup**

▲ **Gang tattoos**

◄ **Modern**

Practice 1

Read the paragraph developed from the previous outline. Circle the main idea. Underline the four sentences that state the major supports.

### Four Types of Tattoos

(1) There are four major types of tattoos: traumatic, amateur, professional, and cosmetic. (2) The first type, traumatic tattoos, is caused by the imbedding of dirt or debris beneath the skin, which leaves an area of pigmentation after healing. (3) For example, this commonly occurs in "road rash" after a motorcycle accident or after a puncture injury from a lead pencil, called a "graphite tattoo." (4) The second type, amateur tattoos, is placed by the person being tattooed or by a friend and often show little artistry or detail. (5) A boyfriend's or girlfriend's name or a gang symbol is tattooed using a pin and India ink, pen ink, charcoal, or ashes as the pigment. (6) The third type, professional tattoos, take two forms: cultural and modern. (7) Cultural tattoos are placed using the time-honored methods of a certain cultural ethnicities. (8) For example, the Samoans use tattoos to display the artistry of their particular heritage. (9) Modern tattoos are performed using a "tattoo gun" and are placed by experienced, paid artists. (10) The fourth type, cosmetic tattoos, is a rapidly growing area of the tattoo industry. (11) Permanent makeup, including eyeliner, lip liner, rouge, and eyebrow pencil, can be placed by a tattoo specialist. (12) Finally, another aspect of cosmetic tattooing is the camouflaging of an undesired tattoo or other physical flaw.

–Adapted from Terrence A. Cronin Jr. *Dermatology Nursing.* Oct 2001 v13 i5 p 380(4).

Read the following paragraph. Then, fill in the sentence outline with the main idea and missing supporting details.

### Alligators and Rocketships

(1) Sharing a boundary with Merritt Island's National Wildlife Refuge on the east coast of Florida, John F. Kennedy Space Center serves as a refuge for several endangered species. (2) For example, the endangered manatee flourishes in the shadows of launch platforms. (3) Just south of launch pad 39A, more than 300 manatees graze protected in a sanctuary in the northern end of Banana River. (4) Manatees are so abundant at the Center that they make up around 30 percent of Florida's total manatee population.

(5) Another endangered species at the center is the beloved sea turtle. (6) Between May and September, thousands of endangered sea turtles come ashore on this barrier island in the dark of night to lay their eggs. (7) With its protected shoreline, Kennedy has one of the most dense turtle populations in the northern hemisphere. (8) Bald eagles also find refuge at the space center. (9) At least five active bald eagle nests exist around the Center. (10) Nests can reach more than six feet in diameter and are usually inhabited from September through May. (11) The eagles usually produce one or two chicks per year. (12) No discussion of wildlife at Kennedy is complete without mentioning

▲ Merritt Island's National Wildlife Refuge

▲ Launch platforms

alligators! (13) While the interactions between man and alligator are few, the biggest problem is during Shuttle landings. (14) Prior to each Kennedy Shuttle landing, it is the task of a special crew to clear the runway of all debris, including any alligators that might be sunning themselves on the runway surface.

–Adapted from *"Alligators and Rocketships."* NASA.
http://www.nasa.gov/centers/kennedy/shuttleoperations/alligators/kscovrv.html

Main idea (Topic Sentence): _____

_____

**A.** Major support: _____

_____

**1.** Minor support: Just south of launch pad 39A, more than 300 manatees graze protected in a sanctuary in the northern end of Banana River.

**2.** Minor support: Manatees are so abundant at the Center that they make up around 30 percent of Florida's total manatee population.

**B.** Major support: _____

_____

    **1.** Minor support: Between May and September, thousands of endangered sea turtles come ashore on this barrier island in the dark of night to lay their eggs.

    **2.** Minor support: _____

_____

**C.** Major support: Bald eagles also find refuge at the space center.

    **1.** Minor support: _____

    **2.** Minor support: _____

_____

    **3.** Minor support: The eagles usually produce one or two chicks per year.

**D.** Major support: _____

_____

    **1.** Minor support: _____

_____

    **2.** Minor support: _____

_____

More practice with outlines and three levels of information in a paragraph
<www.mywritinglab.com>

Practice 3

# Three Parts of a Paragraph

A paragraph is a series of closely related sentences that develop and support the writer's point about a narrowed subject. Often, the paragraph serves as a building block for a longer piece of writing such as an essay, since an essay is composed of two, three, or more paragraphs. In many situations a writer can make a point through one well-developed paragraph. Sometimes, a writer provides a stand-alone paragraph with a title. In addition to a title, a paragraph has three basic parts:

**A Beginning:**
**An introduction of one or more sentences: A topic sentence that states the author's purpose and main point.**

**A Middle:**
**A body of major and minor details that support the topic sentence.**

**An Ending:**
**A conclusion of one or more sentences that reinforces the author's purpose and main point.**

The following graphic describes the function of each part of a paragraph and shows the general format of a paragraph.

**Title:**
Use Key Words or a Phrase to Vividly Describe the Point of Your Paragraph

**The Introduction:**
An introduction is usually one or more sentences that explain the importance of the topic or give necessary background information about the topic.
Your topic sentence states your narrowed subject and your point about the subject.

**The Body:**
The body of a paragraph is made up of a series of sentences that offer major details in support of your topic sentence. If needed, provide minor details that support the major details. Link sentences within the paragraph with clear transitions so your reader can easily follow your thoughts.

**Conclusion:**
The conclusion restates or sums up your paragraph's main idea in one or more sentences.

*Practice 4*

**PARTS OF A PARAGRAPH**

The following student essay by Adam Stewart illustrates the use of a title and the three parts of a paragraph. Underline the topic sentence. Circle each of the three parts of the paragraph: Introduction, Body, and Conclusion. Provide a title for the paragraph.

▲ **Ambitious**

▲ **Mediocre worker**

▲ **Lazy worker**

(1) Although everyone has to work at one point in his or her life and a strong work ethic is looked upon very highly, unfortunately not all workers understand the importance of hard work and a good attitude. (2) Depending upon which category they represent, workers are judged by their coworkers and employers. (3) Three different types of workers make up the workforce, and each type works toward a very different future. (4) First, the ambitious worker comes to work on time, has a good attitude, stays on task, and is always willing to help in any way. (5) Supervisors and coworkers highly value the work ethic of ambitious workers because they always get the job done and do it well beyond expectations. (6) The second type of worker is satisfied with mediocrity. (7) This type of worker comes to work on time, but he or she is not always on the required task. (8) Mediocre workers do what is required and nothing more. (9) Employers and coworkers tolerate mediocre workers because even though they don't always have a good attitude, the job does get done and usually meets expectations. (10) The third type is the lazy worker, also known as the slacker. (11) Everyone hates the slacker. (12) Slackers consistently show up late, rarely accomplish the required task, and continuously try to get the rest of their coworkers off task as well. (13) The slacker, looking for the easy way out, rarely meets expectations. (14) In conclusion, the ambitious workers will be the leaders and high-wage earners; the mediocre workers will likely remain at some dead-end job; and the slackers will probably be fired from job after job, never rethinking their work ethic.

Find more information and practice on each part of the paragraph in the following sections: Introductions—pages 281–283. Topic sentences, major details, and minor details—chapters 4–12. Conclusions—page 294.

More practice with topic sentences and the three parts of the paragraph
<www.mywritinglab.com>

# Developing Your Point Using a Paragraph

An effective paragraph is *focused*, *detailed*, *logical*, and *well expressed*. A writer (1) narrows a topic into a focused main idea; (2) offers only those details that are relevant to the main idea; (3) provides adequate details to support the main idea; (4) organizes these supporting details in a logical flow of information; and (5) uses effective expression through the purposeful choice of words, sentence structure, and grammar.

## The Point: The Main Idea

A focused main idea presents a narrowed subject and the writer's controlling point about the narrowed subject. The controlling point often indicates both the writer's opinion and a pattern of organization. A topic sentence states the focused main idea in a complete sentence.

### Narrow the Topic

Use the following suggestions to guide your thinking as you focus a general topic into a narrowed subject or topic.

- Narrow the topic based on your **opinion**. An opinion is expressed by using words such as *amazing, alarming, beautiful, best, likely, should,* or any other word that states personal values, judgments, or interpretations. Use questions, freewriting, mapping, listing, or another brainstorming technique to discover your opinion about a topic.

  | Example: | General Topic | Narrowed Subject |
  |---|---|---|
  | | Seatbelts | Seatbelts can be dangerous |
  | | | Seatbelts save lives |

- Narrow the topic based on a **pattern of organization**. A writer may use a pattern of organization to narrow a subject and generate details. Patterns of organization are also used to develop, organize, and express a main idea, major details, and minor details in a logical order. The following list provides a few examples of patterns of organization and signal words for each one.

  | Pattern of Organization | Signal Words |
  |---|---|
  | Space Order | *Above, below, next to, underneath, scene* |
  | Time Order | *First, now, then, before, after, process, use* |
  | Example | *For example, exemplify, includes, such as* |
  | Classification | *Types, kinds, levels* |
  | Compare/Contrast | *Similar, likewise, just as / however, in contrast* |
  | Cause/Effect | *Source, origin / results, impact* |

  | Example: | General Topic | Narrowed Subject |
  |---|---|---|
  | | Graffiti | The effects of graffiti |
  | | | The types of graffiti |

- Combine topic, opinion, and pattern of organization to generate a narrowed subject.

  | Example: | General Topic | Narrowed Subject |
  |---|---|---|
  | | Seatbelts | Three reasons seatbelts can be dangerous |
  | | | Proper use of seatbelts saves lives |
  | | Graffiti | The negative effects of graffiti |
  | | | Graffiti: A type of artistic expression |

For more information on each of the patterns of organization, see chapters 4–12.

*Practice 5*

## FOCUS A TOPIC INTO A NARROWED SUBJECT

Combine the topic with an opinion and pattern of organization signal words to narrow the topic.

1. GENERAL TOPIC: *Health Issue: Weightlifting*

   OPINION: *positive*        SIGNAL WORD: *effects*

   NARROWED SUBJECT: _____

2. GENERAL TOPIC: *A Public Figure: Tyra Banks*

   OPINION: *admirable*        SIGNAL WORD: *traits*

   NARROWED SUBJECT: _____

3. GENERAL TOPIC: *Historical Place: Gettysburg*

   OPINION: *most decisive battle in history*    SIGNAL WORD: *scene*

   NARROWED SUBJECT: _____

4. GENERAL TOPIC: *Business: Saving Money*

   OPINION: *smart*        SIGNAL WORD: *steps to*

   NARROWED SUBJECT: _____

## Write the Topic Sentence

Once you have focused a topic into a narrowed subject with your opinion and a pattern of organization, you are ready to write a complete sentence to state the main idea. Each of the following topic sentences offers a subject and a controlling point: a **topic** narrowed by the writer's **opinion** and a suggested **pattern of organization**.

TOPIC          WRITER'S OPINION          PATTERN OF ORGANIZATION
Seatbelts can be dangerous for three reasons.

WRITER'S OPINION          TOPIC          WRITER'S OPINION
Proper use of seatbelts saves lives. ← TOPIC

PATTERN OF ORGANIZATION
TOPIC                    WRITER'S OPINION
Graffiti leads to several negative effects.

PATTERN OF ORGANIZATION
TOPIC              WRITER'S OPINION
Graffiti is a type of artistic expression. ← TOPIC

*Practice 6*

**WRITE A TOPIC SENTENCE**

Write topic sentences for each of the following narrowed subjects.

1. Narrowed Subject: Benefits of aerobic exercise

TOPIC SENTENCE: _____

_____

2. Narrowed Subject: The admirable traits of Tyra Banks

TOPIC SENTENCE: _____

_____

3. Narrowed Subject: Gettysburg: Scene of the Most Decisive Battle in the Civil War

TOPIC SENTENCE: _____

_____

4. Narrowed Subject: Smart Steps to Save Money

TOPIC SENTENCE: _____

_____

More practice with narrowing a subject and writing a topic sentence <www.mywritinglab.com>

# Logical Order

Use a writing plan to establish a logical order for details and a clear flow of ideas. A writing plan includes one or more of the following elements:

*A Pattern of Organization* As discussed on page 58, a writer uses a pattern of organization to arrange major details and minor details in a logical order. The following chart provides a few examples of patterns of organization and signal words for each one (see Chapters 4–12 for in-depth instruction about patterns of organization and signal words):

## Patterns of Organization   Signal Words

| Patterns of Organization | Signal Words |
|---|---|
| Description (Space order) | Above, below, next to, underneath, scene |
| Narrative/Process (Time order) | First, now, then, before, after, next, stage |
| Example | For example, exemplify, includes, such as |
| Classification | Types, kinds, levels |
| Compare/Contrast | Similar, likewise/however, in contrast |
| Cause/Effect | Source, origin/results, impact, reasons |

*Order of Importance* Often, a writer decides upon and arranges details according to his or her opinion about the importance of the details, known as **climatic order**. Usually, climatic order moves from the least important point and builds to the paragraph's climax, the most important point.

***Order of Topic Sentence*** Often the controlling point of the topic sentence divides the subject into chunks of information. The order of the ideas in the topic sentence often reflects a pattern of organization or an order of importance for details.

**Practice 7**

**LOGICAL ORDER**

The following paragraph from a college textbook demonstrates a writing plan based on the logical order of a topic sentence and pattern of organization. Underline the topic sentence. Circle the pattern of organization's signal words.

(1) Interpersonal communication is a continuous series of processes that blend into one another. (2) For convenience of discussion we can separate them into five stages. (3) During the first stage, we sense, we pick up some kind of stimulation. (4) Next, we organize the stimuli in some way. (5) Third, we interpret and evaluate what we perceive. (6) Then, we store it in memory, and finally, in stage five, we retrieve it when needed.
–Adapted from DeVito, *The Interpersonal Communication Book*, 10th Ed., p. 91.

**Practice 8**

**LOGICAL ORDER**

Study the following list of ideas. Label each major support in each group A, B, and C to achieve the most logical order. Discuss the reasons for your choices with a small group of peers.

1. Writing for Everyday Life

Dear Koshanda, we enjoyed our recent visit with you in the great state of Texas.

........... the fun day trips you planned and the great food you cooked

........... the surprise send-off party the night before we left

........... the warm welcome your family provided upon our arrival

2. Writing for Working Life

To Whom It May Concern:  I am writing to register a complaint about the quality of your product, the price of your product, and the attitude of your employees.

........... attitude of your employees

........... price of your product

........... quality of your product

3. Writing for College Life

Political power in the United States, shared equally among three branches of government, actually rests in the hands of relatively few people.

........... Presidential power: One powerful person

........... Legislative power: 535 powerful people

........... Judicial power: 9 powerful people

# Relevant and Adequate Details

Relevant and adequate details support and develop the main idea. As you narrow a topic, usually you generate many ideas before you decide on one main point. You must evaluate each detail based on its relationship to the point you want to make.

*Relevant details* explain and support only the writer's point. Once you narrow a subject into a focused main idea, you then include only those details that relate to your opinion and pattern of organization. Relevant details explain and support only your point as a writer.

## Check for Relevant Details

Apply the following questions to each detail to see if it is relevant to a main idea. If the answers are "no" to these questions, then the detail is most likely irrelevant and should not be included as a support.

- Does the detail reinforce the writer's opinion?
- Does the detail carry out the pattern of organization?
- Does the detail support the main idea?
- Does the detail support a major detail?

*Practice 9*

### RELEVANT DETAILS

The following prewrite list includes a focused main idea and a set of details. Use the "Check for Relevant Details" questions given above to identify the irrelevant detail, and cross it out.

Main Idea: Aerobic exercise leads to several benefits.

| First Benefit | Second Benefit | Third Benefit |
|---|---|---|
| stronger bones | stronger muscles | better health |
| builds bone mass | tones muscles | improved looks |
| reduces brittleness | increases range of motion | reduces body fat |

*Adequate details* offer in-depth explanations and supports for the writer's opinion and pattern of organization. In-depth support of a main idea often requires both major and minor details. Major details directly support the main idea. Minor details support and explain the major details (review the chart on page 51 of this chapter).

## Check for Adequate Details

Apply the following questions to see if you have adequate details to support your main idea. If the answer is "yes" to these questions, then additional details are most likely needed to fully support the main idea.

- Is more information needed to explain the writer's opinion?
- Is more information needed to carry out the pattern of organization?
- Does a major detail need a minor detail of support or explanation?

**ADEQUATE DETAILS**

The following list includes a main idea statement, three major supporting details, and minor details that support each major detail. Circle the major detail that needs more support. Add another minor detail of support for the idea you circled.

Main Idea: Follow three smart steps to save money.

Major Details:   Step one,           Step two,              Step three,
                 avoid debt.         shop with a plan.      cut costs.

Minor Details:   Pay credit          Use a list             Consume fewer
                 cards off.          for groceries.         soft drinks.
                 ................    Avoid impulse buys.    Bring lunch to work.
                 ................    Compare prices.

Many writers use concept maps and other brainstorming techniques to generate enough relevant details to convincingly support a point. Chapters 4 to 12 offer detailed instruction and practice with concept maps and other prewriting activities.

**RELEVANT AND ADEQUATE DETAILS**

Read the following rough draft of a paragraph. Cross out the irrelevant detail. Underline the point that needs more information to adequately support the main idea.

### A Winter Wonder or Winter Haven Vacation?

(1) Many families take advantage of the winter break in school calendars across the country to enjoy a vacation together. (2) A winter-time vacation actually offers distinct choices in activities, food, and clothing. (3) On the one hand, a family may choose to enjoy the wonder of winter. (4) Fresh snow offers plenty of opportunities for winter sports such as skiing, sledding, snowmobiling, snowboarding, or ice skating. (5) Plus, nothing beats the warmth of a fire and a cup of hot soup after a hard day of play in the cold, fresh air. (6) Of course, the family will need to plan on packing additional special

More practice
with relevant and
adequate details
<www.mywritinglab.com>

*Practice 11*

clothing. (7) On the other hand, a family may prefer to visit a winter haven in a tropical climate. (8) Balmy beaches offer plenty of fun options such as sunbathing, snorkeling, surfing, and swimming. (9) Then, after a day drenched in sun and sand, nothing satisfies more than an air-conditioned restaurant serving fresh fish and cold drinks. (10) And the family can travel light. (11) In the tropics, all they really need are their swimsuits and a few causal clothes such as shorts, t-shirts, and sandals. (12) Of course, many people just stay home.

## Effective Expression

Effective expression enhances the writer's purpose through the precise choice and use of words, sentence structure, and grammar.

### Word Choice

Precise word choice communicates exact meaning. Writers choose words that effectively communicate tone, purpose, and order. For example, strong transitions and signal words clue the audience into the logical order of the writer's thoughts. Another example of effective expression is the clear and consistent use of pronouns. In addition, words chosen for their emotional or visual impact create strong mental images in the reader's mind and carry out the writer's purpose.

**Ineffective Expression**

SINGULAR PRONOUN     DISAGREES WITH     PLURAL PRONOUN

Everyone on the soccer team was tired; they were upset about losing.

VAGUE WORDING

**Effective Expression**

SIGNAL WORD

PRONOUNS AND NOUNS AGREE IN NUMBER

As everyone on the soccer team dragged into the locker room, each player drooped her head in defeat.

WORDS CHOSEN FOR EMOTIONAL IMPACT

### Sentence Structure

Four types of sentences serve as the basis for all sentences in the English language: simple sentence, complex sentence, compound sentence, compound-complex sentence. Effective expression uses a variety of sentence types to express ideas in clear and interesting statements. (You will learn more about sentence structure in Chapters 16–17.)

**Simple sentences:**

Michaella had been out of school for years. She was insecure about her abilities.

**Complex sentence:**

Michaella, who had been out of school for years, didn't want to fail.

**Compound sentence:**

She studied for two hours every day; as a result, she earned a 4.0 GPA.

**Compound-Complex sentence:**

Michaella studied for two hours every day because she didn't want to fail; as a result, she earned a 4.0 GPA.

# Grammar

Grammar is a tool of effective expression. Writers use grammar to clarify and polish ideas. Grammar includes a wide variety of language rules such as the following: tense, agreement, and punctuation. (You will learn more about grammar throughout your studies in this text.) During the revision process, many writers focus on one element of expression at a time.

**EFFECTIVE EXPRESSION**

Revise the following paragraph for effective expression through word choice. In a small group of your peers, revise the underlined parts of the following paragraph for effective expression. Use the following word(s) in your revision. Discuss how the revision improves the effectiveness of the paragraph.

suddenly swerved into

landed

Justine's brand new Maxima

A Frightful Moment

*amigo dela          plcasa dele*

(1) Justine was driving her friend Jeremy to his house after a concert last Tuesday evening. (2) An oncoming car <u>is in</u> her lane. (3) Justine jerked her steering wheel to avoid a head on collision. (4) Her car spun 360° off the road. (5) The car <u>lands</u> in the middle of a stand of trees. (6) Thankfully, Justine and Jeremy walked away without injury; unfortunately, <u>their</u> car was totaled.

More practice with evaluating the effectiveness of a paragraph

PART 2 USING PATTERNS OF ORGANIZATION TO DEVELOP PARAGRAPHS

Workshop

# Analyzing the Effectiveness of a Paragraph

Many student writers benefit from the study of a scoring guide. A scoring guide identifies and describes levels of writing effectiveness. The following scoring guide describes the traits of an effective paragraph as discussed in this chapter: A score of "5" indicates a highly effective paragraph. In a small group of your peers, discuss the differences between a "5" paragraph and a "3" level paragraph.

## Scoring Guide for a Paragraph

5   A focused main idea presents the narrowed subject and the writer's point, and suggests a pattern of organization. Relevant and in-depth details convincingly support and develop the main idea. Strong transitions indicate careful ordering of details based on a logical pattern of organization. Effective expression enhances the writer's purpose through the precise choice and use of words, sentence structure, and grammar.

4   A focused main idea presents the narrowed subject and the writer's opinion, and suggests a pattern of organization. Relevant and adequate details support and develop the main idea. Clear transitions indicate an order of details based on a logical pattern of organization. Effective expression carries out the writer's purpose through the competent use and choice of words, sentence structure, and grammar.

3   A focused main idea presents the narrowed subject and the writer's opinion or a pattern of organization. Relevant details offer enough support to develop the main idea. Occasional transitions indicate the use of a pattern of organization, but details are not always logically ordered. Expression does not interfere with the writer's purpose, even though occasional errors in use and choice of words, sentence structure, and grammar occur.

2   The main idea presents a general subject or a broad opinion. Details are generalized statements or lists that do not offer enough information to support the main idea. Weak or misused transitions and confused order of details indicate little use of a pattern of organization. Weak expression interferes with the writer's purpose through frequent errors in use and choice of words, sentence structure, and grammar.

1   The main idea presents a vague, weakly worded opinion about a general subject. Details are missing, superficial, or rambling. Lack of transitions and illogical order of details indicate no use of a pattern of organization. Confused expression interferes with the writer's purpose through pervasive errors in choice and use of words, sentence structure, and grammar.

Use the scoring guide to assign a score to each of the following paragraphs written by students about the following topic: *An Important Lesson Everyone Should Learn*. Be prepared to discuss your reasons for each score.

......... Life is full of changes and drama. Never know what is going to happened next step. With ups and downs I had learn lot of things. At this point of our life you cannot trust anyone. You learn more about life everyday. Experience make us learn something new and give us a lesson what we should expect next. My life was full of thrill but it's good to have something like that in your life. How life has teach me a good lesson and how you can learn something from my experience. I want to tell others that never give up in your life, never think that life is ending when u loose something out of your life, because it's always a hope that bring your confidence back. Never depend on others not even your close family. Trust yourself and you will make it. Success never comes easy it's always tuff ways to find it. Unless you don't give up life goes on.

......... A friendly attitude can bring us more reward than a frown any day. We all need to learn the importance of a smile. Before I learned this lesson, I didn't know how to react at work to a disgruntled person or a grumpy coworker. In fact, most of the time I would simply call on a supervisor for help. Unfortunately, this move made me seem incapable of handling a problem on my own. Then one day, someone smiled at me for no reason. A friendly face in the crowd made me feel good. If one person with a smile on her face could make me feel lighter, then a smile might be a powerful way to change how other people felt. Over the next few months, I smiled at every person who looked in my direction, even the nastiest of patrons. As a result, most people were friendlier towards me, and I even felt better about myself. I also became easily able to handle those pesky daily problems. I wish more of us could learn that we have the opportunity to change the world within in us and outside of us, when we smile.

......... Everyone should learn an important lesson in life. Some lessons about being honest. Everyone should learn honesty. Parents teach honesty. Don't shoplift. Don't cheat on tests. Don't lie to friends, even white lies. Everyone should learn kindness. Parents and friends teach kindness. Peers are not kind to them. Too many school yard bullies hurt people. If everyone learned important lessons in life, they would be better off.

......... My mom taught how to deal with stress. As a young child, I was diagnosed with attention deficit disorder. This condition makes many every day situations very stressful. So mom taught me three things that have helped me reduce stress. First, she taught me to think ahead. For example every evening, I lay out my clothes for the next day. Planning what I want to wear the night before saves me time and gives me one less thing to worry about in the morning rush to get out the door. Second, she taught me to be organized. Not only do I plan what I am going to wear, but I make a daily list of assignments and appointments so I know exactly what I need to do and where I need to be. I also keep a backpack filled with supplies such as bottled water, healthy snacks, pen, paper, or any other item I might need. Finally, mother taught me to ask questions and take notes. Asking questions and taking notes keep me focused on a task and keeps my mind from wandering in a million different directions. I am grateful that my mom taught me how to reduce stress. I bet everyone would be better off if they could learn what my mom taught me about coping with stress.

......... Steeling is wrong! Unfortunately not everyone knows this. If every one respected others' property as they do there own we would have less chaos. If everyone that was caught steeling had a good beating put on them I am sure they would second guess doing it again, I am not saying that is how this problem should be resolved but I think it would work. Whether you are a child or a full grown adult I believe this concept should be stressed, let alone it is against the law. The world would be a better place if no one stole, and we would all have more respect for each other and there property.

More practice with effective expression <www.mywritinglab.com>

# 4

# The Descriptive Paragraph

## A description is an account that creates a vivid mental image.

**Chapter Preview:**

- What's the Point of Description?
- Making a Point Using Description: One Student Writer's Response
- Developing Your Point Using Description
- Using Description in Your Academic Courses
- Workshop: Writing a Description Paragraph Step by Step

The ability to describe people, places, or objects accurately is a useful life skill. Whether you are talking with a stylist about the exact hairstyle you want, sharing a funny or startling scene from your day with a friend in an email, or reporting on the structure of a plant cell for a biology class, you will use description to make your point.

"Snow blows across the highway before me as I walk—little, wavering trails of it swept along like a people dispersed. The snow people—where are they going? Some great danger must pursue them. They hurry and fall, the wind gives them a push, they get up and go on again."

JOHN HAINES, FROM "SNOW"

# What's the Point of Description?

In a descriptive paragraph, the writer uses sensory details such as sights, sounds, smells, tastes, feelings, and textures to create vivid images in the reader's mind. An experienced writer relies on sense memories of a specific experience to call to mind these details. In addition, the writer often uses spatial order to create a clear visual image of a person, place, object, or scene: the location or arrangement in space from top to bottom, bottom to top, right to left, left to right, near to far, far to near, inside to outside, or outside to inside.

Every day, we experience rich sensory details from television, movies, music DVDs, and daily life. Think of a scene that grabbed your attention recently. What is your main impression of the scene? What are several details that make this impression so vivid or memorable?

Description also may include or suggest time order because a person, place, or object usually appears in a situation, or an incident usually occurs or suggests a scene.

Descriptive transition words signal that the details follow a logical order based on one or more of the following elements:

**1.** The arrangement in space of a person, place, object, or scene

**2.** The starting point from which the writer chooses to begin the description

**3.** The time frame as relevant to the description (see Chapter 5 for information about time order)

Getting a mental picture of the person, place, object, scene, or situation helps a writer discover his or her point about the subject being described. Study the following photograph of a popular destination for travelers: the Riverwalk in San Antonio, Texas. Use your sense memory of this or similar scenes to call up sensory details. Fill in the graphic with captions that capture the particular details of specific locations on the Riverwalk. Then answer the question with a one-sentence statement of the overall main idea: "What's the point or impression you are trying to make?"

PHOTOGRAPHIC ORGANIZER: DESCRIPTION

WRITING FROM LIFE

Practice 1

**A** Where is this detail in the scene?

........................................................................................

What are the sensory details?

SIGHT: ..............................................................................

SOUND: ..............................................................................

SMELL: ..............................................................................

TASTE: ..............................................................................

TOUCH: ..............................................................................

**B** Where is this detail in the scene?

........................................................................................

What are the sensory details?

SIGHT: ..............................................................................

SOUND: ..............................................................................

SMELL: ..............................................................................

TASTE: ..............................................................................

TOUCH: ..............................................................................

**C** Where is this detail in the scene?

........................................................................................

What are the sensory details?

SIGHT: ..............................................................................

SOUND: ..............................................................................

SMELL: ..............................................................................

TASTE: ..............................................................................

TOUCH: ..............................................................................

**D** Where is this detail in the scene?

......................................................................................................

What are the sensory details?

SIGHT: ...........................................................................................

SOUND: ........................................................................................

SMELL: ..........................................................................................

TASTE: ...........................................................................................

TOUCH: .........................................................................................

**E** Where is this detail in the scene?

......................................................................................................

What are the sensory details?

SIGHT: ...........................................................................................

SOUND: ........................................................................................

SMELL: ..........................................................................................

TASTE: ...........................................................................................

TOUCH: .........................................................................................

**What's the point?**

......................................................................................................

......................................................................................................

......................................................................................................

Practice 1

## My First Thoughts: A Prewriting Activity

Brainstorm about the images you just studied. Set a time limit, such as five minutes, and write in your notebook about the images you just studied and the details you generated. Write as quickly as you can without stopping.

# Making a Point Using Description: One Student Writer's Response

The following descriptive paragraph, written as an online review for tourists, offers one writer's point about the Riverwalk in San Antonio. Read this description and the explanations; complete the activities. Then, read the writer's journal entry about her experience writing the paragraph.

*strung. past Tense string.*

**Spatial Order:**
The phrase "left bank" establishes spatial order. Circle four more words or phrases that indicate spatial order.

**Main Idea:**
The main idea is the point the author is making. The topic is "Paseo Del Rio, the San Antonio Riverwalk." Underline the author's point.

**Relevant Details:**
Relevant details describe elements of the scene to support the point "shimmers with color and light." Underline additional details that support this point.

**Effective Expression:**
Sensory details such as "cool, damp evenings," "spicy fajitas," "salty margaritas," "lights" and "sunset glimmer" create a vivid mental picture. Underline 3 more sensory details.

### Paseo Del Rio: A Festival of Color and Light

(1) The Texas spirit of fun and hospitality lights up Paseo Del Rio, the San Antonio Riverwalk. (2) This festive and popular travel destination shimmers with color and light. (3) Along the left bank, two lines of brightly colored café umbrellas—tropical red, Cancun blue, emerald green, lemon yellow—shelter outdoor diners and adorn the cobblestone walk. (4) Above the rainbow rows of umbrellas, white lights *saltau-hascu* strung between oak trees along the walking path glimmer softly in the dusk. (5) Miniature white lights rim the eaves and roofs of the buildings behind the diners and illuminate the graceful drape of the oak branches bending over them. (6) Diners can stay warm on cool, damp evenings with spicy fajitas and salty margaritas as they watch the lights of the Riverwalk and the sunset glimmer upon the water. (7) As they watch, a steady flow of purple trimmed boats putter to midstream from under the bridge on the right side of the river. (8) On this side of the river, the rock walls and the footbridge showcase the rough beauty of the area's natural elements and earth tones. (9) Colorful lights trace the arch under the footbridge. (10) Luminaries sit atop both sides of the bridge's stone-grey railings. (11) At the far side of the bridge, more luminaries light the path along the water's edge. (12) People fill the path with laughter and conversation as they stroll beneath trees shimmering with countless tiny lights. (13) All along the river, this canopy of lights buffers the Riverwalk from the buildings rising in the distance. (14) The lights, the good food, the water, the spectacle of color, the festive atmosphere provide a luscious retreat—Texas style!

The student writer of "Paseo Del Rio: A Festival of Color and Light" completed the following reflection to record her thinking through the writing process. Read her writer's journal that describes a few key choices she made as she wrote.

MAIN IDEA: I spent a good deal of time studying this picture before I began writing, and I still needed several revisions to get the effect I wanted. My first thoughts were about the vivid colors and lights and how much fun the Riverwalk looks—like a festival. The place just seems like a carefully created retreat away from the hectic world that lies just a few blocks away. I found a graphic organizer very helpful during prewriting. Since I have visited the Riverwalk, I used sense memory to recall details, and the graphic organizer helped me focus my point and map out the order of details without having to worry about wording, sentence structure, or punctuation.

RELEVANT DETAILS: During one revision, I discovered that my sentence about the boats wasn't relevant to my point. I had included the boats because they were in the picture, not because they supported the point I wanted to make. So I revised that sentence to include the color of the boats, which does add to the festive atmosphere of the Riverwalk and directly supports my point.

LOGICAL ORDER: I devoted one revision to the words that signal spatial order; I wanted to guide the reader's attention from the left bank to the right bank of the river. I had to really think about how to word these signals so the mind's eye could create a picture and follow my point. So my mental eye went from the lower left bank of umbrellas, to above the umbrellas, and then behind them. Next, I directed the reader's attention to the river in the middle of the picture by focusing on what the diners would be watching—the boat tours. To describe the right side of the river, I moved from "near" to "far" based on the location of the bridge.

EFFECTIVE EXPRESSION: During my last revision, I focused on my word choice. By referring to my thesaurus, I was able to use a variety of verbs and nouns for "light." I wanted to emphasize the beautiful effect of the lights throughout the paragraph.

For a blank version of this form for your own reflections about your writing:
<www.mywritinglab.com>

For more information on time order, Chapter 5, "Narration."

# Developing Your Point Using Description

Writers use descriptive paragraphs to make a point through the vivid details they observe and share about a person, place, object, scene, or situation. To make a point by describing details, a writer often relies on spatial order transitions and sensory details. At times, a writer also uses time order to describe an experience.

## The Point: The Main Idea

When you write a description, you limit your topic to concrete details based on sight, sound, smell, taste, and touch. Your opinion or attitude about the subject you are describing is your point or main idea. In a description, your main idea may also include logical order signal words; other times, the logical order is implied without including the signal words.

For example, the first of the following two topic sentences includes (1) the topic, (2) the writer's opinion about the topic, and (3) spatial order signal words. The second topic sentence only includes (1) the topic and (2) the writer's attitude about the topic.

*PATTERN OF ORGANIZATION: SPATIAL ORDER*     *THE TOPIC*

**From head to toe, Latoya** dressed to appear
**professional and confident.**

*THE WRITER'S OPINION*

**Miguel's office** reveals **his careful attention to organization.**

*THE TOPIC*          *THE WRITER'S OPINION*

*Practice 2*

### TOPIC SENTENCES

Practice creating topic sentences. The first two items below present a topic, an opinion, and logical order signal word(s). Combine the ideas in each group to create a topic sentence for a descriptive paragraph. Then, complete the practice by composing your own topic sentences.

**1.** TOPIC: (a favorite place) _Grandmother's kitchen_

OPINION: _offered a haven of old-fashioned country warmth_

LOGICAL ORDER SIGNAL WORDS: _A small room at the rear of the house_

TOPIC SENTENCE: _____

_____

_____

More practice with
creating topic sentences:
<www.mywritinglab.com>

**2.** TOPIC: (a treasured possession) _The handmade well–pump lamp_

OPINION: _is an eye-catching and whimsical family treasure_

LOGICAL ORDER SIGNAL WORDS: _implied: such as in top to bottom_

TOPIC SENTENCE: _____

_____

_Sleek – smooth_
_or glossy._

**3.** TOPIC: (a useful product) _____

OPINION: _sleek, lightweight, flexible, easy to use_

LOGICAL ORDER SIGNAL WORDS (as needed): _____

_____

TOPIC SENTENCE: _____

_____

**4.** TOPIC: (a person of character) My mother (or father, brother, sister, friend, etc.)

OPINION: _kindness_

LOGICAL ORDER SIGNAL WORDS (as needed): _____

_____

TOPIC SENTENCE: _My mother_

**5.** TOPIC: _____

OPINION: _____

LOGICAL ORDER SIGNAL WORDS (as needed): _____

_____

TOPIC SENTENCE: _____

_____

Practice 2

Practice 2

**6.** TOPIC: ....................................................................................................................

OPINION: ..............................................................................................................

LOGICAL ORDER SIGNAL WORDS (as needed): ..............................................

....................................................................................................................

TOPIC SENTENCE: ................................................................................................

....................................................................................................................

**7.** TOPIC: ....................................................................................................................

OPINION: ..............................................................................................................

LOGICAL ORDER SIGNAL WORDS (as needed): ..............................................

....................................................................................................................

TOPIC SENTENCE: ................................................................................................

....................................................................................................................

....................................................................................................................

## Transition Words Used to Signal Visual Description

| | | | | | |
|---|---|---|---|---|---|
| above | at the top | beyond | farther | left | right |
| across | back | by | front | middle | there |
| adjacent | behind | center | here | nearby | under |
| around | below | close to | in | next to | underneath |
| at the bottom | beneath | down | inside | outside | within |
| at the side | beside | far away | | | |

# Logical Order

Once you have chosen a topic and focused on a main idea, you are ready to generate and organize details. To organize visual details, spatial order transition words are helpful during the prewriting phase as well as during the drafting part of the writing process. During prewriting, spatial signal words such as *top*, *middle*, or *bottom* can be used as headings to list details. During the drafting stage, explicitly stating spatial transition words creates a mental picture in your reader's mind of how your subject is arranged in space. Strong transition words establish coherence—a clear and easy-to-follow flow of ideas.

Practice 3

**SPATIAL ORDER DETAILS**

Determine the logical order of the following details taken from Maya Angelou's autobiography *I Know Why the Caged Bird Sings*. Rewrite the paragraph, organizing the details by spatial order. *Hint:* Underline the words that signal spatial order. Complete the exercise by answering the question "What's the point?"

............ And when they put their hands on their hips in a show of jauntiness, the palms slipped the thighs as if the pants were waxed.

............ When they tried to smile to carry off their tiredness as if it was nothing, the body did nothing to help the mind's attempt at disguise.

............ In the store the men's faces were the most painful to watch, but I seemed to have no choice.

............ Their shoulders drooped even as they laughed.

_____

_____

_____

_____

_____

_____

What's the point Maya Angelou makes with her use of spatial details?

_____

_____

More practice with spatial order details:
<www.mywritinglab.com>

# Relevant Details

A writer narrows a topic into a focused main idea by generating descriptive details that answer questions such as *who, what,* and *where.* As a writer brainstorms, the thinking process brings to mind many sensory as well as spatial details. A writer evaluates the relevancy of each detail and uses only those that illustrate the main idea. Some relevant details describe the appearance of a person, object, place, or scene; other relevant details explain the author's opinion about the topic. Many descriptive details appeal to sight, sound, smell, taste, and touch. A **concept map**, or **graphic organizer**, helps in several ways. First, the graphic can prompt your thinking, memory, and creativity. In addition, the graphic helps to order ideas as they occur to you. A graphic organizer also allows you to visualize the details and see if you have enough details to make your point. Irrelevant details do not explain, support, or illustrate the focused point of the paragraph. In addition to the graphic organizer, writers use the revision process to double check details for relevancy and to eliminate irrelevant details.

## Concept Chart: Description

TOPIC: Latoya and professional attire for a job interview

| WHERE | SIGHT | SMELL | SOUND | TASTE | TOUCH |
|---|---|---|---|---|---|
| Top: Hair | hair gathered and smoothed into a neat and stylish twist | | | | |
| Face | light touch of blush and lip gloss; small gold earrings | | calm, assured tone of voice | | |
| Middle: Blouse and Jacket | white dress cotton button-up collared shirt; dark blue jacket with a rich pin stripe | | | | firm handshake |
| Skirt | below the knee; dark blue, A-line | | | | |
| Bottom: Shoes | dark blue, polished, low heels, attractive | | | | |

During the prewriting phase of writing, a writer naturally generates irrelevant details. In fact, an effective writer evaluates the details and uses only the details that support the main idea. All descriptive details should work together to create a strong, unified impression, a mental image of the author's main point.

**Practice 4**

**RELEVANT CONCRETE DETAILS**

The following paragraph develops the ideas recorded in the graphic organizer about Latoya and her professional attire. Circle the main idea. Underline the spatial signal words and the sensory details. Cross out the two details that are not relevant to the main idea.

### Dressed to Impress

(1) Latoya Bond had been job hunting for months; finally, she landed an interview with a company that she was eager to join. (2) Latoya felt confident that she was well qualified for the position. (3) After all, she was one of the three final candidates chosen from over 100 applications, yet she also knew the importance of making a good impression. (4) From head to toe, Latoya dressed to appear professional and confident. (5) Latoya gathered her hard-to-manage curls into a neat and stylish twist. (6) To complement her no-nonsense hairstyle, Latoya used makeup sparingly but effectively. (7) A little black mascara on her lashes, a touch of blush across her cheeks, and bit of tinted lip balm brought attention to her interested eyes and her earnest smile. (8) She would also be sure to speak with a calm and assured voice. (9) The neatly pressed collar of a white cotton shirt contrasted nicely with her tailored blue pinstriped jacket. (10) Her dark blue A-line skirt reached to just below her knees. (11) Latoya finished her outfit with a flattering pair of blue low-heeled pumps that matched her briefcase and purse. (12) She would offer her prospective employer a firm handshake. (13) Latoya looked as professional and confident as she felt.

More practice with relevant, concrete details in descriptive paragraphs: <www.mywritinglab.com>

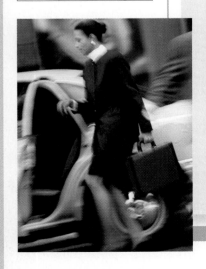

# Effective Expression: Concrete Word Choice

Precise word choice communicates exact meaning. Words chosen for a specific emotional or visual impact create strong mental images in the reader's mind and carry out the writer's purpose. As you move through the writing process, think about the impact you want to have on your reader. For the greatest impact, choose concrete and precise words and phrases instead of general or vague expressions. Choose words that *show* instead of *tell*. Consider the following examples:

**General or vague words that tell:**

> This property has curb appeal.

**Concrete words that show:**

> This beachfront cottage charms potential buyers with its colorful garden, wrap-around porch, and ocean view.

**CONCRETE WORD CHOICE**

Each item below presents a general sentence using vague words. The phrase in parentheses before each sentence—"(A customer to a mechanic)" in item 1, for example—describes the speaker of the sentence and the person hearing it. Revise each sentence to eliminate vague wording. Consider the point of the writing situation; express ideas with words that have concrete and precise meanings for a specific impact. Discuss your revisions with your class or with a small group of peers.

**1.** (A customer to a mechanic):  My car makes a funny sound sometimes.

- - - - - - - - - - - - - - - - - - - - - - - - - - - - - - - - - - - - - - - - - - - - - - - - - - - - - -

**2.** (A student commenting to his or her companion): The restaurant was disappointing.

- - - - - - - - - - - - - - - - - - - - - - - - - - - - - - - - - - - - - - - - - - - - - - - - - - - - - - -

- - - - - - - - - - - - - - - - - - - - - - - - - - - - - - - - - - - - - - - - - - - - - - - - - - - - - - -

**3.** (A weather reporter to a commuter):  The weather is nice (or horrible).

- - - - - - - - - - - - - - - - - - - - - - - - - - - - - - - - - - - - - - - - - - - - - - - - - - - - - - -

- - - - - - - - - - - - - - - - - - - - - - - - - - - - - - - - - - - - - - - - - - - - - - - - - - - - - - -

**4.** (A staff assistant to Technology Support):  The printer is broken.

- - - - - - - - - - - - - - - - - - - - - - - - - - - - - - - - - - - - - - - - - - - - - - - - - - - - - - -

- - - - - - - - - - - - - - - - - - - - - - - - - - - - - - - - - - - - - - - - - - - - - - - - - - - - - - -

- - - - - - - - - - - - - - - - - - - - - - - - - - - - - - - - - - - - - - - - - - - - - - - - - - - - - - -

Practice 5

More practice with concrete word choice in descriptive paragraphs: <www.mywritinglab.com>

# Using Description in Your Academic Courses

Many college courses such as literature, composition, history, psychology, ecology, and biology use description. As you study these courses, you will read descriptions of historical places, influential people, natural elements, and scientific experiments. In addition, you will write descriptions to learn or demonstrate what you have learned.

Practice 6

### USING DESCRIPTION IN A HISTORY ASSIGNMENT

Student writer Jean Powell composed the following descriptive paragraph of an important historical site for a report in her American History course. Complete the following activities: (1) Insert appropriate transition words in the blanks. (2) Underline the words or phrases used to create sensory details. (3) Discuss the point of her report with a small group of peers or with your class.

The Vietnam Memorial is made up of two black granite walls joined in a wide-angled V shape. A study of just one of the walls reveals the significance of the memorial. A polished black granite slab stretches hundreds of feet long. At its highest tip, it stands 10 feet tall and then tapers to a height of 8 inches at its end point. Its low tip points ............ the Lincoln Memorial. ............ its polished face are the carved names of service men and women who gave their lives during the Vietnam War. Starting at the highest point on the first panel, thousands of names are listed in chronological order. The high polish of the black granite reflects the image of the world ............ the wall. The reflection of earth, sky, and visitors are seen along with the inscribed names. On the wall, the present and the past mingle. A path runs ............ the base of the wall so visitors can walk the path to read the names. Many create pencil rubbings or leave tokens such as flowers, flags, and personal notes. To the side of the path, a wide grassy park adds to the sense of serenity. The memorial is a quiet place where one can come to terms with loss and grief. Its tranquility is a fitting memorial to a controversial war that cost so many their lives.

More practice with writing descriptive paragraphs: <www.mywritinglab.com>

# Workshop: Writing a Description Paragraph Step by Step

*Workshop*

## Prewrite Your Paragraph

The various activities below will walk you through the steps of the prewriting stage of the writing process: choosing a topic; focusing your point; and generating and organizing relevant details.

### Choose Your Topic

The following activities are designed to help you choose a topic.

1. Create a bank of topics. Use the following headings and brainstorm or list as many topics as you possibly can. Don't analyze your thoughts; just jot down topics as quickly as they occur to you. Compare your bank of topics with those of your classmates.

   - The Scene of an Accident
   - A Nature Scene
   - A Pop Icon
   - An Advertisement
   - Emotions (such as fear)

2. Reread the freewrite you composed based on the photograph of the San Antonio Riverwalk. Underline ideas that could be used for a descriptive paragraph. Map out the logical order of details.

3. Select a photograph of a special place. Write captions, brainstorm sensory details, and freewrite about the photograph. Remember to ask "What are the sensory details and how are the details arranged in space?" and "What's the point?" as you generate ideas.

### Focus Your Point

Think about a prewrite you have generated for a descriptive topic. Underline or generate words that suggest your values, opinions, or attitudes about what you described. Think about what strikes you as important about your subject. Consider your audience. Who would be interested in this information and why? Choose a purpose. Write a list of adjectives and sensory details that describe the essence of what you are describing. Use a thesaurus and choose several vivid words to express your thoughts. State in one sentence the point of your description:

AUDIENCE: ........................................................................................................

PURPOSE: ...........................................................................................................

WHAT'S THE POINT? ...........................................................................................

........................................................................................................................

## Generate and Organize Relevant Details

Using the ideas you have already recorded and the concept chart for a description, generate and organize sensory and spatial details that support your point. (*Hint*: Fill in the "Where" column with spatial signal words such as *left*, *right*, *near*, *far*, *above*.)

| Concept Chart: Description | | | | | |
|---|---|---|---|---|---|
| TOPIC: | | | | | |
| WHAT'S THE POINT? | | | | | |
| WHERE | SIGHT | SMELL | SOUND | TASTE | TOUCH |
| | | | | | |
| | | | | | |
| | | | | | |
| | | | | | |
| | | | | | |

## Write a Draft of Your Paragraph

Using ideas you generated during the prewriting phase, compose a draft of your paragraph. Return to the prewriting process at any time to generate additional details as needed. Use your own paper.

## Revise Your Draft

Once you have drafted a description, read the draft and answer the questions in the "Questions for Revising a Descriptive Paragraph" box that follows on the next page. Indicate your answers by annotating your paper. If you answer "yes" to a question, underline, check, or circle examples. If you answer "no" to a question, write needed information in the margins and draw lines to indicate placement of additional details. Revise your paragraph as necessary based on your reflection. (*Hint*: Experienced writers create several drafts as they focus on one or two questions per draft.)

## Questions for Revising a Descriptive Paragraph

☐ Have I stated or implied a focused main idea? Have I created a strong impression? Can I state my point in one sentence?

☐ Is the logical order of the details clear? Have I used strong transitions to indicate spatial order? Time order?

☐ Have I created a vivid mental image through the use of sensory details?

☐ Have I made my point with adequate details?

☐ Do all the details support my point?

☐ Have I chosen concrete words to make my point?

## Proofread Your Draft

Once you have made any revisions to your paragraph that may be needed, proofread your paper to eliminate unnecessary errors, such as dangling or misplaced modifiers.

### Grammar in Action: Eliminate Dangling or Misplaced Modifiers

Modifiers are words and phrases that describe other words. A **dangling modifier** occurs when a writer uses a modifier without including the word that the modifier describes.

- **Dangling modifier:**

  **INCORRECT:** Entering the museum of shrunken heads, my stomach lurched with queasiness.

  *(The missing word is "I": It was I, not my stomach, that entered the museum.)*

- **Revised sentence:**

  **CORRECT:** As I entered the museum of shrunken heads, my stomach lurched with queasiness.

A **misplaced modifier** occurs when a writer separates the modifier from the word it is describing.

- **Misplaced modifier:**

  **INCORRECT:** Scattering in a million directions, Tyrone hustled to scoop up the spilled ball bearings.

  *(The ball bearings scattered, not Tyrone)*

- **Revised sentence:**

  **CORRECT:** Tyrone hustled to scoop up the spilled ball bearings scattering in a million directions.

> For more information on dangling and misplaced modifiers, see Chapter 23.

*Workshop*

Edit the following student paragraph to eliminate one dangling modifier and two misplaced modifiers.

## The Amazing Ruby Falls

(1) The caves at Ruby Falls are one of the wonders of the world, eerie yet intriguing. (2) Our tour group was a small one of about ten people. (3) We all piled onto an elevator, stuffy from all the bodies and stinking like a dirty sock, to sink 250 feet underground. (4) We exited the elevator, gasping for air because of the lack of oxygen and the dampness of the cave. (5) The cave was dark with barely any light. (6) We wore helmets mounted with lights. (7) I looked like a real spelunker. (8) We saw stalactites hanging from the ceiling and stalagmites growing up from the ground. (9) The columns, drapes, and flow stone were phenomenal. (10) We walked through an onyx jungle flowing with layers of limestone. (11) The massive monuments were smooth and damp. (12) Some were slimy like a snail. (13) Water trickled from the ceiling in my hair and down my face, a kiss from the cave. (14) We squeezed through stone pathways littered with rock shapes resembling everything from bacon, to a dragon foot, to a form that looked like New York City, all natural. (15) We came across a huge formation; that appeared to be lifelike; the ice sickle stalactites looked like they could break free and assault us. (16) A breathtaking formation that appeared to be lifelike. (17) The caves are amazing.

More practice with correcting dangling and misplaced modifiers:
<www.mywritinglab.com>

**REVIEW OF WRITING A DESCRIPTIVE PARAGRAPH:** DEVELOP YOUR POINT USING THE WRITING PROCESS

Use the following form to record your thinking about writing a descriptive paragraph. Select and focus a topic for your writing situation, audience, and purpose.

Choose a person, place, object, or scene and identify its significance.

What is your point?

TOPIC, PERSON, PLACE, OBJECT, OR SCENE: ....................................................................

AUDIENCE: ....................................................................................................................

PURPOSE: ......................................................................................................................

...................................................................................................................................

...................................................................................................................................

State your main idea in a topic sentence.

TOPIC: ..........................................................................................................................

OPINION: ......................................................................................................................

...................................................................................................................................

...................................................................................................................................

Generate relevant details:

REPORTER'S QUESTIONS: WHO, WHAT, WHERE, WHEN? ................................................

...................................................................................................................................

...................................................................................................................................

...................................................................................................................................

...................................................................................................................................

...................................................................................................................................

Generate sensory details:

LOCATION (TOP, MIDDLE, BOTTOM, LEFT, RIGHT): .................................................................................................

..........................................................................................................................................................................................

SIGHT: ...............................................................................................................................................................................

..........................................................................................................................................................................................

SMELL: ..............................................................................................................................................................................

..........................................................................................................................................................................................

SOUND: .............................................................................................................................................................................

..........................................................................................................................................................................................

TASTE: ...............................................................................................................................................................................

..........................................................................................................................................................................................

TOUCH: ..............................................................................................................................................................................

..........................................................................................................................................................................................

Use logical order. Use transition words to signal organization of details and relationships between ideas.

SPACE ORDER: ..................................................................................................................................................................

TIME ORDER: .....................................................................................................................................................................

Use effective expression. Choose words for clear, precise meaning.

CONCRETE WORDS THAT SHOW INSTEAD OF TELL: .......................................................................................................

..........................................................................................................................................................................................

CORRECTED DANGLING OR MISPLACED MODIFIERS: ..................................................................................................

Review

# Writing Assignments

More ideas for writing a descriptive paragraph: <www.mywritinglab.com>

## Considering Audience and Purpose

Study the photographs at the beginning of the chapter. Assume you are a member of the Riverwalk business community, and the community leaders have asked you and other interested parties for needed safety improvements along the Riverwalk. Suggest and describe one or more specific safety improvements.

## Writing for Everyday Life

Assume you are separated from your family or loved ones during a holiday or a special occasion. Write a letter in which you describe a significant element of the event. For example, describe the decorations of the season or event, a bride's dress, a favorite birthday gift, or the spread of food at a party or dinner. Choose words that reflect one of the following: (1) approval and enjoyment or (2) disapproval and disappointment.

## Writing for College Life

Assume you are writing a report in your psychology class about how a person's mood is reflected in the clothes he or she chooses on any given day. Describe an outfit that reflects an individual's mood.

## Writing for Working Life

Assume you have invented a product that will make life much easier; also assume that the Small Business Association finances the production and marketing of useful new inventions. Write a paragraph describing your product to submit your idea to the Small Business Association.

# 5

## The Narrative Paragraph

## Narration is an account of events told in chronological order to make a specific point.

All of us love a good story. Think of a good story that you have heard, read, or watched on TV or in a theater.

A good story is about personalities or characters, whether real or imagined. A good story is full of vivid action and details. A good story makes a point.

A writer uses narration to tell a story to make a specific point. Often we tell stories to warn about dangers, to teach important lessons, to record important historical events, or to amuse and entertain each other. Narration is a chain of events. These events unfold in chronological order—the order in which they occur. Thus, details follow a logical order based on time. The writer presents an event and then shows when and how each of the subsequent events flows from the first event. In addition to relaying an event, a writer also uses vivid actions and details to show the point of the story. Vivid details may include specific sights, sounds, smells, tastes, textures, feelings, and actions.

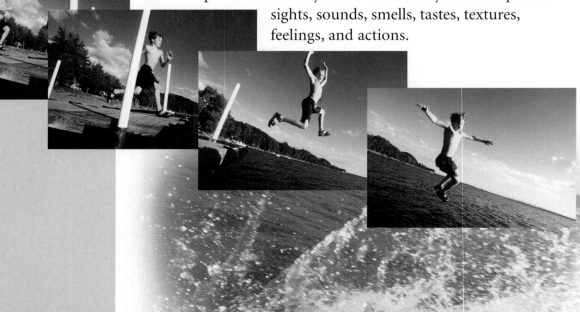

# What's the Point of Narration?

Getting a mental picture of the event helps a writer to discover the point he or she wishes to make. The following sequence of photographs documents a series of events that took place in the life of Jennifer Hudson over the course of three years. Study each photograph in the timeline. Write a caption that states the topic of each picture. Answer the question "What's the point?" with a one-sentence statement of the overall main idea.

*Practice 1*

WRITING FROM LIFE

PHOTOGRAPHIC ORGANIZER: NARRATION

**FIRST EVENT**

What happened?

_____

_____

_____

▲ *American Idol*, April 21, 2004

**SECOND EVENT**

What happened?

_____

_____

_____

▲ *Dreamgirls*, December 25, 2006

**THIRD EVENT**

What happened?

_____

_____

_____

◄ *Oscar ceremony*, February 25, 2007

**What's the point?**

TOPIC SENTENCE: _____

_____

_____

PREWRITING

## My First Thoughts: A Prewriting Activity

Set a time limit, such as five minutes, and write in your notebook about the images you just studied. Do not let your pen or pencil stop. Even if you must repeat ideas, keep writing until the time limit is up. Let the ideas flow freely. Getting your first thoughts about a topic on paper is one excellent way to kick-start your writing process.

# Making a Point Using Narration: One Student Writer's Response

The following paragraph offers one writer's narrative inspired by photographs of Jennifer Hudson. Read the narrative paragraph; read the explanations and follow the directions that are given in the annotations of the paragraph. Then, read the writer's journal that describes a few key choices she made as she wrote.

**Chronological Order**
Chronological order is established with the phrase "in the moment." Circle four more words or phrases that indicate time order.

**Main Idea**
The main idea is the point of the narration. Notice the topic is Jennifer Hudson. Underline the author's point.

**Vivid Verbs**
Vivid verbs such as "exploded" creates a mental image and emphasizes action. Underline three more vivid verbs.

**Relevant Details**
Relevant details describe events to support the point about Hudson's success. Underline another supporting detail about her success.

### Jennifer Hudson: Achieving a Dream

(1) All of us, at some point in our lives, face the disappointment of failure. (2) And in the moment of disappointment, we are tempted to give up, give in, and settle for less. (3) Fortunately, Jennifer Hudson's story teaches us that success can follow failure. (4) On April 21, 2004, fans booted Hudson off of the third season of *American Idol*. (5) Many critics of the show had expected Hudson, Fantasia Barrino or La Toya London, the other two female African-American power talents, to be the winner. (6) Suddenly, Hudson became the sixth of 12 finalists sent home by the fans. (7) Ultimately, she finished in seventh place. (8) She was a loser. (9) But she didn't give up; she kept on working. (10) For the most part, the general public forgot about Jennifer Hudson, but she did not give in to the pressure. (11) She kept working and looking for the next big break. (12) Then, on December 25, 2006, Hudson exploded back onto the national stage with the release of the smash-hit movie *Dreamgirls*, a film about the struggles of a popular 1960s girl group similar to The Supremes.(13) In the film, Hudson sings a gut-wrenching, show-stopping version of the song "And I Am Telling You I'm Not Going." (14) Her five minute emotional performance pulsed with power. (15) Then, on February 25, 2007, Hudson won the Academy Award for Best Supporting Actress for her role as Effie White in *Dreamgirls*. (16) During her acceptance speech she gushed with gratitude, "thank you all for helping me keep the faith." (17) Jennifer Hudson never gave up, gave in, or settled for less. (18) She offers living proof of success after failure.

The student writer of "Jennifer Hudson: Achieving a Dream" completed the following reflection to record her thinking through the writing process. Read her writer's journal that describes a few key choices she made as she wrote.

MAIN IDEA: I think that Jennifer Hudson's story shows why American Idol is so popular. It gives ordinary people a shot at becoming rich and famous based on their talent and guts. Yet, for every person who succeeds, hundreds of others fail to achieve their dreams. Hudson seemed to fail on American Idol, yet she came back and showed everybody that "success can follow failure." She is a real inspiration, and that is the main point I wanted to make.

RELEVANT DETAILS: I have watched American Idol from Season One, and I have followed Jennifer Hudson's rise to success because she was on the show. Because I knew so much, I kept putting in details that didn't really relate to my main point. For example, I included this detail in an earlier draft to show how successful Hudson had become: "The film Dreamgirls starred Beyonce Knowles and Eddie Murphy." But it really put more focus on the film, and I wanted to focus on Hudson, during one revision, I decided to delete it.

LOGICAL ORDER: When I read over my first draft, I noticed that the paragraph didn't really flow smoothly. I had used contrast and addition transition words instead of time order words. So I revised to include chronological transitions because this is a narrative. For example, the signal word "suddenly" replaced the contrast signal word "however," and the signal word "ultimately" replaced the addition signal word "and."

EFFECTIVE EXPRESSION (Vivid Verbs): I have a bad habit of using too many verbs like "are," "is," and "was." Our teacher pointed out that too many of these verbs can make a paper boring, and they don't give the reader very much information about the main point. So I revised to replace "to be" verbs with vivid verbs. For example, I revised the verb in sentence 14 from "was powerful" to "pulsed with power." And I revised the verb in sentence 16 from "said" to "gushed with gratitude."

For a blank version of this form for your own reflections about your writing:
<www.mywritinglab.com>

# Developing Your Point Using Narration

A narrative tells a story. The story illustrates the writer's point or main idea. To make a point by telling a story, a writer relies on the use of time order transitions, relevant sensory details, and vivid word choice.

## The Point: The Main Idea

When you choose to write a narrative, you limit your topic to the details of a specific event based on time order. Most likely, you also have an opinion or point of view about the event. Your opinion or attitude about the event is your point or main idea. Many writers of a narrative paragraph create a topic sentence to state the point illustrated by the events.

For example, the following topic sentence contains (1) the topic, (2) the writer's opinion about the topic, and (3) the pattern of organization used to organize details.

Aaron Ralston bravely survived a five-day ordeal.

TOPIC IS AARON RALSTON

WRITER'S OPINION IS STATED WITH THE WORDS BRAVELY AND ORDEAL

PATTERN OF ORGANIZATION: NARRATION TIME ORDER IS ESTABLISHED WITH THE PHRASE FIVE-DAY ORDEAL

The above chart illustrates the relationship between the topic, the author's opinion, and the pattern of organization in this particular topic sentence. Note that the word "ordeal" suggests both time order and the writer's opinion.

## Practice 2

### TOPIC SENTENCES

Practice creating topic sentences. The first two items present a topic, an opinion, and time order signal word(s). Combine the ideas in each group to create a topic sentence for a narrative. Then, complete the practice by making your own topic sentences.

**1.** TOPIC: _Jeff Gordon_

OPINION: _squeaked to narrow victory_

TIME ORDER SIGNAL WORDS: _during the last few laps of the Daytona 500_

TOPIC SENTENCE: _____

**2.** TOPIC: _honesty_

OPINION: _I learned the value of_

TIME ORDER SIGNAL WORDS: _during my first job interview_

TOPIC SENTENCE: _____

More practice with creating topic sentences:
<www.mywritinglab.com>

More practice with
creating topic sentences:
<www.mywritinglab.com>

**3.** TOPIC: _memory of my childhood_

OPINION: _the happiest_

TIME ORDER SIGNAL WORDS: ............................................................

TOPIC SENTENCE: ............................................................

............................................................

**4.** TOPIC: _a lesson_

OPINION: _I am glad I learned_

TIME ORDER SIGNAL WORDS: ............................................................

TOPIC SENTENCE: ............................................................

............................................................

**5.** TOPIC: ............................................................

OPINION: ............................................................

TIME ORDER SIGNAL WORDS: ............................................................

TOPIC SENTENCE: ............................................................

............................................................

**6.** TOPIC: ............................................................

OPINION: ............................................................

TIME ORDER SIGNAL WORDS: ............................................................

TOPIC SENTENCE: ............................................................

............................................................

Practice 2

# Logical Order

Once you have selected your topic and focused on a main idea, you are ready to generate additional details and organize your ideas into a logical sequence based on time order. Each event in a narrative is developed by describing the individual actions and details that make up that event. Just as time order words in the topic sentence signal a narrative, time order transition words also show the flow of events as they unfold in the narrative. Strong transitions establish coherence, a clear and understandable flow of ideas.

## Transition Words Used to Show Time Order

| | | | | |
|---|---|---|---|---|
| after | during | later | previously | ultimately |
| afterward | eventually | →meanwhile | second | until |
| as | finally | next | since | when |
| before | first | now | soon | while |
| currently | last | often | then | |

**Practice 3**

---

**TIME ORDER SIGNAL WORDS**

The following paragraph was first published by Linda M. Hasselstrom in *High Country News* to explain her choice for self-defense. Fill in the four blanks in the following paragraph with appropriate time order signal words based on the logical order of ideas.

**A Peaceful Woman Explains**
**Why She Carries a Gun**

(1) As I drove home one night, a car followed me. (2) It passed me on a narrow bridge ........... a passenger flashed a blinding spotlight in my face. (3) I braked sharply. (4) The car stopped, angled across the bridge, and four men jumped out. (5) I realized the locked doors were useless if they broke the windows of my pickup. (6) I started forward, hoping to knock their car aside so I could pass. (7) Just ............ another car appeared, and the men hastily got back into their car. (8) They continued to follow me, passing and repassing. (9) I dared not go home because no one else was there. (10) I passed no lighted houses. (11) ............... they pulled over onto the roadside, and I decided to use their tactic: fear. (12) Speeding, the pickup horn blaring, I swerved as close to them as I could ......... I roared past. (13) It worked: they turned off the highway. (14) But I was frightened and angry. (15) Even in my vehicle I was too vulnerable.

More practice with time order:
<www.mywritinglab.com>

# Relevant Details

A writer narrows a topic into a focused main idea by generating details that answer questions such as *who, what, when, where, why,* and *how.* A writer evaluates the relevancy of each detail and uses only those that illustrate the main idea. Some relevant details show the action of the event; other details explain the author's opinion about the event. Relevant details also often include sensory details, which appeal to sight, sound, smell, taste, and touch. These vivid details work together to create a mental image of the author's main point. During the prewriting phase, a timeline can help a writer organize ideas as they are generated. Study the following concept map used to generate details about the topic "Aaron Ralston's Ordeal."

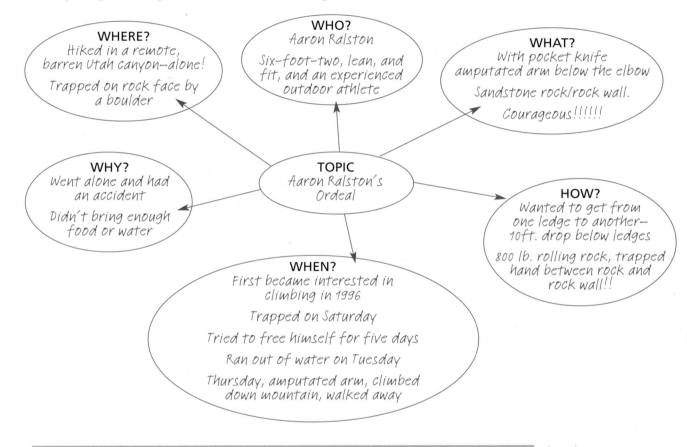

**WHERE?**
Hiked in a remote, barren Utah canyon—alone!
Trapped on rock face by a boulder

**WHO?**
Aaron Ralston
Six-foot-two, lean, and fit, and an experienced outdoor athlete

**WHAT?**
With pocket knife amputated arm below the elbow
Sandstone rock/rock wall.
Courageous!!!!!!

**WHY?**
Went alone and had an accident
Didn't bring enough food or water

**TOPIC**
Aaron Ralston's Ordeal

**HOW?**
Wanted to get from one ledge to another—10ft. drop below ledges
800 lb. rolling rock, trapped hand between rock and rock wall!!

**WHEN?**
First became interested in climbing in 1996
Trapped on Saturday
Tried to free himself for five days
Ran out of water on Tuesday
Thursday, amputated arm, climbed down mountain, walked away

---

**RELEVANT DETAILS**

Using the details in the concept map above about the topic "Aaron Ralston's Ordeal," complete the timeline below to show the proper time order of events.

1 ...................................................................................................

2 ...................................................................................................

3 ...................................................................................................

4 ...................................................................................................

5 ...................................................................................................

*Practice 4*

During the prewriting phase of writing, a writer naturally generates irrelevant details. In fact, an effective writer often produces far more details than can be used to make a specific point. Irrelevant details do not explain, support, or illustrate the focused point of the paragraph. Often, writers use the revision process to double check details for relevancy and to eliminate irrelevant details.

**RELEVANT DETAILS**

The following paragraph develops the ideas recorded in the brainstorming list about Aaron Ralston. Circle the main idea. Underline the relevant sensory details. Cross out the two details that are not relevant to the main idea.

### The Courage to Survive

(1) Aaron Ralston courageously survived a five-day ordeal. (2) Ralston began his ordeal Saturday morning when he made an attempt to climb over a ten-foot drop between two ledges. (3) Suddenly, an 800-pound rock roared down upon him from above. (4) He quickly scrambled to get out of its path in time. (5) In the next second, the mammoth stone trapped him on the barren rock face. (6) The boulder had smashed and pinned his right hand between it and a sandstone wall. (7) Six-foot-two, lean, and fit, Ralston is an experienced outdoor athlete. (8) He first became interested in climbing in 1996. (9) For five days, Ralston chipped away at the boulder with a pocket knife. (10) Finally, on Tuesday, he ran out of his meager ration of food and water. (11) By Thursday rescue seemed unlikely, so Ralston, parched with thirst, made the gutsy decision to amputate his own hand. (12) Knowing his flimsy pocket knife would not cut through bone, he used the force of the rock to snap his bones just below the elbow. (13) Then after applying a tourniquet, Ralston cut through his own muscles, veins, and arteries. (14) Once he completed the hour long amputation, he rappelled down the mountain. (15) At last, a haggard Ralston hiked out of the canyon.

More practice with relevant details: <www.mywritinglab.com>

# Effective Expression: Vivid Verbs

Show; don't tell! Some of the verbs most commonly used by student writers belong to the *to be* family of verbs. However, *to be* verbs such as *am, is, are, was,* and *were* are vague and lifeless. They *tell* instead of *show* action, as in the following sentence: *Ivan was angry.* This sentence tells us about Ivan's emotion, but it doesn't show how he acts when he is angry or how his anger fits into the flow of events.

A writer draws a mental picture for the main idea through the use of vivid verbs.

**Vivid verbs show the action that is taking place:**

Ivan stomped to the trash can and hurled the report into it.

*The verbs "stomped" and "hurled" are biased words. Another witness may have chosen objective language to describe Ivan's actions:*

**Vivid verbs reflect the author's opinion:**

Ivan walked to the trash can and tossed the report into it.

**Vivid verbs express sensory details:**

Ivan snorted with contempt.

Many writers dedicate one full revision to focus on word choices.

---

**VIVID VERBS**

Revise each of the following sentences by replacing *to be* verbs such as *am, is, are, was,* and *were* with vivid verbs.

**1.** The coffee was hot.

-------------------------------------------------------------------------------

**2.** Ryanne was injured during the race.

-------------------------------------------------------------------------------

**3.** Lance Armstrong was the winner of Tour De France six times.

-------------------------------------------------------------------------------

**4.** We were so excited; we were screaming and jumping all around like lunatics.

-------------------------------------------------------------------------------

**5.** I am afraid of my next door neighbor's pit bull.

-------------------------------------------------------------------------------

Practice 6

**VIVID VERBS**

Revise the following paragraph by replacing *to be* verbs, such as *are* and *is*, with vivid verbs.

> (1) Robert and his mother, Maxine, are angry at each other again.
> (2) Seventeen-year-old Robert is sitting silently. (3) His arms are crossed, and he is frowning. (4) His mother is flying around the kitchen; she is slamming the cabinet doors, and pots and pans are rattling.
> (5) Suddenly, she is yelling at him, and like every other time they fight, Robert leaves.

More practice with
vivid verbs:
<www.mywritinglab.com>

# Using Narration in Your Academic Courses

Many college courses in subjects such as history, psychology, composition, and literature use narration. As you study these subjects you will read narrations of historical events, case studies, short stories, and novels. In addition, you will write narratives to demonstrate what you have learned. For example, an essay exam may ask you to relate the key events of a major war or the important events in the life of an influential person. Some college writing assignments ask you to draw upon your personal experience and relate it to what you are learning.

Read the following information from a college communications textbook. On a separate sheet of paper, write a response to the writing assignment, given in the last sentence of the text.

### Ethics in Interpersonal Communication

Because communication has consequences, interpersonal communication involves ethics, a moral aspect of right or wrong. It is believed that there are certain universal ethical principles: you should tell the truth, have respect for another's dignity, and not harm the innocent.

In the U.S. legal system, you have the right to remain silent and to refuse to incriminate yourself. But you don't have the right to refuse to reveal information about the criminal activities of others that you may have witnessed. Psychiatrists and lawyers are often exempt from this general rule. Similarly a wife can't be forced to testify against her husband nor a husband against his wife. In interpersonal situations, however, there aren't any written rules so it's not always clear if or when silence is ethical.

What would you do? While at the supermarket, you witness a mother verbally abusing her three-year-old child. You worry that the mother might psychologically harm the child, and your first impulse is to speak up and tell this woman that verbal abuse can have lasting effects on the child and often leads to physical abuse. At the same time, you don't want to interfere with a mother's right to say what she wants to her child. Nor do you want to aggravate a mother who may later take out her frustration on the child. Write a short narrative that illustrates what you would do in this situation.

More practice with
writing narrative
paragraphs:
<www.mywritinglab.com>

# Workshop: Writing a Narration Paragraph Step by Step

Workshop

## Prewriting for Your Paragraph

The various activities that follow will walk you through the steps of the prewriting stage of the writing process: choosing a topic; focusing your point; and generating and organizing relevant details.

### Choose Your Topic

The following activities are designed to help you choose a topic.

1. Create a bank of topics. Use the following headings and either brainstorm or list as many topics as you possibly can. Don't be critical of what you write; just get as many topics written down as quickly as possible. As you think of new topics, add them to the list. Compare your bank of topics with your peers.

   - Heroes
   - Health
   - Pop Culture
   - Memories

2. Generate ideas with a freewrite. Choose one of the topics from your topic bank and think of an event related to the topic. Write about the event for ten minutes without stopping. Include sensory details: sight, sound, smell, taste, and touch.

3. Select a photograph of a special event. Write a caption, brainstorm topics, and freewrite about the photograph. Remember to ask, "What happened?" and "What's the point?" as you generate ideas.

### Focus Your Point

Read a freewrite you have generated for a narrative. Underline words that suggest your values, opinions, or attitudes about the event. Think about what interests you about the event. Use a thesaurus and choose several vivid words to express your thoughts. Identify your audience and purpose. Write a list of vivid verbs that show the actions that occur during the event. State in one sentence the point of the story you are going to tell.

AUDIENCE: ...............................................................................

.......................................................................................................

PURPOSE: ...............................................................................

.......................................................................................................

VIVID VERBS: ...............................................................................

.......................................................................................................

WHAT'S THE POINT? ...............................................................................

.......................................................................................................

## Generate and Organize Relevant Details

Using ideas you have recorded so far and the time line graphic, generate and organize details that support your point.

### What's the point?

TOPIC SENTENCE: _____

_____

_____

_____

### What happened?

| 1 |
|---|

↓

| 2 |
|---|

↓

| 3 |
|---|

↓

| 4 |
|---|

↓

| 5 |
|---|

 ## Write a Draft of Your Paragraph

Using the ideas you generated during the prewriting phase, compose a draft of your paragraph. Return to the prewriting process at any time to generate additional details as needed. Use your own paper.

 ## Revise Your Draft

Once you have created a draft of a narrative, read it and answer the following questions. Indicate your answers by annotating your paper. If you answer "yes" to a question, underline, check, or circle examples. If you answer "no" to a question, write additional details in the margins and draw lines to indicate their placement. Revise your paragraph based on your reflection. (*Hint:* Experienced writers create several drafts as they focus on one or two questions per draft.)

Workshop

# Questions for Revising a Narrative Paragraph:

☐ Have I stated or implied a focused main idea? Have I created a strong impression? Can I state my point in one sentence?

☐ Is the logical order of the events clear? Have I used strong transitions to indicate time? And space?

☐ Have I made my point with adequate details?

☐ Do all the details support my point?

☐ Have I used vivid verbs to keep my readers interested in what I am saying? Have I used sensory details to make my point?

☐ What impact will my paragraph make on my reader?

For more information on correcting unnecessary shifts in verb tense, see Chapter 19.

## Proofread Your Draft

Once you have made any revisions to your paragraph that may be needed, proofread your paragraph to eliminate careless errors such as shifts in verb tense.

### Grammar in Action: Unnecessary Shifts in Verb Tense

Verb tense tells your reader when an event occurred. "Sandra laughed" is past tense. "Sandra laughs" is present tense. "Sandra will laugh" is future tense. A shift in tense for no logical reason is confusing to the reader.

- **A Shift in Verb Tense:**

  **INCORRECT:** Jennifer sighed loudly, rolled her eyes, and stomps off angrily.

- **Consistent Use of Tense:**

  **CORRECT:** Jennifer sighs loudly, rolls her eyes, and stomps off angrily.

*Workshop Practice 9*

**TENSE SHIFTS**

Edit these sentences for unnecessary shifts in tense.

**1.** Raul works two jobs and attends a community college. He wanted to become a registered nurse and join the Peace Corps.

**TENSE SHIFTS**

More practice with correcting unnecessary shifts in verb tense: <www.mywritinglab.com>

**2.** Hurricane Ivan destroyed property along the coast in Pensacola, Florida. The hurricane force winds and waves would batter hotels to pieces and rip roofs off restaurants and homes.

**3.** Vitali and Carl had fun at the Daytona 500 race. They always pay to sit in the infield. They will grill hamburgers and hot dogs. As they ate, they watched the cars zoom around them.

**4.** Joe and Jarvonna had a wonderful first date. Joe makes reservations at the Japanese Steak House. After dinner, he surprises her with tickets to watch her favorite team, the Orlando Magic, play the Miami Heat. On the way home, Jarvonna suggested stopping for coffee. Losing track of time, the two talk for hours.

Practice 9

Review

**REVIEW OF WRITING A NARRATIVE PARAGRAPH:** DEVELOP YOUR POINT USING THE WRITING PROCESS

Use the following form to record your thinking about writing a narrative paragraph.
Select and focus a topic for your writing situation, audience, and purpose.
Choose a person, place, object, or scene and identify its significance.

PREWRITING DRAFTING **What is your point?**

TOPIC, SITUATION, OR EVENT: .......................................................................................

AUDIENCE: .......................................................................................

PURPOSE: .......................................................................................

PREWRITING DRAFTING **State your main idea in a topic sentence.**

TOPIC: .......................................................................................

OPINION: .......................................................................................

PREWRITING DRAFTING **Generate relevant details.**

REPORTER'S QUESTIONS: WHO, WHAT, WHEN, WHERE, WHY, AND HOW? .......................................................................................

.......................................................................................

.......................................................................................

SENSORY DETAILS: .......................................................................................

.......................................................................................

PREWRITING DRAFTING REVISING **Use logical order. Use transition words to signal organization of details and relationships between ideas.**

SPACE ORDER: .......................................................................................

More ideas for writing
a narrative paragraph:
<www.mywritinglab.com>

TIME ORDER: .......................................................................................

REVISING  PROOFREADING  Use effective expression. Choose words for clear, precise meaning.

VIVID VERBS: ....................................................................................................................

CONSISTENT VERB TENSE: ......................................................................................................

....................................................................................................................................

*Review*

## Writing Assignments

### Considering Audience and Purpose

Study the sequence of photographs of Jennifer Hudson at the beginning of the chapter. Assume the pictures are to be used to document her achievements on a website designed to promote her career. Write a narrative that will be recorded as a voice-over and heard as the pictures flash on the screen.

### Writing for Everyday Life

Assume you or someone you know recently took action in an emergency situation. Write a paragraph for a letter to a friend relaying the event as it unfolded. Choose words that reflect one of the following: (1) approval of a courageous act or (2) concern for a foolish act.

### Writing for College Life

Assume you have witnessed an important historical event such as the invention of the wheel, the first flight into space, landing on the moon, the last battle fought in the Civil War, or 9/11. Write a paragraph for a local paper documenting the event as it occurred.

### Writing for Working Life

Assume you are filing for worker's compensation for an injury that occurred on the job. Write a paragraph for a report to your supervisor in which you record the events as they occurred.

# 6

## Chapter Preview

# The Process Paragraph

## A process is a series of steps, occurring in chronological order.

Every day we repeat countless processes, from cooking a meal to flossing our teeth. Effective use of processes allows us to perform efficiently in every aspect of our lives. In our personal lives, we follow specific processes to file our taxes or enhance our health. In our professional lives, most of us go through an interview process to secure a job and an evaluation process to get a raise. In our academic lives, we follow set procedures to enroll in classes, learn, and achieve high GPAs.

A process may describe the steps necessary to complete a task such as changing a tire, activating an iPod, or creating a web page. A process may also describe the phases, stages, or cycle of a recurring event such as the phases of the moon, the stages of human development, or the cycle of grief. To write a process paragraph, a writer identifies and explains the logical time order of the individual steps or stages in the task or cycle. An effective process also relies heavily on concrete descriptive details and vivid images so the reader can mentally see the process as it unfolds.

# What's the Point of Process?

Visualizing a process helps a writer discover his or her point about the procedure. The following sequence of photographs documents a series of steps in a set of Pilates exercises called "spine stretch and roll like a ball." Study each photograph in the time line. Write a caption that briefly describes each picture.

WRITING FROM LIFE

Practice 1

**PHOTOGRAPHIC ORGANIZER: PROCESS**

STEP ONE

What is happening?

_____

_____

_____

STEP TWO

What is happening?

_____

_____

_____

STEP THREE

What is happening?

_____

_____

_____

STEP FOUR

What is happening?

_____

_____

_____

**What's the point?**

_____

_____

_____

## My First Thoughts: A Prewriting Activity

Set a time limit, such as five minutes, and write in your notebook about the images you just studied. Do not let your pen or pencil stop. Even if you must repeat ideas, keep writing until the time limit is up. Let the ideas flow freely. Getting your first thoughts about a topic on paper is one excellent way to overcome writer's block and set your mind to thinking.

# Making a Point Using Process: One Student Writer's Response

The following paragraph offers one writer's point about the set of exercises depicted in the photographs. Read the process and the explanations; answer the questions. Then, read the writer's journal that records decisions made during the writing process. Answer the question "What's the point?"

**Main Idea:**
The main idea is the point the author is making about the topic. The topic is "an exercise sequence." Underline the author's point about this topic.

**Chronological Order:**
The transition "First" signals time order. Circle four more time order signal words.

**Effective Expression:**
Vivid details such as "sitting tall and straight... as if you were sitting next to a wall" creates a mental picture for the reader. Draw a box around two more vivid descriptive details.

**Relevant Details:**
Relevant details explain specific steps that build strength and flexibility. Strength is required to curve the spine and pull in the stomach. Underline a step in the process that builds flexibility.

Spine Stretch and Roll Like a Ball

(1) "Spine stretch and roll like a ball" is an exercise sequence that builds strength and flexibility in the core area of your body supported by the spine. (2) First, assume the proper starting position. (3) Begin by sitting tall and straight on your mat as if you were sitting next to a wall. (4) Open your legs slightly wider than hip-width apart, placing your heels on the outside edges of the mat. (5) Pull your navel up and in. (6) Extend your arms at shoulder height parallel to your legs and flex your feet, pressing through your heels and pointing your toes toward the ceiling. (7) Next, tighten your buttocks and round your torso up and over. (8) Continually press your lower back behind you and scoop in your abdominals. (9) As you deepen the curve of your spine, press your navel further in as if it could kiss your spine. (10) Imagine your body forming a U-shape. (11) Once you are fully extended, hang your head between your shoulders, and hold the stretch. (12) To roll like a ball from this position, bend your knees and draw both ankles toward the core of your body and balance on your sit bones. (13) Grasp an ankle in each hand; pull your feet close to your buttocks, and place your head snugly between your knees. (14) Imagine your body taking the shape of a small, tight C. (15) Then, inhale and roll back. (16) As you roll, keep your feet close to your body and your head tucked between your knees. (17) Roll until you are balanced on your shoulder blades, but do not roll onto your neck. (18) Throughout the roll, maintain your C-shape and keep your navel pressed into your spine. (19) Finally, exhale as you roll back into your starting position.

The student of "Spine Stretch and Roll Like a Ball" completed the following reflection to record his thinking through the writing process. Read his writer's journal that describes a few key choices he made as he wrote.

MAIN IDEA: I loved writing this paragraph about exercising! I decided to assume the role of a coach who was writing an article for a fitness newsletter so I could directly address the reader using the pronoun "you" in an instructional tone.

RELEVANT DETAILS: As a prewriting activity, I carefully observed the posture of the woman in each photo sequence and listed concrete descriptive details of how her body was arranged in space in each photograph. I made a separate list for each photograph. By doing so, I found that I needed to explain that each of the four steps is actually made up of several movements. For example, the first step "assume the proper starting position" is made up of three movements. I also drew on my own personal experience of performing similar exercises to generate details suggested by the images. For example, I knew that her flattened stomach was evidence that she had contracted her stomach muscles by pulling her navel in toward her spine.

LOGICAL ORDER: I used my first draft to capture the order of steps represented by each photograph. Then, when I revised, I inserted the time order transitions "first" and "next" to indicate the first two major steps of the exercise sequence. As I revised, it occurred to me that the four steps could be divided into two phases. Phase 1 describes the process of the spine stretch, and phase 2 describes the process of rolling like a ball. So, I used the transitional phrase "to roll like a ball from this position" to signal the beginning of the third step of moving from the spine stretch into the roll. I used the transition "then" to signal the fourth step of the exercise. The transition "finally" signals my conclusion.

EFFECTIVE EXPRESSION: I was surprised by how much I needed to rely on descriptive words to fully explain the process. I think concrete, vivid expressions such as "kiss your spine," "forming a U-shape," and "a tight, small C" add interest and help the reader understand the process.

# Developing Your Point Using Process

A process shows how to do something or how something works. To describe a process, a writer uses chronological order (also called time order), relevant concrete descriptive details, and vivid images.

## The Point: The Main Idea

When you write a process paragraph, you limit your topic to a specific set of details based on time order. Most likely, you also have an opinion or point of view about the process, and this opinion or attitude is your point or main idea. A topic sentence states the point or purpose of the steps, directions, or phases.

For example, the following topic sentence contains (1) the topic, (2) the writer's opinion about the topic, and (3) the pattern of organization used to organize details.

The topic is *grief*. The writer's opinion is stated with the phrase *emotional work* and time order is established with the phrases *the six phases* and *in progress*.

The six phases | of grief | represent an emotional work | in progress.

PATTERN OF
ORGANIZATION:
TIME ORDER

TOPIC

AUTHOR'S OPINION

PATTERN OF
ORGANIZATION:
TIME ORDER

The above chart illustrates the relationship of the topic, the author's opinion, and the pattern of organization in this particular topic sentence. Note that the phrase *the six phases of grief* combines the topic and the pattern of organization.

Practice 2

### TOPIC SENTENCES

Practice creating topic sentences. The first two items present a topic, an opinion, and time order signal word(s). Combine the ideas in each group to create a topic sentence for a process. Complete the practice by making your own topic sentences.

1. TOPIC: *Test-taking anxiety*

OPINION: *can be overcome*

TIME ORDER SIGNAL WORDS: *in several steps*

TOPIC SENTENCE: ......................................................

2. TOPIC: *Checking the oil and changing the oil in a car*

OPINION: *easy and quick*

TIME ORDER SIGNAL WORDS: *process*

TOPIC SENTENCE: ......................................................

**3.** TOPIC: *Sexual harassment*

OPINION: *important to report*

TIME ORDER SIGNAL WORDS: *company procedures*

TOPIC SENTENCE: 

More practice with
creating topic sentences:
<www.mywritinglab.com>

**4.** TOPIC: 

OPINION: 

TIME ORDER SIGNAL WORDS: 

TOPIC SENTENCE: 

**5.** TOPIC: 

OPINION: 

TIME ORDER SIGNAL WORDS: 

TOPIC SENTENCE: 

**6.** TOPIC: 

OPINION: 

TIME ORDER SIGNAL WORDS: 

TOPIC SENTENCE: 

**7.** TOPIC: 

OPINION: 

TIME ORDER SIGNAL WORDS: 

TOPIC SENTENCE: 

*Practice 2*

More practice with creating topic sentences: <www.mywritinglab.com>

# Logical Order

Once you have selected your topic and focused on a main idea, you are ready to generate additional details and organize your ideas into a logical sequence based on time order. A process describes the individual actions that make up each step or phase within the process. Just as time order words in the topic sentence signal a process, time order transition words show the flow of events as the process unfolds. Strong transitions establish coherence, a clear and understandable flow of ideas.

## Transition Words Used to Show Time Order

| | | | | |
|---|---|---|---|---|
| after | during | later | previously | ultimately |
| afterward | eventually | meanwhile | second | until |
| as | finally | next | since | when |
| before | first | now | soon | while |
| currently | last | often | then | |

Practice 3

**TIME ORDER**

The following information appears in the safety publication *How to Survive a Submerging Car* sponsored by the Florida Highway Patrol. Determine the logical order of the sentences. Rewrite the paragraph, organizing the details by chronological order. *Hint:* Underline the time order transition words. Complete the exercise by answering the question "What's the point?"

Save Your Life: P.O.G.O. a Sinking Car

........ Although the window should open, do not waste time trying to open the door because the water pressure will keep the doors firmly shut.

........ Then, while the car is still floating, **get out**; crawl through the opened window and swim to shore.

........ The first thing to do in a floating car is to **push** the button to unbuckle your seatbelt.

........ Next, **open** the window; electric windows should still work while the car is floating.

........ When a car plunges into a lake or river, it should float for about three minutes, giving you enough time to safely exit the car before it sinks.

More practice
with time order:
<www.mywritinglab.com>

........ P.O.G.O. stands for Push, Open, and Get Out.

........ Once the car sinks, the P.O.G.O. method still works.

........ Wait until the water reaches your neck so that the water pressure inside and outside the car are equal.

........ In a submerged car, first **push** the button that releases your seatbelt.

........ Finally, **get out**; push yourself out of the car and quickly swim to the surface.

........ Then, **open** your car door.

**What's the point?**

........................................................................

........................................................................

*Practice 3*

# Relevant Details

As a writer narrows a topic into a focused main idea about a process, the thinking process brings to mind many details of time and space. A writer evaluates the relevance of each detail and uses only those that illustrate the main idea. Some relevant details show the action of the process; other details explain the author's opinion about the process. Relevant details also include vivid descriptive and sensory details. These details work together to create a vivid mental image of the author's main point about the process. During the prewriting phase, a time line can help a writer organize ideas as they are generated. Study the following time line used to generate details about the phases of grief.

**The Six Phases of Grief**

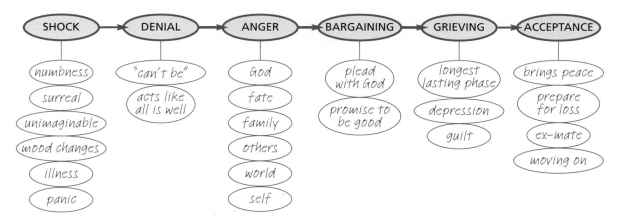

During the prewriting phase of writing, a writer naturally generates irrelevant details. In fact, an effective writer often produces far more details than can be used to make a specific point. Irrelevant details do not explain, support, or illustrate the focused point of the paragraph. A careful writer uses the revision process to double check details for relevancy and to eliminate irrelevant details.

Practice 4

**RELEVANT DETAILS**

The following paragraph develops the ideas recorded in the brainstorming list about the six phases of grief. Circle the main idea. Underline at least three concrete details. Cross out the two details that are not relevant to the main idea.

### The Phases of Grief

(1) In her book, *On Death and Dying*, Dr. Elizabeth Kübler-Ross explains the phases of grief we experience when we learn that a loved one is terminally ill. (2) The six phases of grief represent an emotional work in progress. (3) The first phase is shock. (4) During this initial phase, we experience a fog of numbness; life seems surreal as it crumbles around us, and the chore ahead of us seems unimaginable. (5) Throughout the second phase, denial, we work hard to erect the illusion that recovery is possible or that life is still normal. (6) We simply think, "This can't be happening to me." (7) Once we move past denial, we then grapple with the third phase of grief—anger. (8) We aim our anger at God, fate, doctors, family, the world, or even ourselves. (9) Thoughts such as "If only I had…" or "How can others just go on with their lives?" occupy our minds. (10) During traumas such as divorce, we often become angry with our ex-mate. (11) During the fourth phase, known as bargaining, we negotiate with God to cure the problem in exchange for our good behavior. (12) The fifth phase, usually the longest lasting, is grieving. (13) We often labor in mourning for months or years. (14) Chipping away at depression, guilt, physical illness, loneliness, panic, and abrupt mood changes employs all our energies. (15) The final phase of grief occurs as acceptance. (16) Often, for those of us facing our own death, acceptance brings the wage of peace. (17) As survivors of loss, such as divorce, we usually find ourselves working to re-build our lives and move on.

More practice with relevant, concrete details: <www.mywritinglab.com>

# Effective Expression: Vivid Images

Show; don't tell! Create vivid word pictures that deepen your reader's understanding of your point. Two figures of speech create vivid images: simile and metaphor.

A **simile** is an indirect comparison between two different ideas or things that uses *like, as, as if,* or *as though.*

### Example:

As Robin crossed the finish line, his legs pumped like pistons.

A **metaphor** is a direct comparison between two different ideas or things that does *not* use *like, as, as if,* or *as though.* Often a metaphor uses words such as *is, are,* or *were* to make the direct comparison between the two ideas.

### Example:

As Robin crossed the finish line, his legs were pumping pistons.

---

**VIVID IMAGES**

Revise each of the following sentences to create vivid images by using similes and metaphors suggested by the photos. Discuss your work with your class or in a small group of your peers.

**1.** To ensure a healthful serving size, limit meat portions to 3 ounces.

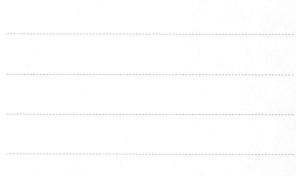

---------------------------------

---------------------------------

---------------------------------

---------------------------------

**2.** Adolescence is a stage of human development made up of great change leading to adulthood.

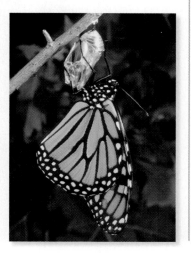

---------------------------------

---------------------------------

---------------------------------

---------------------------------

*Practice 5*

More practice with
vivid images:
<www.mywritinglab.com>

**3.** A successful election campaign is based on a series of strategic decisions.

**4.** Overcoming addiction requires one to understand and control dangerous inner emotions.

Practice 5

# Using Process in Your Academic Courses

Many college courses such as biology, ecology, history, political science, psychology, and composition use process in their discussions. As you study these courses you will learn about processes involving the physical world, mental health, government, and writing. In addition, you will record processes to learn or demonstrate what you have learned. For example, a science lab may require you to conduct an experiment, record the steps you took, and evaluate the process. Some college writing assignments ask you to reflect upon your personal writing process so you can strengthen your writing skills.

**Practice 6**

**USING PROCESS IN A COMPOSITION ASSIGNMENT**

During a composition class, a student wrote the following paragraph in her writer's journal to reflect upon the effectiveness of her writing process. Assume you are her peer editor, and, based on what you have learned in this chapter about writing a process and in Chapter 2 about the writing process, offer advice about her writing process.

Kristen Elizabeth Spengler

Writing 101

September 27, 2007

My Writer's Journal: My Writing Process

(1) I start my writing process by mapping. (2) I make what is like a spider web with one basic idea in the middle of the page and supporting ideas branching off all around it. (3) After brainstorming for a while, I go on the computer and put the ideas I came up with into sentences. (4) Usually, I like to lay it all out on the computer and print it out because it is easier for me to see it while I'm typing my draft. (5) After I type up all the ideas I brainstormed, I write my paragraph, print it out, and turn it in.

More practice with writing process paragraphs: <www.mywritinglab.com>

# Workshop: Writing a Process Paragraph Step by Step

*Workshop*

## Prewrite Your Paragraph

The various activities below will walk you through the steps of the prewriting stage of the writing process: choosing a topic; focusing your point; and generating and organizing relevant details.

### Choose Your Topic

The following activities are designed to help you choose a topic.

1. Create a bank of topics. Use the following headings and brainstorm or list as many processes about each topic as you possibly can. Don't criticize your thoughts; just get as many relevant processes written down as quickly as possible. Compare your bank of topics with those of your peers.

   - Recycling Trash
   - Auditioning
   - Studying
   - Training an Animal

2. Generate ideas with a freewrite. Choose one of the topics from your topic bank and think of the steps necessary to complete the process. Write about the process for ten minutes without stopping.

3. Select a photograph or series of photographs that illustrate a process. Write captions; brainstorm steps, directions, or phases; and freewrite about the photograph(s). Remember to ask, "What is happening?" and "What's the point?" as you generate ideas.

### Focus Your Point

Read a freewrite you have generated for a process. Underline words that suggest your values, opinions, or attitudes about the process. Use a thesaurus and choose several vivid words to express your thoughts. Think about why the steps are important. Identify your audience and purpose. Create a list of concrete details and vivid images that show the actions that occur during the process. State in one sentence the point of the process:

AUDIENCE: .................................................................................................

PURPOSE: .................................................................................................

.................................................................................................

WHAT'S THE POINT? .................................................................................................

.................................................................................................

## Generate and Organize Relevant Details

Using ideas you have recorded so far and the process flowchart, generate and organize details that support your point.

**What's the point?**

TOPIC SENTENCE: _____

_____

_____

**What is happening?**

| First Step |
| --- |
| |

| Second Step |
| --- |
| |

| Third Step |
| --- |
| |

| Fourth Step |
| --- |
| |

 DRAFTING

# Write a Draft of Your Paragraph

Using the ideas you generated during the prewriting phase, compose a draft of your process paragraph. Return to the prewriting process at any time to generate additional details as needed. Use your own paper.

 REVISING

# Revise Your Draft

Once you have created a draft of a process, read the draft to answer the following questions. Indicate your answers by annotating your paper. If you answer "yes" to a question, underline, check, or circle examples. If you answer "no" to a question, write needed information in margins and draw lines to indicate placement of additional details. Revise your paragraph as necessary based on your reflection. (*Hint:* Experienced writers create several drafts as they focus on one or two questions per draft.)

*Workshop*

Workshop

# Questions for Revising a Process Paragraph

☐ Have I stated or implied a focused main idea? Have I created a strong impression? Can I state my point in one sentence?

☐ Is the order of the steps, directions, or phases within the process clear? Have I used strong transitions?

☐ Have I made my point with adequate details? Have I included only the details that are relevant to my topic sentence?

☐ Have I used vivid images to make the process clear to my readers? Have I used concrete details to make my point?

# Proofread Your Draft

Once you have made any revisions to your paragraph that may be needed, proofread your paragraph to eliminate careless errors such as run-on sentences.

## Grammar in Action: Eliminating Run-on Sentences

A **run-on sentence** occurs when two or more independent clauses are punctuated as one sentence. Correct a run-on sentence by applying any of the following four edits: (1) separate independent clauses with a period and capital letter; (2) insert a coordinating conjunction (*and*, *but*, or *nor*, *for*, *so*, or *yet*) and a comma between independent clauses; (3) insert a semicolon between the independent clauses; or (4) insert a semicolon with an appropriate transition between independent clauses.

- **A run-on sentence:**

   Plants take in water through their roots they take in the gas carbon dioxide through their foliage plants use sunlight to turn water and carbon dioxide into food through the process of photosynthesis.

- **Two ways to correct the above run-on sentence:**

*ADDED COMMA AND COORDINATING CONJUNCTION "AND" TO SEPARATE INDEPENDENT CLAUSES*

**(1)** Plants take in water through their roots, and they take in the gas carbon dioxide through their foliage; plants use sunlight to turn water and carbon dioxide into food through the process of photosynthesis.

*ADDED SEMI-COLON TO SEPARATE INDEPENDENT CLAUSES*

*ADDED SEMICOLON AND TRANSITION WORD "THEN" TO SEPARATE INDEPENDENT CLAUSES*

**(2)** Plants take in water through their roots. In addition, they take in the gas carbon dioxide through their foliage; then, plants use sunlight to turn water and carbon dioxide into food through the process of photosynthesis.

*ADDED PERIOD TO SEPARATE INDEPENDENT CLAUSES; THE FIRST LETTER OF THE SECOND INDEPENDENT CLAUSE IS NOW CAPITALIZED*

For more information on run-ons, see Chapter 21.

*Practice 7*

### ELIMINATING RUN-ONS

Edit these sentences to eliminate run-ons.

**1.** Using anabolic steroids is a fast way to increase body size some athletes are willing to cheat at a sport they take these steroids to increase body mass beyond what hard work alone could produce.

-------------------------------------------------------------------

-------------------------------------------------------------------

-------------------------------------------------------------------

**2.** Effective questioning occurs in an order that draws out the exact information needed questions should focus on easy-to-answer factual information that puts the person at ease then the interviewer can move to ideas that can't be stated as a fact.

-------------------------------------------------------------------

-------------------------------------------------------------------

-------------------------------------------------------------------

More practice with correcting run-ons:
<www.mywritinglab.com>

*Review*

### REVIEW OF WRITING A PROCESS PARAGRAPH: DEVELOP YOUR POINT USING THE WRITING PROCESS

Use the following form to record your thinking about writing a process paragraph. Select and focus your topic for your writing situation, audience, and purpose. Choose a process made up of several steps or phases and identify its significance.

 What is your point?

TOPIC, PROCESS OF STEPS OR PHASES: _____

-------------------------------------------------------------------

AUDIENCE: _____

-------------------------------------------------------------------

PURPOSE: _____

-------------------------------------------------------------------

-------------------------------------------------------------------

**PREWRITING DRAFTING** State your main idea in a topic sentence.

TOPIC: ..............................................................................................................................................

..............................................................................................................................................

OPINION: ..........................................................................................................................................

..............................................................................................................................................

..............................................................................................................................................

**PREWRITING DRAFTING** Generate relevant details.

REPORTER'S QUESTIONS: HOW, WHEN, WHAT, WHERE, AND WHO? ..........................................................

..............................................................................................................................................

..............................................................................................................................................

DESCRIPTIVE DETAILS: ........................................................................................................................

..............................................................................................................................................

..............................................................................................................................................

**PREWRITING DRAFTING REVISING** Use logical order. Use transition words to signal organization of details and relationship between ideas.

TIME ORDER: .....................................................................................................................................

..............................................................................................................................................

SPACE ORDER: ...................................................................................................................................

..............................................................................................................................................

..............................................................................................................................................

*Review*

**REVISING PROOFREADING** Use effective expression. Choose words for clear, precise meaning. Eliminate run-on sentences.

VIVID IMAGES: ..................................................................................................................................

..................................................................................................................................

CORRECTED RUN-ON SENTENCES: ................................................................................................

..................................................................................................................................

..................................................................................................................................

*Review*

# Writing Assignments

## Considering Audience and Purpose

Study the sequence of photographs about the set of Pilates exercises at the beginning of the chapter. Draft a process paragraph based on one of the following two writing situations:

Assume you are keeping a personal exercise journal. Write a paragraph in which you describe the steps in your exercise sequence. Include the challenges you might face in each phase of the process.

Assume you are an instructor of an exercise class for an elderly group. Think about specific movements in each step of the exercise that might have to be adapted due to poor balance or stiffness of joints. Write a paragraph for the Senior Citizens' Health Club Newsletter that describes the exercises adapted for the elderly.

## Writing for Everyday Life

Assume that a friend or family member has asked you for advice about how to open a bank account; write a paragraph that explains how to do so. Be sure to include information about necessary personal identification and available banking services. Choose words that reflect one of the following: (1) endorsement of the banking services or (2) warning against possible problems.

## Writing for College Life

Assume you are in a college course called Student Success, and you have been assigned to write a brief oral report about how to study. Write a paragraph that records the text for your speech in which you describe the most effective way to take notes during class.

## Writing for Working Life

Assume you are the director of the Human Resources department for a corporation, and you are volunteering your services at a job fair designed to help unemployed citizens secure jobs. You have agreed to teach participants how to handle the interviewing process. Write a paragraph as part of your handout that describes the steps necessary to prepare for an interview.

# 7

# The Example Paragraph

An example, also called an exemplification, is a specific illustration of a more general idea.

When we communicate – with family members, employers, teachers, or friends – we often use examples to clarify a point we want to make. Think of a situation you were in recently where you used examples to make a point. What makes an example effective?

In everyday life, we illustrate our decorating ideas with paint chips and swatches of fabric. In working life, we offer examples of our hard work and successes when we apply for jobs and promotions. In college life, professors and textbook authors use examples to teach concepts in every discipline.

To write an example paragraph, a writer moves from a general idea to specific examples that support and clarify the main point. Sometimes, as in a science lab report, a writer may present the specific examples first and then come to a general conclusion based on the examples. An effective example paragraph also relies heavily on concrete details, the logical order of importance, and, often, parallel expression.

# What's the Point of Examples?

Generating and organizing examples help a writer to discover his or her point about a particular topic. The following photographs offer three examples of people who have overcome barriers to achieve success. Study each photograph. Write a caption that briefly lists examples of barriers each person might have overcome and examples of the success each has achieved. Then, answer the question, "What's the point?" with a one-sentence statement of the overall main idea.

*WRITING FROM LIFE*

*Practice 1*

**PHOTOGRAPHIC ORGANIZER: EXAMPLES**

PEOPLE WHO HAVE OVERCOME BARRIERS

| Who is this? | Who is this? | Who is this? |
| --- | --- | --- |
| Barriers? | Barriers? | Barriers? |
| Achievements? | Achievements? | Achievements? |

**What's the point?**

## My First Thoughts: A Prewriting Activity

*PREWRITING*

Set a time limit, perhaps five minutes, and write in your notebook about the images you just studied. Do not let your pen or pencil stop. Even if you must repeat ideas, keep writing until the time limit is up. Let ideas flow freely.

# Making a Point Using Examples: One Student Writer's Response

The following paragraph offers one writer's point about what the people in the photographs exemplify. Read the exemplification. Read the explanations and follow the directions that are given in the annotations of this exemplification paragraph. Then, read the writer's journal entry that records decisions made during the writing process.

**Main Idea:**
The main idea is the point the author is making about the topic. The topic is "those who have overcome." Underline the author's point about this topic.

**Listing Order:**
The transitional phrase "for example" signals that the paragraph is developed by examples. Circle two more transitional phrases that indicate a list of examples. This paragraph ends with the author's most important example. Underline the word(s) that suggest the last example is the most important example.

**Relevant Concrete Details:**
Concrete details list specific examples of each person's successes and barriers. Draw a box around two more concrete examples of success. Place check marks above an example of a barrier each person faced.

**Effective Expression:**
Parallelism refers to the way items in a list are worded. To achieve parallelism, a writer uses the same style of wording for a series of items. Using the same form of words in a list makes your ideas easier to follow. Double underline two more sets of details that are listed in parallel form.

## Icons of Hope

(1) Have you ever faced an overwhelming barrier that you felt you just couldn't overcome? (2) If so, take heart—you are not alone, and you are not destined to defeat. (3) Others have endured to triumph despite obstacles such as physical disabilities, life-threatening diseases, or poverty and abuse. (4) Those who have overcome serve as icons of hope. (5) For example, singer, songwriter, composer, and instrumentalist Stevie Wonder has inspired millions with albums like *Talking Book* and singles like "Superstition." (6) In addition to his flexible and unique voice, Wonder mastered a multitude of instruments including the guitar, piano, drums, synthesizers, and harmonica. (7) So far he has earned nearly two dozen Grammys and one Academy Award. (8) And he accomplished all this despite being blind since infancy. (9) Another example of hope is professional road bicycle racer Lance Armstrong. (10) Armstrong has won the prestigious Tour de France an historic seven times from 1999 to 2005. (11) According to the official Tour de France website, the three week bike race, consisting of around 20 stages, ranges from 1800 to 2500 miles in total length. (12) Riders complete each stage in the course of one day, and stages run through both mountainous and flat terrain. (13) Though the race itself is a testimony to endurance, Armstrong's achievement offers hope to millions fighting cancer. (14) In 1996, Armstrong underwent surgery and chemotherapy to treat the testicular cancer that had spread to his brain and lungs. (15) Perhaps no greater example of overcoming exists than that of Oprah Winfrey. (16) Winfrey has attained global fame, multi-million dollar wealth, and astonishing influence. (17) Her power reaches far beyond previous levels achieved by a single working woman. (18) Her numerous awards document her excellence as talk show host, actor, producer, editor, and humanitarian. (19) Born to poverty in Mississippi and sexually molested as a young girl, Winfrey emerged into success out of adversity. (20) The next time you feel overwhelmed, remember Stevie, Lance, and Oprah—all icons of success, determination, and hope.

The student writer of "Icons of Hope" completed the following reflection to record her thinking about the writing process. Read her writer's journal that describes a few key choices she made as she wrote.

MAIN IDEA: Writing this paragraph took longer than I thought it would. Because I already knew so much about each of these individuals, my brainstorming process produced a lengthy time order list of examples of their challenges and successes. However, when I began my first draft, I kept choosing words that focused on the effects of their barriers and the causes of their successes. So I ditched that draft and began again with my list of examples by my elbow. This draft seemed more like mini-biographies or narratives rather than a paragraph of examples. So I went back to brainstorming. Then, I realized, aha, I didn't have a purpose or audience for the paragraph. I had plenty of details, really more than I could use in one paragraph, but without a purpose and audience, I struggled with the order of ideas and wording. So I decided to assume the role of a an advice columnist for a women's magazine like "Redbook" or "Woman's World." My purpose was to encourage discouraged readers with examples of people who had overcome obstacles—each of us can reach our potential despite any barrier life may present.

LOGICAL ORDER: Now that I had a purpose, I could finally break away from time order. So I rearranged the details using order of importance for impact: moving from least important to most important examples. The accomplishments of these people take on a deeper meaning when considered in the light of the barriers they faced, so I began with examples of each one's success and ended with examples of each one's barrier. Deciding whom to list first was tough. Blindness, cancer, poverty and sexual abuse are all important and difficult to overcome. However, because I had chosen women as my main audience, I wanted to end with Oprah, so I created the following outline:

For a blank version of this form for your own reflections about your writing:
<www.mywritinglab.com>

Topic: Icons of Hope

A.      Introduction and topic sentence

B.      Stevie Wonder (Major Supporting Detail)

        1. Examples of accomplishments  (Minor Supporting Detail)

        2. Example of barrier (Minor Supporting Detail)

C.      Lance Armstrong (Major Supporting Detail)

        1.  Examples of accomplishments (Minor Supporting Detail)

        2.  Example of barrier  (Minor Supporting Detail)

D.      Oprah Winfrey   (Major Supporting Detail)

        1.  Examples of accomplishments (Minor Supporting Detail)

        2.  Example of barriers  (Minor Supporting Detail)

RELEVANT DETAILS: Once the organization jelled, I eliminated irrelevant details. For example, I deleted the details about the charity work of these public figures.

EFFECTIVE EXPRESSION: During several revisions, I focused on word choice. I chose the word "icon" as a synonym for "example." I signaled each major detail with listing and example signal words. And I revised to take advantage of the power of parallel language. For example, the last sentence originally stated, "The next time you feel overwhelmed, remember Stevie, Lance, and Oprah—each one examples of hope, people who have reached success through determination."

# Developing Your Point Using Examples

An exemplification illustrates a main point with one or more examples. To exemplify a point, a writer lists the examples, often according to the order of importance; explains each example with relevant concrete details; and often uses parallel expression.

## The Point: The Main Idea

When you write an exemplification, you limit your topic to a set of specific examples, instances, or cases. Most likely, you also have an opinion or point of view about the examples, and this opinion or attitude is your point or main idea. You may reveal your opinion by listing the examples in a particular order of importance. A topic sentence states the point or purpose of the examples.

For example, the following topic sentence contains (1) the topic; (2) the writer's opinion about the topic; and (3) the pattern of organization used to organize details.

The topic is *body art*. The pattern of organization is established with the phrase *such as tattooing and piercing* and the verb *exemplifies*. The writer's opinion is stated with the phrase *self-expression*.

Sometimes, in an example paragraph, a topic sentence only implies the pattern of organization as in the following version:

When the example pattern of organization is only implied by the topic sentence, then transitions that signal and list examples establish the pattern of organization within the body of the paragraph. Notice in the following example that the two major detail sentences state the topic, pattern of organization, and writer's opinion.

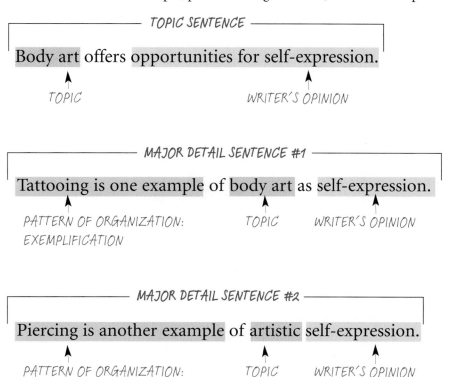

*Practice 2*

## TOPIC SENTENCES

The first four items present a topic, an opinion, and example signal word(s). Combine the ideas in each group to create a topic sentence for an example paragraph. Then, complete the practice by making your own topic sentences. (*Hint:* Not all topic sentences for example paragraphs need to include example signal words.)

**1.** TOPIC: *Foods*   OPINION: *inflame the condition diverticulitis*

EXAMPLE (OR LISTING) SIGNAL WORDS: *Certain*

TOPIC SENTENCE: _____

_____

_____

**2.** TOPIC: *A friend*   OPINION: *compassion and honesty*

EXAMPLE (OR LISTING) SIGNAL WORDS: *illustrates*

TOPIC SENTENCE: _____

_____

_____

**3.** TOPIC: *Solar energy*   OPINION: *is versatile and cheap*

EXAMPLE (OR LISTING) SIGNAL WORDS: *not included; only implied*

TOPIC SENTENCE: _____

_____

_____

**4.** TOPIC: *SUV drivers*   OPINION: *rugged, aggressive*

EXAMPLE (OR LISTING) SIGNAL WORDS: _____

TOPIC SENTENCE: _____

_____

_____

More practice with
creating topic sentences:
<www.mywritinglab.com>

**5.** TOPIC: .................................................. OPINION: ..................................................

EXAMPLE (OR LISTING) SIGNAL WORDS: ..................................................

TOPIC SENTENCE: ..................................................

..................................................

**6.** TOPIC: .................................................. OPINION: ..................................................

EXAMPLE (OR LISTING) SIGNAL WORDS: ..................................................

TOPIC SENTENCE: ..................................................

..................................................

**7.** TOPIC: .................................................. OPINION: ..................................................

EXAMPLE (OR LISTING) SIGNAL WORDS: ..................................................

TOPIC SENTENCE: ..................................................

..................................................

*Practice 2*

# Logical Order

Once you have selected your topic and focused on a main idea, you are ready to generate additional details and list your ideas based on their order of importance. To use examples to illustrate a main point, a writer moves from a general idea to a major support to a minor support. To signal the movement between these levels of ideas, a writer uses transitions to signal or list examples. Strong transitions establish coherence, a clear and understandable flow of ideas.

## Transitions Used to Signal Examples

| | | | |
|---|---|---|---|
| an illustration | for instance | once | to illustrate |
| for example | including | such as | typically |

## Transitions Used to List Examples

| | | | | |
|---|---|---|---|---|
| also | final | for one thing | last of all | second |
| and | finally | furthermore | moreover | third |
| another | first | in addition | next | |
| besides | first of all | last | one | |

Practice 3

## LISTING ORDER

The following information was published on a government website for consumer protection. Determine the logical order of the sentences. Complete the exercise by answering the question "What's the point?" Discuss your answers with your class or with a small group of peers.

### Consumer Beware!

......... The third and most common example of fraud is phishing.

......... Phishing is an email message that lures a consumer to a phony website.

......... The email sender pretends to be from a legitimate government organization, bank, or retailer.

......... The phishy email stated, "We recently reviewed your account, and we need more information to help us provide you with secure service."

......... The message also directed the receiver "to visit the Resolution Center and complete the 'Steps to Remove Limitations.'"

......... A recent instance of phishing came from a phony PayPal site.

......... A second example of fraud is the phone scam; a caller pretends to represent a trusted organization or company.

......... In one instance, a caller claims to work for the court and says the listener has been called for jury duty.

......... The caller then demands personal information such as a social security number, birth date, and credit card numbers.

......... The first and least common example of fraud is the handyman sting.

......... The handyman offers to fix the problem, such as replacing a roof or removing a fallen tree, for a cash fee lower than any reputable company could offer.

......... The handyman shows up on the doorstep of a home in obvious need of repair, usually after severe weather such as a tornado or hurricane.

......... Most often, the money is paid upfront, and the work is never completed.

### What's the point?

.................................................................................................

.................................................................................................

.................................................................................................

.................................................................................................

More practice with listing order:
<www.mywritinglab.com>

# Relevant Details

As a writer narrows a topic into a focused main idea, the thinking process brings to mind many details that answer the questions *who, what, when, where, why,* and *how.* A writer evaluates the relevancy of each detail and uses only those that exemplify the main idea. Some relevant details express major examples of the main point; minor details may further illustrate major examples. Some major and minor details may explain the author's opinion about the examples. During the prewriting phase, a list can help a writer organize ideas as they are generated. Study the following list generated about the topic "Examples of State Gun Laws."

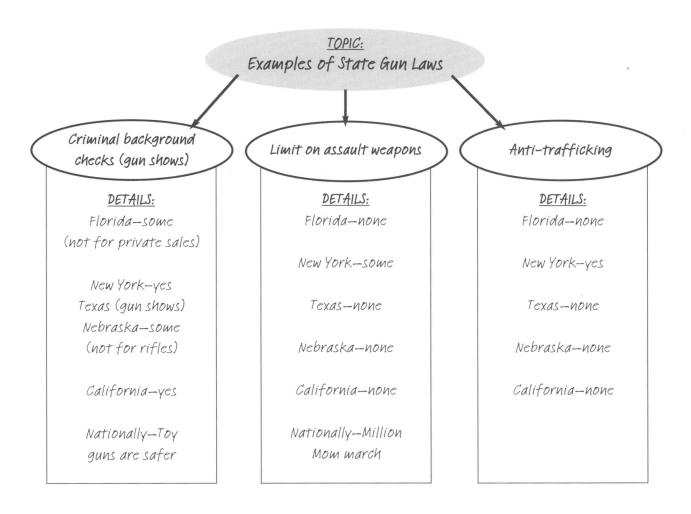

During the prewriting phase of writing, a writer naturally generates irrelevant details. In fact, an effective writer often produces far more details than can be used to make a specific point. Irrelevant details do not exemplify, explain, or support the focused point of the paragraph. A careful writer uses the revision process to double check details for relevancy and to eliminate irrelevant details.

Practice 4

The following paragraph, adapted from the <stategunlaws.org> website, develops the ideas recorded in the brainstorming list about state gun laws. Circle the main idea. Underline three concrete major examples. Cross out the two details that are not relevant to the main point.

## State Gun Laws

(1) New York, Florida, Texas, Nebraska, and California gun control laws vary greatly from state to state. (2) For example, of the five states—New York, Florida, Texas, Nebraska, and California—only New York has an anti-trafficking law that places a one-handgun-per-month limit on gun sales. (3) In the other four states, anyone can easily traffic guns to criminals by buying as many handguns as they want from gun stores and turning them over for profit on the streets. (4) Unbelievably, toy guns face stricter safety regulations than do real guns. (5) In addition, only two states, California and New York, require criminal background checks at gun shows. (6) Florida and Nebraska require partial background checks; for example, Florida requires a criminal background check for handguns, but no background check is necessary to purchase an assault rifle such as AK47. (7) Alarmingly, Texas does not require background checks at gun shows. (8) Perhaps the most alarming example of our uneven approach to gun control is the overall lack of limits on assault weapons. (9) Of the five states, only California bans the sale of semiautomatic assault weapons such as the Uzi. (10) New York has a partial limit on such sales; for example, the state does not ban the sale of "rapid fire ammunition magazines that hold up to 100 rounds." (11) Texas, Nebraska, and Florida have no limits on assault weapons and magazines. (12) A national network of volunteers known as the Million Mom March work to strengthen and unify gun laws.

More practice with relevant details: <www.mywritinglab.com>

# Effective Expression: Parallel Language

Parallel language is the use of similar and balanced expressions in a pair or series of words, phrases, or clauses. Parallelism makes a piece of writing more enjoyable, more powerful, and more readable. Study the following examples from a student's first thoughts about the seasons of the year:

For more information on parallelism, see Chapter 20.

More practice with parallel language:
<www.mywritinglab.com>

**Non-parallel words:**

> Summer temperatures are ideal for swimming, boating, and a picnic.

**Revised Words for Parallelism:**

> Summer temperatures are ideal for swimming, boating, and picnicking. ◄

*THIS SERIES OF WORDS (NOUNS) ALL END IN —ING.*

**Non-parallel phrases:**

> The seasons can go from the fire of summer, to the chilly fall, to the freezing winter, to the birds chirping and flowers blooming.

**Revised Phrases for Parallelism:**

> The seasons can go from the fire of summer, to the chill of fall, to the freeze of winter, to the breeze of spring.

*THIS SERIES OF IDEAS REPEAT A PATTERN OF PREPOSITIONAL PHRASES.*

**Non-parallel clauses:**

> I love the fall because the leaves turn colors, because the air turns crisp, and it's football season.

**Revised Clauses for Parallelism:**

> I love the fall because the leaves turn colors, because the air turns crisp, and because television programming turns to football.

*THESE CLAUSES ARE NOW ALL DEPENDENT CLAUSES THAT BEGIN WITH THE SAME SUBORDINATING CONJUNCTION ("BECAUSE") AND USE THE SAME VERB ("TO TURN").*

---

**PARALLEL EXPRESSION**

Revise each of the following sentences so ideas are expressed in parallel language. Discuss your work with your class or with a small group of peers.

**1.** Examples of activities that strengthen the heart include jogging, swimming, and jump rope.

Practice 5

**2.** A healthy heart lifestyle includes the following: getting plenty of sleep, eating a balanced diet, and regular exercise. *exercising regularly*

**3.** In my current position, I am responsible for training new employees, to balance the cash registers, and the work schedules for the week. *balance  Scheduling  working*

**4.** Tongue piercing is not risk free; for example, a tongue piercing can become infected, cracking a tooth. *crack a tooth*

**5.** The professor gave us a choice between two options for our final exam: a final written exam or giving a ten minute speech with a PowerPoint presentation. *or need given*

# Using Examples in Your Academic Courses

Every college course uses examples to clarify ideas. As you study these courses, you will study examples of governments, important historical figures, psychological concepts, scientific principles, effective speeches, and so on. In addition, you will prove what you have learned by providing examples of the concepts and skills you have studied.

### USING EXAMPLES IN A SHORT-ANSWER COMMUNICATION ESSAY EXAM

Assume your college professor of communication has given your class a set of practice study questions to help you prepare for an upcoming mid-term exam. A peer in your study group prepared the following answer to one of the study questions. Based on what you have learned about writing an effective example paragraph, offer suggestions to strengthen her paragraph.

**Sample Question:** According to page 115 of your textbook, *The Interpersonal Communication Textbook,* 10th ed., by Joseph A. DeVito, effective listening has several "major purposes and payoffs." In one paragraph, identify three of these purposes and payoffs.

### Listening: The Purposes and Payoffs

(1) According to Joseph A. DeVito, effective listening has several major purposes and payoffs. (2) For example, one major purpose of effective listening is to learn about others, the world, and oneself. (3) By being open to ideas other than one's own, one avoids problems and deepens logical thinking. (4) Another purpose of effective listening is to relate to others. (5) By being kind and helpful and loving, one develops long lasting relationships. (6) A third purpose of effective listening is to influence others. (7) By respecting the opinions of others, one earns the trust and respect of others. (8) One should always remember that hearing is not listening because hearing is merely a passive, physical process.

More practice with writing example paragraphs: <www.mywritinglab.com>

# Workshop: Writing an Example Paragraph Step by Step

Workshop

## Prewrite Your Paragraph

The various activities that follow will walk you through the steps of the prewriting stage of the writing process: choosing a topic; focusing your point; and generating and organizing relevant details.

### Choose Your Topic

The following activities are designed to help you choose a topic.

1. Create a bank of topics. Use the following headings to brainstorm or list as many examples about each topic as you possibly can. Don't criticize your thoughts; just get as many relevant examples written down as quickly as possible. Add more topics and examples as they occur to you. Compare your bank of topics with those of your peers.

   - Pollution
   - Job Skills
   - Effective Teachers
   - Alternative Energy Supplies

2. Generate ideas with a freewrite. Choose one of the topics from your topic bank and think of the examples that illustrate the topic. Write about the topic and examples for ten minutes without stopping.

3. Select a photograph or series of photographs that illustrate a topic. Write a caption, brainstorm examples, freewrite about the photograph(s). Remember to ask, "What does the picture illustrate?" and "What's the point?"

### Focus Your Point

Read a prewrite you have generated for an exemplification. Underline words that suggest your values, opinions, or attitudes about the topic and the examples. Think about why the details are important. Identify your audience and purpose. Write a list of additional concrete examples that illustrate your point. State in one sentence the point of the examples.

AUDIENCE: ............................................................................................................

PURPOSE: ..............................................................................................................

............................................................................................................................

WHAT'S THE POINT? ..............................................................................................

............................................................................................................................

............................................................................................................................

## Generate and Organize Relevant Details

Using ideas you have recorded so far and the following idea map, generate and organize details that support your point.

**Example: Illustrations of an Idea**

**What's the point?**

Topic:

| Example 1 | Example 2 | Example 3 |

Minor Details

Minor Details

Minor Details

## Write a Draft of Your Paragraph

Using ideas you generated during the prewriting phase, compose a draft of your example paragraph. Return to the prewriting process at any time to generate additional details as needed. Use your own paper.

## Revise Your Draft

Once you have created a draft of an example paragraph, read the draft and answer the questions in the "Questions for Revising an Example Paragraph" box that follows. Indicate your answers by annotating your paper. If you answer "yes" to a question, underline, check, or circle examples. If you answer "no" to a question, write additional details in the margin and draw lines to indicate their placement. Revise your paragraph based on your reflection. (*Hint:* Experienced writers create several drafts as they focus on one or two questions per draft.)

Workshop

# Questions for Revising an Example Paragraph

☐ Have I stated or implied a main idea? Have I made my point? Can I state my point in one sentence?

☐ Have I used concrete details to make my point?

☐ Have I included only the details that are relevant to my point?

☐ Have I used order of importance effectively? Have I used strong transitions?

☐ Have I used parallel language to make my ideas clear to my readers?

 **Proofread Your Draft**

Once you have made any revisions to your paragraph that may be needed, proofread your paragraph for proper usage and punctuation, such as using commas in a series.

### Grammar in Action: Using Commas in a Series

Use commas to separate three or more words, phrases, or clauses in a series. One of the following conjunctions is used between the last two items of a series: *but, or, yet, so, for, and,* or *nor:* for example, *sending, receiving,* and *forwarding emails.* Some experts state that the comma before the conjunction is optional. However, leaving the last comma of the series out may cause confusion, so many experts advise including it. In writing for college, we suggest you include it. Study the following examples:

For more information on using commas in a series, see Chapter 29.

- **Using Commas to Separate Three or More Words:**

    David Chappell is candid, creative, and comical.

    *Coordinating conjunction*

- **Using Commas to Separate Three or More Phrases:**

    Texas offers vacation experiences that are enjoyable and educational: exploring Big Ben National Park, visiting The Alamo, and touring the NASA Space Center.

    *Coordinating conjunction*

- **Using Commas to Separate Three or More Clauses:**

    Our company is looking for employees who can find solutions, who can work as a team, and who can excel in their roles.

    *Coordinating conjunction*

Workshop

### USING COMMAS IN A SERIES

Edit these sentences for proper use of commas in a series.

**1.** I only need three pairs of shoes—running shoes low heeled pumps and reef sandals.

_____

_____

**2.** The study of psychology includes units such as the biology of the brain the development of the mind and the social behaviors of a human being.

_____

_____

**3.** Those who snore are those who are more likely to have heart attacks who are more likely to be in an automobile accident and who are more likely to suffer from daytime fatigue.

_____

_____

_____

More practice with using commas in a series:
<www.mywritinglab.com>

### REVIEW OF WRITING AN EXAMPLE PARAGRAPH: DEVELOP YOUR POINT USING THE WRITING PROCESS

Use the following form to record your thinking about writing an example paragraph. Select and focus your topic for your writing situation, audience, and purpose.

Choose a topic that is best explained with examples and identify its significance.

 What is your point?

TOPIC, EXAMPLES: _____

AUDIENCE: _____

PURPOSE: _____

_____

_____

State your main idea in a topic sentence.

TOPIC: .......................................................................................................................................................................

OPINION: ...................................................................................................................................................................

...................................................................................................................................................................................

...................................................................................................................................................................................

Generate relevant details.

REPORTER'S QUESTIONS: WHO, WHAT, WHERE, WHEN, WHY, HOW? ..........................................................

...................................................................................................................................................................................

CONCRETE EXAMPLES: ...............................................................................................................................................

...................................................................................................................................................................................

Use logical order. Use transition words to signal organization of details and relationship between ideas.

TRANSITIONS TO SIGNAL EXAMPLES: ......................................................................................................................

...................................................................................................................................................................................

TRANSITIONS TO LIST EXAMPLES: ...........................................................................................................................

...................................................................................................................................................................................

Use effective expression. Use parallel expressions. Correctly use commas in a series.

PARALLEL EXPRESSIONS: .............................................................................................................................................

CORRECT USE OF COMMAS IN A SERIES: ...............................................................................................................

...................................................................................................................................................................................

Review

# Writing Assignments

More ideas for writing an
example paragraph:
<www.mywritinglab.com>

## Considering Audience and Purpose

Study the sequence of photographs about the examples of people who have
overcome barriers at the beginning of the chapter. Choose one of the following
writing situations and compose a paragraph.

Assume you are part of a committee that is creating and burying a time
capsule. The committee chose these pictures to place in the time capsule. Write
a paragraph that explains how one or all of these individuals exemplify
American culture in the early 21$^{st}$ century.

Assume you are a fan of one of the individuals depicted in the photographs.
Write a one-paragraph letter of appreciation in which you list and explain
examples of his or her admirable traits.

## Writing for Everyday Life

Assume that you are keeping a personal journal and you want to capture the
essence of your daily life so your children and grandchildren will know about
the customs, fashions, or nature of this time in your life and our society. Use
examples to make your point. Choose words that reflect one of the following
attitudes: (1) realistic, (2) idealistic.

## Writing for College Life

Assume you are a member of the Student Government Association, and
you are helping with freshman orientation. Identify two or three aspects of
college life about which new students should be aware. Use examples to make
your point.

## Writing for Working Life

Assume a peer is applying for a job as a supervisor of a sales team at Best Buy
or Radio Shack (or some other job that requires leadership and commitment)
and has asked you for a recommendation. Interview the peer; then write a
one-paragraph recommendation in which you use examples to support your
recommendation.

# 8

# The Classification Paragraph

## A classification is a division of a topic into one or more subgroups.

Whether we are grocery shopping, studying, job hunting, or searching for that special someone, we often gather and group information based on types. For example, most of us have experienced or observed the social cliques that form in high schools, neighborhoods, and on the job.

A writer uses classification to sort, group, and label items and ideas based on shared traits or types. In everyday life, we fulfill various social roles such as life-partner, parent, sibling, friend, employee, or student. In working life, we promote people to higher levels of responsibility and pay based on particular types of skills and attitudes. In college life, each of us probably prefers certain kinds of courses, likes certain types of teachers, and does better on certain types of tests.

To write a classification paragraph, a writer divides a topic into subgroups based on shared traits or qualities. The writer lists and often labels each subgroup, describes its traits, and offers examples that best represent the group. Because groups and subgroups are listed, transitions are often used to signal logical order and ensure coherence. An effective classification uses details of description and examples, logical order, and (as in any effective paragraph) sentence variety.

# What's the Point of Classification?

Identifying and labeling groups or types helps a writer to discover his or her point about a particular topic. Study the following set of photographs: In the space provided (1) identify the major fashion "look" represented by the three photographs. (2) List the traits of each subgroup. (3) Describe specific examples based on the outfits in the photographs. (4) Answer the question "What's the point?"

Practice 1

WRITING FROM LIFE

PHOTOGRAPHIC ORGANIZER: CLASSIFICATION

TOPIC: TYPES OF FASHION

| 1ST TYPE | 2ND TYPE | 3RD TYPE |

**1.** What is the best label for the fashions shown in each of these images?

---------------------------------- ---------------------------------- ----------------------------------

**2.** Traits:      Traits:      Traits:

---------------------------------- ---------------------------------- ----------------------------------

---------------------------------- ---------------------------------- ----------------------------------

---------------------------------- ---------------------------------- ----------------------------------

**3.** Examples:      Examples:      Examples:

---------------------------------- ---------------------------------- ----------------------------------

---------------------------------- ---------------------------------- ----------------------------------

**What's the point?**

----------------------------------------------------------------------------------------------

----------------------------------------------------------------------------------------------

PREWRITING

## My First Thoughts: A Prewriting Activity

Brainstorm about the images you just studied. Set a time limit, such as five minutes, and write in your notebook about the images and the details you generated. Write as quickly as you can without stopping. Let the ideas flow freely. Getting your first thoughts about a topic on paper is one excellent way to kick-start your writing process.

# Making a Point Using Classification: One Student Writer's Response

The following paragraph offers one writer's point about the types of fashions illustrated by the photographs. Read the classification paragraph below and the annotations. Complete the activities in bold type given in the annotation. Some responses may vary. Then, read the writer's journal that records decisions she made during the writing process.

### 3° of Cool

**Main Idea:**
The main idea is the point the author is making about the topic. The topic is fashion.
**Underline the author's point about this topic.**

**Effective Expression:**
Parallelism refers to the way ideas are worded. To achieve parallelism in this sentence, the writer repeated a *who-clause* three times.
**Underline two additional sentences that repeat a *who-clause* three times.**

**Listing Order:**
The transitional phrase, "another type" signals that the paragraph is developed by listing types of fashion.
**Underline one or more transitional words or phrases that signal a list of types, traits, or examples.**

(1) Fashion offers a wide variety of styles for personal expression. (2) Obviously, designers create fashion collections to appeal to specific styles. (3) Interestingly, styles reflect the values of a culture and a person. (4) In the first part of the 21st century, fashion reveals a mass devotion to cool. (5) Three high-name-recognition designers offer pop-culture cool to the socialite, the urbanite, and the professional. (6) First, Jennifer Lopez appeals to the socialite who seeks the trendy, high-fashion cool in her JLO Collection. (7) The JLO look is for the sociable woman who is comfortable with herself, who doesn't look exactly like everyone else, and who is sexy, fun, and fashionable. (8) One outfit featured in a runway show illustrates JLO's trendy style. (9) The outfit sported mid-thigh brown boots; skin-tight red leggings; black short-shorts; a body-hugging tan sweater top; a wide waist-cinching brown belt; a luxurious fur collar and luxurious fur puffed long-sleeves. (10) Offering another type of pop-culture cool, P. Diddy appeals to the urbanite who seeks sophisticated, laid-back cool in his Sean John Collection. (11) The Sean John look is for the man on the street who exudes confidence, who stands out from the crowd, and who thrives in both urban and suburban settings. (12) One of his casual sportswear outfits epitomizes urban cool. (13) The outfit is simple yet distinctive: loose-fit, dark rinse denims; a large, dark silver buckle on a black belt; a crisp, white cotton tee-shirt; a matching bleached white windbreaker; and sleek dark glasses. (14) Finally, Tommy Hilfiger appeals to the professional

who seeks chic, in-control cool in his H Hilfiger Collection. (15)
The Hilfiger look is for the career woman who knows what she
wants, who leads by example, and who values quality. (16)
Separate pieces combine to create a tailored, elegant outfit: a soft
melon-colored, knee-length pencil skirt in a rich no-wrinkle fabric;
a starched and fitted berry and white striped shirt; and a tailored
blazer in the same soft melon-colored, no-wrinkle fabric as the
skirt. (17) Each designer put his or her own spin on the cool look,
so the socialite, the urbanite, and the professional can all be cool.

**Relevant Details:**
Relevant details include descriptive details of traits
and examples. Descriptive details include sensory
details such as "melon" and "starched."
**Circle two more details that appeal to the senses.**

---

**THE WRITER'S JOURNAL**

The student writer of "3° of Cool" completed the following reflection to record her
thinking through the writing process. Read her writer's journal that describes a few key
choices she made as she wrote.

MAIN IDEA: _I experimented with my writing process with this paragraph._
_Instead of just beginning to type or freewrite, this time I used a_
_classification photographic organizer to generate several lists of_
_details. Once I generated and labeled my ideas, I still had trouble starting_
_a draft. I needed an introduction, a purpose for writing about these_
_particular looks. Finally, I decided to assume I was writing an assignment_
_for a sociology class, and my purpose was to describe a cultural value_
_reflected in fashion. Finally, I composed a draft. Sometimes, I could_
_quickly write the lists in parallel language; other times, the lists seemed_
_awkwardly worded. Instead of getting stuck on wording, I continued to_
_write out my ideas. Once the first draft was completed, I took a much_
_needed break!_

RELEVANT DETAILS: _First, I filled in the boxes labeled "Traits" with a list of_
_adjectives that described the outfit in each picture. Then, in the boxes_
_labeled "Example," I described a specific detail from the outfit that_
_illustrated the adjective. This approach helped me to create and label_
_the following groups of details:_

| NAME | JLO |
| --- | --- |
| TRAITS: | Cool, fun, sexy, trendy, fashionable, youthful |
| EXAMPLE: | Luxurious fur, body-hugging, wide belt, waist-cinching, skin-tight red leggings, mid-thigh high boots |

| NAME | Sean John |
| --- | --- |
| TRAITS: | urban wear, casual, sophisticated, sporty |
| EXAMPLE: | crisp, white tee-shirt, loose-fit denims, large silver belt buckle |

| NAME | Hilfiger |
| --- | --- |
| TRAITS: | hip, chic, spirited, elegant, youthful, tailored, finished |
| EXAMPLE: | pencil straight/knee-length fitted skirt, no-wrinkle, soft-berry/white stripes melon-colored shirt/blazer |

After brainstorming these details, I put my pencil down, walked around, and thought about what labels best describe each fashion look. Suddenly, it hit me that these were all cool, hip looks that reflect pop culture. The JLO look seemed best suited for a social event like a concert or a club, so I labeled it the socialite look. The Sean John look seemed perfect for hanging in the neighborhood, catching a movie, or going to a comedy club in the city, so I labeled it the urbanite look. The Hilfiger look seemed ideal for the up-and-coming career woman, so I labeled it the professional look.

LOGICAL ORDER: I decided to order my discussion of the styles from trendy to traditional.

EFFECTIVE EXPRESSION: Later when I reread my paragraph, I underlined the sentences I wanted to revise for parallel expression. I decided to *describe each fashion group with the same sentence structure: The _____ look is for the _____ woman (or man) who _____, who _____, and who _____. I also used parallel expressions to describe each outfit. For example, the sentence that describes Sean John's outfit reads, "The outfit is simple yet distinctive: loose-fit, dark rinse denims; a large, dark silver buckle on a black belt; a crisp, white cotton tee-shirt; a matching bleached white windbreaker; and sleek dark glasses." This sentence uses adjective-noun phrases separated by semicolons. I enjoyed writing this paragraph and had fun creating parallel expressions.*

# Developing Your Point Using Classification

A classification makes a main point by grouping or sorting ideas. To support a point through classification, a writer divides a topic into subgroups based on common traits or principles. Writers offer relevant concrete details of descriptions and examples, and (as in every piece of writing) control sentence structure.

## The Point: The Main Idea

When you write a classification, you limit your topic to a set of ideas or groups based on types, shared traits, and common principles. Most likely, you also have an opinion or point of view about the groups, traits, or common principles. This opinion or attitude is your point or main idea. You also reveal your opinion by discussing the groups or traits in a particular order of importance. A topic sentence states the point or purpose of the groups, types, or traits.

For example, the following topic sentence contains (1) the topic; (2) the writer's opinion about the topic; and (3) the pattern of organization used to organize details.

The topic is *friendship*. The pattern of organization is established with the phrase *three types of*. The writer's opinion is stated with the phrase *equally important interpersonal relationships*.

TOPIC
PATTERN OF ORGANIZATION:
CLASSIFICATION SIGNAL WORDS
WRITER'S OPINION

Friendships offer three types of equally important interpersonal relationships.

The example above illustrates the relationship between the topic, the writer's opinion, and the pattern of organization in this particular topic sentence.

Practice 2

## TOPIC SENTENCES

Practice creating topic sentences. The first three items present a topic, an opinion, and classification signal word(s). Combine the ideas in each group to create a topic sentence for a classification. Then, complete the practice by writing your own topic sentences.

**1.** TOPIC: *leisure activities*   OPINION: *relaxing and inexpensive, strengthen family ties*

CLASSIFICATION SIGNAL WORDS: *two types of*

TOPIC SENTENCE: _____

_____

**2.** TOPIC: *diet*   OPINION: *healthful*

CLASSIFICATION SIGNAL WORDS: *several traits*

TOPIC SENTENCE: _____

_____

**3.** TOPIC: *credit*   OPINION: *a wise consumer must understand*

CLASSIFICATION SIGNAL WORDS: *types of*

TOPIC SENTENCE: _____

_____

**4.** TOPIC: *singer Faith Hill*   OPINION: _____

CLASSIFICATION SIGNAL WORDS: _____

TOPIC SENTENCE: _____

_____

**5.** TOPIC: _____   OPINION: _____

CLASSIFICATION SIGNAL WORDS: _____

TOPIC SENTENCE: _____

_____

**6.** TOPIC: .................................. OPINION: ..................................

CLASSIFICATION SIGNAL WORDS: ..................................

TOPIC SENTENCE: ..................................

..................................

**7.** TOPIC: .................................. OPINION: ..................................

CLASSIFICATION SIGNAL WORDS: ..................................

TOPIC SENTENCE: ..................................

..................................

*Practice 2*

# Logical Order

Once you have divided a topic into groups, types, or traits and focused on a main idea, you are ready to generate additional details and list your ideas in their order of importance. To make a point using classification, a writer moves from a general idea (the group) to a major support (a particular trait of the group) to a minor support (an example of the trait). To signal the movement between these levels of ideas, a writer uses transitions to signal or list groups, types, or traits. Strong transitions establish coherence, a clear and understandable flow of ideas.

**Words That Are Used to Signal Groups, Types, or Traits**

| | | | | |
|---|---|---|---|---|
| aspect | classify | group | quality | style |
| attribute | classification | ideal | rank | trait |
| brand | collection | kind | section | type |
| branch | division | level | set | typical |
| categories | element | order | sort | variety |
| characteristic | feature | part | status | class |
| form | principle | stratum | | |

**Transitions That Combine with Signal Words to List Groups, Types, or Traits**

| | | | | |
|---|---|---|---|---|
| also | final | for one thing | last of all | second |
| and | finally | furthermore | moreover | third |
| another | first | in addition | next | |
| besides | first of all | last | one | |

**LISTING ORDER**

The following information appears in a college science textbook. Determine the logical order of the sentences. *Hint:* Underline the transitions that signal or list groups, types, or traits. Complete the exercise by answering the question "What's the point?" Discuss your answers with your class or with a small group of peers.

---

### Two Types of Tumors

_____ First, benign tumors are not cancerous; they are abnormal masses of essentially normal cells.

_____ Another type of tumor is the malignant tumor.

_____ Third, benign tumors always remain at their original site in the body.

_____ One type of tumor is the benign tumor. Benign tumors have several traits.

_____ Malignant tumors have several distinct traits.

_____ Second, arising from a single cancer cell, a malignant tumor displaces normal tissue as it grows.

_____ First, this tumor is cancerous; it is a mass of cancer cells.

_____ Third, cells may also split off from the malignant tumor, invade the circulatory system (lymph vessels and blood vessels), and travel to new locations, where they can form new tumors.

_____ Second, benign tumors can cause problems if they grow in certain organs like the brain, but usually they can be removed by surgery.

_____ If the tumor is not killed or removed, some of the cancer cells spread into surrounding tissues, enlarging the tumor.

—Adapted from Campbell, Reece, Taylor, and Simon.
*Biology: Concepts & Connections,* 5th ed. Benjamin Cummings 2008. p.135.

**What's the point?**

---

## Relevant Details

As a writer narrows a topic into a focused main idea, the thinking process brings to mind many details that answer the questions such as *who, what, when, where, why,* and *how.* A writer evaluates the relevancy of each detail and uses only those that clarify or support the main idea based on classification. Some relevant details identify subgroups, types, or traits of the main point. Minor details may offer examples of subgroups, types, or traits. Some major and minor details may explain the writer's opinion about the topic and how it is being classified. During the prewriting phase, a list can help a writer organize ideas as they are generated. Study the following concept map used to generate ideas about the topic "Two types of comedy that dominate television."

**Concept Map**

| Topic: | *Two types of comedy that dominate television.* | |
|---|---|---|
| | **Type 1:** *Sketch comedy* | **Type 2:** *Situation comedy* |
| Traits: | Better for adult audience | Better for family |
| Performer: | Ensemble routine | Ensemble routine |
| Origin: | Evolved from vaudeville | Evolved from radio |
| Length: | Short scenes or sketches (1–10 mins.) | 30 min. story line |
| Material: | Actors improvise/write scripts Avoids violence, uses bad language | Writers create scripts Avoids violence and bad language |
| Focus: | Politics, current events, issues | Social relationships at home and work |
| Examples: | Colgate Comedy Hour, Monty Python's Flying Circus, SNL, Mad TV, Chappelle's, Ed Sullivan (best show of all) | I Love Lucy, Friends, Seinfeld, Everybody Hates Chris |

During the prewriting phase of writing, a writer naturally generates irrelevant details. In fact, an effective writer often produces far more details than can be used to make a specific point. Irrelevant details do not explain or support the focused point of the paragraph. A careful writer uses the revision process to double-check details for relevancy and to eliminate irrelevant details.

The following paragraph develops the ideas recorded in the brainstorming list about comedy. Circle the main idea. Underline two traits for each group. Cross out the two details that are not relevant to the main point.

## Television Comedy: Sketches and Sitcoms

(1) Two types of comedy have long dominated television. (2) One type is sketch comedy. (3) Sketch comedy is an ensemble routine that evolved from vaudeville into a bit for television on variety shows as the *Colgate Comedy Hour* and the *Ed Sullivan Show*. (4) Sketch comedy is a series of short comedy scenes that typically range from one to ten minutes. (5) Often the actors improvise the sketch, making it up as they go; then they write the script based on their improvisation. (6) This kind of humor avoids violence, often uses offensive language, and focuses on politics, issues, and current events. (7) Well-known examples of sketch comedy include *Monty Python's Flying Circus*, *Saturday Night Live*, *Mad TV*, and *Chappelle's Show*. (8) However, the *Ed Sullivan Show* remains the all time best variety show to have appeared on television. (9) A second type of comedy dominating television is the sitcom or situation comedy, also an ensemble routine. (10) The sitcom evolved from radio shows such as *Amos and Andy*; sitcoms continue to flourish on television. (11) Sitcoms are usually set in a specific location such as a home or office, and they present amusing story lines about a group of characters such as a family, friends, or co-workers in an office. (12) Often episodes are self-contained stories that are resolved in less than 30 minutes; some sitcoms do use ongoing story lines based on

developing relationships between characters. (13) This type of humor avoids violence, rarely uses offensive language, and focuses on social relationships. (14) Well-known examples of situation comedy include *I Love Lucy*, *Friends*, *Seinfeld*, and *Everybody Hates Chris*. (15) Overall, sitcoms are more appropriate for family viewing than sketch comedy.

# Effective Expression: Controlled Sentence Structure

Control of sentence structure enhances effective expression. You can express ideas through the use of four sentence types: simple, compound, complex, and compound-complex. Study the following definitions and examples of these four types of sentences:

**1**. A **simple sentence** contains one independent clause.

INDEPENDENT CLAUSE

Two types of comedy have long dominated television.

**2**. A **compound sentence** contains two or more independent clauses. These clauses can be joined with:

**a.** A comma and a coordinating conjunction (*for, and, nor, but, or, yet, so*: FANBOYS),

INDEPENDENT CLAUSES

Sitcoms are usually set in a specific location such as a home or office, and they present amusing story lines about a group of characters such as a family and neighbors or co-workers in an office.

**b.** A semicolon,

The sitcom evolved from radio shows such as *Amos and Andy*; they continue to flourish on television.

INDEPENDENT CLAUSES

OR

**c.** A semicolon with a conjunctive adverb.

INDEPENDENT CLAUSE

Often the ensemble of actors improvises the sketch; then they write the script based on their improvisation.

INDEPENDENT CLAUSE

**3**. A **complex sentence** contains one independent clause and one or more dependent clauses. A dependent clause begins with a subordinating conjunction (such as *although, because, when, who, which,* and *that*) placed immediately before a subject and verb. Sometimes, the subordinating conjunction also serves as the subject of the verb in the dependent clause.

INDEPENDENT CLAUSE

Sketch comedy is a series of short comedy scenes that often range between one and ten minutes.

DEPENDENT CLAUSE

**4.** A **compound-complex** sentence contains two or more independent clauses and one or more dependent clauses. This sentence type combines the traits of the compound and complex sentences.

INDEPENDENT CLAUSE

Often episodes are self-contained stories

that are resolved in less than 30 minutes;

some sitcoms do use ongoing story lines based

on developing relationships between characters.

DEPENDENT CLAUSE                    INDEPENDENT CLAUSE

Practice 5

### SENTENCE VARIETY

Label each of the following sentences as a simple, compound, complex, or compound-complex sentence. Revise each sentence into the new type of sentence indicated. Discuss your work with your class or with a small group of your peers.

............................ **1.** Foods from wheat, rice, oats, cornmeal, barley, or another cereal grain are grain products. Bread, pasta, oatmeal, breakfast cereals, tortillas, and grits are examples of grain products.

REVISE INTO A COMPOUND SENTENCE: ...................................................................

..................................................................................................................................

..................................................................................................................................

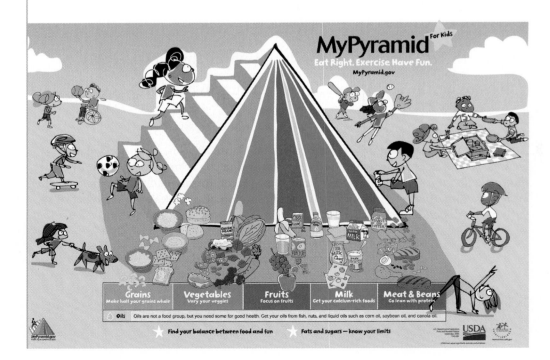

**2.** Oils are fats that are liquid at room temperature, like canola, olive, and other vegetable oils used in cooking.

More practice with
sentence variety:
<www.mywritinglab.com>

REVISE INTO A COMPOUND-COMPLEX SENTENCE: _____

_____

_____

**3.** Vegetables are organized into subgroups. These subgroups include dark green vegetables, orange vegetables, dry beans and peas, and starchy vegetables.

REVISE INTO A COMPLEX SENTENCE: _____

_____

_____

**4.** The new food pyramid, which includes steps to illustrate the need for physical activity, classifies food into six food groups; these groups include grains, vegetables, fruits, oils, milk, and meats and beans.

REVISE INTO SIMPLE SENTENCES: _____

_____

_____

*Practice 5*

# Using Classification in Your Academic Courses

Often, writing in college requires research. Research deepens your understanding of a topic in several ways: (1) you locate facts; (2) you consider the opinions of experts; (3) you weed out false facts; and (4) you clarify your own point about a topic based on the information you collect. Classification plays a key role in research because information is organized based on types. Two well-known methods of classifying information are the Dewey Decimal System and the Library of Congress System. Your college library uses one of these two types to arrange books on the shelves by labeling them with a system of letters and numbers. When you are assigned a research topic, you will use classification to find the information you need.

## USING CLASSIFICATION FOR LIBRARY RESEARCH:
CLASSIFICATION OF INFORMATION—THE LIBRARY OF CONGRESS SYSTEM

Listed below are the letters and titles of the main classes and one subgroup of the Library of Congress Classification. Study the list and answer the questions.

A – GENERAL WORKS

B – PHILOSOPHY. PSYCHOLOGY. RELIGION

C – AUXILIARY SCIENCES OF HISTORY

D – HISTORY (GENERAL) AND HISTORY OF EUROPE

E – HISTORY: AMERICA

F – HISTORY: AMERICA

G – GEOGRAPHY. ANTHROPOLOGY. RECREATION

H – SOCIAL SCIENCES

   H – Social Sciences (General)

   HA – Statistics

   HB – Economic theory. Demography

   HC – Industries. Land use. Labor

   HE – Transportation and communications

   HF – Commerce

   HG – Finance

   HJ – Public Finance

   HM – Sociology (General)

   HN – Social history and conditions. Social problems. Social reform

HQ – The family. Marriage. Women

HS – Societies: secret, benevolent, etc.

HT – Communities. Classes. Races

HV – Social pathology. Social and public welfare. Criminology

HX – Socialism. Communism Anarchism

J – POLITICAL SCIENCE

K – LAW

L – EDUCATION

M – MUSIC AND BOOKS ON MUSIC

N – FINE ARTS

P – LANGUAGE AND LITERATURE

Q – SCIENCE

R – MEDICINE

S – AGRICULTURE

T – TECHNOLOGY

U – MILITARY SCIENCE

V – NAVAL SCIENCE

Z – BIBLIOGRAPHY. LIBRARY SCIENCE. INFORMATION RESOURCES (GENERAL)

—"Library of Congress Classification Outline." *Library of Congress* 5 July 2005.
2 March 2006 http://www.loc.gov/catdir/cpso/lcco/lcco.html

**1.** Write the letter of the group that would contain the following book titles:

............... *Dealing with Relatives (—even if you can't stand them): Bringing Out the Best in Families at Their Worst* by Rick Brinkman and Rick Kirschner.

............... Encyclopedia of Family Health

**2.** Write the letter of the group that you would search for the following information:

............... The principles of Islam

............... The author Toni Morrison, winner of the Nobel Prize for Literature

More practice using classification:
<www.mywritinglab.com>

# Workshop: Writing a Classification Paragraph Step by Step

*Workshop*

## Prewrite Your Paragraph

The various activities below will walk you through the steps of the prewriting stage of the writing process: choosing a topic; focusing your point; and generating and organizing relevant details.

### Choose Your Topic

The following activities are designed to help you choose a topic.

1. Create a bank of topics. Use the following headings to brainstorm or list as many categories and subgroups about each topic as you possibly can. Don't analyze your thoughts; just get as many relevant categories written down as quickly as possible. Add more topics and categories as they occur to you. Compare your bank of topics with those of your peers.

   • Birth Order (traits of oldest, middle, youngest, only child)
   • Music
   • Technology
   • Vehicles
   • Life Roles

2. Generate ideas with a freewrite. Choose one of the topics from your topic bank and think of the traits that set a group or subgroup apart. Write about the traits of the group and subgroups for ten minutes without stopping.

   OR

   Select a photograph or series of photographs that illustrate a group or subgroup. Write a caption, brainstorm traits, and freewrite about the photograph(s). Remember to ask, "What is the group or subgroup represented by this picture(s)?" and "What's the point?"

### Focus Your Point

Read a freewrite you have generated for a classification. Underline words that suggest your values, opinions, or attitudes about the topic and its subgroups or categories. Think about why the traits are important. Think about what examples best represent the group, categories, or subgroups. Identify your audience and purpose. Write a list of additional concrete traits and examples that explain your point. State in one sentence the point of the groups, traits, and examples:

AUDIENCE: _____

PURPOSE: _____

## Generate and Organize Relevant Details

Use the graphic organizer below to either organize the ideas you have already created or to generate details to support your point.

| Types (groups) of |
|---|

| 1st Type/group | 2nd Type/group | 3rd Type/group |
|---|---|---|

| Traits: | Traits: | Traits: |
|---|---|---|

| Examples: | Examples: | Examples: |
|---|---|---|

**What's the point?**

# Workshop

## Write a Draft of Your Paragraph

Using the ideas you generated during the prewriting phase, compose a draft of your classification paragraph. Return to the prewriting process at any time to generate additional details as needed. Use your own paper.

## Revise Your Draft

Once you have created a draft of a classification paragraph, read the draft and answer the following questions. Indicate your answers by annotating your paper. If you answer "yes" to a question, underline, check, or circle examples. If you answer "no" to a question, write additional details in the margins and draw lines to indicate their placement. Revise your paragraph based on your reflection.

# Questions for Revising a Classification Paragraph

- ☐ Have I made my point? Can I state my point in one sentence?
- ☐ Have I divided my topic into types, groups, or categories? Have I clearly labeled each group? Have I discussed the common traits and examples of each group?
- ☐ Have I used strong transitions of classification?
- ☐ Have I used concrete details to make my point?
- ☐ Have I included only the details that are relevant to my topic sentence?
- ☐ Have I used the following to make my ideas clear to my readers: vivid verbs and images, parallel language, controlled sentence structure?

## Proofread Your Draft

Once you have made any revisions to your paragraph that may be needed, proofread your paper to eliminate distracting errors such as comma splices.

For more information on eliminating comma splices, see Chapter 22.

### Grammar in Action: Eliminating Comma Splices

Comma splices and run-on sentences have been categorized as two of the most common errors in student writing. Both the comma splice and the run-on occur when writers join ideas without the proper punctuation.

A **comma splice** occurs when a writer uses *only a comma* to join two or more independent clauses.

Americans enjoy many vacation options, some choose family bonding activities such as trips to family reunions or theme parks, others choose special interest activities such as Bike Week in Daytona Beach or spring break in Cancun.

*Workshop*

Workshop Practice 7

A **comma splice** can be corrected in three different ways.

---

**Three Rules for Properly Joining Two or More Independent Clauses**

A writer can properly join two or more independent clauses in several ways:
1. Use a comma AND a coordinating conjunction (*for, and, nor, but, or, yet, so,*: FANBOYS).
2. Use a semicolon.
3. Use a semicolon with a transition (*for example, in addition, however, therefore, thus,* etc.).

---

Study the following examples:

1. Americans enjoy many vacation options; some choose family bonding activities such as trips to family reunions or theme parks, but others choose special interest activities such as Bike Week in Daytona Beach or spring break in Cancun.

2. Some choose family bonding activities such as trips to family reunions or theme parks; others choose special interest activities such as Black College Reunion (BCR) in Daytona Beach or spring break in Cancun.

3. Americans enjoy many vacation options; for example, some choose family bonding activities such as trips to family reunions or theme parks.

---

**ELIMINATING COMMA SPLICES**

Edit these sentences to eliminate comma splices. *Hint:* Underline subjects once and verbs twice to identify independent clauses.

**1.** My car matches my personality, we are both dependable and conservative.

----------------------------------------

**2.** Both of us are dependable, for example, I have perfect attendance, put in long hours, and meet my goals.

----------------------------------------

----------------------------------------

**3.** I have perfect attendance, put in long study hours, and maintain a high GPA, my Toyota Camry has a perfect maintenance record, gets great gas mileage, and lives up to its reputation.

----------------------------------------

----------------------------------------

----------------------------------------

More practice with eliminating comma splices: <www.mywritinglab.com>

Use the following form to record your thinking about writing a classification paragraph. Select and focus your topic for your writing situation, audience, and purpose. Choose a topic that is best explained through classification and identify its significance.

**What is your point?**

TOPIC, GROUPS, TYPES, TRAITS: ....................................................................................

.................................................................................................................................

AUDIENCE: ...............................................................................................................

PURPOSE: ................................................................................................................

.................................................................................................................................

**State your main idea in a topic sentence.**

TOPIC: ....................................................................................................................

OPINION: .................................................................................................................

.................................................................................................................................

**Generate relevant details.**

REPORTER'S QUESTIONS: WHO, WHAT, WHERE, WHEN, WHY, HOW? .............................

.................................................................................................................................

SUBGROUPS (Use vivid labels for each group): ..............................................................

.................................................................................................................................

TYPES: ....................................................................................................................

.................................................................................................................................

TRAITS: ...................................................................................................................

.................................................................................................................................

PREWRITING DRAFTING REVISING

Use logical order. Use transition words to signal organization of details and relationship between ideas.

TRANSITIONS TO LIST SUBGROUPS, TYPES, OR TRAITS: ........................................................................

....................................................................................................................................................

TRANSITIONS TO SIGNAL EXAMPLES: ..............................................................................................

....................................................................................................................................................

REVISING PROOFREADING

Use controlled sentence structure. Avoid comma splices.

CONTROLLED SENTENCE STRUCTURE (Types of sentences used): ........................................................

....................................................................................................................................................

ELIMINATED COMMA SPLICES: ........................................................................................................

....................................................................................................................................................

....................................................................................................................................................

Review

# Writing Assignments

## Considering Audience and Purpose

Study the set of photographs about the types of fashion at the beginning of the chapter. Assume you are the emcee for a local charity fashion show to be held in the mall. Write a paragraph in which you record the text of what you will say as the models walk down the runway. Create your own label for each outfit or look. Describe the traits of each look and give examples of where each outfit could be worn.

## Writing for Everyday Life

Assume you have just experienced an event as an invited guest, and you would like to follow up with a written thank-you note. Write a one-paragraph thank-you note in which you include the following information: the type of event, the quality of your experience, the most vivid aspects of the event, and the traits of your host that you appreciate. Choose words that reflect one of the following: (1) polite and reserved or (2) warm and enthusiastic.

## Writing for College Life

Assume you are in a college psychology class. Your teacher has assigned a chapter on "The Six Basic Emotions and Their Combinations" as the basis of discussion for your next class meeting. The teacher also requires you to keep a learning log. You have decided to record in your learning log what you currently know about these ideas before you begin your reading assignment. Write one paragraph in which you identify, describe, and exemplify six basic types of emotions you have observed or experienced.

## Writing for Working Life

Assume you are compiling information for a résumé for a position as manager trainee at a business such as Target, Best Buy, or Olive Garden. Use the following categories to create your résumé.

**Personal Information:** Name, address, phone number, and email address

**Objective:** Manager Trainee position with <u>name of business</u>

**Education:**

**Work Experience:**

**Activities:**

# 9

## The Comparison and Contrast Paragraph

### Chapter Preview

- What's the Point of Comparison and Contrast?

- Making a Point Using Comparison and Contrast: One Student Writer's Response

- Developing Your Point Using Comparison and Contrast

- Using Comparison and Contrast in Your Academic Courses

- Workshop: Writing a Comparison and Contrast Paragraph Step by Step

A comparison examines how two or more things are similar. A contrast looks at how two or more things are different.

Comparing and contrasting ideas is an essential part of critical thinking. When we choose between Subway and McDonald's or Apple and Dell computers, we are weighing the similarities or differences of products and services and making a choice by comparison shopping. What are some basic comparable points for any consumer to consider when shopping? What are some other situations in which we use comparable points as the basis of our thinking or actions?

In everyday life, we compare or contrast the neighborhoods and prices of homes we want to buy, or the honesty and policies of political candidates as we decide for whom we will vote. In working life, we compare or contrast the salaries, benefits, and working conditions among several career opportunities. In college life, we compare and contrast leaders, governments, cultures, literature, technology, writers, or philosophies in a wide range of courses.

To write a comparison or a contrast paragraph, identify the comparable points between two (or more) topics. Once you identify the points of comparison, brainstorm a list of similarities and differences for each one. Then, list and explain examples of each similarity or difference.

▲ Hurricane Katrina

▲ Hurricane Rita

# What's the Point of Comparison and Contrast?

Often ideas become clearer when they are analyzed based on how they relate to one another. The comparison and contrast patterns of organization allow a writer to explore the ways in which ideas are related. The following set of photographs document some similarities and differences between Hurricane Katrina and Hurricane Rita. These two hurricanes both hit the Gulf Coast in the summer of 2005. Study the sets of images. Answer the following questions about each comparable point.

PHOTOGRAPHIC ORGANIZER: COMPARE AND CONTRAST: POINTS OF SIMILARITIES AND DIFFERENCES

WRITING FROM LIFE

Practice 1

Comparable
Topics: ........................................ ........................................

  Similar to or

different from

What is the 1st comparable point? ........................................

........................................ ........................................

........................................ ........................................

  Similar to or

different from

What is the 2nd comparable point? ........................................

........................................ ........................................

  Similar to or

different from

What is the 3rd comparable trait? ........................................

........................................ ........................................

........................................ ........................................

**What's the point?** ........................................

........................................

167

## My First Thoughts

Brainstorm about the images you just studied. Set a time limit, such as five minutes, and write in your notebook about the images and the details you generated. Write as quickly as you can without stopping. Let the ideas flow freely. Getting your first thoughts about a topic on paper is one excellent way to kick-start your writing process.

# Making a Point Using Comparison and Contrast: One Student Writer's Response

The following paragraph offers one writer's point about the similarities and differences between hurricanes Katrina and Rita as illustrated by the photographs. Read the comparison and contrast paragraph below and the annotations. Complete the activities in bold type given in the annotation. Then, read the writer's journal that records decisions made during the writing process.

**MAIN IDEA:**
The main idea is the point the author is making about the topic.
Circle the two topics being compared and contrasted and underline the author's point about the two topics.

**LOGICAL ORDER:**
Words of comparison or contrast signal similarities or differences.
Underline three more transitions of comparison or contrast.

**RELEVANT DETAILS:**
Relevant details include descriptive details about similarities or differences between comparable points.
Underline two more details of similarities or differences.

**EFFECTIVE EXPRESSION:**
This sentence gives equal weight to the hurricanes by joining two sentences with a semicolon.
Underline another sentence that expresses balanced ideas with the use of a semicolon.

### Their Eyes Were Watching Storms

(1) The 2005 hurricane season produced over two dozen named storms. (2) Although two of those storms—Hurricane Katrina and Hurricane Rita—revealed the devastating power of Gulf Coast hurricanes, they prompted very different evacuation experiences. (3) Both hurricanes became major category 5 storms with well-formed eyes and wide spirals of wind and rain, and both hurricanes weakened before hitting landfall. (4) For example, Hurricane Katrina produced sustained winds between 125 and 175 mph, storm surges between 13 and 30 feet, and affected the entire Gulf Coast region. (5) Likewise, Hurricane Rita produced sustained winds of 175 mph, storm surges of 15–20 feet, and also affected major portions of the Gulf Coast region. (6) Another similarity occurred in the aftermath of both storms: massive flooding. (7) Hurricane Katrina's storm surges gushed into communities like New Orleans and destroyed homes, businesses, and entire neighborhoods; similarly, Hurricane Rita's storm surge leveled the entire coastal community of Holly Beach. (8) Even though both storms left a swath of destruction, a degree of difference in the destruction is visible. (9) Katrina left New Orleans completely submerged with no land in sight; Rita left patches and ribbons of dry ground along the coast. (10) Despite the similar dangers posed by these two storms, the evacuation response differed greatly. (11) Thousands of people did not evacuate before Katrina hit land. (12) As a result, they were trapped and stranded for days at the Superdome, in hospitals, and in their homes. (13) In contrast, people did decide to evacuate before Hurricane Rita hit land. (14) As a result, thousands of people were trapped for hours in their cars on the Interstate as they tried to flee the storm. (15) The shared fury of storms and differences between the evacuation responses serve as warnings about the need for uniform evacuation plans.

The student writer of "Their Eyes Were Watching Storms" completed the following reflection to record her thinking through the writing process. Read her writer's journal that describes a few key choices she made as she wrote.

MAIN IDEA: *Before writing anything, I really studied the details of each set of pictures. The power of the images and the importance of the event forced me to stop and think. Although I feel deeply about the topic, I did not want my emotions to limit my understanding of the similarities and differences between the two storms. So I assumed the role of a researcher reporting on the situation in a detached tone. To help me generate details, I used the graphic organizer in the chapter opening.*

RELEVANT DETAILS: *The pictures jolted my memory about the horror of these storms, and I wanted to use what I lived through and saw on the news to make my point. To help me organize details and figure out how to present my ideas, I created two types of outlines: comparable point by point and topic block by topic block.*

| POINT BY POINT | TOPIC BLOCK BY TOPIC BLOCK |
|---|---|
| **A. Size and Scope** | **A. Katrina** |
| 1. Katrina | 1. Size and scope |
| 2. Rita | 2. Evacuation |
| **B. Evacuation** | 3. Aftermath |
| 1. Katrina | **B. Rita** |
| 2. Rita | 1. Size and scope |
| **C. Aftermath** | 2. Evacuation |
| 1. Katrina | 3. Aftermath |
| 2. Rita | |

LOGICAL ORDER: *I used the point-by-point outline. I revised several times to improve my word choice and get better control of my flow of ideas. I also carefully controlled sentences to give equal weight to comparable points. In one revision, I changed the order of points. Instead of listing the comparable points based on time order, I listed them in order of importance. I began with the two points of similarities to establish the significance of the storms. For emphasis, I ended with a major difference between the two experiences.*

For a blank version of this form for your own reflections about your writing:
<www.mywritinglab.com>

EFFECTIVE EXPRESSION: On my last draft, I changed the adjective for "evacuation plans" in the last sentence from "effective" to "uniform." To give the two ideas equal weight, I revised the following sentence from "While Katrina left parts of New Orleans completely submerged with no land in sight, Rita left patches and ribbons of dry land all along the coastal city it destroyed" to "Katrina left parts of New Orleans completely submerged with no land in sight; Rita left patches and ribbons of dry land all along the coastal city it destroyed." I really like my title. It's a play on the word "eye," and it's a literary reference in honor of author Zora Neale Hurston and her novel _Their Eyes Were Watching God._

# Developing Your Point Using Comparison and Contrast

A **comparison** makes a point by discussing the *similarities* between two or more topics. A **contrast** makes a point by discussing the *differences* between two or more topics. To support a point through comparison or contrast, a writer identifies the comparable points of the topic, offers relevant and concrete descriptions and examples for each comparable point, and effectively uses coordination and subordination of ideas.

## The Point: The Main Idea

When you write a comparison or a contrast piece, you limit your thoughts to a set of topics based on their relationship to each other. Most likely you have an opinion or belief about the two topics and their comparable points. Your opinion is your point or main idea. In a comparison or contrast paragraph, you also reveal your opinion by discussing the topics and their points of similarities or differences in the order of your own choosing. A topic sentence states the overall point of the comparison or the contrast between the two topics.

For example, the following topic sentence contains (1) the comparable topics, (2) the writer's opinion about the topic, and (3) the pattern of organization used to organize the details.

The comparable topics are *Giada De Laurentiis* and *Rachael Ray, celebrity chefs*. The pattern of organization is established with words *even though* and *differ*. The writer's opinion is stated with the clause *styles differ greatly*.

PATTERN OF ORGANIZATION: TRANSITION WORDS THAT SIGNAL CONTRAST                    TOPIC

Even though Giada De Laurentiis and Rachael Ray are both celebrity chefs, their styles differ greatly.

WRITER'S OPINION

**TOPIC SENTENCES**

Practice creating topic sentences. The first two items present a topic, an opinion, and comparison and contrast signal word(s). Combine the ideas in each group to create a topic sentence for a comparison or a contrast. Then, complete the practice by making your own topic sentences.

**1.** TOPIC: *The communication styles of men and women*

OPINION: *significant*

COMPARISON OR CONTRAST SIGNAL WORDS: *differ three ways*

TOPIC SENTENCE: 

**2.** TOPIC: *Two 2008 hybrid cars the Toyota Prius and the Honda Civic*

OPINION: *equal value*

COMPARISON OR CONTRAST SIGNAL WORDS: *similar ratings for safety and fuel economy*

TOPIC SENTENCE: 

**3.** TOPIC: *Private diary; blog*

OPINION: *fulfill purposes*

COMPARISON OR CONTRAST SIGNAL WORDS: *Although share similar traits, differences*

TOPIC SENTENCE: 

**4.** TOPIC: *Nonverbal gestures; spoken language*

OPINION: *believable*

COMPARISON OR CONTRAST SIGNAL WORDS: *more, than*

TOPIC SENTENCE:

More practice with
creating topic sentences:
<www.mywritinglab.com>

**5.** TOPIC: *Surfing; skateboarding*

OPINION: ....................................................................

COMPARISON OR CONTRAST SIGNAL WORDS: ....................................

TOPIC SENTENCE: ........................................................

....................................................................................

**6.** TOPIC: ..............................................................

OPINION: ....................................................................

COMPARISON OR CONTRAST SIGNAL WORDS: ....................................

TOPIC SENTENCE: ........................................................

....................................................................................

Practice 2

# Logical Order

Once you have identified the comparable points between your topics and have focused on a main idea, you are ready to generate and organize additional details. To make a point using comparison or contrast, a writer moves from a general idea (the comparison or contrast of two or more topics) to a major support (a comparable point about the topics) to minor supports (details or examples of the comparable point about the topics). To signal the movement among these levels of ideas, a writer uses transitions to signal similarities or differences and examples. Strong transitions establish coherence, a clear and understandable flow of ideas.

## Words That Signal Comparison

| | | | | |
|---|---|---|---|---|
| alike | in a similar fashion | just as | resemble | similarly |
| as | in a similar way | just like | same | |
| as well as | in like manner | like | similar | |
| equally | in the same way | likewise | similarity | |

## Words That Signal Contrast

| | | | | |
|---|---|---|---|---|
| although | conversely | differently | nevertheless | to the contrary |
| as opposed to | despite | even though | on the contrary | unlike |
| at the same time | difference | in contrast | on the one hand | yet |
| but | different | in spite of | on the other hand | |
| by contrast | different from | instead | still | |

The following information appears as a paragraph in a college literature textbook. Determine the logical order of the sentences. Complete the exercise by answering the question "What's the point?"

### The Fable and the Parable

.......... The fable and the parable are age-old literary forms of fiction that grew out of the oral tradition of story-telling.

.......... Although these two types of stories may seem similar, they differ in several important ways.

.......... This universal truth is the basis of a moral lesson that is clearly stated at the end of the story.

.......... First, the fable is a short story that illustrates a universal truth.

.......... In addition, to make its point, a fable uses fantastical plots and mythical creatures, talking animals, animate objects, and people as characters.

.......... For example, in Aesop's fable "The Tortoise and the Hare," the main characters are a talking turtle and rabbit in an absurd race against each other, and the point or lesson is that "steady progress brings success while arrogance leads to loss."

.......... Like a fable, the parable is a short story designed to teach a lesson or convey a moral based on a universal truth.

.......... In another contrast to a fable, a parable uses human beings as characters and realistic situations for the plot.

.......... However, while a fable clearly states its moral as a fitting end to its story, a parable implies its lesson and leaves room for various interpretations.

.......... For example, the parables Jesus used in his teachings have at least two levels of meaning.

.......... In "The Parable of the Prodigal Son," Jesus told a story about a realistic, everyday situation that anyone in the audience could easily understand, and he told the story in a way that also had a symbolic meaning for his disciples or followers.

.......... Ultimately, both the fable and the parable are told to create a vivid and unforgettable word-picture.

**What's the Point?**

..............................................................................................

..............................................................................................

More practice
with logical order:
<www.mywritinglab.com>

# Relevant Details

As a writer narrows a topic into a focused main idea, the thinking process brings to mind many details that answer the questions *who, what, when, where, why,* and *how.* A writer evaluates the relevancy of each detail and uses only those that clarify or support the main idea. In a comparison or contrast paragraph, some relevant major details include those that identify comparable topics or points. Relevant minor details offer examples and explanations of the similarities or differences between comparable points. Relevant details include descriptions, explanations, and examples of similarities or differences between two or more topics. Details are logically ordered to best support the point.

**Comparable Topics in a Venn Diagram**

Mothers (my mom, Maxine )

Unique Traits

Mature behaviors

LOYAL: habitually avoids
family gossip

FAIR: treats everyone with
equal love and respect

HUMBLE: puts us first

Us (mom/me)

Shared Trait

BAD HABIT: Thumb-
rolling; unaware of
habit; action and
sound annoy others

Daughters (me, Sandra)

Unique Traits

Immature behaviors

FICKLE: enjoy family gossip; want
to be more like mom

BIASED: still have family favorites;
learning to be more like mom

PRIDEFUL: Often need to be right;
want to be like mom!

During the prewriting phase of writing, a writer naturally generates irrelevant details. In fact, an effective writer often produces far more details than can be used to make a specific point. Irrelevant details do not explain or support the focused point of the paragraph. A careful writer uses the revision process to double check details for relevancy and to eliminate irrelevant details.

RELEVANT CONCRETE DETAILS

The following paragraph explains and illustrates the ideas generated using the Venn diagram. Circle the main idea. Underline the words that signal similarities or differences and three supporting points of similarities discussed in the paragraph. Cross out two details that are not relevant to the main point.

### Bonds of Habits Tie Us Together

(1) I never realized how similar parents and their children can be. (2) My mother, Maxine, has a habit of rolling her thumbs. (3) She sits with her hands clasped, fingers laced, and thumbs rolling. (4) The action creates a soft rhythmic swish as the pad of one thumb brushes the top of her other thumb. (5) I don't know why, but the sight and sound of mother's thumb-rolling drives me to distraction. (6) Sometimes, I can hardly concentrate on my thoughts. (7) She remains completely unaware of the habit or how much it bothers me. (8) The one time I mentioned the behavior, she was embarrassed, and she tried for a while to break herself of the habit. (9) Although I vowed never to develop any such quirk, I recently caught myself in the middle of my own mother-like thumb roll. (10) As my husband described his golf swing, his eyes kept darting to my hands in the same way my own eyes react to Mom's thumb roll. (11) Suddenly he fell silent mid-sentence. (12) We heard a sound just like the one made by mother's thumb roll. (13) Just like my mother, I sat with my hands clasped, fingers-laced, and thumbs rolling. (14) My husband asked, "Maxine," (he called me by mother's name instead of my name!) "Maxine, are you aware that you are a thumb-roller? (15) And that, for some reason, it gets on my nerves?" (16) My habit of leaving lids loose on containers also drives my husband nuts. (17) Now I know just how maddeningly similar parents and their children can be.

More practice with relevant details:
<www.mywritinglab.com>

175

# Effective Expression: Use of Coordination and Subordination

Effective expression reflects a writer's thoughtful match of ideas to words and structure. Two types of sentence structures enable effective expression of comparison or contrast: coordination and subordination.

**Coordination** expresses an **equal** relationship between **similarities** with words such as: *and, likewise, similarly, also.* Coordination expresses an **equal** relationship between **differences** with words such as *but, yet, or, however, in contrast.*

A **compound sentence** is an example of **coordination.**

**Subordination** expresses an **unequal** relationship between **similarities** with words such as: *as, just as, just like, like.* **Subordination** expresses an **unequal** relationship between **differences** with words such as *although, even though, while.*

A **complex sentence** is an example of **subordination.**

For more information on coordination and subordination, see Chapters 17 and 21.

### Example

An athlete trains the body for competitions; *likewise,* a student trains the mind for final exams.

### Example

*Just as* an athlete trains the body for competitions, a student trains the mind for final exams.

## Practice 5

### USING COORDINATION AND SUBORDINATION

Label each of the following sentences as a compound or a complex sentence. Identify the pattern of organization expressed by each sentence as comparison, contrast, or both. Revise sentence 5 from a compound sentence into a complex sentence. Discuss your work with your peers.

**1.** Although the pessimist and the optimist face many of the same challenges in life, they differ greatly in their actions, words, and thoughts.

SENTENCE TYPE: ..............................................................................................

PATTERN OF ORGANIZATION: ..............................................................................

**2.** Just as the pessimist faces rejection and disappointments, the optimist endures those same hardships common to all humans.

SENTENCE TYPE: ..............................................................................................

PATTERN OF ORGANIZATION: ..............................................................................

**3.** The pessimist focuses on problems and remains passive; in contrast, the optimist focuses on solutions and takes action.

SENTENCE TYPE: ..............................................................................................

PATTERN OF ORGANIZATION: ..............................................................................

**4.** The pessimist speaks words of condemnation and complaints, yet the optimist speaks words of affirmation and thanksgiving.

SENTENCE TYPE: _____

PATTERN OF ORGANIZATION: _____

**5.** The pessimist assumes the worst outcome as a given; the optimist expects a positive result as a probability.

REVISED INTO COMPLEX SENTENCE: _____

_____

More practice with relevant details: <www.mywritinglab.com>

# Using Comparison and Contrast in Your Academic Courses

College writing assignments are often based on information gathered through class lectures, textbook reading assignments, and research. For example, essay exams often test students on material given in class or assigned in readings. Note-taking is an excellent pretest and prewriting activity. When you take or revise notes, set up a graphic organizer into which you can plug information from your class notes or reading assignments. A popular note-taking graphic divides an 11-inch by 8.5-inch page into three sections: a 8-inch by 3-inch left margin for key words; a 8-inch by 5-inch right margin for notes; and a 3-inch by 8.5-inch wide bottom margin for a summary. This format allows you to write, reflect, and write for understanding as you study.

**USING COMPARISON AND CONTRAST IN AN ART APPRECIATION COURSE: TAKING NOTES**

Study the following set of notes taken during a lecture in a college art appreciation class. In the bottom margin (on the next page), write a short paragraph that states and supports the main idea of the notes.

| Tragic hero | Virtuous, admirable, rich, powerful, and male, but flawed; inner conflict and guilt; accepts responsibility for suffering; loses all. |
|---|---|
| Example | 5th Century BCE: In <u>Oedipus the King</u>, Oedipus loses power, wealth, family, and independence due to his limited wisdom and great pride. |
| Melodramatic hero | A symbol of good, male or female, a stereotype of courage and honesty, etc. No flaws; no inner conflict or guilt; fights against and defeats evil; all ends well. |
| Example | Pauline, the heroine of <u>Perils of Pauline</u>, is a "damsel in distress" who escapes many life-threatening, thrilling perils (dangers) due to her courage and ingenuity. |

More practice using comparison and contrast: <www.mywritinglab.com>

*Practice 6*

*Summary What are the differences between a tragic hero and a melodramatic hero?*

---

Workshop

PORTFOLIO

# Workshop: Writing a Comparison and Contrast Paragraph Step by Step

## WRITING A COMPARISON AND CONTRAST PARAGRAPH STEP BY STEP

### Choose Your Topic

The following activities are designed to help you choose a topic.

1. Create a bank of topics. Use the headings given below to brainstorm, or list as many similarities or differences about sets of topics as you possibly can. Don't criticize your thoughts. Add more topics, similarities, or differences as they occur to you. Revisit topic banks created during your study of previous chapters and identify comparable topics. Compare your bank of topics with those of your peers.

   - Family Members
   - Natural Disasters
   - Neighborhoods
   - Movies

2. Generate ideas with a freewrite. Choose one of the topics from your topic bank and think about the points of similarities or differences. Write about the similarities or differences for ten minutes without stopping.

   OR

   Select a set of photographs that illustrate the similarities or differences between two topics. Write a caption, brainstorm comparable points, and freewrite about the photograph(s). Remember to ask, "What are the similarities or differences represented by these images?" and "What's the point?"

### Focus Your Point

Read a prewrite you have generated for a comparison or contrast paragraph. Identify your audience and purpose. Annotate the text: underline or insert words that suggest your values, opinions, or attitudes about the topics and their points of similarity or difference. State in a sentence or two the importance of each similarity or difference between the comparable topics. Generate one or more concrete examples for each comparable point. Finally, state the point of comparison or contrast in one sentence.

AUDIENCE: ........................................................................

PURPOSE: ..........................................................................

## Generate and Organize Relevant Details

Using ideas you have recorded so far and the concept chart below, generate and organize details that support your point.

| Concept Chart: Comparison/Contrast | | | |
|---|---|---|---|
| COMPARABLE TOPICS: | TOPIC A | LIKE OR UNLIKE | TOPIC B |
| 1st attribute, point, basis of comparison | | Like or unlike | |
| 2nd attribute, point, basis of comparison | | Like or unlike | |
| 3rd attribute, point, basis of comparison | | Like or unlike | |

**What's the point?**

_____

_____

_____

 # Write a Draft of Your Paragraph

Using the ideas you generated during the prewriting phase, compose a draft of your comparison or contrast paragraph. Return to the prewriting process at any time to generate additional details as needed. Use your own paper.

 # Revise Your Draft

Once you have created a draft of your comparison or contrast paragraph, read the draft and answer the following questions. Indicate your answers by annotating your paper. If you answer "yes" to a question, underline, check, or circle examples. If you answer "no" to a question, write additional details in the margins and draw lines to indicate their placement. Revise your paragraph based on your reflection.

Workshop

# Questions for Revising a Comparison and Contrast Paragraph

☐ Have I chosen appropriately comparable topics? Have I clearly labeled each comparable point as a similarity or a difference?

☐ Have I made my point? Can I state my point in one sentence?

☐ Are my ideas logically and clearly ordered? Have I used strong transitions of comparison or contrast?

☐ Have I used concrete details to make my point?

☐ Have I included only the details that are relevant to my topic sentence?

☐ Have I used the following to make my ideas clear and interesting to my readers: vivid verbs and images, parallel language, controlled sentence structure, coordination, or subordination?

# Proofread Your Draft

Once you have revised your paragraph, proofread to ensure precise usage and grammar, such as editing for proper use of a comma after introductory elements.

### Grammar in Action:
### Commas after Introductory Elements

Commas are used after introductory elements: a word, phrase, or dependent clause that comes before an independent clause.

A dependent clause—an incomplete thought containing a subject and a verb—is signaled by a subordinating conjunction (*although, because, while…*) or a relative pronoun (*who, which, that…*).

An independent clause is a complete thought containing a subject and a verb.

- **Introductory word used with independent clause**

   Similarly, Sandra twiddles her thumbs.

- **Introductory phrase used with independent clause**

   In contrast, comedy's main purpose is to entertain.

- **Introductory dependent clause used with independent clause**

   Although Bob and Tom are both baby boomers, they differ greatly in values and lifestyles.

For more information on using commas after introductory elements, see Chapter 29.

Workshop

## COMMAS AND INTRODUCTORY ELEMENTS

Edit the following sentences for proper use of a comma after an introductory element. Identify the type of introductory element used in each sentence.
*Hint:* To identify a dependent clause, look for subordinating conjunctions and relative pronouns immediately in front of a subject and verb. To identify an independent clause, underline subjects once and verbs twice; then check to be sure a subordinating conjunction or relative pronoun does not come first.

..........    1. Unlike those who are habitually late  Consuelo has received three merit raises for prompt, efficient work.

..........    2. Like a fire hydrant opened full force  Deborah poured out her grief.

..........    3. However  the traveling nurse program offers better pay and greater mobility.

..........    4. The oldest child enjoyed the full attention of her parents; in contrast  the youngest child always had to share her parent's attention with her siblings.

More ideas for writing a comparison and contrast paragraph:
<www.mywritinglab.com>

## REVIEW OF WRITING A COMPARISON OR CONTRAST PARAGRAPH: DEVELOP YOUR POINT USING THE WRITING PROCESS

Use the following form to record your thinking about writing a comparison or contrast paragraph.

Select and focus your topic for your writing situation, audience, and purpose. Choose a topic that is best explained through comparison or contrast and identify its significance. What is your point?

TWO (OR MORE) COMPARABLE TOPICS: ................................................................................

................................................................................................................................................

AUDIENCE: .................................................................................................................................

PURPOSE: ...................................................................................................................................

................................................................................................................................................

State your main idea in a topic sentence.

TWO (OR MORE) COMPARABLE TOPICS: ................................................................................

OPINION: ...................................................................................................................................

................................................................................................................................................

Generate relevant details.

REPORTER'S QUESTIONS: WHO, WHAT, WHERE, WHEN, WHY, HOW? ........................................................................

....................................................................................................................................................................................

POINTS OF SIMILARITIES: ..............................................................................................................................

....................................................................................................................................................................................

POINTS OF DIFFERENCE: ..............................................................................................................................

....................................................................................................................................................................................

Use logical order. Use transition words to signal organization of details and relationship between ideas.

TRANSITIONS OF COMPARISON: ..................................................................................................................

....................................................................................................................................................................................

TRANSITIONS OF CONTRAST: ........................................................................................................................

....................................................................................................................................................................................

Use coordination and subordination. Use commas to set off introductory elements.

USE OF COORDINATION AND SUBORDINATION: ..........................................................................................

COMMAS WITH INTRODUCTORY ELEMENTS: ..............................................................................................

....................................................................................................................................................................................

INTRODUCTORY WORDS: ..............................................................................................................................

INTRODUCTORY PHRASES: ............................................................................................................................

....................................................................................................................................................................................

INTRODUCTORY DEPENDENT CLAUSES: ......................................................................................................

....................................................................................................................................................................................

Review

# Writing Assignments

## Considering Audience and Purpose

Study the set of photographs about hurricanes Katrina and Rita at the beginning of the chapter. Write a letter to the editor of your local newspaper. Contrast what happened with both, what should have happened, and what must happen in the future. Answer the question, "What can we do better?" Call for action! Use a reasonable tone and avoid name calling.

## Writing for Everyday Life

Assume that you have just experienced a life-altering event, such as a near-death experience, a graduation, a marriage, the birth of a child, a severe loss, or the breaking of a bad habit. You have been asked to talk about "Change" to a specific audience such as the Rotary Club, a civic group. Identify your audience and write a short speech in which you discuss three before-and-after comparable points. Allow your tone through word choice to reflect either sadness and regret or pride and encouragement.

## Writing for College Life

Assume you are in a biology class and you read the following textbook question on the study guide for the final exam: "In what ways did the human skeleton change as upright posture and bipedalism evolved? Describe the changes by comparing the human skeleton and the skeleton of a quadruped such as a baboon." – Campbell, Mitchell, and Reece. *Biology: Concepts and Connections*, 5th ed. 2005 Longman. p. 620.

Test what you already know about the subject by writing a paragraph. Identify the comparable points of similarities and/or differences between the two topics. Look up words in your dictionary as needed.

## Writing for Working Life

Assume that you are applying for a management position at a local business or mid-sized company. You had the following positions and experiences, which are listed on your résumé: Treasurer, Student Government Association; Certified in various computer programs and software; Member of Toastmasters, a public-speaking organization. Write a paragraph in which you compare the skills you've developed with the skills needed at the job for which you are applying.

# 10

# The Definition Paragraph

## A definition explains what a word or concept means.

We are all familiar with the word *definition*. In fact, we apply or create definitions in every aspect of life. Call to mind what you already know about a definition. Answer the following questions: How would you define "a good life"? What are the traits and examples of "a good life"? What information should be included in a definition?

The definition pattern of organization is helpful in all areas of life. In personal life, you rely upon a doctor's definition of your symptoms when you seek medical treatment. In working life, you define your job duties to ensure your best performance. In college life, you will define the specialized meanings and examples of words in each content area.

To write a definition, the writer names a concept, explains its traits, describes the concept using similar terms, and offers examples of the concept. Often a contrast clarifies meaning; thus, a writer may also include an example and explanation of what the term or concept is *not*.

# What's the Point of a Definition?

The following definition-concept chart shows three visual examples of a concept and one visual example of what the concept is not. Study the chart and the visual examples. Then, write answers to the questions asked in the chart. Consider these questions as you write your answers: What is the concept being defined? What are some examples? What traits does each example represent? Then, answer the question, "What's the point?" with a one-sentence statement of the overall main idea.

**WRITING FROM LIFE**

**Practice 1**

**PHOTOGRAPHIC ORGANIZER: DEFINITION-CONCEPT CHART**

What does the concept represent?

What are some examples?

What is it NOT?

Concept?

What is this concept? Synonyms? Traits?

**What the point?**

*Concept map adapted from following sources:*

Frayer, D., Frederick, W. C., and Klausmeier, H. J. (1969). *A Schema for Testing the Level of Cognitive Mastery.* Madison, WI: Wisconsin Center for Education Research.

Schwartz, R., & Raphael, T. (1985). "Concept of definition: A Key to Improving Student's Vocabulary." *The Reading Teacher*, 39, 198-205.

## My First Thoughts: A Prewriting Activity

Brainstorm about the images you just studied. Set a time limit, such as five minutes, and write in your notebook about the images and the details you generated. Write as quickly as you can without stopping. Let the ideas flow freely. Getting your first thoughts about a topic on paper is one excellent way to kick-start your writing process.

# Making a Point Using Definition: One Student Writer's Response

The following paragraph offers one writer's point about the concept depicted in the photographs. Read the definition and the paragraph's annotations. Complete the activities in bold type given in the annotations. Then read the writer's journal entry that records decisions made during the writing process.

**MAIN IDEA:**
The main idea states the author's point about a concept. The concept being defined is "hero."
**Underline the writer's point about the concept.**

**RELEVANT DETAILS:**
Relevant details include descriptive details about traits and examples.
**Circle three additional traits of a hero.**

**LISTING ORDER:**
The transition "third" indicates that at least three traits are listed.
**Underline the two transitions that introduce supporting details.**

**EFFECTIVE EXPRESSION:**
Figurative language paints a vivid image for your reader. "Bravery bobbling on a bungee" gives a human trait to the concept "Bravery."
**Circle one other phrase that uses figurative language.**

## An Everyday Hero

(1) An everyday hero is one who dies to self to live for others. (2) We need more everyday heroes. (3) First, we need compassionate, brave, hard-working men and women to feed the poor, tend to the sick, or confront a crisis. (4) Second, we need people of humility who value the needs of others above their own, and we need people of valor who risk all to meet those needs. (5) Third, we need people of dedication who toil no matter how hard and how daunting the labor may be. (6) We do not need mere thrill-seekers, people who contrive a risk for fun, who fly high on adrenaline, and who find bravery bobbling on a bungee. (7) Indeed, we need heroes like Mother Teresa. (8) This humble servant chose to live among the poorest of the poor in Calcutta, India, so she could care for "the unwanted, the unloved, the uncared for." (9) Certainly, we need more heroes like the rescue workers of 9/11. (10) Heroic responders from all parts of the country rushed to the fallen towers of the World Trade Center, and with diligence and reverence, they moved our mountain of grief. (11) Without doubt, we need more heroes like the unpaid workers of the Red Cross. (12) Selfless volunteers from all walks of life risk their own lives to give aid to the sick and dying in the muddy, ransacked villages of the world. (13) These few examples represent thousands and thousands of unnamed heroes across the globe. (14) Even so, most assuredly, we need more everyday heroes.

**THE WRITER'S JOURNAL**

The student writer of "An Everyday Hero" completed the following reflection to record her thinking through the writing process. Read her writer's journal that describes a few key choices she made as she wrote.

MAIN IDEA: This paragraph is the result of careful planning and many revisions. The definition chart helped me identify the traits and descriptive details of the examples of heroes during my prewriting session. Interestingly, by filling in the map, I discovered my own views about what makes a person a hero. The images made me feel sad for the victims, yet inspired by the volunteers. My purpose is to call the reader to become an everyday hero in everyday life.

RELEVANT DETAILS: The map enabled me to think about my feelings and record some descriptive synonyms such as "compassionate, brave, and hard-working."

LOGICAL ORDER: As I read my first draft, I noticed that I had not used strong transitions. Instead, I had relied upon repeating key phrases such as "we need..." to unite the ideas. Although I liked the effect of the repeated phrases, I decided to experiment by adding listing transitions for the traits in the first several sentences. Then, I chose to use emphatic signal words to introduce the examples: "indeed, certainly, without doubt, most assuredly." During this revision, I also moved the topic sentence; originally, I thought I would end the paragraph with the actual definition of "everyday hero." I wanted to build up to the definition at the end, but it seemed to sound better when I placed it as the first sentence.

EFFECTIVE EXPRESSION: In my final revision, I focused on effective expression. Since the topic "heroes" seems like a lofty ideal to me, I wanted to use figurative language. So I used "moved our mountain of grief" to describe the rubble of the towers and suggest the emotional significance of the event and the 9/11 heroes. The bungee jumper is a great example of what a hero is not, so I used the phrase "bravery bobbling on a bungee" to depict the selfish risk bungee jumping seems to be (in my opinion, anyway!). I wanted the alliteration of the "b" sound to create a silly contrast to the serious images of heroes. At the last minute, I wanted to change every instance of the word "everyday hero" to "hero." I wonder which version would best reach a general audience? I need feedback! Due date looming—this draft is a go!

For a blank version of this form for your own reflections about your writing:
<www.mywritinglab.com>

# Developing Your Point Using Definition

A definition clarifies the meaning of a concept. A definition makes a point by classifying a concept, describing its traits, describing what it is *like*, describing what it is *not like*, and illustrating it with examples. To support a point by definition, a writer classifies a concept, offers relevant and concrete descriptions and examples of what it is and what it is not, and may also use figurative language.

## The Point: The Main Idea

When you write a definition paragraph, you limit your thoughts to a set of details that clarify the meaning of a concept. Most likely, you have an opinion or belief about the concept, characteristics, or examples. Your opinion is your point or main idea. A topic sentence states the overall point of the definition. Often a definition topic sentence emphasizes one aspect of the definition: its class, its traits, what it is like, or what it is not like.

For example, each of the following three topic sentences contains (1) a concept, (2) the writer's attitude about the concept, and (3) the pattern of organization.

### Definition by Classification: Group or Traits

TOPIC    PATTERN OF ORGANIZATION: DEFINITION SIGNAL WORDS    WRITER'S OPINION

A classical hero is a male character who suffers tragic loss due to his pride and ignorance.

### Definition by Comparison: Synonyms or Analogies

TOPIC    PATTERN OF ORGANIZATION: DEFINITION SIGNAL WORDS    WRITER'S OPINION

Faith is like the sap of a tree or the fountainhead of a flowing well.

### Definition by Contrast: Negation or What It Is Not

TOPIC    PATTERN OF ORGANIZATION: DEFINITION SIGNAL WORDS    WRITER'S OPINION

A compassionate intervention is not an accusing, condemning, or violent action.

**TOPIC SENTENCES**

The first three items present a topic, an opinion, and definition signal words. Combine the ideas in each group to create a topic sentence for a definition. Then, complete the practice by making your own topic sentences.

**1.** TOPIC: *Depression*

OPINION: *treatable illness that affects the body and mind*

DEFINITION SIGNAL WORDS: *is a*

TOPIC SENTENCE:

**2.** TOPIC: *A hypocrite*

OPINION: *a spy or traitor*

DEFINITION SIGNAL WORDS: *is*

TOPIC SENTENCE:

**3.** TOPIC: *Forgiveness*

OPINION: *denial of the wrong, but rather acceptance of the apology*

DEFINITION SIGNAL WORDS: *does not mean*

TOPIC SENTENCE:

**4.** TOPIC: *sociology*

OPINION: *Neutral*

DEFINITION SIGNAL WORDS: *is*

TOPIC SENTENCE:

More practice with
creating topic sentences:
<www.mywritinglab.com>

**5.** TOPIC: ........................................................................................................................................................

OPINION: ........................................................................................................................................................

DEFINITION SIGNAL WORDS: ........................................................................................................................

TOPIC SENTENCE: ........................................................................................................................................

**6.** TOPIC: ........................................................................................................................................................

OPINION: ........................................................................................................................................................

DEFINITION SIGNAL WORDS: ........................................................................................................................

TOPIC SENTENCE: ........................................................................................................................................

**7.** TOPIC: ........................................................................................................................................................

OPINION: ........................................................................................................................................................

COMPARISON OR CONTRAST SIGNAL WORDS: ......................................................................................

TOPIC SENTENCE: ........................................................................................................................................

Practice 2

# Logical Order

Once you have narrowed your topic into a focused subject, you are ready to generate and organize additional details. To make a point using definition, a writer moves from a general idea (the concept to be defined) to major and minor supporting details. These include traits and examples of *what it is, what it is like,* or *what it is not like.* To signal the relationship between these levels of ideas, a writer often uses the following pattern of wording: "A concept is…"; "A term means…"; "for example."   Strong signal words establish coherence, a clear and understandable flow of ideas.

## Key Words and Transition Words That Signal Definition

| **Key words:** | are | constitutes | indicates | means |
|---|---|---|---|---|
| | connotes | defined as | is | suggests |
| | consists of | denotes | is not | |
| **Transition words:** | also | in addition | one trait | |
| | another trait | in particular | specifically | |
| | for example | like | such as | |

The following ideas were published on a government Website. Determine the logical order of the following sentences.

### Sexual Harassment

......... Sexual harassment is a form of sex discrimination that violates the Civil Rights Act of 1964.

......... Furthermore, unwelcome sexual advances, requests for sexual favors, and other verbal or physical conduct of a sexual nature constitutes sexual harassment when submission to or rejection of this conduct explicitly or implicitly affects an individual's employment, unreasonably interferes with an individual's work performance or creates an intimidating, hostile or offensive work environment.

......... Fourth, unlawful sexual harassment may occur without economic injury to or discharge of the victim.

......... In addition, sexual harassment can occur in a variety of circumstances, including but not limited to the following:

......... The following two examples of sexual harassment illustrate a demand for sexual favor and the creation of a hostile working envoirnment:

......... First, the victim as well as the harasser may be a woman or a man; the victim does not have to be of the opposite sex.

......... Second, the harasser can be the victim's supervisor, an agent of the employer, a supervisor in another area, a co-worker, or a non-employee.

......... Third, the victim does not have to be the person harassed, but could be anyone affected by the offensive conduct.

......... Fifth, the harasser's conduct must be unwelcome.

......... After weeks of this, the supervisor makes it known to the employee that the only way the employee will get the promotion he or she is seeking is to date the supervisor.

......... In one example, an employee feels threatened by his or her supervisor because of the persistent teasing and sex-related hints that occur.

......... In another example, a co-worker constantly tells sexually explicit jokes and makes demeaning comments about male coworkers and clients.

—Adapted from United States Equal Employment Opportunity Commission.
*"Facts about Sexual Harassment."* 13 March 2006

More practice
with logical order:
<www.mywritinglab.com>

# Relevant Details

As a writer narrows a topic into a focused main idea, the thinking process brings to mind many details that answer questions such as *who, what, when, where, why,* and *how.* A writer evaluates the relevancy of each detail and uses only those that clarify or support the main idea. In a definition paragraph, some relevant major details include those that classify and describe the traits of a term or concept. Relevant minor details offer examples and illustrations of the term or concept as defined. Some major and minor details may explain the writer's opinion about the concept. Relevant details include types, traits, descriptions, and examples of the concept being defined.

During the prewriting phase, a concept chart can help a writer organize ideas. Study the following Definition Concept Chart about the topic "graffiti."

**Definition Concept Chart**

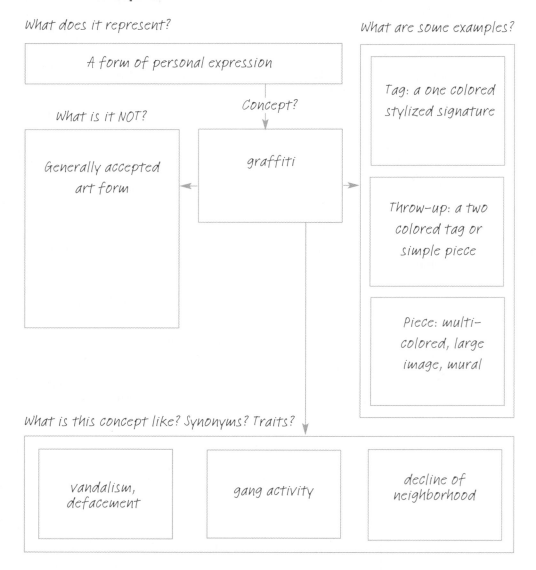

What does it represent?

A form of personal expression

What is it NOT?

Concept?

Generally accepted art form

graffiti

What are some examples?

Tag: a one colored stylized signature

Throw-up: a two colored tag or simple piece

Piece: multi-colored, large image, mural

What is this concept like? Synonyms? Traits?

vandalism, defacement

gang activity

decline of neighborhood

During prewriting, a writer naturally generates irrelevant details. In fact, an effective writer often produces far more details than can be used to make a specific point. Irrelevant details do not explain or support the focused point of the paragraph. A careful writer uses the revision process to double-check details for relevancy and to eliminate irrelevant details.

The following paragraph develops the ideas generated about graffiti during the brainstorming and prewriting phase. Circle the main idea. Underline the three major details. Cross out two details that are not relevant to the main point.

### Graffiti

(1) Although graffiti is a common sight, many do not understand its true nature: vandalism. (2) Graffiti, a form of personal expression, is the unlawful markings of an individual or group on private and public surfaces. (3) One type of graffiti is known as a tag, a stylized signature of a tagger or writer. (4) A tag is quickly created with one color that starkly contrasts with the background upon which it is written. (5) Tags can be written with spray paint, fat-tipped markers, etching tools, or pre-tagged stickers. (6) Another kind of graffiti is the throw-up, a two-dimensional image made with large bubble letters that are outlined in black or white and filled in with another color. (7) A writer often uses throw-ups to bomb an area in a short amount of time. (8) A third type of graffiti, similar to a mural, is the piece, short for masterpiece. (9) Time-consuming to create, a piece is a large, colorful, and complex image that usually reflects a political or social issue. (10) Piecing demonstrates a high level of aerosol paint control. (11) Unlike more widely accepted forms of art, graffiti is not generally regarded as aesthetically pleasing, nor is it thought of as a means to explore or enhance the appreciation of beauty. (12) Graffiti is much more likely to be labeled as vandalism and defacement, and seen as evidence of a gang or a neighborhood in decline. (13) Instances of graffiti are evident in both urban and suburban public areas such as parks, restrooms, buildings, and trains. (14) Graffiti can be removed by scraping, power washing, chemically treating, or painting the affected surface. (15) Many communities fight graffiti by offering legal walls as concrete canvases for graffiti writers.

More practice with relevant details:
<www.mywritinglab.com>

# Effective Expression:
# Sound Structure and Vivid Images

Effective expression reflects a writer's thoughtful match of ideas to words and structure. Writers rely heavily on the various forms of the *to be* verb (such as *is*) to write a definition. Often the use of *is* leads to nonstandard phrasing or bland expressions. To add interest and maintain clarity, consider the following hints:

**Hint 1:** Avoid *is when* and *is where* to construct your definition. One way to revise to eliminate *is when* and *is where* is to follow the verb with a synonym that renames the subject of the sentence.

**Nonstandard**

Addiction is when a person has a compulsive need for a habit-forming substance such as alcohol, nicotine, or heroin.

**Revised**

Addiction is a compulsive need for a habit-forming substance such as alcohol, nicotine, or heroin.

**Nonstandard**

Utopia is where a person can find perfect laws and social conditions.

**Revised**

Utopia is an ideal society made up of perfect laws and social conditions.

**Hint 2:** Use *is* to create a vivid image. A vivid image often allows the writer to express a point about the concept being defined.

Addiction is a self-made prison of compulsive need.

Utopia is a paradise made up of perfect laws and social conditions.

**Hint 3:** Replace *is* with an action verb. An action verb often allows the writer to express a point about the concept being defined.

Addiction imprisons a person in the compulsive need for habit-forming substances such as alcohol, nicotine, and heroin.

Utopia promises an ideal society made up of perfect laws and social conditions.

**SOUND STRUCTURE AND VIVID IMAGES**

Revise the following sentences to avoid nonstandard phrasing or bland expressions. Discuss your work with your class or with a small group of your peers.

.

**1.** An input device is where a machine feeds data into a computer, such as a keyboard.

REVISED: ......................................................................................................

......................................................................................................

**2.** A character is when any symbol requires a byte of memory or storage in computer software.

REVISED: ......................................................................................................

......................................................................................................

**3.** A cursor is where a special symbol such as a blinking underline character signifies where the next character will be displayed on the screen; to type in different areas of the screen, you must move the cursor.

REVISED: ......................................................................................................

......................................................................................................

......................................................................................................

**4.** Located at the top of a computer's keyboard and labeled F1 through F12, function keys are where you can find shortcuts to certain tasks in the Windows operating system; for example, on some keyboards, F1 is the "help" shortcut key.

REVISED: ......................................................................................................

......................................................................................................

......................................................................................................

**5.** A computer virus is when a program or code (written computer instructions) is loaded onto a computer without the consent of the user; a computer virus can quickly use up all of the computer's memory and bring the system to a halt.

REVISED: ......................................................................................................

......................................................................................................

......................................................................................................

......................................................................................................

More practice with sound sentence structure and vivid images.

# Using Definition in Your Academic Courses

The definition paragraph serves as an excellent way to write for understanding. By defining key concepts and specialized vocabulary in your content courses, you will deepen your learning.

Practice 6

**USING DEFINITION IN A COMMUNICATIONS ASSIGNMENT: DEFINING SPECIALIZED VOCABULARY**

The following definition concept chart is based on information taken from a college communications textbook. Demonstrate your understanding of the concept and the relationship among the details in the definition. Using your own words, write a definition of the concept in the space below.

**What does it represent?**

non-verbal communication, facial expressions

**What is it NOT?**

verbal messages

**Concept?**

Affect displays

**What are some examples?**

anger: furrowed forehead; clinched jaw

happiness and surprise: wide eyes; smile

worry and fatigue: furrowed forehead; slack jaw

**Traits**

Interactive, as when people respond to your feelings: "You look angry. What's wrong?"

Unintentional, as when they give away even when you don't want to show your feelings

Intentional, as when you want to show surprise, anger, or love; actors intentionally use affect displays

—DeVito, Joseph A. *The Interpersonal Communication Book, 10th ed.* Allyn & Bacon, 2004, p. 182.

More practice with writing definition paragraphs: <www.mywritinglab.com>

# Workshop: Writing a Definition Paragraph Step by Step

## Choose Your Topic

The following activities are designed to help you choose a topic.

1. Create a bank of topics. Use the headings below to brainstorm or list as many concepts to be defined as you possibly can. Don't analyze your thoughts; just get as many topics written down as quickly as possible. Add more topics as they occur to you. Revisit topic banks created during your study of previous chapters for terms or concepts you could define. Compare your bank of topics with those of your peers.

   - Hip Hop Music
   - Role Models
   - Pollution
   - Success

2. Generate ideas with a freewrite. Choose one of the topics from your topic bank and think about the following: To what group does the concept belong? What are the characteristics of the concept? What are some examples of the concept?

   OR

   Select a set of photographs that illustrates the essence of a concept. For each photo: brainstorm types, traits, synonyms, contrasts, and examples. Freewrite about the photograph(s). Remember to ask, "What's the point?"

## Focus Your Point

Read a freewrite you have generated for a definition. Underline words that suggest your values, opinions, or attitudes about the concept and its traits. Think about why the concept is important. Think about what examples best represent each trait and a situation that best illustrates the concept. Identify your audience and purpose. Write a list of additional concrete examples that explain your point. State in one sentence the point of the definition:

AUDIENCE: ....................................................................................................

PURPOSE: ....................................................................................................

....................................................................................................

....................................................................................................

....................................................................................................

....................................................................................................

....................................................................................................

# Generate and Organize Relevant Details

Using ideas you have recorded so far and the following definition concept chart, generate and organize details that support your point.

**Definition Concept Chart**

What does the concept represent?

What are some examples?

What is it NOT?

Concept?

What is this concept like?

Synonyms?

Traits?

WHAT'S THE POINT?

## Write a Draft of Your Paragraph

Using the ideas you generated during the prewriting phase, compose a draft of your definition paragraph. Return to the prewriting process at any time to generate additional details as needed. Use your own paper.

 ## Revise Your Draft

Once you have created a draft of a definition paragraph, read the draft and answer the following questions. Indicate your answers by annotating your paper. If you answer "yes" to a question, underline, check, or circle examples. If you answer "no" to a question, write additional details in the margins and draw lines to indicate their placement. Revise your paragraph based on your reflection.

## Questions for Revising a Definition Paragraph

☐ Have I chosen an important concept to define? Have I clearly classified and illustrated the concept?

☐ Have I stated or implied a focused main idea? Can I state my point in one sentence? Have I created a strong impression?

☐ Have I effectively used order of importance? Have I used strong transitions of definition?

☐ Have I made my point with adequate details? Have I used concrete details to make my point?

☐ Have I included only the details that are relevant to my topic sentence?

☐ Have I used the following to make my ideas clear and interesting to my readers: vivid verbs and images, parallel language, controlled sentence structure, coordination, or subordination?

 ## Proofread Your Draft

Once you have made any revisions to your paragraph that may be needed, proofread your paragraph for proper usage and punctuation, such as using commas to set off nonessential information.

Workshop

For more information on using commas with nonessential information, see Chapter 29.

*Workshop*

# Grammar in Action:
# Proper Use of Commas with Nonessential Information

In a sentence, some information that describes or modifies a word is nonessential. Nonessential information doesn't restrict the meaning of the word being described or modified. Nonessential information can be words, phrases, or clauses. If you can leave the information out of the sentence without changing the meaning of the sentence, then the information is nonessential. Use **commas before** and **after** nonessential words, phrases, and clauses. Use commas after nonessential words, phrases, and clauses that introduce a sentence.

- **Nonessential Word:**
  Regular physical activity, moreover, promotes health, psychological well-being, and a healthy body weight.

  My husband, Bob, runs six miles every other day.

- **Nonessential Phrase:**
  For example, a healthful diet includes a variety of fruits and vegetables each day.

  Janine, eating a healthful diet and exercising, has lost 25 pounds.

- **Nonessential Clause:**
  My great-grandmother, who is nearly 90 years old, goes bowling every week.

  Sandra's diet, which is laden with high-fat, high-calorie foods, must change to ensure her good health.

*Practice 7*

**PROPER COMMA USE WITH NONESSENTIAL INFORMATION**

Edit these sentences for proper use of commas before and after nonessential words, phrases, or clauses. Underline the nonessential information and insert the commas as needed.

**1.** Patience however is not tolerance of harmful wrongdoing.

**2.** Jerome who has been my friend since childhood does not tolerate gossip.

**3.** Jerome wanting to stand on his principles broke up with a girl who was a gossip.

**4.** Patience is on the other hand acceptance based on forgiveness.

**5.** Once Iva who was a gossip until Jerome broke up with her changed her ways, Jerome asked her out again.

More practice with using commas with nonessential information: <www.mywritinglab.com>

**REVIEW OF WRITING A DEFINITION PARAGRAPH:** DEVELOP YOUR POINT USING THE WRITING PROCESS

Use the following form to record your thinking about writing a definition paragraph. Select and focus your topic for your writing situation, audience, and purpose. Choose a topic that is best developed through definition and identify its significance.

 What is your point?

CONCEPT TO BE DEFINED: ...................................................................................................

AUDIENCE: ...........................................................................................................................

PURPOSE: .............................................................................................................................

........................................................................................................................................

........................................................................................................................................

State your main idea in a topic sentence.

CONCEPT TO BE DEFINED: ...................................................................................................

OPINION: ..............................................................................................................................

........................................................................................................................................

........................................................................................................................................

Generate relevant details.

REPORTER'S QUESTIONS: WHO, WHAT, WHERE, WHEN, WHY, HOW? ...............................

........................................................................................................................................

TRAITS OF THE CONCEPT: ...................................................................................................

DESCRIPTION OF THE CONCEPT (what is the concept *like*: synonyms): ..........................

........................................................................................................................................

WHAT THE CONCEPT IS NOT: ..............................................................................................

EXAMPLES OF THE CONCEPT: ..............................................................................................

Review

  Use logical order. Use transition words to signal organization of details and relationship between ideas.

TRANSITIONS THAT SIGNAL DEFINITION: ........................................................................................

TRANSITIONS THAT LIST DETAILS: ............................................................................................

.................................................................................................................................................

Use effective expression. Use standard sentence structure and vivid images. Correctly use commas with nonessential information..

STANDARD SENTENCE STRUCTURE AND VIVID IMAGES:.......................................................

.................................................................................................................................................

PROPER USE OF COMMAS WITH NONESSENTIAL INFORMATION: ...........................................

.................................................................................................................................................

# Writing Assignments

## Considering Audience and Purpose

Study the set of photographs about the people and situations at the beginning of the chapter. Assume you have benefited personally from the efforts of one of the people depicted in the images. Brainstorm a list of attributes of this person. Write a one-paragraph thank-you letter to this person in which you define what he or she means to you.

## Writing for Everyday Life

Assume that you have agreed to seek counseling to improve a relationship with a family member or co-worker. The counselor has asked you to define your role in the relationship. Identify the type of relationship you have with your family member or co-worker, the major traits of the relationship, and examples or incidents that illustrate the nature of your relationship. Allow your tone—through your word choice—to reflect one of the following: (1) concern or (2) resentment.

## Writing for College Life

Assume you are a first-semester college student who is enrolled in a study skills class, and you have been assigned to write a paragraph that defines student success. Based on your experience and observations, write a definition of student success that addresses attitudes, behaviors, and skills.

## Writing for Working Life

Assume that you work in a retail store that sells clothes, electronics, or some other specialized merchandise. Also assume that sales and morale are down. Write a one-paragraph memo to your supervisor in which you define the morale problem.

More ideas for writing a definition paragraph: <www.mywritinglab.com>

# 11

# The Cause and Effect Paragraph

A cause is the reason an event took place. An effect is the result of an event. Cause leads to effect. *agredir: bater em greve locomi*

Understanding the relationship between cause and effect is a vital critical thinking skill used in all aspects of life. For example, when an illness strikes us, we must correctly identify the cause of our symptoms in order to treat it. In addition, we must take into account the side effects of any medication we take to treat the illness. What are some other instances in which we consider causes and effects?

Thinking about cause and effect points out the relationship between events based on reasons and results. For example, in your personal life, you may have identified that stress causes you to eat for comfort. In working life, you may have identified the need to master certain software programs to be competitive in the job market. In college life, you may have identified how logical causes and effects play a role in the study of history, science, or economics. To write a cause and effect paragraph, identify a set of related events, objects, or factors. Then, label each event, object, or factor within the group as either a cause or an effect. Be sure to test each event as a true cause. Events that occur at or near the same time may be coincidental and unrelated. Then, present your details in a logical order that explains why each cause leads to a specific effect.

# What's the Point of Cause and Effect?

Often ideas become clearer when they are analyzed based on how they relate to one another. The cause and effect pattern of organization allows a writer to explore the ways in which ideas are related based on reasons and results. The following set of photographs documents a set of causes and effects. Study the images and write captions that identify the appropriate causes and effects illustrated. Answer the following questions: What is this? Why did this happen? What is the further effect? Answer the question "What's the point?" with a one-sentence statement of the overall main idea.

**PHOTOGRAPHIC ORGANIZER: CAUSE AND EFFECT**

What is this?

Why did it happen?

What is this further effect?

Why did it happen?

▲ *A volunteer organization*

▲ *Volunteers building homes*

What is this?

Why did it happen?

What is this?

Why did it happen?

What's the point?

## My First Thoughts: A Prewriting Activity

Brainstorm about the images you just studied. Set a time limit, such as five minutes, and write in your notebook about the images and the details you generated. Write as quickly as you can without stopping. Let the ideas flow freely. Getting your first thoughts about a topic on paper is one excellent way to kick-start your writing process.

# Making a Point Using Cause and Effect: One Student Writer's Response

The following paragraph offers one writer's point about the causes and effects illustrated by the photographs. Read the cause and effect paragraph; complete the activities. Then read the writer's journal that records decisions made during the writing process.

**EFFECTIVE EXPRESSION:**
Precise word choice makes your point credible. Writers often confuse the word "affect," a verb that means to influence with "effect," a noun which means result.
Circle a verb that can be replaced with "affects." Circle two nouns that can be replaced with "effect."

**STRONG TRANSITIONS:**
The transitional word "because" signals that "natural disasters and poverty" occur as causes before "Habitat for Humanity calls for volunteers." Underline three more transitional words or phrases that signal cause or effect.

**RELEVANT DETAILS:**
Relevant details include descriptive details that describe the qualities of a cause or effect. "Quality and affordable" are important traits of the homes built by Habitat for Humanity. These traits become the effect or goals. Circle three more relevant details that describe a cause or effect.

**MAIN IDEA:**
The main idea is the point the author is making about the topic. The topic is Habitat for Humanity. Underline the author's point about this topic.

A Noble Response: A Joyous Result

(1) Volunteer work is a noble response to human need, and one basic human need is safe and comfortable shelter. (2) Habitat for Humanity affects this basic need. (3) Because of the impact of natural disasters and poverty on housing, Habitat for Humanity calls for volunteers to build quality and affordable houses that results in home ownership for those in need. (4) In recent years, natural disasters such as earthquakes, mudslides, hurricanes, and tsunamis have caused countless homes to be reduced to rubble or obliterated. (5) As a result, hundreds of thousands of people are left homeless and without resources to rebuild. (6) Currently, poverty influences many around the world by causing families to live in shoddy structures with little hope of improving their living conditions. (7) Habitat for Humanity was established to meet these very needs. (8) Consequently, strangers voluntarily come together to accomplish one goal: to build a house for a family. (9) The end results are obvious. (10) First, the family, who also helped build their home, owns their home. (11) In addition, and just as importantly, along with home ownership comes the joy and pride of an improved quality of life. (12) Habitat for Humanity is a noble response to human need with joyous results.

The student writer of "A Noble Response: A Joyous Result" completed the following reflection to record his thinking through the writing process. Read his writer's journal that describes a few key choices he made as he wrote.

MAIN IDEA: At first, I had a hard time focusing my topic. I couldn't decide if I wanted to write about the cause and effects of volunteering in general, or the reasons and results of volunteering for Habitat for Humanity. Since I had a week to write my paragraph, I took a couple of days just thinking about how to focus the topic. As I drove to school, worked on my car, or cooked supper, I found myself thinking about which way to go. Finally, I figured out that the topic of volunteering was too broad for one paragraph, and I decided to explore the causes and effects of HH.

RELEVANT DETAILS: Once I decided on my focus, the graphic organizer really helped me generate ideas, and, as a result, I composed the first draft fairly quickly. I divided my discussion into two groups: (1) two reasons Habitat for Humanity was established and (2) a few of the impacts of HH.

LOGICAL ORDER: While the body of the paragraph came quickly and easily, I spent a great deal of time thinking about how to start and end the paragraph. Finally, I decided to use some of the ideas that came to me as I thought about volunteering in general—meeting human needs. And then it occurred to me how noble HH is, and what joy HH brings to people's lives—perfect ideas with which to begin and end a paragraph about HH. These ideas helped me with my title, too!

EFFECTIVE EXPRESSION: I revised several times for effective word choice. For example, in the sentence about natural disasters, I changed the wording from "homes to be destroyed" to "homes reduced to rubble or obliterated." The revised wording seemed to best describe the details in the photographs. For the same reasons, I also revised the sentence about poverty to change the wording from "substandard houses" to "shoddy structures."

For a blank version of this form for your own reflections about your writing:
<www.mywritinglab.com>

# Developing Your Point Using Cause and Effect

A cause and effect paragraph makes a point by discussing the reasons and results among a set of events, objects, or factors. To support a point through cause and effect, a writer identifies a set of events, objects, or factors. A writer then identifies the specific details of cause and effect between each of the events, objects, or factors. The writer tests each reason and result to weed out true causes and effects from coincidence. The writer discusses the specific details in the order that reflects the logical relationship among causes and effects. In addition, the writer uses precise word choice for effective expression.

## The Point: The Main Idea

When you write a cause and effect paragraph, you limit your thoughts to a set of topics based on their relationship to each other. Most likely you have an opinion or belief about the topics and their causes and effects; your opinion is your point or main idea. A topic sentence states the overall point of the causes and effects.

For example, the following topic sentence contains (1) the topic, (2) the writer's opinion about the topic, and (3) the pattern of organization used to organize the details.

TOPIC    PATTERN OF ORGANIZATION: SIGNAL WORDS    WRITER'S OPINION

Addiction to television has led to several negative effects on American students.

The topic is the *addiction to television of American students*. The pattern of organization is established with the signal words *led to several effects*. The writer's opinion is stated with the modifier *negative*.

---

**TOPIC SENTENCES**

The first four items present a topic, an opinion, and cause or effect signal word(s). Combine the ideas in each group to create a topic sentence for a cause and effect. Then, complete the practice by making your own topic sentences.

**1.** TOPIC: *smoking cigarettes*

OPINION: *adverse*

CAUSE OR EFFECT SIGNAL WORDS: *leads to physical effects*

TOPIC SENTENCE:

**2.** TOPIC: *bullying*

OPINION: *low*

CAUSE OR EFFECT SIGNAL WORDS: *stems from low self-esteem and anger*

TOPIC SENTENCE: _____

**3.** TOPIC: *violence and sex in television programming*

OPINION: *popular demand by the audience*

CAUSE OR EFFECT SIGNAL WORDS: *is due to*

TOPIC SENTENCE: _____

_____

**4.** TOPIC: *alternative sources of energy*

OPINION: *must be developed*

CAUSE OR EFFECT SIGNAL WORDS: *for several reasons*

TOPIC SENTENCE: _____

**5.** TOPIC: *the war in Iraq*

OPINION: _____

CAUSE OR EFFECT SIGNAL WORDS: _____

TOPIC SENTENCE: _____

_____

**6.** TOPIC: _____

OPINION: _____

CAUSE OR EFFECT SIGNAL WORDS: _____

TOPIC SENTENCE: _____

*Practice 2*

More practice with
creating topic sentences:
<www.mywritinglab.com>

# Logical Order

Once you have identified a topic, a set of factors, their relationships based on cause and effect, and have focused on a main idea, you are ready to generate and organize additional details. To make a point using cause or effect, a writer moves from a general idea (the overall causal relationship) to a major support (a specific cause or effect of the topic) to minor supports (details or examples of a specific cause or effect). To signal the movement among these levels of ideas, a writer uses transitions to signal causes, effects, and examples. Strong transitions establish coherence, a clear and understandable flow of ideas.

## Transitions That Signal Cause and Effect

| | | | | |
|---|---|---|---|---|
| accordingly | consequently | hence | on account of | so |
| as a result | due to | if…then | results in | therefore |
| because of | for that reason | leads to | since | thus |

## Verbs That Signal Cause and Effect (sample list)

| | | | | | |
|---|---|---|---|---|---|
| affect | constitute | create | force | institute | restrain |
| cause | construct | determine | induce | preclude | stop |
| compose | contribute | facilitate | initiate | prevent | |

## Nouns That Signal Cause and Effect (sample list)

| | | | | |
|---|---|---|---|---|
| actor | consequence | end | influence | product |
| agent | creation | event | issue | result |
| author | creator | grounds | outcome | source |
| condition | effect | impact | outgrowth | |

Practice 3

**ORDER OF CAUSES AND EFFECTS**

The following ideas appeared in an article published by the *National Women's Health Information Center*. Number the sentences by logical order. Complete the exercise by answering the question: "What's the point?"

### How Is A Stroke Prevented?

.......... Along with taking needed medications, eating a healthful diet lowers your risk for a stroke.

.......... The more stroke risk factors you have, the greater the chance that you will have a stroke.

.......... A stroke is the result of cerebrovascular disease, which is a disease of the blood vessels in the brain.

.......... You can't control some risk factors, such as aging, family health history, race and gender.

.......... However, you do control habits that may affect the likelihood of having a stroke.

.......... If you have any of these conditions, then take your medication as prescribed by your health care provider.

.......... Therefore, eat a diet low in saturated fat and rich in fruits, vegetables, and whole grains.

.......... For example, habits that lead to health conditions such as heart disease, high blood pressure, high cholesterol, and diabetes can contribute to a stroke.

.......... For example, eating too many animal foods and whole milk dairy products can result in high cholesterol which raises your risk for a stroke.

.......... Finally, aspirin therapy may reduce the risk of strokes due to blood clots, but check with your health care provider before starting to take aspirin on a daily basis.

.......... In addition to watching what foods you eat, you can also reduce your stroke risks by exercising for at least 30 minutes a day on most days of the week.

.......... In addition, smoking is a significant risk factor leading to strokes; so, if you smoke, stop!

.......... If it is hard to quit on your own, then nicotine patches, support groups, and programs are available to help you stop smoking.

.......... Regular exercise reduces cholesterol and the build up of fatty plaque that causes the blood clots that lead to strokes.

—Adapted from United States Department of Health and Human Services. *"Stroke." Women's Health.gov* The National Women's Health Information Center. 26 March 2006. http://www.4woman.gov/faq/stroke.htm#4

What's the Point?

_____

_____

_____

_____

More practice with logical order:
<www.mywritinglab.com>

*Practice 3*

# Relevant Details

As a writer narrows a topic into a focused main idea, the thinking process brings to mind many details that answer the questions such as *who, what, when, where, why,* and *how*. A writer evaluates the relevancy of each detail and uses only those that clarify or support the main idea. In a cause and effect paragraph, some relevant major details include those that identify a specific cause or effect. Relevant minor details offer examples and explanations of the cause or effect. Relevant details include descriptions, examples, and explanations of the causal relationship between a set of events, situations, objects, or factors.

One writer generated these ideas while brainstorming using a fishbone cause and effect concept map.

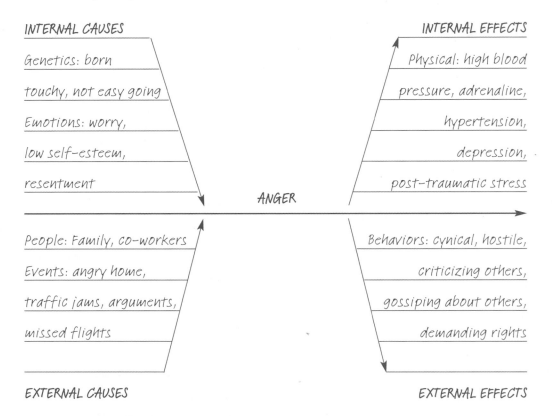

INTERNAL CAUSES

Genetics: born touchy, not easy going

Emotions: worry, low self-esteem, resentment

ANGER

INTERNAL EFFECTS

Physical: high blood pressure, adrenaline, hypertension, depression, post-traumatic stress

People: Family, co-workers

Events: angry home, traffic jams, arguments, missed flights

EXTERNAL CAUSES

Behaviors: cynical, hostile, criticizing others, gossiping about others, demanding rights

EXTERNAL EFFECTS

During the prewriting phase of writing, a writer naturally generates irrelevant details. In fact, an effective writer often produces far more details than can be used to make a specific point. Irrelevant details do not explain or support the focused point of the paragraph. A careful writer uses the revision process to double-check details for relevancy and to eliminate irrelevant details.

**RELEVANT DETAILS**

The following paragraph develops the ideas generated about anger during the brainstorming phase using the fishbone cause and effect concept map shown on page 212. Circle the main idea. Underline two causes and two effects. Cross out two details that are not relevant to the main point.

### Anger Inside and Out

(1) Anger can be a normal, healthy emotion, yet anger can also spiral out of our control and lead to problems that affect our work, our families, and our lives. (2) To control anger, we need to understand its causes and effects. (3) Basically, anger is the result of both internal and external forces. (4) Genetics and emotions are two internal forces that give rise to anger. (5) According to experts, some people are born innately touchy and easily angered. (6) Others of us are born with mild, easy-going tendencies. (7) Another internal force is the complex mixture of our emotions. (8) Worry, low self-esteem, anxiety, or resentment can cause anger to flare. (9) In addition, external forces such as people and events can trigger anger. (10) For example, if we have been raised in an environment of anger without learning how to cope with negative feelings, we are much more likely to be easily angered. (11) As a result, a disagreement with a family member or co-worker, a traffic jam, or a cancelled airline flight ignites angry feelings. (12) Not only does our anger arise from internal and external forces, but also our anger has internal and external effects. (13) Anger has immediate physical effects: it causes our heart rate, blood pressure, and adrenaline to rise. (14) Ultimately, chronic anger can lead to hypertension or depression. (15) Post-traumatic stress syndrome also leads to depression. (16) Chronic anger also may result in cynical and hostile behavior towards others. (17) When we feel angry, we may act out our hostility by criticizing others, gossiping about them, or rudely demanding our rights. (18) Ultimately, uncontrolled anger damages our relationships with others and diminishes our quality of life. (19) We need to understand the reasons and results of our anger before we can hope to control this volatile emotion.

More practice with relevant details:
<www.mywritinglab.com>

# Effective Expression: Correct Use of Words

Effective expression reflects a writer's thoughtful choice of words for impact on the reader. Some words, such as *affect* and *effect,* seem closely related because they are similar in their sounds and spellings. These similarities often cause confusion and lead to the misuse of the words. However, their meanings are clearly distinct, so thoughtful writers use the correct word for effective expression.

*Affect* is a verb that means **to influence.**

**Example**

Video games **affect** learning by improving concentration and visual skills.

*Effect* is a noun that means **result.**

**Example**

Video games have a positive **effect** on learning by improving concentration and visual skills.

*Effect* is a verb that means **to bring about.**

**Example**

The new law will **effect** a change in the sentencing of sex offenders.

## Practice 5

### CORRECT USE OF AFFECT AND EFFECT

Complete the following sentences with the correct use of the words *affect* and *effect*. (*Hint:* Substitute the words *influence* or *result* as a test for exact meaning in the context of the sentence.)

**1**. The lack of bright light during winter months produces an ........................ known as Seasonal Affective Disorder (SAD), a form of depression.

**2**. The long, dark hours of winter ........................ as much as 6 percent of the population.

**3**. The ........................ of SAD include loss of energy, social withdrawal, overeating, weight gain, and difficulty concentrating.

**4**. Researchers believe that reduced sunlight ........................ the biological rhythms that control the body's internal clock.

**5**. Researchers also believe that heredity, age, and the body's chemical balance ........................ the onset of SAD.

**6**. Exposure to sun and sun lamps for one to three hours a day ........................ a positive change in the mood of one who suffers from SAD.

More practice with commonly confused words: <www.mywritinglab.com>

# Using Cause and Effect in Your Academic Courses

Often college writing assignments require that you combine information you learn from your textbooks with your observations about how that information applies to real-world situations. Textbooks may provide graphic organizers to emphasize key concepts and make them easy to understand. Use these graphic organizers to learn and apply the concept. A good way to review your textbook notes is to add examples you have observed in life to the concept you are studying.

**USING CAUSE AND EFFECT IN A SOCIOLOGY ASSIGNMENT**

Study the following graphic taken from a college sociology textbook. In a small group or with a peer, add examples of each concept that you and your peer(s) have observed. Then, write a paragraph in answer to the question at the end of the practice. Use a dictionary as necessary.

—Jaffe, Michael L. *Understanding Parenting, 2nd Ed.* Allyn & Bacon. 1997 p. 241.

EXAMPLE OF PARENTAL STANDARD: ...................................................................................

..............................................................................................................................................

EXAMPLE OF CHILD'S VIEW OF SUCCESS AND FAILURE: ....................................................

..............................................................................................................................................

EXAMPLE OF FEEDBACK: .......................................................................................................

..............................................................................................................................................

EXAMPLE OF PARENTING STYLE: ..........................................................................................

..............................................................................................................................................

Practice 6

Practice 6

PORTFOLIO

Workshop

EXAMPLE OF FURTHER CHALLENGE: ..............................................................

..............................................................

EXAMPLE OF ADJUSTMENT: ..............................................................

..............................................................

On a separate sheet of paper, answer the following question:
What factors influence children's self-esteem and self-confidence?

# Workshop: Writing a Cause and Effect Paragraph Step by Step

## WRITING A CAUSE AND EFFECT PARAGRAPH STEP BY STEP

**PREWRITING**

## Choose Your Topic

The following activities are designed to help you choose a topic.

**1.** Create a bank of topics: Use the following headings to brainstorm or list as many causes and effects as you possibly can. Don't criticize your thoughts; just get as many relevant causes and effects written down as quickly as possible. Add more topics, causes, or effects as they occur to you. Revisit topic banks created during your study of previous chapters; identify causes and effects. Compare your bank of topics with those of your peers.

- You Tube
- Friendship
- Fuel-efficient Cars
- Romance

**2.** Reread a freewrite you created (such as the one based on the photographs of the people in the chapter opening or the one generated in Practice 3). Underline ideas that you could use for a cause and effect paragraph. Number the points you recorded to indicate a logical order. Add major or minor details of explanation and examples as needed.

OR

Select a set of photographs that illustrate a set of related events, situations, objects, or factors. Generate a list that identifies the details of each event, situation, object, or factor as either a cause (reason) or an effect (result). Freewrite about the photograph(s). Remember to ask, "What's the point?"

## Clarify Your Point

Read a prewrite you have generated for a cause and effect. Underline words that suggest your values, opinions, or attitudes about the events. Think about why the information is important. Think about what examples best represent each cause or effect. Think about a situation that best illustrates the concept. Identify your audience and purpose. Write a list of additional concrete examples that explain your point. In one sentence, state the point of the cause and effect.

AUDIENCE: ......................................................................................................................

PURPOSE: ........................................................................................................................

WHAT'S THE POINT? ........................................................................................................

................................................................................................................................

## Generate and Organize Relevant Details

Use the graphic organizer below to either organize the ideas you have already created or to generate details to support your point.

CAUSE                                                                    EFFECT

CAUSE                                                                    EFFECT

WHAT'S THE POINT?:........................................................................................

................................................................................................................................

# Write a Draft of Your Paragraph

Using the ideas you generated during the prewriting phase, compose a draft of your cause and effect paragraph. Return to the prewriting process at any time to generate additional details as needed. Use your own paper.

# Revise Your Draft

Once you have created a draft of your cause and effect paragraph, read the draft and answer the following questions. Indicate your answers by annotating your paper. If you answer "yes" to a question, underline, check, or circle examples. If you answer "no" to a question, write additional details in the margins and draw lines to indicate their placement. Revise your paragraph based on your reflection.

Workshop

# Questions for Revising a Cause and Effect Paragraph

☐ Have I chosen an important set of related events, situations, objects, or factors?

☐ Have I made my point? Can I state my point in one sentence?

☐ Have I effectively used a logical order based on short-term, long-term, most important, least important, obvious, or subtle causes and effects? Have I used strong transitions of cause and effect?

☐ Have I included only the details that are relevant to my topic sentence?

☐ Have I used the following to make my ideas clear and interesting to my readers: vivid verbs and images, parallel language, controlled sentence structure, coordination, subordination, precise use of words such as *affect* and *effect*?

☐ Have I used concrete details to make my point?

# Proofread Your Draft

Once you have made any revisions to your paragraph that may be needed, proofread your paper to eliminate unnecessary errors, such as editing for commonly confused words.

### Grammar in Action: Commonly Confused Words

As you learned earlier in this chapter, some words, such as *affect* and *effect,* seem closely related because they are similar in their sounds and spellings. These similarities often cause these words to be confused with one another and lead to their misuse. However, their meanings are clearly distinct, so thoughtful writers choose the precise word for effective expression. The following list presents a group of words that are commonly confused. Memorize this list of words and their meanings so you can use each one precisely in your writing.

| | |
|---|---|
| **its, it's** | **its** (possessive form of it); **it's** (contraction of *it is* or *it has*) |
| **their, they're, there** | **their** (possessive of they); **they're** (contraction of *they are*); **there** (points to a place) |
| **to, two, too** | **to** (suggests movement or direction); **two** (a number); **too** (also) |
| **whose, who's** | **whose** (possessive form of *who*); **who's** (contraction of *who is* or *who has*) |
| **your, you're** | **your** (possessive form of *you*); **you're** (contraction of *you are*) |

Workshop

## PRECISE USE OF COMMONLY CONFUSED WORDS

Edit these sentences by crossing out the word used incorrectly and inserting the correct word. (*Hint:* Some words are used correctly.)

1. Who's purse is over their on the counter by the refrigerator?

2. You too are two young to see an R rated movie.

3. Michealle and Koshanda have cut and donated their hair to Locks of Love, a non-profit organization that makes wigs for cancer patients.

4. Devon, who's brother is an NFL linebacker, has to tickets too the playoffs.

5. The supervisors said that your going to leave you're car at the airport while your traveling because there willing to pay for the parking charges.

More practice with commonly confused words: <www.mywritinglab.com>

## REVIEW OF WRITING A CAUSE AND EFFECT PARAGRAPH: DEVELOP YOUR POINT USING THE WRITING PROCESS

Use the following form to record your thinking about writing a cause and effect paragraph. Select and focus your topic for your writing situation, audience, and purpose. Choose a topic that is best developed through cause and effect and identify its significance.

 PREWRITING DRAFTING    **What is your point?**

CAUSES (REASONS FOR AN EVENT, OBJECT, OR FACTOR): ............................................

..........................................................................................................................

EFFECTS (RESULTS OF AN EVENT, OBJECT, OR FACTOR): ............................................

..........................................................................................................................

CAUSES LEADING TO EFFECTS: ....................................................................................

AUDIENCE: ...................................................................................................................

PURPOSE: .....................................................................................................................

PREWRITING DRAFTING    **State your main idea in a topic sentence.**

TOPIC: ..........................................................................................................................

OPINION: ......................................................................................................................

Generate relevant details.

REPORTER'S QUESTIONS: WHO, WHAT, WHERE, WHEN, WHY, HOW? ....................................................

..........................................................................................................................................................................

CAUSES, DESCRIPTIONS, EXAMPLES, EXPLANATIONS: ................................................................

..........................................................................................................................................................................

EFFECTS, DESCRIPTIONS, EXAMPLES, EXPLANATIONS: ................................................................

..........................................................................................................................................................................

Use logical order. Use transition words to signal organization of details and relationship between ideas.

TRANSITIONS THAT SIGNAL CAUSES: ............................................................................................

..........................................................................................................................................................................

TRANSITIONS THAT SIGNAL EFFECTS: ............................................................................................

..........................................................................................................................................................................

Use effective expression. Use words precisely. Avoid misuse of commonly confused words.

AFFECT: ...............................................................................................................................................

EFFECT: ...............................................................................................................................................

ITS, IT'S: ..............................................................................................................................................

THEIR, THEY'RE, THERE: ....................................................................................................................

TO, TWO, TOO: ..................................................................................................................................

WHOSE, WHO'S: ................................................................................................................................

YOUR, YOU'RE: ..................................................................................................................................

..........................................................................................................................................................................

Review

# Writing Assignments

More ideas for writing a cause and effect paragraph: <www.mywritinglab.com>

## Considering Audience and Purpose

Study the set of photographs at the beginning of the chapter. Assume you are the one who now owns the home built by Habitat for Humanity. Assume that as you worked beside the volunteers to build your home, you became friendly with the project director, Wilma Weindmyer. Write a one-paragraph thank-you letter to Ms. Weindmyer that explains the impact of building and owning your own home.

## Writing for Everyday Life

Assume that you are the mentor of a young person who is a member of your family or community. Assume the young person is making some choices that can have lasting negative consequences. Perhaps the youth is hanging out with the wrong crowd, or skipping school, or experimenting with drugs. Write a one-paragraph letter that explains the dangers of the wrong choices or the benefits of mature choices. Choose your words to reflect one of the following: (1) stern warning or (2) warm encouragement.

## Writing for College Life

Assume you are applying for a scholarship set up to aid a person currently enrolled as a full-time college student with at least a 3.0 GPA. Assume you must compete with other students to win the scholarship by writing a one-paragraph essay on the topic "Education Matters." Write a paragraph that explains one or both of the following: (1) the impact the education has had and will have on you; (2) the impact you hope to have as an educated member of society.

## Writing for Working Life

Assume that you are applying for a job with a company or organization. Perhaps you are applying for a job as a health care provider, teacher, office manager, or computer programmer. Write a one-paragraph cover letter that explains the impact you can have on the job due to your skills, work ethic, and character.

# 12

## The Persuasive Paragraph

## A persuasive claim is a strong stand on a debatable topic supported by facts, examples, and opinions.

In almost every area of our lives, we engage in some form of persuasion. Whether convincing a friend to see a particular movie or proving we are the right candidate for a particular job, we use reasons, logic, and emotion to get others to agree with our views. What are some other situations that use persuasion to influence our beliefs and behaviors? Why are certain arguments or points of view so persuasive?

To be persuasive, a writer asserts a strong stand on one side of a debatable issue. Then the writer supports that stand by offering convincing evidence such as reasons, facts, examples, and expert opinions. In everyday life, our court system is based on proving claims of guilt or innocence. In working life, we use reasons to resolve workplace disputes. In college life, we encounter debatable claims in every discipline. In addition to asserting a claim and supporting it with evidence, a persuasive writer acknowledges and rebuts (disproves, challenges) the opposition.

# What's the Point of Persuasion?

The purpose of persuasion is to convince the reader to agree with a particular claim about a debatable topic. Persuasion is a call to action or a call to a change of mind. The following posters are designed to persuade young women about smoking cigarettes. Study the photographs. In the space provided, identify the claim, reasons, and an opposing point of view about smoking. Answer the question "What's the point?" with a one-sentence statement of the overall main idea.

**PHOTOGRAPHIC ORGANIZER: PERSUASION**

What is this idea?

-------------------------------

-------------------------------

-------------------------------

What is this reason?

-------------------------------

-------------------------------

-------------------------------

What is this reason?

-------------------------------

-------------------------------

-------------------------------

What is this opposing

point? -------------------------

-------------------------------

-------------------------------

**What's the point?**

-------------------------------

-------------------------------

-------------------------------

## My First Thoughts: A Prewriting Activity

Brainstorm about the images you just studied. Set a time limit, such as five minutes, and write in your notebook about the images and the details you generated. Write as quickly as you can without stopping. Let the ideas flow freely. Getting your first thoughts about a topic on paper is one excellent way to kick-start your writing process.

# Making a Point Using Persuasion: One Student Writer's Response

The following paragraph offers one writer's point about the argument against smoking as illustrated by the photographs. Read the persuasive paragraph below and the annotations. Complete the activities in bold type given in the annotations. Then, read the writer's journal that records decisions made during the writing process.

**EFFECTIVE EXPRESSION:**
To persuade a reader, an author uses subjective words that qualify ideas and express opinions and value judgments. The word "always" qualifies the action of tobacco companies as absolute and unwavering. **Circle three more subjective words.**

**RELEVANT DETAILS:**
In persuasion, relevant details include facts, consequences, and information from experts or authorities on the topic. This detail does all three. **Underline another factual detail.**

**STRONG TRANSITION:**
The transition phrase "in truth" signals that the author is offering a reason in support of the claim. **Circle three more transitional words or phrases that signal a reason of support.**

**MAIN IDEA:**
The main idea is the point or claim the author is making about the topic. The topic is "smoking." **Underline the writer's point about this subject.**

### Calling All Girls: Tell Tobacco Companies to Butt Out

(1) Tobacco companies spend millions of dollars each year to convince young women to smoke. (2) Their aim is to lure teenage girls into a lifetime of addiction that will generate billions of dollars in profit. (3) In 1999, nearly 165,000 American women died prematurely from smoking-related diseases such as lung cancer and heart disease ("Women and Smoking"). (4) Advertisements always depict women who smoke as icons of "In." (5) For example, a particular Newport poster depicts a beautiful, thin young woman with a wide smile holding a cigarette while dancing with a guy as good looking and wide-smiling as she. (6) They seem cool, popular, and sexy. (7) "Fire it up" with "Newport pleasure" is a call to fire up life with fun. (8) In truth, this image is deceiving. (9) Just as the poster states (by law), smoking has many harmful effects. (10) In fact, according to "Women and Smoking: A Report of the Surgeon General—2001," women who smoke two or more packs of cigarettes a day face a risk for cancer 20 times higher than for women who do not smoke. (11) In truth, nonsmokers do not increase their risk of lung cancer or heart disease. (12) Nonsmokers, when they do become pregnant, do not put the health of their unborn babies at risk. (13) Furthermore, nonsmokers are fashionable. (14) Nonsmokers are creative. (15) Nonsmokers are and do have fun. (16) In fact, nonsmokers have more money than smokers to spend on pleasure such as fashion, video games, music, or special interests like art. (17) Therefore, teenage girls should tell tobacco companies to "butt out" because smoking is out. (18) Not smoking is the real cool, the real in.

### Works Cited

Centers for Disease Control and Prevention. "Women and Smoking: A Report of the Surgeon General—2001." 31 Jan. 2004. 3 Apr. 2006. Path: A-Z Index; Smoking; Smoking and Women; At a Glance; Health Consequences of Tobacco Use Among Women.

The student writer of "Calling All Girls: Tell Tobacco Companies to Butt Out" completed the following reflection to record her thinking through the writing process. Read her writer's journal that describes a few key choices she made as she wrote.

MAIN IDEA: I really enjoyed writing this paragraph because I started smoking as a teenager, and thankfully, was able to quit when I became pregnant with my first child. The only reason I could kick the habit was because the smell and taste of smoke made me sick once I became pregnant. As I studied the photographs and filled out the graphic organizer, the details made it clear to me how important fitting in and being cool is to girls. It seemed apparent to me that the Newport poster would probably be far more appealing and persuasive to most young women, so I wanted to counter that image immediately in my paragraph.

RELEVANT DETAILS: I also wanted to include some compelling facts from a reliable source, so I searched the Centers for Disease Control for information on women and smoking. My works cited entry documents the path that I took to locate relevant information in the site.

LOGICAL ORDER: I decided to order my reasons by countering the opposition. So I began each of my major supports with a discussion about the false image of the Newport poster, and then concluded with the positive ideas illustrated about the "In/Out" poster. It was during my revisions, however, that I included the transition word therefore. I like the way this word gave power to the conclusion.

EFFECTIVE EXPRESSION: During a revision, I noted that I had used a series of three short, parallel sentences about the traits of nonsmokers beginning with "In truth, nonsmokers are..." I played around with a few versions of these ideas. At first, I combined them into one sentence with compound verbs: "Nonsmokers are fashionable, creative, and fun." But I liked the emphasis that the three short, parallel sentences gave to these details. After all, these sentences state important reasons that support my claim. I also revised to use subjective words. Words such as lure, almost, and deceiving depict negative views of the tobacco advertisers. I also edited for proper use of point of view. I was tempted to shift into the use of you to call the reader to action. But I decided that I wanted to appeal to the family and friends of young women as well. So I stuck with the third person point of view and used girls, woman, she, smokers, nonsmokers, and they.

For a blank version of this form for your own reflections about your writing:
<www.mywritinglab.com>

# Developing Your Point Using Persuasion

A persuasive paragraph makes a point by supporting one side of a debatable topic and refuting the opposing side. The details that support and refute the point include reasons based on facts, examples, effects, and expert opinions on the topic. In addition, a writer uses effective expression to qualify ideas and control the point of view.

## The Point: The Main Idea

When you write a persuasive paragraph, you limit your thoughts to the reasons that support one side and refute the opposing side of a debatable topic or issue. A persuasive paragraph gives your opinion or stand on the issue. A topic sentence states the debatable topic, the writer's persuasive opinion, and, possibly, a pattern of organization. Because persuasion is a purpose, the writer may choose any particular pattern of organization to support a claim. Often, the pattern of organization is only suggested rather than stated. In addition, the writer's persuasive opinion is frequently signaled by the following types of subjective words or phrases: *all, always, only, must, must not, should, should not,* or *too.* These subjective words qualify an idea as debatable.

For example, the following topic sentence contains (1) the debatable topic, (2) the writer's persuasive opinion, and (3) a pattern of organization.

DEBATABLE TOPIC          WRITER'S OPINION          DEBATABLE TOPIC

Colleges and universities should provide substance free housing for students for several reasons.

PATTERN OF ORGANIZATION

The debatable topic or issue is *substance free housing for students at colleges and universities.* The writer's opinion is expressed with the verb phrase *should provide.* Note that the verb *provide* calls for action, and the helping verb *should* qualifies the action. The phrase *for several reasons* signals a list that will most likely contain facts, examples, effects, expert opinion, and reasons against the opposing view.

*Practice 2*

### TOPIC SENTENCES

The first four items present a debatable topic, the writer's opinion, and a pattern of organization. Combine the ideas in each group to create a topic sentence for a persuasive paragraph. Then, complete the practice by making your own topic sentences.

**1.** TOPIC: *education about crystal meth*

OPINION: *horrific, is our best hope to end this plague*

PATTERN OF ORGANIZATION: *the consequences of*

TOPIC SENTENCE:

**2.** TOPIC: consumers, hybrid vehicles

OPINION: should demand

PATTERN OF ORGANIZATION: due to their economic and environmental benefits

TOPIC SENTENCE: _____

_____

**3.** TOPIC: procrastination by students, academic

OPINION: is the leading, failure

PATTERN OF ORGANIZATION: cause of

TOPIC SENTENCE: _____

_____

**4.** TOPIC: breakfast

OPINION: is important

PATTERN OF ORGANIZATION: more than any other meal of the day.

TOPIC SENTENCE: _____

_____

**5.** TOPIC: graffiti

OPINION: _____

PATTERN OF ORGANIZATION: _____

TOPIC SENTENCE: _____

_____

Practice 2

More practice with
creating topic sentences:
<www.mywritinglab.com>

Practice 2

**6.** TOPIC: ....................................................................................................................................

OPINION: ...............................................................................................................................

PATTERN OF ORGANIZATION: ...........................................................................................

TOPIC SENTENCE: ..............................................................................................................

....................................................................................................................................................

....................................................................................................................................................

**7.** TOPIC: ....................................................................................................................................

OPINION: ...............................................................................................................................

PATTERN OF ORGANIZATION: ...........................................................................................

TOPIC SENTENCE: ..............................................................................................................

....................................................................................................................................................

....................................................................................................................................................

# Logical Order

Once you have identified a debatable topic, you are ready to generate and organize the details. To make a persuasive point, a writer moves from a general idea (the claim) to a major support (a reason, fact, example, expert opinion, or reason against the opposing view) to a minor support (also a reason, fact, example, expert opinion, or reason against the opposing view). Transitions and signal words indicate the importance and movement among details. Strong transitions and signal words establish coherence, a clear and understandable flow of ideas.

## Transitions That Signal Persuasion

| | | | | |
|---|---|---|---|---|
| accordingly | finally | in conclusion | obviously | thus |
| admittedly | first (second, | indeed | of course | to be sure |
| although | third, etc.) | in fact, in truth | on the one hand | truly |
| because | for | in summary | on the other hand | undoubtedly |
| but | furthermore | last | since | |
| certainly | granted | meanwhile | some believe | |
| consequently | hence | nevertheless | some may say | |
| despite | however | nonetheless | therefore | |
| even so | | | | |

# Signal Words That Qualify an Idea as Persuasive (sample list)

| all | every | might | only | seem | too |
|-----|-------|-------|------|------|-----|
| always | has/have to | must | ought to | should | usually |
| believe | it is believed | never | possibly, possible | sometimes | |
| could | may | often | probably, probable | think | |

More practice with logical order: <www.mywritinglab.com>

## ORDER OF SUPPORTS FOR A CLAIM

Number each sentence according to the logical order of the ideas. Complete the exercise by answering the question "What's the point?"

**For the Sake of the Children**

_____ Obviously, in addition to risk of injury from explosions during the cooking process, a drug made from such materials has devastating health effects.

_____ A few of these risks include fire hazards, chemical explosions, physical and sexual abuse, and medical neglect.

_____ According to John W. Gillis, the director of the Office for Victims of Crime, "children who live at or visit home-based meth labs face acute health and safety risks."

_____ Crude home labs make crystal meth from common household products such as paint thinner, rubbing alcohol, battery acid, lye-based cleaning products, gasoline, kerosene, fertilizer, and chlorine bleach.

_____ As these chemicals are cooked with a heat source, they become volatile and explosive.

_____ In addition, because of the natural hand-to-mouth behavior of young children, they are likely to absorb or ingest toxic chemicals used to make the drug.

_____ Of course, removal of a child from his or her home is a traumatic experience; however, the dangers posed by the "meth" lifestyle far outweigh the risks posed by removing the child from these chaotic homes.

_____ For example, many of these chemicals damage vital organs, cause cancer, and lead to other severe health problems.

_____ In that same year, 26 were injured and two died as a direct result of meth-lab activities in the home.

_____ According to the El Paso Intelligence Center, in 2001, over 2,000 children lived in meth homes.

—Swetlow, Karen. *"Children at Clandestine Methamphetamine Labs: Helping Meth's Youngest Victims."* OVC Bulletin. Office for Victims of Crime. U.S. Department of Justice. June 2003. 3 April 2006. <http://www.ojp.usdoj.gov/ovc/publications/bulletins/children/197590.pdf>.

**What's the point?**

_____

_____

_____

# Relevant Details

As you narrow a topic into a focused main idea, you generate supporting details that answer the questions such as *who, what, when, where, why,* and *how.* Evaluate the relevancy of each detail and use only those that clarify or support the main idea. The supports of a persuasive claim are reasons, facts, examples, effects, expert opinions, and details that refute the opposing view.

Compare the following chart of Persuasive Supporting Details with the ideas in the persuasive thinking map about metal detectors in public schools.

| Persuasive Supporting Details | |
|---|---|
| REASON | A cause of an event or action. An explanation. A basis or foundation of an idea. |
| FACT | A specific detail that is true based on objective proof. Objective proof can be physical evidence, an eyewitness account, or the result of accepted scientific investigation. |
| EXAMPLE | An illustration or instance of a general idea. |
| EFFECT | A result or consequence of an event or action. Consider positive effects of claim and negative effects of opposing views. |
| EXPERT OPINION | A view based on much training and extensive knowledge in a given field. Be sure to stay with opinions of experts in the field of the topic that is being debated. For example, a physician, an expert in medicine, is not an expert in criminal justice. |
| SUPPORTS THAT REFUTE | To refute is to disprove or counter an opposing point; supports include reasons, facts, effects, examples, and expert opinions. |

**Persuasive Thinking Map**

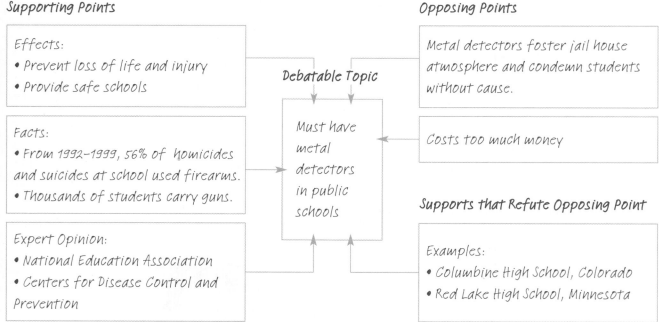

During the prewriting phase of writing, a writer naturally generates irrelevant details. In fact, an effective writer often produces far more details than can be used to make a specific point. Irrelevant details do not explain or support the focused point of the paragraph. A careful writer uses the revision process to double-check details for relevancy and to eliminate irrelevant details.

More practice with relevant details:
<www.mywritinglab.com>

The following paragraph develops the ideas about metal detectors in public schools generated using a persuasive thinking map. Circle the main idea. Underline one example of each of the following: fact, example, effect, and a support that refutes the opposing view. Cross out the detail that is not relevant to the main point.

## Pay the Price: Stop the Shootings

(1) Public school officials should use metal detectors to screen students for possession of firearms in order to reduce the numbers of injuries and deaths. (2) The use of metal detectors signals students that safety measures are in place and that violence will not be tolerated. (3) Some oppose the use of metal detectors as a step that fosters a jail house atmosphere and condemns students as guilty without cause. (4) These opponents to metal detectors also decry the economic cost of screening students for possession of firearms. (5) Unfortunately, evidence indicates that the need to provide a safe school and the right to a safe school far outweigh these concerns. (6) According to the Centers for Disease Control and Prevention, from 1992 to 1999, 56% of homicides and suicides occurring at school involved firearms. (7) In addition, the National Education Association estimates that "on a daily basis, 100,000 students carry guns to school, 160,000 miss classes due to fear of physical harm, and 40 are injured or killed by firearms." (8) Tragic school shootings have already occurred and signal that the danger is clear and present. (9) For example, in 1999 at Columbine High School, in Colorado, two students massacred 12 fellow students and a teacher, injured 24 other people, and then committed suicide. (10) As recently as 2005, at Red Lake High School in Minnesota, a student killed five students and injured seven others after he had killed his grandfather and his grandfather's girlfriend at home. (11) He also shot himself. (12) All of these shooters obviously suffered mental health problems. (13) Though these incidents are extreme, they are not isolated. (14) These incidents show that public schools must screen students for weapons. (15) The cost of not doing so is too high!

## Works Cited

Centers for Disease Control and Prevention. "Source of Firearms Used by Students in School-Associated Violent Deaths—United States, 1992–1999." Morbidity and Mortality Weekly Report. 7 March 2003. 52(09); 169-72. <http://www.cdc.gov/mmwr/mmwr/preview/mmwrhtml//mm5209a1.htm>.

"School Violence." National Education Association. Washington, D. C. 1993.

# Effective Expression: Use of Subjective Words to Persuade

Effective expression is the result of a writer's thoughtful choice of words for impact on the reader. Subjective words reflect a strong stand because they express opinions, emotions, value judgments, and interpretations. Because subjective words express personal opinions, they can bring meanings and stir reactions in the reader not intended by the writer. Therefore, a thoughtful writer carefully chooses subjective words for effective expression. Note the differences between the neutral words and the subjective words in the following list:

| Neutral Words | Subjective Words |
| --- | --- |
| injury | wound, gash |
| perpetrator | criminal, delinquent, achiever |
| shelter | haven, hut |

**Practice 5**

### EFFECTIVE EXPRESSION: USE OF SUBJECTIVE WORDS TO PERSUADE

Use your dictionary and thesaurus to find an effective biased word to fill in the blank in each sentence. In the spaces after each sentence, describe the impact you intend to have on your reader through your choice of words. Discuss your work with your class or small group.

**1.** Spanking is a ................................................................................................................

................................................................................................................................

**2.** Laws that require cyclists to wear helmets are ..............................................

................................................................................................................................

**3.** Completion of a college education requires ....................................................

................................................................................................................................

**4.** Burning the United States flag is an act of .....................................................

................................................................................................................................

**5.** President George W. Bush is .............................................................................

................................................................................................................................

More practice with
using subjective words:
<www.mywritinglab.com>

# Using Persuasion in Your Academic Courses

Often college textbooks present graphics to help you think critically and come to your own conclusions about a debatable topic. An excellent study technique is to write a paragraph in response to the information and questions. Many professors of these courses will also ask you to write an essay in which you explain your understanding of a controversial issue. You may find that you can use the information from the textbook as a resource for your writing assignment.

*Practice 6*

**USING PERSUASION IN AN AMERICAN GOVERNMENT ASSIGNMENT:** RESPONDING TO A CONTROVERSIAL ISSUE

Study the following information and graphic taken from an American Government college textbook about the campaign for the Senate, 2002. You may want to discuss your interpretation of the information with your class or small group. On a separate sheet of paper, write a paragraph that answers the questions and supports a claim about the given information.

Take a few moments to study the breakdown of a sample budget for a typical senate campaign, shown below, and then answer the following critical thinking questions: Where does the majority of campaign funding come from? What constitutes the single largest expense for the typical campaign? About what proportion of campaign funds comes from PACs? (A PAC is a Political Action Committee, which is a special interest group such as a labor union, tobacco company, or gun association.) Is this proportion smaller or larger than you thought?

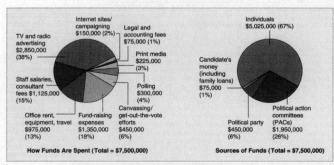

—From Sabato O'Connor and Keith Haag, *American Government: Continuity and Change*, 2004, Texas Edition, Pearson 2004, p.558.

More practice with writing persuasion paragraphs: <www.mywritinglab.com>

# Workshop: Writing a Persuasive Paragraph Step by Step

*Workshop*

**PREWRITING**

## Choose Your Topic

The following activities are designed to help you choose a topic.

1. Create a bank of topics: Use the following debatable topics to brainstorm or list as many facts, effects, and examples as you possibly can. Don't analyze your thoughts; just get as many ideas written down as quickly as possible. Add more debatable topics and examples as they occur to you. Revisit topic banks created during your study of previous chapters. Compare your bank of topics with those of your peers.

   - Violence in Cartoons
   - Sex Education
   - Teenage Drivers
   - Conserving Energy

2. Choose a list of topics from activity 1. Brainstorm possible points the opposition could use to challenge your ideas. Identify relevant expert opinions you will need to include. Determine where you could locate those opinions. For example, can you interview an expert? Locate an expert opinion on the Internet? Read a newspaper or magazine article?

   OR

   Select a set of photographs that illustrate a debatable topic. Generate a list that includes facts, effects, examples, and opposing points. Search for expert opinions to include. Freewrite about the photograph(s). Remember to ask, "What's the point?"

## Focus Your Point

Read a prewrite you have generated for a persuasive paragraph. Underline words that suggest your values, opinions, or attitudes about the events, situations, objects, or factors. Why is the subject important? Think about the reasons, facts, effects, and examples that best represent your claim. Identify your audience. Think about what specific reaction you want from your audience. Do you want to change your audience's mind about an issue, raise your audience's awareness about an issue, or call your audience to take a specific action? In one sentence, state the claim of your persuasion.

AUDIENCE: ................................................................................................

PURPOSE—AUDIENCE REACTION: ...................................................................

# Generate and Organize Relevant Details

Use the persuasive thinking map below to either organize the ideas you have already created or to generate details that support your point.

**Persuasive Thinking Map**

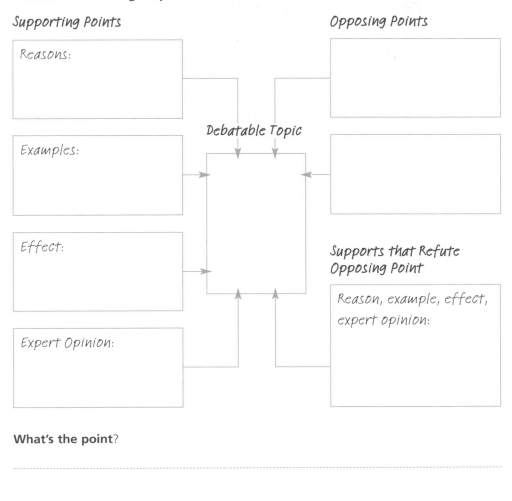

Supporting Points

Opposing Points

Reasons:

Examples:

Debatable Topic

Effect:

Supports that Refute Opposing Point

Reason, example, effect, expert opinion:

Expert Opinion:

**What's the point**?

---------------------------------------------------------------------

---------------------------------------------------------------------

# Write a Draft of Your Paragraph

Using the ideas you generated during the prewriting phase, compose a draft of your persuasion paragraph. Return to the prewriting process at any time to generate additional details as needed. Use your own paper.

# Revise Your Draft

Once you have created a draft of a persuasion paragraph, read the draft and answer the following questions. Indicate your answers by annotating your paper. If you answer "yes" to a question, underline, check, or circle examples. If you answer "no" to a question, write additional details in the margins and draw lines to indicate their placement. Revise your paragraph based on your reflection.

Workshop

# Questions for Revising a Persuasive Paragraph

☐ Have I chosen an important debatable topic?

☐ Have I made my point? Can I state my point in one sentence?

☐ Have I effectively used reasons, facts, effects, examples? Have I used strong signal words of persuasion?

☐ Have I used concrete details to make my point?

☐ Have I included only the details that are relevant to my topic sentence? Have I used effective and relevant expert opinions? Have I addressed important opposing points effectively? Have I documented my sources properly?

☐ Have I used the following to make my ideas clear and interesting to my readers: vivid verbs and images, parallel language, controlled sentence structure, coordination, subordination, precise use of words such as *affect* and *effect,* and thoughtful use of biased words?

☐ Have I used subjective words to persuade my reader?

Make any revisions to your paragraph that may be needed. Once that's done, turn your attention to the matter of editing for consistent use of point of view.

# Proofread Your Draft

Once you have made any revisions to your paragraph that may be needed, proofread you paper to ensure appropriate usage and grammar, such as the consistent use of point of view.

### Grammar in Action: Consistent Use of Point of View

Point of view is established with the use of personal pronouns. Personal pronouns identify three points of view: first person, second person, and third person.

### Personal Pronouns and Points of View

- **First Person** (informal tone)
  I, me, mine, myself, my,
  we, us, ours, our, ourselves

- **Second Person** (informal tone)
  you, your, yours, yourselves

- **Third Person** (formal tone)
  he, him, his, himself,
  she, her, hers, herself,
  it, its, itself
  they, them, their, theirs, themselves

Workshop

Common sense tells us that we cannot shift between several individuals' points of view. However, often, we shift point of view carelessly, as in the following sentence:

> Television addiction contributes to our obesity. When you choose to sit in front of a television from the minute you get home until you go to bed, you leave no time for exercise.

Consistent use of point of view strengthens coherence or the clear flow of ideas. Therefore, we should carefully edit our writing to ensure consistent use of point of view, as in the following edited version of the sentence above.

> Television addiction contributes to our obesity. When we choose to sit in front of a television from the minute we get home until we go to bed, we leave no time for exercise.

*Workshop*

PORTFOLIO

*Practice 7*

**CONSISTENT USE OF POINT OF VIEW**

Edit these sentences for consistent use of point of view. Cross out the pronoun that causes a shift in point of view and insert a noun or pronoun that establishes consistent use of point of view. Discuss your answers with a small group of peers or with your class.

**1.** A parent must monitor children's access to the Internet because you are vulnerable to predators in chat rooms and virtual communities like MySpace.com.

**2.** Some people believe that abstinence is the only way you can prevent unwanted pregnancies and the spread of sexually transmitted diseases.

**3.** People should not talk on the cell phone and drive at the same time. I was run off the road by a man who was obviously having an intense cell phone conversation while he was driving.

**4.** Getting enough sleep is crucial to a person's long-term health. When you deprive yourself of sleep, you deprive the body of its ability to repair itself through rest.

**5.** Women should limit their intake of alcohol to one serving of red wine per day; keep in mind that one serving is five ounces.

More practice with point of view consistency: <www.mywritinglab.com>

Review

**REVIEW OF WRITING A PERSUASIVE PARAGRAPH:** DEVELOP YOUR POINT USING THE WRITING PROCESS

Use the following form to record your thinking about writing a persuasive paragraph. Select and focus your topic for your writing situation, audience, and purpose. Choose a topic that can be stated as a debatable claim and identify its significance.

PREWRITING  DRAFTING   **What is your point?**

DEBATABLE CLAIM: ...........................................................................................................

AUDIENCE: .......................................................................................................................

PURPOSE: .........................................................................................................................

PREWRITING  DRAFTING   **State you main idea in a topic sentence.**

TOPIC: ..............................................................................................................................

OPINION, DEBATABLE CLAIM: ...........................................................................................

PREWRITING  DRAFTING   **Generate relevant details.**

REPORTER'S QUESTIONS: WHO, WHAT, WHERE, WHEN, WHY, HOW? ..................................

..........................................................................................................................................

PERSUASIVE SUPPORTING DETAILS: ...................................................................................

REASONS: .........................................................................................................................

FACTS: ..............................................................................................................................

EXAMPLES: ........................................................................................................................

EFFECTS: ...........................................................................................................................

EXPERT OPINIONS: ............................................................................................................

OPPOSING POINTS: ..............................................................................................................................................

SUPPORTS THAT REFUTE OPPOSING POINTS: ...........................................................................................

..............................................................................................................................................................................

PREWRITING · DRAFTING · REVISING    Use logical order. Use transition words to signal the
relationship among supporting details and to qualify ideas.

TRANSITIONS THAT SIGNAL PERSUASION: ....................................................................................................

SIGNAL WORDS THAT QUALIFY IDEAS: .........................................................................................................

REVISING · PROOFREADING    Use effective expression. Use subjective words for a thoughtful effect.
Use a consistent point of view.

SUBJECTIVE WORDS: ............................................................................................................................................

POINT OF VIEW: ...................................................................................................................................................

FIRST PERSON: ......................................................................................................................................................

SECOND PERSON: .................................................................................................................................................

THIRD PERSON: .....................................................................................................................................................

Review

# Writing Assignments

## Considering Audience and Purpose

Study the set of photographs at the beginning of the chapter. Assume you are an advertiser, and you have been asked to write a brochure to go along with one of the posters. Choose which side of the topic you wish to represent (the tobacco company or the anti-smoking public health announcement). Write a one-paragraph argument in support of the side of the issue you represent.

## Writing for Everyday Life

Assume that you and your family, or you and a group of your friends, have decided to take a vacation together. Each of you has a different destination and activity in mind. Write a one-paragraph email to your family or group of friends in which you convince them to travel to your choice of destinations. Be sure to include facts, effects, examples, expert opinions, and reasons that counter any opposition to your choice. Allow your word choice and tone to reflect your enthusiasm.

## Writing for College Life

Assume that you disagree with a grade you have received for a course or an assignment. Write a one-paragraph letter to your professor in which you argue for the grade you believe you have earned. Be sure to include facts that prove what you have learned, examples of what you have learned, and the benefits of what you have learned. As part of your proof, include ideas and concepts you have learned from your professor (as an expert in the field). Allow your word choice and tone to reflect both respect for the professor and self-confidence in your abilities.

## Writing for Working Life

Assume that you are a supervisor of a shift of workers at a fast food restaurant or at a department store. Assume that you are short of staff, and the busy season is approaching: you need more workers. Write a one-paragraph memo to your district manager, Derwood Kuntz, persuading him to authorize you to hire three additional workers. Be sure to include reasons, facts, examples, effects, and points that will counter any opposition he may pose.

More ideas for writing a persuasive paragraph: <www.mywritinglab.com>

# Writing
# an Essay

# 13

## Understanding the Essay

## An essay is a series of closely related ideas.

All of us of have had some experience studying, writing, or reading essays. What do you already know about essays? Where do you see essays? What are the traits of an essay?

Perhaps the most common and flexible form of writing, an essay allows powerful personal expression. The essay is used for academic papers, business reports, business letters, newspaper and magazine articles, Web articles, and personal letters, as well as letters to the editor of a paper or journal. By mastering the task of writing an essay, you empower your ability to think, to reason, and to communicate.

# What's the Point of an Essay?

Like a paragraph, an **essay** is a series of closely related ideas that develop and support the writer's point about a topic. In fact, the paragraph serves as a building block for an essay since an essay is composed of two, three, or more paragraphs. Therefore, the skills you developed to write a paragraph will also help you write an effective essay.

## The Four Parts of an Essay

An essay has four basic parts: a **title**; a beginning, made up of an **introductory paragraph**; a middle, made up of **body paragraphs**; and an ending, often made up of a **concluding paragraph**. The following chart shows the general format of an essay.

**Hook the reader's interest. Use key words or a phrase to vividly describe your essay.** → **1. The Title**

An introduction usually consists of a brief paragraph in which you do the following: Introduce the topic. Explain the importance of the topic or give necessary background information about the topic. Hook the reader's interest. State your main idea in a thesis statement—a sentence that contains your topic and your point about the topic. → **2. The Introduction**

The body of an essay is usually made up of a series of longer paragraphs. Most body paragraphs follow a similar pattern. Focus on one aspect of your main idea. State the focus of the paragraph in a topic sentence. Use the topic sentence to state the point you are making in the paragraph and relate the point of the paragraph to your thesis statement. Offer major details that support the topic sentence. If needed, offer minor details that support the major details. Link body paragraphs with clear transitions so your reader can easily follow your thoughts. → **3. The Body**

The conclusion restates or sums up the essay's main idea. In longer essays, the conclusion may be a separate paragraph. In shorter essays, the conclusion may be a powerful sentence or two at the end of the last body paragraph. → **4. The Conclusion**

For more on creating effective introductions, conclusions, and titles, see Chapter 14.

# Making a Point Using an Essay: One Writer's Response

Read the following essay from the U.S. Bureau of Labor Statistics' Web site. Study the annotations and complete the activities suggested in the annotations.

**The Introduction:**
The writer begins with a bold statement designed to hook the reader's interest. The next several sentences offer important background information about an associate degree. The introduction ends with the thesis statement. Notice that the thesis statement states the topic, "associate degree," and the writer's focus, "many advantages" and "many resources."

**The Title:**
The writer used a phrase to appeal to the reader's desire to get a "jump start" on the future. The title introduces the topic "Associate Degree" and sums up the point of her essay in just a few words.

### Associate Degree: Two Years to a Career or a Jump Start to a Bachelor's Degree

by Olivia Crosby

(1) In two years, you can increase your earnings, train for some of the fastest growing jobs in the economy, and pave the way for further education. (2) How? (3) Earn an associate degree. (4) An associate degree is a college degree awarded after the completion of about 20 classes. (5) It either prepares students for a career after graduation, or it allows them to transfer into a bachelor's degree program. (6) An associate degree offers many advantages, and many resources exist to help you decide upon a specific degree and college.

**The Body:**
The body of this essay is made up of several paragraphs. This topic sentence states a primary support for the thesis–one advantage of an associate degree: "increased earning power." By repeating the key term "advantage," the writer ties this body paragraph to the thesis statement.

**This detail** supports the topic sentence and is introduced with the transition "First."

This sentence is a minor detail that supports a major detail.
**Underline the phrase that introduces this detail.**

**Second major detail** that supports the topic sentence. Note the transition word "also."

**Third major detail** that supports the topic sentence is introduced with the transition "However."

(7) One advantage of an associate degree is increased earning power. (8) First, people with associate degrees earn more money. (9) For example, compared with workers whose highest held degree was a high school diploma, workers with an associate degree averaged an extra $128 a week in 2001, according to the Bureau of Labor Statistics (BLS). (10) People with associate degrees are also more likely to find jobs. (11) The unemployment rate in 2001 was more than 30 percent lower for people with associate degrees compared with high school graduates. (12) And, according to several academic studies, advantages in the job market might be even greater for those just starting their careers and for those who work in a career related to their degree. (13) However, for most people, the best part about earning an associate degree is the opportunity to enter interesting professions. (14) Training is available for those with nearly any interest, from technical fields like electronics and health care to liberal arts areas, such as design and social work. (15) And according to the BLS, careers in which workers often are required to have an associate degree are growing faster than careers that require other types of training.

(16) Another advantage of an associate degree is that it is widely ◄ available, offering a variety of experiences. (17) Degrees are available from public community colleges, private two-year colleges, for-profit technical institutes, and many four-year colleges and universities. (18) Taking classes from home is more common in associate degree programs than in any other type of educational program. (19) More than 9 percent of associate degree students used distance learning in 1998, according to the U.S. Department of Education. (20) Other students have a more traditional college experience. (21) These students choose schools that offer on-campus housing and meals. (22) And nearly all schools offer extracurricular activities—such as sports, clubs, and volunteer groups—as well as academics.

(23) In addition to the many advantages of an associate degree, many ◄ resources exist to help you make the best decisions about your career and how to train for it. (24) First, most libraries and career centers have the Encyclopedia of Associations and the *Occupational Outlook Handbook.* (25) These books offer information about work-related associations. (26) The *Handbook* also describes hundreds of careers and how to train for them. (27) Second, counselors at colleges and career centers have information about local associate degree programs, labor markets, and financial aid. (28) Third, the easiest way to learn about specific degree programs is to request information from the schools that offer them. (29) Nearly every school provides free publications, and many maintain Web sites describing programs and facilities. (30) For more details, consider calling, writing, or visiting prospective teachers. (31) Faculty and counselors are usually happy to speak with would-be students about courses and careers.

(32) An associate degree increases your chance for financial power ◄ and personal fulfillment—in just two years. (33) And with the many resources to help you decide on a degree and school along with the flexible paths to access, a bright future awaits you. (34) So don't delay; begin today!

—Adapted from Olivia Crosby, "Associate Degree: Two Years to a Career or a Jump Start to a Bachelor's Degree," US Department of Labor.

---

**This topic sentence** states another primary support for the thesis–"another advantage" of an associate degree. This phrase links this paragraph to the previous paragraph with the transition "another," and the word "advantage" ties this body paragraph to the thesis statement. Underline the words in the topic sentence that state the author's point in this paragraph.

**This topic sentence** offers another primary support for the thesis. The sentence begins with a transitional phrase "In addition to the many advantages of an associate degree." This phrase links this paragraph to the previous paragraphs and the thesis statement. Circle the words that state the author's focus in this paragraph. Underline the three major supporting details in this paragraph. Remember to look for transition words.

**The Conclusion:** This essay ends by restating the writer's main idea and calling the reader to action. Underline the words that restate the essay's main point.

Test your understanding of the essay's structure. Read the student essay below straight through once. Complete the activities beneath the essay as you read the essay a second time. After reading, complete the outline with information from the essay.

Lacey Durrance

Professor Ragan

ENC 1101: Section 47

October 10, 2007

### Traits of a Successful College Student

(1) First-time college students don't realize the reality shock they will receive when they get to college. (2) High school and college atmospheres are extremely different in many ways. (3) College campuses and classes are often larger, college teachers have different expectations, and college students face many new challenges. (4) College is a big part of growing up, and with growing up comes certain traits needed to make it in college. (5) To get through college successfully, all first-time college students must be dedicated, responsible, and independent. (6) Many won't realize this until it is too late, and without these traits, they won't succeed.

(7) Dedication is a primary part of being successful in college. (8) Students must want a good grade and know what they need to do to achieve it. (9) Students must work hard and take action to learn at a college level. (10) Assignments can't be left until the last minute like they might have been in high school. (11) College students must be willing to speak up in class and ask questions when they don't understand, even if they are afraid they will look foolish. (12) Dedication means setting priorities for success; dedication means putting off going out with friends; dedication means caring about producing the best work possible. (13) Dedicated students will do their work and do it well, spending hours reading textbooks, reviewing notes, and revising essays. (14) College is very different in the sense that much is expected from students, and they won't be walked through anything.

(15) For many, being responsible during high school wasn't really necessary. (16) Students could forget to do their homework and "blame it on the dog," yet the teacher most likely would extend the deadline. (17) In contrast, college students must be responsible for their actions and accept the consequences. (18) Paying attention to what's due and when assignments should be turned in is a prime example. (19) Most college teachers stick to their deadlines and expect students to do so also. (20) Being on time to class is another example of being responsible. (21) Unlike high school, there are no bells or signals that start college classes. (22) Students must manage their time to get themselves to class on time. (23) Responsibility plays a key role in a successful college career.

(24) However, having dedication and being responsible aren't the only traits college students need to survive. (25) College students must also be independent in everything they do. (26) Teachers expect students to take notes without assigning them to do so. (27) In high school, teachers often gave out notes to study from or told students where and when to take them. (28) This isn't the story in college. (29) College students must do their work without being reminded everyday. (30) However, teachers are there to help their students understand the class material. (31) They will guide their students yet not help complete their work. (32) Being independent is a skill to acquire for college success, as well as life-long success.

(33) College is hard work, and students must have these traits to be successful. (34) Most first-time college students will struggle with the new experience, yet by being dedicated, responsible, and independent, they will thrive in the college world.

**1.** Based on the title of the essay, what is the writer's topic and main point?

------------------------------------------------------------

------------------------------------------------------------

**2.** In the introduction, how does the writer "hook" the reader's interest?

------------------------------------------------------------

------------------------------------------------------------

*Practice 1*

**3.** Underline the thesis statement. Rewrite the thesis statement using your own words here.

---

---

**4.** What ideas did the writer restate in her conclusion?

---

---

**5.** The writer used a brief outline to plan and organize her ideas before she wrote her essay. Recreate her plan by completing the following outline. Fill in the blanks with her thesis statement and topic sentences.

**I.** INTRODUCTION

THESIS STATEMENT: _____

---

---

**II.** FIRST BODY PARAGRAPH TOPIC SENTENCE: _____

---

---

**III.** SECOND BODY PARAGRAPH TOPIC SENTENCE: _____

---

---

**IV.** THIRD BODY PARAGRAPH TOPIC SENTENCE: _____

---

---

**V.** CONCLUSION TOPIC SENTENCE: _____

---

---

Practice 1

# Developing Your Point: Writing an Essay

## The Four Levels of Information in an Essay

### Types of Details

Two types of details are often needed to thoroughly explain a main idea: primary and secondary details. **Primary details** directly explain or support the thesis statement. **Secondary details** indirectly support the thesis statement. In an essay, topic sentences of the body paragraphs are the primary supports for the thesis statement. The examples, reasons, and facts within the body of a paragraph support the topic sentence. They serve as secondary details that support the thesis statement.

### Levels of Details

Secondary supports can also be divided into two levels: major details and minor details. A **major detail** supports a topic sentence. A **minor detail** supports a major detail. Thus, a topic sentence supports the thesis statement, and secondary supports explain a topic sentence. The following flow chart illustrates these levels of information in an essay. This chart represents a basic three-paragraph essay. This format is often expanded to include two or more body paragraphs.

| Levels of Information in an Essay |
| --- |
| **Introduction:** Offers important background information about the topic. Offers the reader a reason to read about the topic. Hooks the reader's interest |

For more on outlining, see Chapter 2.

| **Thesis Statement:** | States the main idea of the essay in a complete sentence |
| --- | --- |
| | Uses specific, effective wording |
| | Covers all the details in the essay ◄ |

**Introductory Paragraph**

| **Topic Sentence** | Offers one primary support for the thesis statement |
| --- | --- |
| | States the author's main idea of the paragraph |
| | Covers all the details in the paragraph |

| **Major Detail** | Explains or supports the topic sentence |
| --- | --- |
| | Is a secondary support for the thesis statement |
| | Is more general than a minor detail |

**Body Paragraph:** Most essays have two or more body paragraphs. The ideas in a body paragraph often move from general to specific: from topic sentence to major support to minor support. This pattern is often repeated in each body paragraph.

| **Minor Detail** | Explains or supports a major detail |
| --- | --- |
| | Is a secondary support for the thesis |
| | Is one of the most specific ideas in the paragraph ◄ |

**The Conclusion:** A short essay may require just a sentence or two at the end of the final body paragraph. Longer essays often need a separate short paragraph to summarize the major points of the essay.

| **Conclusion:** Refers to the main idea of the essay: Sums up the primary supports of the essay |
| --- |
| Reinforces the writer's overall point ◄ |

IDENTIFYING THE LEVELS OF DETAIL IN AN ESSAY

An outline can help you see the levels of information in your essay. Read the following three-paragraph essay. Underline the thesis statement. Next, underline the three major details in the body paragraph. Then, complete the outline with information from the essay.

## Street Luging for the Extreme Thrill

(1) Extreme sports take athletic competition to new levels of danger and excitement. (2) They often offer a combination of speed, height, danger, and mind-blowing stunts. (3) Street luging illustrates the allure of extreme sports.

(4) Street luging, like many extreme sports, involves high levels of speed, danger, and adrenaline. (5) First, street luging is all about speed. (6) A pilot lies on his or her back on a luge (a type of skateboard, eight and a half feet long) and flies through a street course at speeds of around 70 miles per hour. (7) As a result, the urethane wheels of the luge may actually flame fire and melt during a run due to the high speeds. (8) Second, street luging courses are known for their rough, hazardous road surfaces and obstacles. (9) For example, very dangerous courses are known as *bacon* while less dangerous ones are labeled *scrambled eggs*. (10) And frequently, luges snag or hook together, wobble, wipe out, or slam into barriers that mark the course. (11) Finally, the dangers of street luging are related to another important attraction of extreme sports—the thrilling rush of an adrenaline high. (12) The adrenaline rush is due to high levels of dopamine, endorphins, and serotonin produced by the body in response to the danger. (13) Adrenaline floods the body with additional surges of energy, power, and well-being so that a person can either fight or flee the danger. (14) Many extreme sports participants are called adrenaline junkies. (15) Luge pilots refer to this feeling as being "amped."

(16) Extreme sports include a wide variety of thrill-seeking sports such as wave surfing, wind surfing, BASE jumping (jumping from buildings, antennas or towers, spans or bridges, or cliffs), parachuting, and drag racing. (17) Overall, street luging offers athletes all the dangers and thrills that all extreme sports enthusiasts find so attractive.

**I.** (Introduction) Extreme sports take athletic competition to new levels of danger and excitement. They often offer a combination of speed, height, danger, and mind-blowing stunts.

Thesis Statement: Street luging illustrates the allure of extreme sports.

**II.** (Body) Street luging, like many extreme sports, involves high levels of speed, danger, and adrenaline.

    **A.** ........................................................................................................................

        **1.** A pilot lies on his or her back on a luge (a type of skateboard, eight and a half feet long) and flies through a street course at speeds of around 70 miles per hour.

        **2.** As a result, the urethane wheels of the luge may actually flame fire and melt during a run due to the high speeds.

    **B.** ........................................................................................................................

      ........................................................................................................................

        **1.** Very dangerous courses are known as *bacon* while less dangerous ones are labeled *scrambled eggs*.

        **2.** Frequently, luges snag or hook together, wobble, wipe out, or slam into barriers that mark the course.

    **C.** ........................................................................................................................

      ........................................................................................................................

        **1.** ...........................................................................................................

          ...........................................................................................................

          ...........................................................................................................

        **2.** Adrenaline floods the body with additional surges of energy, power, and well-being so that a person can either fight or flee the danger.

        **3.** Many extreme sports participants are called adrenaline junkies.

        **4.** ...........................................................................................................

          ...........................................................................................................

**III.** (Conclusion) Extreme sports include a wide variety of thrill-seeking sports such as wave surfing, wind surfing, BASE jumping (jumping from buildings, antennas or towers, spans or bridges, or cliffs), parachuting, and drag racing. Overall, street luging offers athletes all the dangers and thrills that all extreme sports enthusiasts find so attractive.

*Practice 2*

# The Traits of an Effective Essay

The word essay means attempt, to make an effort to accomplish an end. An essay is a writer's attempt to share his or her unique and specific point about a specific subject to a specific audience for a specific purpose. An effective essay supports a **main idea** with **relevant details** in **logical order,** using **effective expression.**

## The Point: Main Idea

What's the point of a focused main idea? To make a clear and powerful point to your reader! An effective essay makes a clear point by focusing on a main idea. A focused main idea is the result of several thinking steps: selecting and narrowing a topic and writing a thesis statement.

### Select and Narrow a Topic

For more on using prewriting techniques and selecting a topic, see Chapter 2.

Many writers break this step into two parts. First, a writer often generates a list of topics. This list serves as a bank of ideas that can be applied to a wide variety of writing situations. Second, a writer considers the writing situation.

Understanding the writing situation helps the writer narrow the topic. For example, the length of an essay often depends on your audience and purpose. A paper for an academic audience such as a history professor may have a required length of 1,000 words. In contrast, a local newspaper may limit the length of letters to the editor to 500 words. The scope of the topic needs to match the required length. For example, the 500-word letter to the editor cannot cover all the reasons one should volunteer at the local soup kitchen for the poor. Instead, you would need to narrow the topic to just two or three reasons. And you would choose only those details that are of interest to your specific audience.

For more on the writing situation, and topic, purpose, and audience, see Chapter 2.

*Practice 3*

### THE WRITING SITUATION

The following pictures present specific writing situations. Each picture represents an audience, and each caption states the purpose for writing to that audience. First, match the audience and purpose to its appropriate topic. Then, write the letter of the topic in the appropriate space. Finally, discuss your answers with your class or in a small group.

Topics:  a. The importance of a specific lesson

b. Wisdom gained from an education

c. The proper way to discipline a child

d. Why voting is important

.......... Writing Situation 1: To Inform – to share, explain or demonstrate information

.......... Writing Situation 2: To Persuade – to change this audience's opinion or call them to action

.......... Writing Situation 3: To Express – to share personal opinions, feelings or reactions

.......... Writing Situation 4: To Reflect – to record your understandings about what you have experienced or learned

Your purpose for writing is another important part of the writing situation. Most likely you write for three general purposes: to inform, to entertain, or to persuade. A specific writing situation may call for a more specific purpose such as to express a personal opinion or to reflect upon the significance of an event.

### TOPIC, PURPOSE, AND AUDIENCE

Generate a list of topics appropriate for each of the following writing situations. Discuss your answers with your class or in a small group.

Situation **1:**

PURPOSE: *To inform*

AUDIENCE: *Speech class teacher and peers*

TOPICS: _____

_____

_____

_____

_____

Situation **2:**

PURPOSE: *To express displeasure or satisfaction*

AUDIENCE: *A manager or supervisor*

TOPICS: _____

_____

_____

_____

Situation **3:**

PURPOSE: *To persuade*

AUDIENCE: *The general public*

TOPICS: _____

_____

_____

_____

Practice 4    Practice 5

Situation **4:**

PURPOSE: _To reflect upon personal growth_

AUDIENCE: _Self, as in a journal_

TOPICS: _____

_____

_____

_____

_____

_____

**WRITING FOR WORKING LIFE**

The following chart lists several occupations and possible writing situations for each one. Work with a peer or a small group of your classmates to complete the chart with information about the writing situation for each occupation.

| Writing Situations in Working Life | | | |
|---|---|---|---|
| **Occupation** | **Topic** | **Purpose** | **Audience** |
| Police officer | an accident report | | |
| Nurse | appropriate ways to draw blood | | |
| Lawyer | closing argument in a trial | | |

## Draft a Thesis Statement

After choosing and narrowing a topic, a writer composes a working draft of the thesis statement. A **thesis statement** shares the same traits of a topic sentence for a paragraph. Just as the topic sentence states the main idea of a paragraph, the thesis sentence states the main idea of the essay. Both statements answer the question "What's the point?" This point is the opinion about the topic that you are explaining and supporting in the essay. In fact, your point further narrows your topic. The writer's point or opinion is often referred to as the controlling idea.

The controlling idea often includes a pattern of organization as well as the writer's opinion. You learned about patterns of organization as you studied how to develop paragraphs in Chapters 3 to 12, and you will study them again later in this chapter. The following graphic illustrates an effective thesis statement.

*TOPIC*        *WRITER'S POINT: CONTROLLING IDEA*

A near-death experience  dramatically  changes a person.

*OPINION*        *PATTERN OF ORGANIZATION*

The word *dramatically* is an opinion that must be explained or supported. In addition, the word *changes* suggests a pattern of organization. This word indicates that the writer is going to compare what the person was like before the near-death experience to what the person is like after the near-death experience. The controlling idea answers the question "what's the point?" of the essay.

| **Hints for Drafting a Thesis Statement** |
| --- |
| Use specific statements. Replace vague, general words with vivid, exact words. "Football is a dumb game" is too vague and general. "Football glorifies violence" is specific and vivid. |
| Always state your thesis statement as a complete sentence. |
| Avoid announcing your topic. Never say, "I am going to write about football and violence," or "My essay is about football and violence," or "My topic is football violence." |
| Review and, if necessary, revise your thesis statement after you have written a rough draft. As you think about a topic, the point you want to make often becomes clearer. |

### CREATING AND REVISING THESIS STATEMENTS

The first five items present a topic and a writer's point about the topic. Combine the ideas in each group to create a thesis statement. Revise the next five thesis statements to make them specific and effective. Discuss your ideas with your class or in a small group.

**1.** TOPIC: *Workplace aggression*

WRITER'S POINT: *is on the rise and takes on several forms of behavior.*

THESIS STATEMENT:

**2.** TOPIC: *Cardiovascular disease*

WRITER'S POINT: *although certain factors are unavoidable, other factors we can influence*

*Practice 6*

Practice 6

THESIS STATEMENT: ..................................................................................

..................................................................................

**3.** TOPIC: *Major depressive disorder*

WRITER'S POINT: *a common type of mood disorder with several*

*long-term effects*

THESIS STATEMENT: ..................................................................................

..................................................................................

**4.** TOPIC: *Use of chat rooms and online discussion boards*

WRITER'S POINT: *Five tips for effectiveness*

THESIS STATEMENT: ..................................................................................

..................................................................................

**5.** TOPIC: *Weight training machines and free weights*

WRITER'S POINT: *similarities and differences*

THESIS STATEMENT: ..................................................................................

..................................................................................

**6.** Cell phones cause a lot of problems.

REVISED THESIS STATEMENT: ..................................................................................

..................................................................................

..................................................................................

..................................................................................

**7.** Smoking is a bad habit.

REVISED THESIS STATEMENT: ..................................................................................

..................................................................................

**8.** The football team the Houston Texans are a bunch of losers.

REVISED THESIS STATEMENT: .........................................................

..........................................................................................

..........................................................................................

**9.** My job at Cypress Gardens in Winter Haven, Florida, was very interesting.

REVISED THESIS STATEMENT: .........................................................

..........................................................................................

..........................................................................................

**10.** I am going to talk about the dangers of compulsive gambling on the gambler and his family.

REVISED THESIS STATEMENT: .........................................................

..........................................................................................

..........................................................................................

*Practice 6*

# Relevant Details

In an effective essay, the writer provides enough relevant details to adequately or thoroughly support the essay's main idea.

## Generate Details with a Writing Plan

Most writers generate details during the prewriting stage by listing or freewriting. Once you have generated an adequate amount of details, you need to organize them into a writing plan. Many writers use clustering or outlining to help them create a plan for the essay. Clustering and outlining are excellent ways to see if you have enough details to support the point of your essay.

> For more on listing and freewriting, see Chapter 2.

Some writers begin the writing process by generating details, then drafting a thesis statement, while other writers draft a working thesis statement first and then generate details. The following two practices offer you an opportunity to work with both approaches. In your own writing, you should experiment to see which approach works best for you.

> For concept maps of specific patterns of organization, such as narration, classification, and definition, see Chapters 4-12.

Practice 7

## DRAFTING A THESIS, GENERATING DETAILS, AND CREATING A WRITING PLAN

Read the thesis statement. Note that the thesis statement suggests three body paragraphs with the controlling idea "three simple steps." First, study the following set of details created during a brainstorming session. Then, group the details into chunks of information by completing the outline with details from the list. Finally, state the main idea of each paragraph in a topic sentence.

THESIS STATEMENT: *Three simple steps can lead to a long, healthy life.*

DETAILS: *eating healthy          being active          managing stress*

*need thirty minutes of moderate exercise nearly every day*

*managing stress reduces cardiovascular disease, chronic fatigue,*

*and psychological disorders*

*eat five or more servings of fruit or vegetables daily*

*healthful diet reduces the risk of cancer/other chronic diseases*

*exercise reduces obesity, diabetes, high blood pressure, heart disease,*

*and stroke*

*start slow, build up gradually*

*balance obligations*

*get plenty of rest*

*make time for recreation and fun*

*control portions*

*drink plenty of water*

*stay committed*

*dance, garden, swim, walk, jog, lift weights, etc.*

*talk over problems/challenges with a friend or counselor*

**I.** INTRODUCTION

THESIS STATEMENT: *Three simple steps can lead to a long, healthy life.*

**II.** TOPIC SENTENCE: *The first step to a long, healthy life is a healthful, balanced diet.*

    **A.** SUPPORTING DETAIL: *Healthful diet reduces the risk of cancer and other chronic diseases.*

    **B.** SUPPORTING DETAIL: _____

    **C.** SUPPORTING DETAIL: _____

    **D.** SUPPORTING DETAIL: _____

**III.** TOPIC SENTENCE: *The second step to long-term health is being active.*

    **A.** SUPPORTING DETAIL: _____

    _____

    **B.** SUPPORTING DETAIL: _____

    **C.** SUPPORTING DETAIL: _____

    **D.** SUPPORTING DETAIL: _____

    **E.** SUPPORTING DETAIL: _____

**IV.** TOPIC SENTENCE: _____

    **A.** SUPPORTING DETAIL: _____

    _____

    **B.** SUPPORTING DETAIL: _____

    **C.** SUPPORTING DETAIL: _____

    **D.** SUPPORTING DETAIL: _____

    **E.** SUPPORTING DETAIL: _____

**5.** CONCLUSION

Practice 7

For more on creating and using concept maps, see Chapter 2.

Often, a writer uses a prewriting technique, such as a concept map, to generate primary and secondary details. Then, the writer drafts a working thesis statement to summarize the point of the details generated with the concept map.

*Practice 8*

**GENERATE DETAILS, DRAFT A THESIS, CREATE A WRITING PLAN**

Study the following list of details. Create a writing plan by filling in the concept map with groups of details from the list. Then, write a one-sentence summary (a thesis statement) of the main point that they support. Next, write topic sentences to state the main idea of each group of details. Finally, fill in the outline based on the concept map. Use complete sentences.

| | | |
|---|---|---|
| respects others | builds consensus | seeks solutions |
| stays on point | fosters team work | remains professional |
| avoids gossip | diffuses confrontations | sticks with facts, not feelings |
| functions of effective communication on the job | gets to the point quickly | encourages input from others |
| | states clear expectations | |

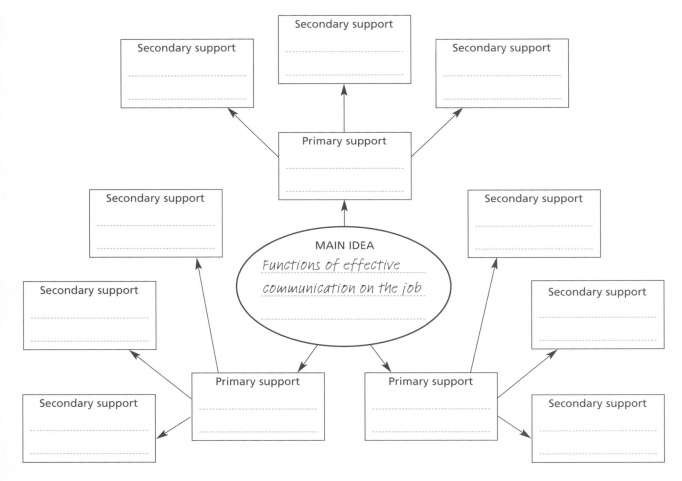

One-sentence summary of primary supports:

......................................................................................................................................

......................................................................................................................................

I. INTRODUCTION

THESIS STATEMENT: *To succeed on the job, you need effective communication skills.*

II. .........................................................................

    A. .................................................................

    .........................................................................

    B. .................................................................

    .........................................................................

    C. .................................................................

III. ........................................................................

    A. .................................................................

    B. .................................................................

    .........................................................................

    C. .................................................................

    .........................................................................

IV. ........................................................................

    A. .................................................................

    .........................................................................

    B. .................................................................

    C. .................................................................

    .........................................................................

**V.** CONCLUSION

Practice 8

# Evaluate Details

In an effective essay, every detail supports the thesis statement. *All* the details work together as a unit to explain and support the writer's point. During the prewriting process, a writer brainstorms many details, some of which may not be related to the focus of the main idea. Therefore, as you create your writing plan, you should test the details to be sure that each one is relevant to the thesis statement. Drop those details that do not support either the thesis statement or the thesis statement's primary supports. You also may want to check details for relevance once more during the revision stage of the writing process.

*Practice 9*

### TESTING DETAILS FOR RELEVANCE

Study the following writing plan. Cross out details that are not relevant to the thesis statement. The following questions will help you test details for unity. Share your work with your class or in a small group of peers.

- What is the topic and controlling idea of the thesis statement? Circle the topic. Underline the controlling idea.

- Which details are the primary supporting details (the ones that will be used as topic sentences for body paragraphs)? Number the three primary supports A, B, and C.

- What are the secondary details? Number each secondary detail to correspond to a primary point: A1, A2, and so on; B1, B2, and so on; and C1, C2, and so on.

THESIS STATEMENT: *Due to the nature of lightning, you must follow lightning safety guidelines to reduce risk of injury or death.*

_____ Lightning is a complex event.

_____ A spark of lightning can reach over five miles in length, soar to temperatures of approximately 50,000 degrees Fahrenheit, and contain 100 million electrical volts.

_____ Lightning is described as having two components: leaders and strokes.

_____ The leader is the probing feeler sent from the cloud.

_____ The return streaks of light are a series of strokes that produce the actual lightning bolt or flash that we see.

_____ Fires are usually started by unusually long-lasting hot lightning bolts.

_____ Lightning is also common, unpredictable, and dangerous.

_____ At any given moment, there are 1,800 thunderstorms in progress somewhere on the earth. This amounts to 16 million storms each year.

_____ An average of 25 million flashes of lightning from the cloud to ground occur every year.

_____ Lightning has been seen in volcanic eruptions, extremely intense forest fires, surface nuclear detonations, heavy snowstorms, and in large hurricanes.

_____ No one can predict the location or time of the next stroke of lightning.

_____ Lightning has been the second largest storm killer in the U.S. for the last 40 years, exceeded only by floods.

_____ Lightning strikes can cause paralysis, brain damage, and cardiac arrest.

_____ Following proven lightning safety guidelines can reduce your risk of injury or death.

_____ Seek safe shelter when you first hear thunder or see dark threatening clouds developing overhead or lightning.

_____ Count the seconds between the time you see lightning and the time you hear the thunder.

_____ You should already be in a safe location if that time is less than 30 seconds.

_____ The safest location during lightning activity is an enclosed building.

_____ Stay inside until 30 minutes after you last hear thunder.

_____ Rain will not kill you.

_Practice 9_

# Logical Order

In an effective essay, body paragraphs are arranged in a clear, logical order for a coherent flow of ideas. Likewise, effective writers link each paragraph to the next so that readers can follow their chain of thought.

You can achieve a coherent flow of ideas in several logical ways.

1. _Follow the order of ideas as presented in the thesis statement._ Often the controlling idea of the thesis statement divides the topic into chunks of information.

2. _Follow space order._ At times, a writer describes how something is arranged in space to develop a main idea. Description moves from top to bottom, side to side, front to back, or the reverse of these.

3. _Follow time order._ A writer may record an event or a process as it unfolds in time.

4. _Present ideas in order of importance._ Often, a writer decides upon and arranges details according to his or her opinion about the importance of the details, known as **climactic order**. Usually, climactic order moves from least important point in the first body paragraph and builds to the essay's climax, the most important point in the final body paragraph.

**COHERENCE TECHNIQUES: THESIS-STATEMENT, SPACE, TIME, AND CLIMACTIC ORDER**

Complete the exercises, and share your responses with your class or in a small group.

1. **Follow the order of ideas as presented in the thesis statement.** Underline the three chunked parts of the controlling idea. Then, write and arrange in coherent order three topic sentences (primary supports) suggested by the thesis statement.

**I.** Introduction

THESIS STATEMENT: .............................................................................

.............................................................................

.............................................................................

**II.** .............................................................................

**III.** .............................................................................

**IV.** .............................................................................

.............................................................................

**V.** Conclusion

2. **Follow space order**. Write and arrange in space order three topic sentences (primary supports) suggested by the following thesis statement. Use the photographs to generate your primary supports.

**I.** Introduction

THESIS STATEMENT: *Although Goth fashion varies widely, the look makes a bold, nontraditional fashion statement.*

**II.** _____

**III.** _____

**IV.** _____

**V.** Conclusion

3. **Follow time order.** Write and arrange in time order three topic sentences (primary supports) suggested by the following thesis statement. Use the photographs to generate your primary supports.

**I.** Introduction

THESIS STATEMENT: *Technology plays a key role in the restoration of Sand Key Beach, Florida.*

**II.** _____

_____

**III.** _____

**IV.** _____

**V.** _____

_____

**VI.** Conclusion

▲ Before restoration

▲ During restoration

▲ After restoration

**4. Present ideas in order of importance.** Write and arrange in climactic order three topic sentences (primary supports) suggested by the following thesis statement.

**I.** Introduction

THESIS STATEMENT: *Stress challenges us in almost every aspect of our lives.*

**II.**

**III.**

**IV.**

**V.** Conclusion

Practice 10

## ORDERING PARAGRAPHS

Study the following writing plans. In the space provided next to each primary support (topic sentence) number the statements in each group II, III, or IV to show the most coherent order. Then, indicate which coherence technique you used in the numbered spaces:

TSO = Thesis Statement Order;
TO = Time Order; SO = Space Order;
CO = Climactic Order.

........... **1.** I. Introduction

THESIS STATEMENT: *The sunrise blazed in a belt of fire.*

........... Below the smoldering belt, the sea flared in reflected waves of orange, yellow, and red.

........... The entire canopy of the earth glowed like the underside of a red hot ember.

........... Where sky met earth, the sun paused, a perfect, brilliant ball of flame upon a belt of smoky purple.

V. Conclusion

........... **2.** I. Introduction

THESIS STATEMENT: *iPods are an excellent investment because they are*

*equipped with the ability to store and play large libraries of music,*

*store and play movies, and store personal information through*

*calendars, address books, and personal notes.*

........... iPods are able to store and play large libraries of music.

........... iPods can store and play movies.

........... iPods organize personal information through calendars, address books, and personal notes.

V. Conclusion

........... **3.** I. Introduction

THESIS STATEMENT: *Ballroom dancing is popular for several reasons.*

........... Most importantly, according to many people, ballroom dancing provides them with a life-long hobby.

........... A significant reason that many people begin ballroom dancing is the rigorous exercise required to accomplish the moves.

........... Many people take up ballroom dancing just to meet new friends and have a good time.

V. Conclusion

........... **4.** I. Introduction

THESIS STATEMENT: *Real learning occurs before, during, and after each*

*class.*

......... After class, review class notes, compare class notes to your reading notes, and summarize what you learned in your own words.

......... During class, listen actively, take notes, and ask questions.

......... Before class, read the assigned material, take notes, and think of questions to ask during class.

V. Conclusion

## Connecting Paragraphs

In addition to ordering paragraphs coherently, writers clearly connect each paragraph to the next so that readers can follow their chain of thought. You can use several options to connect paragraphs to each other. The following chart lists and illustrates each option.

| Connecting Paragraphs |
| --- |
| **Echo or repeat important words or phrases from the thesis statement in body paragraphs.** |
| I. Thesis statement:      We can *ease* the *pain* that occurs from illness or injury in several different ways. |
| II. Topic sentence:      *Pain* can be *eased* by deep breathing. |
| III. Topic sentence:      Visualization and imagery *ease pain.* |
| **Refer to the main idea of the previous paragraph in the topic sentence of the present paragraph.** |
| I. Thesis statement:      Applying the principles of computer ergonomics reduces the chances of injury and fatigue. |
| II. Topic sentence:      The *computer screen* should be *placed properly* to avoid painful injuries to the neck. |
| III. Topic sentence:      *Proper placement* of the *monitor* not only *reduces* the possibility of *neck injury* but also eases eye fatigue. |
| **Use transitional words, phrases, or sentences.** |
| I. Thesis statement:      Sleep disorders can deprive sufferers of much needed rest and complicate their lives. |
| II. Topic sentence:      *One type* of sleep disorder is known as night terrors. |
| III. Topic sentence:      *Another type* of sleep disorder, nightmares, torments many people. |
| IV. Transition sentence and topic sentence:      *At least the previous two disorders occur in the privacy of one's home.* Narcolepsy, a *third kind* of sleep disorder, can occur suddenly anywhere, and at any time without warning. |
| **Tie the last idea in one paragraph to the opening of the next paragraph.** |
| I. Thesis statement:      Hurricane activity is on the rise, is likely to increase, and calls for new methods of preparation. |
| II. Topic sentence and ending idea of paragraph:      Hurricane activity is on the rise because of higher ocean temperatures and lower vertical wind shear.<br>Therefore, these *climate changes* are likely to continue for as many as 10 to 40 years. |
| III. Topic sentence:      *These shifts in climate* call for new methods of hurricane preparation. |

Read the following essay. Underline the connections between paragraphs. Circle the key ideas that are repeated throughout the essay. Discuss with your class or in a small group the different types of connections the writer used and evaluate their effectiveness.

## A Song of Humility

(1) The neighborhood of my youth hummed with the songs of our carefree play. (2) The beat of hammers building forts and the zings of the over-ripe ammunition of our orange wars in Winter Haven, Florida, blended beautifully with the music of the times. (3) The Beatles, and all the other really far-out groups, deafened us to any world but our very own. (4) No one was more deaf than I.

(5) At that time, I was particularly deaf to the family that lived two streets over and halfway down a dusty clay side road. (6) This out of sync family lived poorer than we did. (7) They grew their own food, raised chickens, and loved loud country music. (8) Every time I passed their house, I felt sorry for them, in a smug sort of way. (9) One afternoon the mama of that family labored up the hill to our house. (10) Her son had cut a record, and she "would be obliged if we was to listen to it" and tell her what we thought. (11) I was too busy marveling at her stained clothes and dusty feet to hear how respectfully my mother responded.

(12) Mother treated everyone with respect and tried to teach her children to do so as well. (13) She insisted that the whole family listen to the twangy tune about love and shirttails, but only I took great joy in mocking it. (14) Mother told me to return the record and say she thought it "a fine tune." (15) When I objected, she said, "Consider this an avoidable duty!" (16) I stood a long time studying the rusty door of that family's dust-covered house, wondering why I hadn't the courage to do my duty.

(17) Finally, my good friend Florence appeared at the end of the alley. (18) "Florence," I cried in great relief, "come here quick." (19) I ran to meet her, and we stood a few feet away with our backs turned from the door I so dreaded. (20) In the loud, exuberant tones of an inconsiderate child, I belted out the details of my dilemma. (21) "You ought to hear this … stupid … only hicks … and I have to … Hey, wait for me," I said to her retreating back. (22) I had hoped to push my obligation into her hands. (23) "Naw," she said without looking back, "I'm already late."

(24) So, I turned to do my hated duty. (25) Then I saw the son, the singer, dart from the door into the shadows of the house. (26) I wheeled about and cried, "Florence, come back." (27) I ran to her, begging, "He heard me. (28) What should I do? (29) He heard everything I said." (30) Florence shrugged and turned away. (31) I pivoted and marched to the steps. (32) The son stepped out to meet me. (33) My words resonated in the silence that loomed between us, and I cursed the supper time desertion of the dusky streets. (34) "Young lady," he said gently. (35) I looked at him. (36) "Thank ya for bringing back my demo."

(37) To this day, the timbre of his voice shames me. (38) I had mocked him, yet he sought to soothe my soul. (39) And, now, when I feel the deafness of prejudice threaten me, I remember the song of humility I learned that day from a fine young singer.

# Effective Expression: Using a Thesaurus

One aspect of effective expression is choosing the precise word to convey your point with power and clarity. Effective writers often refer to a thesaurus to avoid repetition and to find the exact words needed to make their point. A thesaurus is a collection of words, their synonyms (words of similar meaning), and their antonyms (words of opposite meaning). Some thesauruses list words alphabetically: A–Z. Other thesauruses list words by types or groups of related words. You can find both kinds on the Internet. For example, *Roget's II: The New Thesaurus* 3rd ed. online at Bartleby.com offers both versions. You can find words by looking at the headwords as in the following two illustrations:

| **Alphabetical Index:** | | | **Categorical Index:** |
|---|---|---|---|
| A-1 | to | all right | like, dislike |
| all-round | to | atrocity | restraint, unrestraint |
| atrophy | to | big | explosion, collapse |

Features vary from thesaurus to thesaurus, so be sure to read the instructions on how to use a specific one. Some features include a main entry, parts of speech, a definition, a list of synonyms, a list of antonyms, field or usage labels (such as Law or slang), and a *see also* cross reference.

### EFFECTIVE EXPRESSION: USING A THESAURUS

Study the two entries from *Roget's II: The New Thesaurus* 3rd ed.* Then, answer the questions.

**spew**

VERB: To send forth (confined matter) violently: belch, disgorge, eject, eruct, erupt, expel. Geology : extravasate. See EXPLOSION.

**extravasate**

VERB: Geology. To send forth (confined matter) violently: belch, disgorge, eject, eruct, erupt, expel, spew. See EXPLOSION.

1. What part of speech are these two words? _____

2. Is the word "Geology" a synonym, an antonym, or a field label? _____

3. Is the word "Explosion" in both entries a field label, a cross reference,

or a synonym? _____

4. Insert a word from the entries that best completes the point of the following statement:
   Jeremiah's parents _____ their breath in relief as he safely completes his parachute jump.

*All examples from *Roget's II: The New Thesaurus* 3rd ed. Boston: Houghton Mifflin, 1995.

# Workshop: Writing an Essay Step by Step

### WRITING AN ESSAY STEP BY STEP

To create an effective essay, use the complete writing process. Begin by prewriting; then, move on to drafting, revising, and editing. Writing rarely develops in a neat and orderly process. Some writers need to generate details before they can compose a working thesis statement. Others have to know exactly what their main point is before they can generate details. The following series of workshops encourages you to follow the prewriting steps in a certain order. Feel free to move between steps or to return to any step in the process as needed.

## Prewriting

During the prewriting stage, you figure out what you want to say, why you want to say it, and to whom you want to say it.

**TOPIC**
What you write

**AUDIENCE**
Who reads
what you write

**PURPOSE**
Why you write

For an overview of the writing process, see Chapter 2.

For more on the prewriting stage of the writing process, see Chapter 2.

### Select and Narrow Your Topic

Select a topic on your own, pick a topic from a previous practice or workshop, or choose one of the following topics. Identify your audience and purpose.

- Movie heroes (or villains)
- Violence in sports
- Technology everyone should own
- A great achievement
- A fun activity
- Common fears

### Create a Tentative Thesis

Then, draft a tentative thesis statement.

TOPIC: ..............................................................................................

AUDIENCE: ..........................................................................................

PURPOSE: ...........................................................................................

....................................................................................................

THESIS STATEMENT: ...............................................................................

....................................................................................................

....................................................................................................

....................................................................................................

Workshop

## Generate Supporting Details

Generate primary and secondary supporting details by listing or using the concept map. Use the reporter's questions *who? what? when? where? how?* and *why?* to produce details.

For more information on patterns of organization, see Chapters 4-12 and Chapter 15.

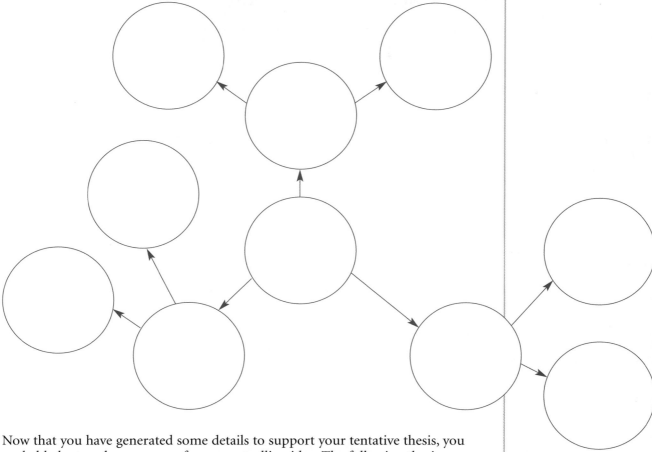

Now that you have generated some details to support your tentative thesis, you probably have a clearer sense of your controlling idea. The following thesis statement has been revised to focus the topic by including the writer's opinion and a pattern of organization.

TOPIC          WRITER'S POINT: CONTROLLING IDEA

Voter turnout remains dismal for several reasons.

OPINION          PATTERN OF ORGANIZATION

## Revise Your Thesis Statement

Revise your thesis so that it includes the topic, your point about the topic, and, if appropriate, a pattern of organization.

REVISED THESIS STATEMENT:

.......................................................................................

.......................................................................................

Workshop

# Evaluate Your Details

Use a writing plan to test your details. Complete the following outline with your revised thesis statement and details from your list or concept map. Make sure you have an adequate amount of details to convince your reader of your point. If you do not have the necessary major and minor details to support each topic sentence, brainstorm additional details. Delete details that are not related to your thesis statement or to the topic sentences (the primary supports for your thesis statement).

**I.** INTRODUCTION

THESIS STATEMENT: ................................................................................

............................................................................................................

............................................................................................................

............................................................................................................

............................................................................................................

............................................................................................................

**II.** ........................................................................................................

............................................................................................................

    **A.** ..............................................................................................

    **B.** ..............................................................................................

**III.** .......................................................................................................

............................................................................................................

    **A.** ..............................................................................................

    **B.** ..............................................................................................

**IV.** .......................................................................................................

............................................................................................................

    **A.** ..............................................................................................

    **B.** ..............................................................................................

**V.** CONCLUSION

PORTFOLIO

Workshop

# Write a Draft of Your Essay

Often, a writer pauses during the drafting stage of the writing process to scan what has been written so far, particularly when using a computer to write. Sometimes, while scanning, a writer may begin to make small revisions. Scanning may help a writer stay focused and can help with expression. However, you should resist the urge to spend very much time revising at this point. Your main purpose is to get a rough draft written. You can make effective revisions once you have a working draft.

For more on the drafting stage of the writing process, see Chapter 2.

Using your writing plan, write a rough draft of the body of your essay. Don't worry about the introduction and conclusion for now. Have a dictionary and thesaurus nearby just in case you get stuck trying to think of a word.

# Revise Your Essay Draft

Revision is much more than simply recopying the essay so that it is neater. A good revision requires time. So, put your essay aside for an hour or two, or even better, a day or two. You want to look at your essay with fresh eyes. Then, set aside enough time to revise your essay more than once—that way, you do not have to think of everything in one sitting. During the revising stage of your writing, think about your essay on two different levels: logic and style. The following chart offers you some helpful questions to guide you through your revision.

For more on the revising stage of the writing process, see Chapter 2.

# Questions for Revising an Essay

- [ ] Does the essay have a clearly stated thesis statement?
- [ ] Are my topic sentences clearly stated?
- [ ] Have I provided relevant support?
- [ ] Is each body paragraph fully developed with major and minor details as needed?
- [ ] Which ideas need more support?
- [ ] Is each topic sentence directly related to my thesis statement?
- [ ] Is each detail in each body paragraph related to its topic sentence?
- [ ] Have I used logical order?
- [ ] Have I provided clear connections between paragraphs?
- [ ] Have I provided clear connections between sentences within paragraphs?
- [ ] Have I used effective expression?
- [ ] Do my sentences vary in type and length?

For more information about sentence variety, see Chapter 18.

Reread your essay, and as you revise, mark up your rough draft with the changes you intend to make: (1) cross out irrelevant details and vague, weak, or trite expressions, and write stronger words directly above or near them; (2) draw arrows to show where you want to move information; (3) add more details in the margin and draw a line to indicate where you will put them.

# One Student Writer's Revision Process

At the beginning of this chapter, you read the essay Lacey Durrance composed for her English class. Take a moment to reread her final draft on page 246–247. Then, study her revisions of one draft of the essay's first two paragraphs. How does this draft differ from her final draft?

## Traits of a Successful College Student

(1) First-time college students don't realize the reality shock they will receive when they get to college. (2) High school and college atmospheres are extremely different in many ways. (3) Schools are larger; there are different teachers with different expectations, and different experiences. (4) College is a big part of growing up, and with growing up comes certain traits that you need to have to make it in college. (5) All first-time college students must have dedication, be responsible, and be independent, to get through college successfully. (6) Many won't realize this until it is too late and without these traits, they won't succeed.

(7) Dedication is the biggest part of being successful in college. (8) Students must want a good grade, and know what they need to do to achieve it. (9) Among my own personal experiences of being a first time college student, dedication has played a major part of being successful. (10) I had to change my learning process to adapt to college and so have former students. (11) Students must be hard working and take action to learn at a college level. (12) Things can't be left until the last minute like they might have been in high school. (13) College students can't only want a good grade, but must do the work to get that grade. (14) Dedication will get their work done and do it well. (15) College is very different in the sense that a lot is expected from students, and they won't be walked through anything.

Workshop

# Proofreading Your Essay

For more on the proofreading stage of the writing process, see Chapter 2.

*Workshop Review*

PORTFOLIO

Once you have revised your essay to your satisfaction, take time to carefully proofread your work. Check for the mistakes that you commonly make such as spelling errors, misplaced or missing commas, shifts in verb tense, or shifts in point of view. Publishing a clean, error-free draft proves you are committed to excellence and that you take pride in your work.

Proofread to correct spelling and grammar errors. Mark the corrections you need to make directly on the most recent draft of your essay. Create a neat, error-free draft of your essay.

---

**REVIEW:** UNDERSTANDING THE ESSAY

**1.** What are the four parts of an essay?

a. ...................................................................................................

b. ...................................................................................................

c. ...................................................................................................

d. ...................................................................................................

**2.** What are the four levels of information in an essay?

a. ...................................................................................................

b. ...................................................................................................

c. ...................................................................................................

d. ...................................................................................................

**3.** What are two types of details in an essay?

a. ...................................................................................................

b. ...................................................................................................

**4.** What are the two levels of secondary supports?

a. ...................................................................................................

b. ...................................................................................................

**5.** An effective essay supports a ........................... idea with ........................... details in ........................... order and ........................... expression.

**6.** What are the four phases of the writing process for composing an essay?

a. ...................................................................................................

b. ...................................................................................................

c. ...................................................................................................

d. ...................................................................................................

# 14

## Effective Introductions, Conclusions, and Titles

### Introductions, conclusions, and titles work together to emphasize the writer's point.

The importance of effective introductions, conclusions, and titles is obvious in the composition of a movie. Think of a good movie you have seen lately. How did its title hook your interest? How did the title relate to the point of the movie? How effective was the opening of the film? How was the conclusion of the movie related to its beginning?

Just as in a successfully constructed movie, an essay with an effective introduction, conclusion, and title is more likely to impact an audience with a well made point.

# What's the Point of Effective Introductions, Conclusions, and Titles?

Effective introductions, conclusions, and titles work together to emphasize the writer's point in an essay.

Practice 1

### PHOTOGRAPHIC ORGANIZER: INTRODUCTIONS, CONCLUSIONS, AND TITLES

Study the following series of pictures of Mount St. Helens before, during, and after an eruption. First, answer the questions below for each of the photographs to identify the major details that could be used in an essay about the event. Then, write captions that provide a title, an introduction, and a conclusion for the point made by the images.

Title: ......................................................................................................

Introduction: ............................................................................................

............................................................................................................

FIRST EVENT · · · · SECOND EVENT · · · · THIRD EVENT ⟶

What is this?

........................................

........................................

What's happening?

........................................

........................................

What is this?

........................................

........................................

What the point?

............................................................................................................

............................................................................................................

Conclusion:

............................................................................................................

............................................................................................................

## My First Thought Box: A Prewriting Activity

Set a time limit, such as five minutes, and write in your notebook about the images you just studied. Do not let your pen or pencil stop. Even if you must repeat ideas, keep writing until the time limit is up. Let the ideas flow freely. Getting your first thoughts about a topic on paper is a great way to start the writing process.

# Making a Point Using Effective Introductions, Conclusions, and Titles: One Student Writer's Response

The following paragraph offers one writer's response to the call to write a title, introduction, and conclusion based on the images of Mount St. Helens' eruption. Read the text below and the annotations. Complete the activities in bold type given in the annotations. Then, read the writer's journal that records decisions she made during the writing process.

**Title:**
An effective title can be a word or phrase that helps the reader understand the writer's point by stating the topic and suggesting the writer's opinion about the topic.
**Underline the topic and circle the writer's opinion.**

→ Nature's Fierce Power Humbles Humanity

**Introduction:**
An effective introduction stirs the reader's interest, establishes the relevance of the topic, and often suggests or states the main idea.
**Underline the sentence that states the main idea.**

→ An ancient Chinese proverb states, "Human will can conquer nature." However, the 1980 eruption of Mount St. Helens in Washington makes a mockery of such a thought. The 1980 eruption of Mount St. Helens demonstrates the devastating power of nature and the powerlessness of humanity.

**Conclusion:**
An effective conclusion restates the main idea to reinforce the writer's point in the reader's memory.
**Underline the words that restate the topic and the writer's opinion.**

→ As Maya Angelou stated, "Nature has no mercy at all."

### THE WRITER'S JOURNAL

The student who wrote "Nature's Fierce Power Humbles Humanity" wrote the following journal entry to record her thoughts about using an introduction, conclusion, and title. Read her writer's journal that describes a few key choices she made as she wrote. Underline any strategies that you might be able to use in your own writing.

> When I first saw the images of the 1980 eruption of Mount St. Helens, I was blown away by the devastating power of nature. I guess being so coddled by technology, I never really thought about how little control we have over nature. Of course, since then, Hurricane Katrina has made it quite clear to me just how vulnerable we are. Yet, just as we did before Katrina struck, many have forgotten this terrible truth. I had an idea about the point I wanted to make, but I waited until after I composed

*the body of my essay before I worked on my introduction, conclusion, and title. It's really hard for me to introduce a point until I know exactly what that point is, and I like to tie my conclusion to my introduction so that my essay creates an unbroken circle of thought. Hey, I just noticed that my title, introduction, thesis statement, and conclusion create a summary of my essay. I am going to use this strategy when I read information for my academic courses. What a great way to take notes!*

# Developing Your Point Using Effective Introductions, Conclusions, and Titles

Thoughtful introductions, conclusions, and titles enhance the effectiveness of an essay. Often these three aspects of the essay are written after the thesis statement and body paragraphs have been drafted. Although titles are the first part of the essay that catches the reader's attention, many writers create them after the introduction and conclusion.

For more on the parts of an essay, see Chapter 13.

## Effective Introductions

An effective introduction serves the following purposes:

- It introduces the essay topic.
- It explains the importance of the essay topic and/or gives necessary background information about the topic.
- It hooks the reader's interest.
- It presents the essay's main idea in a thesis statement.

For more on thesis statements, see Chapter 13.

Many writers choose to end the introductory paragraph with the thesis statement.

The following chart describes and illustrates several types of introductions you can use to effectively begin your essay. The thesis statement in each introduction is underlined.

For more on using narration to tell an anecdote, see Chapter 5 and Chapter 15.

| Types of Introductions | |
|---|---|
| **An interesting illustration or anecdote** | **EXAMPLE:** The Wooten family makes a point of sharing the evening meal as special family time. Every evening, just as the family begins to dine and enjoy each other's company, the phone begins its non-stop ringing with unwanted harassment from telemarketers. Thankfully, the family can now put a stop to the harassment. <u>The National Do Not Call Registry is open for business, putting consumers in charge of the telemarketing calls they get at home.</u> |

| Types of Introductions …*continued* | |
|---|---|
| **A surprising fact or statement** | **EXAMPLE:** Nearly one in seven Americans has key clinical data missing from their medical files, according to a report in *The Journal of the American Medical Association* (JAMA). And in 44 percent of cases the absent information would have impacted a doctor's diagnosis, potentially putting patients' health at risk. <u>You can take a few simple steps to maintain accurate and accessible personal-health records and safeguard your well-being.</u><br><br>– Adapted from "Read This Before Your Next Doctor's Appointment," First Magazine |
| **A direct quotation** | **EXAMPLE:** In 1961 a copy writer named Shirley Polykoff was working for the Foote, Cone & Belding advertising agency on the Clairol hair-dye account when she came up with the line: "If I've only one life to live, let me live it as a blond!" <u>In a single slogan she had summed up what might be described as the secular side of the Me Decade.</u> "If I've only one life to live, let me live it as _____!" (You have only to fill in the blank.)<br><br>– Tom Wolfe, "The Me Decade and the Third Great Awakening" |
| **A definition** | **EXAMPLE:** Hope is belief that the impossible is possible. Hope is the future counted in the present. Hope is a light, a map, and a compass. <u>Hope gave me the will to fight and survive cancer.</u> |
| **A contradiction or opposing view** | **EXAMPLE:** Many wanna-be runners don't even try because they believe they don't have the right physique. Their legs are too short. Their stomach is too big. Their shoulders are too broad. Their body weight is too much. These people are wrong. The body is unimportant. The mind is everything. Running is not a physical sport. <u>It's mental.</u><br><br>– "Mind Over Body," Running Fit Prevention Guide |
| **A vivid description** | **EXAMPLE:** Two gas stations. A car repair shop barely visible through the rusty open hoods of dismantled race cars. A man clad in overalls selling roasted peanuts from the back of his truck. These are a few sights at the unpretentious intersection that is the small town of Barberville in Northwest Volusia. <u>To some, the settlement along the corner of U.S. 17 and State Road 40 represents one of the area's last strongholds of unspoiled country life.</u><br><br>– Maria Herrera, "Rural Residents Wary of Road Project" |
| **A general or historical background** | **EXAMPLE:** Charles Darwin was born in 1809 the same day as Abraham Lincoln. Even as a boy, Darwin's consuming interest in nature was evident. When he was not reading nature books, he was in the fields and forests fishing, hunting, and collecting insects. His father, an eminent physician, could see no future for a naturalist and sent |

For more on using definition, see Chapter 10 and Chapter 15.

For more on using description, see Chapter 4 and Chapter 15.

Charles to the University of Edinburgh to study medicine. But Charles, only 16 years old at the time, found medical school boring and distasteful. He left Edinburgh without a degree and then enrolled at Christ College at Cambridge University, intending to become a minister. At Cambridge, Darwin became the protégé of the Reverend John Henslow, a professor of Botany. Soon after Darwin received his B.A. degree in 1831, Henslow recommended the young graduate to Captain Robert Fitzroy, who was preparing the survey ship *Beagle* for a voyage around the world. <u>It was a tour that would have a profound effect on Darwin's thinking and eventually on the thinking of the whole world.</u>

– Neil Campbell and Jane Reece, *Essential Biology*

*Practice 2*

## INTRODUCTIONS

Read the following four introductory paragraphs. Underline the thesis statement and identify the type of introduction used in each one. Discuss your answers with your class or in a small group of peers.

**a.** An interesting illustration or anecdote
**b.** A surprising statement or fact
**c**. A direct quotation
**d.** A definition

**e.** A contradiction or opposing view
**f.** A vivid description
**g.** General or historical background

........... **1.** Heat kills! In fact, excessive heat is the number one weather-related killer, causing more fatalities per year than floods, lightning, tornadoes, hurricanes, winter storms, and extreme cold, according to the National Weather Service's storm data from 1994 to 2003. Therefore, when you exercise in warm, humid temperature, protect yourself by taking a few sensible safety measures.

........... **2.** To Frederick Douglass is credited the plea that, "the Negro be not judged by the heights to which he has risen, but by the depths from which he has climbed." Judged on that basis, the Negro woman embodies one of the modern miracles of the modern World.
– *Mary McLeod Bethune, "A Century of Progress of Negro Women"*

........... **3.** The roll of honor read at the 9/11 ceremonies was a tapestry of America, of native-born Americans of all ethnic origins and more recent immigrants. Of course, we know too well that some of the assassins and others plotting against America were immigrants who betrayed our ideas, so it is natural that many people feel we should now close the door altogether, beginning with immigrants from Muslim countries. Natural, and wrong. What is long overdue, however, is a sustained national dialogue on immigration.
– *Mortimer B. Zuckerman, "Our Rainbow Underclass"*

........... **4.** When we first saw Henry, we knew he had to be ours. He had only been recently rescued from a cruel breeder who supplied greyhounds to local race tracks. We were told that the breeder caged Henry in a metal crate with shredded newspaper for bedding for 18-22 hours each day. He feed Henry cheap 4-D meat for Greyhounds. The 'D' stands for dying, diseased, disabled and dead livestock. Henry had barely survived the E. coli poisoning from this feed. At one time, almost every detail of Henry's skeleton could be seen beneath his thin skin. The fact is that these kinds of abuses are more common than not. Greyhound racing should be outlawed.

# Effective Conclusions

An **effective conclusion** fulfills the following purposes:

- It brings the essay to an end.
- It restates the essay's main idea and sums up the major points in the essay.

In longer essays, the conclusion may be a separate paragraph. In shorter essays, the conclusion may be a powerful sentence or two at the end of the last body paragraph. Just remember that a conclusion must stay on point, so don't introduce new information.

The following chart describes and illustrates several types of conclusions you can use to effectively and powerfully end your essay.

| Types of Conclusion | |
|---|---|
| **A question** | **EXAMPLE:** Don't you want to experience the well-being that results from a healthful diet and regular exercise? |
| **A quotation** | **EXAMPLE:** Just as renowned coach of the Green Bay Packers Vince Lombardi said, "The difference between a successful person and others is not a lack of strength, not a lack of knowledge, but rather in a lack of will." |
| **A call to action** | **EXAMPLE:** This is not a time for indecision or hesitation. This is a time for commitment and action. Tell your federal, state, and local governments that you demand a coordinated response plan for natural disasters. |
| **A suggestion** | **EXAMPLE:** Your best friend is the one who will tell you a hard truth for your own good. |
| **A warning about consequences** | **EXAMPLE:** If instruments used for ear and body piercing are not properly cleaned and sterilized between clients, then you could contract HIV, hepatitis B, or hepatitis C. |
| **A vivid image** | **EXAMPLE:** And when this happens, when we allow freedom to ring, when we let it ring, when we let it ring from every village and every hamlet, from every state and every city, we will be able to speed up that day when all God's children, black men and white men, Jews and Gentiles, Protestants and Catholics, will be able to join hands and sing in the word of the Old Negro Spiritual – Free at last! Free at last! Thank God Almighty, we are free at last!<br><br>–Martin Luther King, "I Have a Dream" |
| **A summary** | **EXAMPLE:** Therefore, it is especially important to wash your hands before, during, and after you prepare food, before you eat, after you use the bathroom, after handling animals or animal waste, when your hands are dirty, and more frequently when someone in your home is sick.<br><br>–National Center for Infectious Diseases, "Wash Your Hands Often" |

For more on using description, see Chapter 4 and Chapter 15.

*Practice 3*

**CONCLUSIONS**

Read the following four conclusions. Identify the type of conclusion for each selection. Discuss your answers with your class or in a small group of peers.

**a.** A question
**b.** A quotation
**c.** A call to action
**d.** A suggestion

**e.** A warning about consequences
**f.** A vivid image
**g.** A summary

.............. **1.** Fellow citizens, we will meet violence with patient justice—assured of the rightness of our cause and confident of the victories to come.
*–President George W. Bush, "Address to a Joint Session of Congress and the American People, 2001."*

.............. **2.** The crew of the space shuttle Challenger honored us by the manner in which they lived their lives. We will never forget them, nor the last time we saw them, this morning, as they prepared for their journey and waved goodbye and "slipped the surly bonds of earth" to "touch the face of God."
*—President Ronald Reagan, Eulogy for the Challenger Astronauts, 1986.*

.............. **3.** The measure of a student's achievement is not in the grade from a teacher, too often these days a symbol of high inflation and low value, but in the wisdom gained from learning. Daniel Pederson stated it best in *Newsweek*, March 3, 1997: "When *A* stands for average, do grades mean anything at all?"

.............. **4.** Our life on earth has already reaped many benefits from past and current space exploration. The establishment of a human colony on the moon would further enhance the quality of life on this planet. Products designed for independent life on the moon will someday become part of everyday life on Earth, advancing research in robotics, communications, medicine, computer technologies, food and nutrition, clothing, environmental and architectural design, rocketry, fuel and energy, building materials, and agriculture. We should shoot for the moon!

# Effective Titles

An **effective title** fulfills the following purposes:

- It hooks the reader's interest.
- It vividly describes the topic of your essay.

You should write your essay, reread your essay for its overall impact, and then create your title. Your title should be brief, and you should not use italics, quotations, or underlining for emphasis. Instead, center the title on the page about an inch above the introductory paragraph. Capitalize the first word and other key words of the title, except for prepositions such as *in, on, for, at* and articles such as *a, an,* and *the.* The following chart describes and illustrates several types of effective titles.

| Types of Titles | | |
|---|---|---|
| **The question title:** States the main point as a question. | **EXAMPLES:** | Is Cloning Moral? <br> Why Clone? |
| **The descriptive title:** Uses key words to form the thesis statement. | **EXAMPLES:** | The Arrogance of Cloning <br> Cloning Offers Hope |

For more on using description, see Chapter 4 and Chapter 15.

For more on using patterns of organization to develop paragraphs and essays, see Chapters 4-12 and Chapter 15.

| The recommendation title: Calls for action. | EXAMPLES: | Cloning Must Be Banned<br>Clone On! |
|---|---|---|
| The general-specific title: States the general topic, followed by a controlling point. | EXAMPLES: | Cloning: An Unethical Procedure<br>Cloning: The Scientific Method Working for Progress |
| The pattern(s) of organization title: Uses the words that establish the essay's central pattern(s) of organization. | DESCRIPTION EXAMPLES: | The Town of My Birth<br>The Beauty of the Beach |
| | NARRATION EXAMPLES: | Sojourner Truth's Journey<br>An Unforgettable Memory |
| | PROCESS EXAMPLES: | How to Deal with Cranky Customers<br>Starting Your Own Business |
| | EXAMPLE/ ILLUSTRATION EXAMPLES: | Winning Isn't Easy<br>Pets Are People Too |
| | CLASSIFICATION EXAMPLES: | Types of Sexual Harassment<br>Kinds of Camps for Kids |
| | COMPARISON/ CONTRAST EXAMPLES: | The Differences between Male Talk and Female Talk |
| | DEFINITION EXAMPLES: | The Forgiving Heart<br>The Meaning of Bravery<br>What It Means to Be Compulsive |
| | CAUSE/EFFECT EXAMPLES: | Why Parents Send Their Kids to Camp<br>The Reasons Students Cheat<br>The Effects of Hurricane Katrina |
| | PERSUASION EXAMPLES: | The Need for Smaller Classes in Public Schools<br>We All Have the Right to Die<br>Commit to Life to the Very End |

Practice 4

**TITLES**

Read the following three-paragraph business memo and supply a title in the blank labeled RE (for the topic of the memo).

Memo

To:        Sales Associates

From:      Shanika Thomas, Store Manager

Date:      3 November 2007

RE: ..............................................................................

Do you want to win the $200 bonus promised to each employee of the store which best represents our company's ideals: professional, friendly,

*Practice 4 Review*

fast service? Corporate representatives will be popping in unannounced sometime over the next few weeks to rate us as individuals and as a team.

To ensure our win, keep the following tips in mind. Reflect professionalism in your personal attire, the store's appearance (keep shelves stocked and orderly), and in your work ethic. Reflect friendliness in your attitudes to supervisors, coworkers, and, most importantly, to our customers. Finally, be quick to help each other and the customer. Greet the customer promptly and politely. The moment a customer walks in through our door, make that person feel as if he or she is the most important person on earth.

If each and every one of you continues to do the fine job that has put our store in the finals of this competition, we will all be winners!

**REVIEW:** EFFECTIVE INTRODUCTIONS, CONCLUSIONS, AND TITLES

Complete the chart by filling in the blanks with information from the chapter:

### Types of Introductions

- An interesting illustration or anecdote
- A surprising fact or statement
- A direct quotation
- A definition

- A contradiction or opposing view
- _____
- _____

### Types of Conclusions

- A question
- _____

- _____

- A suggestion
- A warning about consequences
- A vivid image
- A summary

### Types of Titles

- The Question Title
- The Descriptive Title

- _____
- The General-Specific Title

### The Patterns of Organization Title:

_____

- Description
- Narration
- Process
- Example/Illustration
- Classification

- Comparison/Contrast
- Definition
- Cause/Effect
- Persuasion

# 15

# Using Patterns of Organization to Develop Essays

## Patterns of organization help arrange, present, and develop ideas into an essay.

We use patterns of organization to clearly arrange and present thoughts and ideas as we engage in academic, business, and everyday life. Students who go to RateMyProfessor.com are looking for certain traits in and ratings about a teacher and may compare these qualities with those of another teacher. Factory owners must think about the effects of commonly used chemicals in the manufacturing process and train their employees on safety procedures. To make a particular dish or dessert, cooks must closely follow a recipe's steps and instructions and do those steps in order. Similarly, many writers use patterns of organization to develop their ideas into an essay.

# What's the Point of Using Patterns of Organization to Develop Essays?

**PHOTOGRAPHIC ORGANIZER: USING PATTERNS OF ORGANIZATION IN ESSAYS**

Study the following series of pictures. First, answer the questions below each of the photographs to identify the major details that could be used in an essay about the event. Then, write captions that provide a title, an introduction, and a conclusion for the point made by the images.

NARRATION: *A Chain of Events*          TOPIC: *My New York Experience*

FIRST EVENT          SECOND EVENT          THIRD EVENT

What happened?          What happened?          What happened?

------------------------------------

------------------------------------

What's the point of the narration?

------------------------------------

Now that you have used a pattern of organization to brainstorm about a topic, think about how patterns of organization can help you write an essay. Answer the question:

What's the point of learning about using patterns of organization to write an essay?

------------------------------------

------------------------------------

## My First Thoughts: A Prewriting Activity

Set a time limit, such as five minutes, and jot down in your notebook your thoughts about using patterns of organization. In addition to the examples mentioned above, what are some other situations that require thinking about time sequences, comparisons, contrasts, definitions, or persuasive ideas?

# Making a Point Using Patterns of Organization: One Student Writer's Response

Read the following student journal entry that records the writer's thoughts about using patterns of organization to develop an essay.

> Earlier in the semester, I learned about using patterns of organization to develop paragraphs, so I see how useful they will be during the writing of essays. Based on the timeline for "My New York Experience," I can see that an essay uses several paragraphs to discuss a topic. The graphic also shows that each paragraph discusses just one part of the topic. It also occurred to me that the topic is "New York" and the pattern of organization is time order (based on "experience"). So all the details in the essay have to be details of time, but I also think some description is also going to be needed. Patterns of organization can help me limit a topic and think up details of support. Patterns of organization can help me keep on topic and put my ideas in the order that makes the most sense.

# Developing Your Point in a Descriptive Essay

The ability to describe people, places, or things accurately is a useful life skill.

In your personal life, you may need to file a police report or insurance claim about the damage, loss, or theft of your property. You must be able to describe the damaged, lost, or stolen goods.

In your college life, you will rely upon description in many content courses. For example, you may need to describe a natural environment for a science class or a piece of artwork for a humanities class.

In your working life, you may need to describe the physical specifications of office equipment.

To write a **descriptive essay**, a writer describes a person, place, or object based on its location or the way it is arranged in space. Spatial order describes an arrangement of details from top to bottom, from bottom to top, from right to left, from near to far, far to near, from inside out, or outside to inside. The writer also relies upon sensory details such as sight, sound, smell, taste, and touch to create vivid mental images so that the reader can see what is being described. **Descriptive transition words** signal that the details follow a logical order based on two elements:

For information on writing a descriptive paragraph, see Chapter 4.

1. How the person, place, or object is arranged in space.

2. The starting point from which the writer chooses to begin the description.

## Transition Words Used to Signal Description

| | | | | | | |
|---|---|---|---|---|---|---|
| above | at the side | beneath | close to | here | nearby | there |
| across | at the top | beside | down | in | next to | under |
| adjacent | back | beyond | far away | inside | outside | underneath |
| around | behind | by | farther | left | right | within |
| at the bottom | below | center | front | middle | | |

# A Descriptive Essay:
# One Student Writer's Response

Read the following descriptive essay written by student Allyson Melton for an English class. Read the essay a second time, then, complete the activities and answer the questions that follow.

### The Brilliance of Nature

1    (1) Too often, the brilliance of nature goes unnoticed. (2) This became very apparent to me, early one morning, on my way to work. (3) As I merged with the flock of procrastinating people, late as usual, I sped along, aware of the neon yellow dashes on the road flashing by as I sped along. (4) The flock of us grudgingly slowed to a stop as we approached a red light. (5) While waiting impatiently for the signal to go green, I diverted my eyes from the glare of the traffic light. (6) The sights and sounds around me revealed a vision of color and movement.

2    (7) The view to my left filled my vision with color and movement. (8) The road was lined with trees, each one proudly standing tall. (9) Dressed in their brightly colored costumes of jade, olive, emerald, and lime, they stood against the heavens as a magnificent tribute to the earth. (10) Their brown trunks, solid and strong-willed, stood unwaveringly in the face of time.

(11) A skirt of green grass encircled the weathered tree roots. (12) To my right, a gleaming shopping center towered above the people who milled around its base. (13) Shoppers constantly lined in and out of the mall doors; they reminded me of ants carrying grains of sand or tiny crumbs to and from their anthill. (14) The light gray sidewalk provided a path mostly for bicyclists, spinning their wheels in an effort to gain ground, and joggers, bobbing along with the iPod ear buds plugged in like drooping antennae.

3       (15) The view ahead wavered in a vapor of exhaust fumes and noise. (16) The road, packed with cars of all colors and shapes, stretched before me. (17) Everything from the small, bright red sports car to the gigantic, black Hummer had come to a stop on this stretch of asphalt. (18) I rolled my window down to feel the cool morning air only to be greeted by honking horns and obnoxious music from nearby cars. (19) The bass from the music of the car beside me was so loud I could feel the boom, boom, boom move through my frame and land at the top of my head with an extra "boom" for emphasis. (20) Before quickly rolling my window up again, I caught a whiff of the sharp smell of exhaust fumes.

4       (21) The red light still burned brightly, so I ventured a quick look up at the sky and couldn't look away. (22) It contained every hue imaginable, moving from pink to purple, blue to gray, and orange to yellow. (23) The newly risen sun, so yellow it was nearly white, shimmered in the mist of the new day. (24) Golden sun rays sprayed a flock of birds with a splendid display of light and shadow. (25) Their wings had hypnotic powers in their rhythmic beatings. (26) Hundreds, even thousands formed a fluid ribbon of birds, winding through the topaz sky in a graceful stream, never fraying from its curve. (27) Though I couldn't see even one bird up close, I could imagine their feathers blowing in the cool morning air as they swept through the sky. (28) As I watched, the stream continued to speed across the sky without hesitation, as if they all knew exactly where they were going. (29) When I finally broke my gaze, I looked around again.

5       (30) The people in their cars around me were still staring fixatedly forward at that commanding red light while the glory of nature flew over their heads. (31) As the birds continued to flow across the heavens, the light switched to green. (32) As much as I wanted to linger and watch them, I had to move forward again.

Practice 2

**READING AND EVALUATING THE ESSAY**

Complete the activities below after you have read the essay a second time.

**1.** What kind of title does the writer use? _____

**2.** What type of introduction does the writer use? _____

_____

**3.** Underline the thesis statement.

**4.** For each of the body paragraphs, underline the topic sentence. Circle the descriptive transition words. List two major details for each paragraph below.

Major Details (Paragraph 2): _____

_____

Major Details (Paragraph 3): _____

_____

Major Details (Paragraph 4): _____

_____

**5.** What type of conclusion does the writer use? _____

**6.** What is the purpose of the essay? Explain your answer. _____

_____

**7.** Who is the audience for the essay? Explain your answer. _____

_____

**8.** What did you like best about the essay? Why? _____

_____

_____

**9.** What about the essay could be improved? _____

_____

For more on types of titles, introductions, and conclusions, see Chapter 14.

For more on thesis statements, see Chapter 13.

For more on topic sentences, see Chapter 3 and Chapter 13.

For more on purpose and audience, see Chapter 2.

## Writing Assignments for a Descriptive Essay

Plan and illustrate your essay with one or more photographs of your own choosing. Write caption(s) for the photograph(s) that reflect your point(s).

## Considering Audience and Purpose

Assume you are a witness or victim of an ATM robbery, and authorities have asked you to write a description of the two thieves and the getaway car. Your description will be included in the official police report, will be used by a sketch artist to create a picture of the thieves and their car, and may be distributed to the media to alert the public.

## Writing for Everyday Life

Most of us have a favorite spot or place to which we return or that we reminisce about with fondness. Describe your favorite place or the favorite spot of someone you know. Write an essay that describes the site's special qualities for the regional newspaper of this favorite location.

## Writing for College Life

Assume you are writing an essay for a sociology class about popular culture. Describe a person or object that represents an aspect of pop culture: a film actor; the costume or instrument of a singing artist; a cartoon character.

## Writing for Working Life

Assume you work for a travel agency, and your clients—parents with three children ranging in ages from 3 to 15—ask you for advice about where to go for a one-week vacation. The family has expressed an interest in going someplace that offers natural beauty and outdoor activities. Write a letter to the parents describing the destination you recommend for their vacation.

## Additional Descriptive Topics

| | |
|---|---|
| A scene that provokes strong emotions | A person of interest |
| A vandalized or dilapidated neighborhood | An exotic animal and its habitat |
| Ideal gifts for a loved one | The scene after violent weather |

# Developing Your Point in a Narrative Essay

Narration is a fundamental part of everyday life.

- In your personal life, you may wish to share an important moment or event you experienced with a friend or family member in a letter or email.

- In your college life, you will study biographies and write essays about important figures in subjects such as history, science, and the arts. You will also study and narrate significant events that have occurred in various fields of study, such as wars in history or case studies in psychology.

For information on writing a narrative paragraph, see Chapter 5.

- In your working life, you may need to narrate an individual or departmental accomplishment in a report, memo, or letter.

In a **narrative essay,** a writer shows a series of events or actions that occur during a specific period of time. The writer presents an event and then shows when each of the additional events occurred in relation to it. Thus, narrative details follow a logical order based on time or chronological order. The following transition words establish the flow of ideas or coherence of a narration essay by signaling when actions or events occurred and in what order.

## Transition Words Used to Signal Narration

| | | | | |
|---|---|---|---|---|
| after | during | later | previously | ultimately |
| afterward | eventually | meanwhile | second | until |
| as | finally | next | since | when |
| before | first | now | soon | while |
| currently | last | often | then | |

# A Narrative Essay: One Writer's Response

Read the following narrative essay. Read the essay a second time, then, complete the activities and answer the questions that follow.

### The Meanest Fish

1    (1) The Gar is the ugliest of any fresh water fish—olive brown with black spots and a yellow-white belly. (2) These fish have a long crooked snout filled with irregularly spaced and very sharp teeth. (3) They also are the meanest of all fish, a fact which I discovered three days after my eleventh birthday during a fishing trip on the Tomoka River in East Central Florida.

2    (4) Like many rivers in Florida, the Tomoka is a narrow, sluggish, tea colored river that snakes its way through dense hammocks of palms, live oak, and palmettos. (5) Canoes are about the only mode of transportation that can make it through some of the long, almost impenetrable stretches of the river. (6) On weekends, we would launch off from the dock at Sanchez Park and often paddle for hours up and down the river, dropping a fishing line every now and then, and most of the time losing our bait to the catfish living along the banks. (7) This particular trip was a special one. (8) I had just received a new fishing pole for my birthday and was anxious to try it out. (9) I perched on the front seat of the canoe; my brother sat on the bottom in the middle, and my Dad took the back seat, providing most of the momentum and all of the steering. (10) My paddling was enthusiastic, but not very efficient because, whenever possible, I would pull my paddle out of the water to knock down the banana spider webs strung between the low branches of the overhanging trees. (11) I would tell

my brother that the spider was going to fall on his head. (12) He would yell and start jumping around, and then Dad would yell at him to sit still and me to stop teasing him. (13) It was all great fun!

3       (14) Eventually, we pulled around a bend in the river to a favorite fishing hole, known to be home to some extra large catfish. (15) Catfish are great because they always put up a good fight, even the small ones. (16) We decided to eat our baloney sandwiches and drink our root beer before it got too hot. (17) Of course, eager to try out my new fishing gear, I had no desire to eat and was soon threading a hunk of my baloney onto my hook. (18) Catfish will bite at just about anything, but baloney seems to be one of their favorite snacks.

4       (19) I dropped my hook in the water and was just getting ready to settle down when something hit the bait hard. (20) Suddenly, my pole was bent almost double, and I was yelling at the top of my lungs. (21) Since we were in such shallow water, I only had about six feet of line out, and when I yanked back in surprise, a huge Gar fish popped out of the water, back over my head, and into my brother's lap! (22) He started screaming at the large slimy fish, and his sandwich and root beer went sailing over his head and right into Dad's lap.

        (23) "Gar! Gar! Gar!" my brother was screaming.

        (24) "Gar! Gar! Gar!" I was screaming.

        (25) "Sit still or you'll..." was what Dad was screaming, but he didn't get to finish.

5       (26) My brother and I had sort of leapt in opposite directions so for a frozen moment the canoe was counterbalanced, but then, inevitably, time resumed, and over the canoe tipped, taking us, our lunch, our gear, and the Gar along with it. (27) Fortunately, the river was so shallow that our feet hit the mushy bottom, and before we knew what was happening, my Dad's strong hands drug us both up onto the bank. (28) As we spat out the water and baloney and caught our breath, Dad retrieved the canoe and most of our gear, and we managed to paddle back to the dock where we had put in without any more problems. (29) Soaked, covered in mud, and empty handed, we presented quite a sight for Mother when we finally showed up in the kitchen.

6       (30) It was a long while before I went fishing again. (31) My new pole had followed the Gar into some far corner of the river, and I had no desire to meet up again with the meanest of all fish.

**READING AND EVALUATING THE ESSAY**

Complete the activities below after you have read the essay a second time.

**1.** What kind of title does the writer use? _____

**2.** What type of introduction does the writer use? _____

_____

**3.** Underline the thesis statement.

**4.** For each of the body paragraphs, underline the topic sentence. Circle the narrative transition words. List two major details for each paragraph below.

Major Details (Paragraph 2): _____

_____

Major Details (Paragraph 3): _____

_____

Major Details (Paragraph 4): _____

_____

**5.** What type of conclusion does the writer use? _____

**6.** What is the purpose of the essay? Explain your answer. _____

_____

**7.** Who is the audience for the essay? Explain your answer. _____

_____

**8.** What did you like best about the essay? Why? _____

_____

_____

**9.** What about the essay could be improved? _____

_____

> For more on types of titles, introductions, and conclusions, see Chapter 14.

> For more on thesis statements, see Chapter 13.

> For more on topic sentences, see Chapter 3 and Chapter 13.

> For more on purpose and audience, see Chapter 2.

# Writing Assignments for a Narrative Essay

Plan and illustrate your essay with one or more photographs of your own choosing. Write caption(s) for the photograph(s) that reflect your point(s).

## Considering Audience and Purpose

Assume you have been asked to speak to a group of teenagers about peer influences on their development. You have decided to use a personal childhood experience to develop your ideas. Your purpose is to explain how one childhood experience with a peer influenced you.

## Writing for Everyday Life

Most of us, like the writer of "The Meanest Fish," have a vivid memory from childhood that shows the strength of our family, the joy of being young and carefree, or a challenge we have overcome. What does a vivid memory from childhood reveal about you, your family, or someone you know? Recount a vivid memory in an essay that will be published in a newsletter for family members and friends who live far away.

## Writing for College Life

Narrate an important event such as the terrorist attack on 9/11, the swearing in of the President of the United States, the launching of a space shuttle, the civil rights march on Washington and Dr. Martin Luther King's "I Have a Dream Speech," as though you had witnessed it. Write a report for your college history class about the event as you saw it unfold.

## Writing for Working Life

Assume you are applying for a management job with a retail store such as Wal-Mart, Target, or J.C.Penney.  What life and work experiences can you relate that show your ability to listen, solve problems, manage merchandise, and motivate others? Write an essay sharing an incident or series of events that show you are the best candidate for the job.

## Additional Narrative Topics

| | |
|---|---|
| A clash with authority | An ideal day or a horrible day |
| An important lesson learned | The story behind a celebrity's rise to fame |
| A life-changing experience | The time you met someone important to you |

# Developing Your Point in a Process Essay

The ability to clearly communicate the steps in a process is a basic skill for success in all areas of life.

- In your personal life, you may want to share advice with a friend or relative about how to reduce stress or how to handle a job interview.

- In your college life, many academic disciplines, such as biology, sociology, and psychology, rely on process. For example, you may be required to record the process you used in a science lab activity, or you may choose to write a research paper on the stages of grief for a psychology class.

- In your working life, you may need to write a marketing plan, an action plan, or a company procedure.

For information on writing a process paragraph, see Chapter 6.

A **process essay** shows actions that can be repeated at any time, with similar results. Like narration, a process essay is organized by time order (also called chronological order). A writer uses the process pattern of organization for three reasons:

**1.** To give steps, directions, or procedures for completing a task.

**2.** To analyze or study the steps, cycles, or phases of a process.

**3.** To explain how to complete a task and to analyze the process.

The following transition words establish the flow of ideas or coherence of a process essay.

## Transition Words Used to Signal a Process

| | | | | |
|---|---|---|---|---|
| after | during | later | previously | ultimately |
| afterward | eventually | meanwhile | second | until |
| as | finally | next | since | when |
| before | first | now | soon | while |
| currently | last | often | then | |

# A Process Essay: One Writer's Response

Read the following process essay. Read the essay a second time, then, complete the activities and answer the questions that follow.

### How to Find Your Keys

1      (1) In order to find your keys, you must first understand the important role keys play in your life. (2) Fortunately, this important role becomes abundantly clear when you are standing in the hallway ready to dash out the door for work or school and you realize your keys are missing. (3) You cannot lock your door. (4) You cannot start your car. (5) You have nothing to jangle impatiently while waiting in line at Dunkin Donuts for coffee. (6) You are going to be late. (7) Keys are indeed important. (8) However, there is no need

to panic, even though you may lose your job if you are late one more time or fail the midterm or not have time to stop at Dunkin Donuts. (9) OK, perhaps a little panic is warranted. (10) The important thing to remember is that if you approach the search for your keys calmly and logically, none of these catastrophes need occur.

2      (11) The first step is to check your person. (12) Start with your hands. (13) You would not be the first person to scour the house or apartment for something you are already holding. (14) This is very similar to the "glasses perched on top of head" phenomenon. (15) Check your pockets. (16) Better yet, empty your pockets so you don't have to guess what all that stuff in your pockets actually is just by touch. (17) Check your coat pockets. (18) Now check your other coat's pockets even though they couldn't possibly be there because you hate that coat and you never wear it. (19) If you have a purse, see appendix A, "Major Excavations." (20) These procedures will establish that you are not, in fact, in physical contact with your keys.

3      (21) Next you will undertake the process of "retracing your steps" which is essentially a form of backward time travel. (22) You may have to travel back several hours so you must be patient. (23) Sometimes it helps if you actually walk backwards, undress, climb back into bed, etc. (24) But be careful! (25) All this backward motion requires a degree of physical coordination and you haven't had your coffee yet. (26) At some point, you will probably have to venture into the dirty clothes hamper. (27) No one said finding lost keys did not require courage and fortitude. (28) If you travel all the way back to the moment when you walked in the door the previous evening and have still not located your keys, you may have to adopt a more creative strategy. (29) But first you will have to travel forward in time to get back to the present. (30) I will wait.

4      (31) As a last resort, think creatively. (32) If you have pets, remember that they always know more than they let on and should always be suspected. (33) Carefully inspect pet bedding, food bowls, and under the sofa. (34) Even if you have caged birds or fish, check the seed cup and the little castle that bubbles in the aquarium. (35) You never know. (36) If all else fails, you can resort to the SDSM or Slow Desperate Spin Maneuver. (37) This is where you stand in the middle of your apartment and slowly spin around, trying to look on every surface simultaneously, hoping for a glimpse of your keys, sparkling like a gold nugget at the bottom of a mountain stream. (38) This of course never works, but sometimes the dizziness created

by this move will jog your memory and you will remember you left your keys on the kitchen counter next to the empty peanut butter jar.

5      (39) As you can see, by following this careful and thoughtful process, you will never again be separated from your keys for very long.  (40) And keys in hand, you will stride purposefully into a bright and meaningful future or at least until you get to the donut shop.

*Practice 4*

---

### READING AND EVALUATING THE ESSAY

Complete the activities below after you have read the essay a second time.

**1.** What kind of title does the writer use? ...............................................................

**2.** What type of introduction does the writer use? ...........................................

**3.** Underline the thesis statement.

**4.** For each of the body paragraphs, underline the topic sentence. Circle the process transition words. List two major details for each paragraph below.

Major Details (Paragraph 2): .....................................................................................

Major Details (Paragraph 3): .....................................................................................

Major Details (Paragraph 4): .....................................................................................

**5.** What type of conclusion does the writer use? ..........................................

**6.** What is the purpose of the essay? Explain your answer. ........................

....................................................................................................................................................

....................................................................................................................................................

**7.** Who is the audience for the essay? Explain your answer. .......................

....................................................................................................................................................

....................................................................................................................................................

**8.** What did you like best about the essay? Why? ...........................................

....................................................................................................................................................

....................................................................................................................................................

**9.** What about the essay could be improved? .................................................

....................................................................................................................................................

For more on types of titles, introductions, and conclusions, see Chapter 14.

For more on thesis statements, see Chapter 13.

For more on topic sentences, see Chapter 3 and Chapter 13.

For more on purpose and audience, see Chapter 2.

# Writing Assignments for a Process Essay

Plan and illustrate your essay with one or more photographs of your own choosing. Write caption(s) for the photograph(s) that reflect your point(s).

## Considering Audience and Purpose

Assume you are a student-worker in the admissions and registration office at your college. You have been asked to create a brochure for students that illustrates and explains the registration process from a student's point of view. Write several paragraphs that take students through the registration process. Consider creating a brochure based on what you write.

## Writing for Everyday Life

At some point in our lives, all of us suffer the loss of a loved one or a valued object. Tell how you or someone you know coped with such a loss. Write a letter to a friend in which you share the steps you or someone you know took to overcome the grief of loss.

## Writing for College Life

Assume you are enrolled in the college class Introduction to Psychology, and your professor has assigned a chapter about stress. Your professor wants to know what you already know about stress before you read the chapter. Write an essay that explains several steps one can take to reduce stress.

## Writing for Working Life

Assume that you are on a committee at work that is looking into ways in which employees can better manage their time and increase productivity. What recommendations would you make for employees whose tasks include phone calling, emailing, writing reports, filing paperwork, and attending meetings? Interview a staff assistant (such as in the English, science, or some other department at your college) for timesaving tips on the job. Write a report in which you outline several timesaving steps. Insert the appropriate information into the following MLA citation format to document your source:

```
Last Name of Person Interviewed, First Name of Person
    Interviewed. Personal Interview. Day Month Year.
```

## Additional Process Topics

How to win an argument

How to get a promotion or recommendation

How to develop a friendship

How to save money or shop smart

How to make a piece of art, such as a print, woodcut, or an etching

How to set up a program or piece of technology (such as a cell phone, email, website, or blog)

# Developing Your Point in an Illustration Essay

Illustration may be the pattern of organization that you will use most often.

- In your personal life, think about how you often rely on examples and illustrations to make your point, such as when you recommend a restaurant or movie to a friend.

- In your college life, illustrations and examples effectively clarify a main point in all areas of study. For example, for a history class, you may choose to explain the contributions Frederick Douglass made to the civil rights of African Americans by offering several examples or illustrations.

- In your working life, examples and illustrations help prove that you or an employee under your supervision deserve a raise.

For information on writing an example paragraph, see Chapter 7.

In the illustration essay, a writer offers a focused main idea about a particular topic and then offers a series of examples or illustrations to clarify or support the main idea. Example words signal that a writer is giving an instance of a general idea.

## Transition Words Used to Signal Examples and Illustration

| | | | |
|---|---|---|---|
| an illustration | for instance | once | to illustrate |
| for example | including | such as | typically |

## An Illustration Essay: One Student Writer's Response

Read the following example and illustration essay written by student Beth Zivistski for an English class. Read the essay a second time, then, complete the activities and answer the questions that follow.

### Fads: POG-Mania

1     (1) In all areas of life, our society is constantly swept up in the latest craze, and with the rise of every new fad comes the depressing downfall of the former fad. (2) Fads make their way into the world as fast as they are shut out. (3) A fad arises out of a particular culture, becomes intensely popular for a brief time, and then loses popularity suddenly and dramatically. (4) Ironically, fad-mania blindly leads to the retirement of great ideas, such as the fabulous milk cap game now known as POGs.

2     (5) Milk cap games were an excellent example of a fad that arose out of a particular culture. (6) Milk cap games originated when milk and juice were sold in glass bottles rather than the current disposable containers. (7) This fad-game first got its name from a brand of a tropical fruit drink made up of passion fruit, orange, and

guava juice called POG. (8) Kids collected the round wax coated cardboard disks that sealed the bottles and invented simple games that everyone could play. (9) Nearly every household, rich or poor, had access to milk caps, which made the game very inclusive. (10) Children enjoyed this popular form of entertainment until the establishment of screw-on lids and disposable containers virtually put an end to milk caps and these engaging games.

3      (11) Most fads, such as milk games, began as a simple, fun idea. (12) For example, the standard rules for POG playing were simple. (13) Two or more players placed an equal number of POGs into a common stack. (14) The milk caps would be piled artwork side up on a level surface. (15) To determine who would go first, players flipped a POG or played Ro-Sham-Bo (Paper, Scissors, Rock). (16) The first player threw his or her "kini" or slammer, an object used to hit the stack of POGs. (17) Usually a slammer was bigger, thicker, and heavier than a POG, often made of plastic or different types of metal. (18) All of the milk caps that landed face down went to that player. (19) The milk caps left over were restacked for the next player's turn. (20) The players exchanged turns until every milk cap had been won, and the player with the most milk caps was the winner. (21) Like all fads, the POG craze started simply, in this instance, with children using the milk caps for inexpensive fun.

4      (22) POGs were also an illustration of the intense popularity to which a fad could rise. (23) As the fad grew in popularity, companies flooded the market with POG products. (24) In the early 1990s, a number of companies started their own series of game pieces to compete in the new craze. (25) For example, the company Tilt, Poison, and Kapz offered POGs decorated with skulls, crossbones, and eight balls. (26) Even fast food restaurants illustrated POG mania as they latched onto the new fad and included POGs in their kid's meals. (27) POGs were not just a source of entertainment through game play. (28) They became available in sets of original artwork, sports and team logos, or even pictures of the latest Saturday morning cartoons. (29) Purchasing POGs became an obsession. (30) For example, people began collecting POGs, and some felt the need to own every single POG in a series. (31) These factors made POGs collectable as well as tradable. (32) The popularity of POGs was also evident in its international following, as illustrated by the World Pog Federation (WPF), created by players who loved POGs so much that they wanted an official body to direct the craze. (33) The WPF created its own official brand that was printed with the POG logo on the back. (34) The

front artwork carried a variety of designs including cartoons, POG history, and POG incentives.

5        (35) POGs also illustrated the criticism and blame most fads face for fostering undesirable consequences and behaviors. (36) For example, many criticized POGs for fostering overspending. (37) When so many companies offered such a wide range of POG series available for purchase, expenses for a POG devotee quickly mounted up. (38) Children used their allowances to buy POGs; adults spent exorbitant amounts of money ensuring they had complete sets of brand name POGs for sports teams, athletes, or other popular cultural icons. (39) Another example of the criticism against POGs was the belief that the game was a form of gambling. (40) People would play for keeps in the hopes of enlarging their POG holdings. (41) Oftentimes, players would lose their own POGs in the process; then they would have to purchase more. (42) Many critics opposed POGs as an illustration of the antisocial behaviors that a fad can generate. (43) For example, fights sometimes broke out over POGs. (44) This game, for some children, was much more than entertainment; therefore, if these children lost a certain favored POG, they would react as children often do with tears, insults or even fists. (45) POGs, and especially slammers, were often stolen. (46) In addition, many educators complained that POG playing served as a distraction to school work. (47) Eventually, these negative aspects led to the banning of POGs by many public schools in North America.

6        (48) Like all fads, POGs decreased suddenly and dramatically in popularity. (49) Today, instead of lining the shelves in major retail markets, POGs may possibly be found on eBay or in specialty game and card shops. (50) Like fads, POG playing rose out of its culture, began as a way to have fun, reached intense heights of popularity, garnered criticism, and then faded away as just another one of those crazy trends that swept across the nation and over international borders. (51) Even so, POG playing is still fondly remembered by those who still love them to this day. (52) POGs illustrate the irony of fad-mania: the short lived devotion to a really good idea.

Practice 5

Complete the activities below after you have read the essay a second time.

**1.** What kind of title does the writer use? ..............................................................

**2.** What type of introduction does the writer use? ..................................................

**3.** Underline the thesis statement.

**4.** For each of the body paragraphs, underline the topic sentence. Circle the example or illustration transition words. List two major details for each paragraph below.

Major Details (Paragraph 2): ............................................................................

..........................................................................................................................

Major Details (Paragraph 3): ............................................................................

..........................................................................................................................

Major Details (Paragraph 4): ............................................................................

Major Details (Paragraph 5): ............................................................................

..........................................................................................................................

**5.** What type of conclusion does the writer use? ..................................................

**6.** What is the purpose of the essay? Explain your answer. ..................................

..........................................................................................................................

**7.** Who is the audience for the essay? Explain your answer. ................................

..........................................................................................................................

**8.** What did you like best about the essay? Why? ................................................

..........................................................................................................................

..........................................................................................................................

**9.** What about the essay could be improved? ......................................................

..........................................................................................................................

..........................................................................................................................

---

For more on types of titles, introductions, and conclusions, see Chapter 14.

For more on thesis statements, see Chapter 13.

For more on topic sentences, see Chapter 3 and Chapter 13.

For more on purpose and audience, see Chapter 2.

# Writing Assignments for an Illustration Essay

Plan and illustrate your essay with one or more photographs of your own choosing. Write caption(s) for the photograph(s) that reflect your point(s).

## Considering Audience and Purpose

Assume you serve as a member of the Parent-Student-Teacher Association (PSTA), and you have been asked to write a report to be submitted to the principal. The purpose of the report is to explain the improvements your group wants to be funded. Identify and illustrate the need for three improvements at the school.

## Writing for Everyday Life

Think about the creativity and cleverness of the human mind as seen through various inventions. Which invention best represents human achievement in our generation? Write an essay for your local newspaper that illustrates the most helpful invention of our time.

## Writing for College Life

Think about the importance of integrity, reliability, or candor in our culture. What three people in the news illustrate these concepts? Write an essay for a college course in ethics that gives three illustrations of people who epitomize integrity, reliability, or candor.

## Writing for Working Life

Assume that you are a local businessperson and you have been asked to share with a youth group your thoughts on the value of an education. What examples or illustrations would you choose to convince students to make education a top priority? What knowledge or skills did you gain through your education that helped you succeed in your business? Write a speech to be given to the youth and their parents in which you illustrate the importance of an education.

## Additional Illustration Topics

| | |
|---|---|
| Lack of morality on television | A healthful diet or an outlandish diet |
| The best or worst commercials | Good gifts that don't cost much money |
| Annoying or dangerous driving behaviors | Acts of kindness |

# Developing Your Point in a Classification Essay

Classification allows you to order or group your thoughts based on traits of a category.

- In your personal life, you may want to warn a young person in your family or social group about types of peer pressure or dangerous behaviors to avoid.

- In your college life, you will use classification in the sciences to write about classes of species or habitats; in the humanities, to write about styles of artists, artistic movements, modes of architecture, literature, and branches of philosophies; in business and history classes, to write about the kinds of economic systems and governments.

- In your working life, you may need to write reports that identify types of markets for your products, job descriptions based on the nature of the position you need to fill, or a cover letter that describes the set of skills you bring to the workplace.

For information on writing a classification paragraph, see Chapter 8.

Writers use the **classification essay** to sort or divide ideas into smaller groups and then describe the common traits of each subgroup. The writer lists each subgroup, describes its characteristics, and offers examples that represent the group. Because groups and subgroups are listed, transitions that suggest additional categories are often used to ensure coherence.

## Transitions Used to Signal Classification

| | |
|---|---|
| another (group, kind, type) | first (group, categories, kind, type, order) |
| characteristics | second (group, class, kind, type, traits) |

## A Classification Essay: One Student Writer's Response

Read the following classification essay written by Josiah Cobb for a music appreciation class. Read the essay a second time, then, complete the activities and answer the questions that follow.

### Types of Guitars

1     (1) When people think of guitars, they most likely think of an oldies band such as the Beatles and their guitars, or an iconic performer like B.B. King and his guitar "Lucille" or, more currently, Mark Tremonti and his signature Paul Reed Smith guitar. (2) However, most people are unaware of the differences among guitars. (3) Not all guitars are alike. (4) True, guitars share fundamental traits: they are stringed instruments with a neck, a flat back, incurving sides, and a flat peg disc with rear tuning pegs. (5) However, apart from these shared traits, a range of guitars from acoustic to electric have evolved that enable musicians to create an array of distinct sounds.

(6) Currently, four types of guitars allow musicians to produce a variety of sounds in today's music.

2          (7) The acoustic guitar is a favored instrument used in most types of current music. (8) Bands today rely on the bright sound of the acoustic guitar to fill in the gaps with the guitar's unique, deep, full sound. (9) The acoustic guitar is simply a hollow body that has a neck and a set of thick bronze strings which together produce a bigger sound than the other types of guitars. (10) Because most acoustic guitars are not amplified by an external device, their sound is not loud and often cannot compete with other instruments in a band or orchestra. (11) However, one of the secrets to a good sounding acoustic guitar is the pick-up, which detects the mechanical reverberations of the strings and acts as a microphone. (12) A pick-up is mounted on the body of the guitar close to the strings. (13) The Simon & Garfunkel folk song "Fifty-Ninth Street Bridge" offers an excellent example of the rhythmic, strumming sound created with the acoustic guitar.

3          (14) The classical or nylon guitar is a kind of acoustic guitar designed especially for finger picking, which is the art of plucking the string with the fingers instead of using a pick to strum over the strings. (15) The classical guitar has nylon strings instead of bronze strings, and the body of the classical guitar is larger than the other types of guitars. (16) This design produces a reverberation as if it were in a large room. (17) In addition, the neck of the guitar is broader than the ones on steel string guitars, allowing for more complex finger work. (18) Classical guitars do have acoustic pick-ups in them most of the time. (19) One of the most popular examples of the classical guitar's crisp, nimble tones can be heard in "Classical Gas" by Mason Williams.

4          (20) A third kind of guitar is the electric guitar. (21) The unique design of the electric guitar makes it a versatile instrument. (22) The body of the electric guitar is solid, small, and can be any shape. (23) Most electric guitars today have two pick-ups. (24) The modern day pick-ups are usually small rectangular pieces of plastic with six small magnets. (25) These pick-ups use the magnets to feel the vibrating string and then transfer the sound through an amplifier so the player can hear the pitch of the strings. (26) Many guitarists love the electric guitar because they can get any sound out of it they want. (27) For instance, by using the neck pick-up, the guitarist can get the really low end sound of a hardcore band, or by using the bridge pick-up, he

or she can get the bright high end sound of ska music. (28) The electric guitar also lets the musician mimic the sounds of other types of guitars such as the acoustic, Dobro, or the classical. (29) One illustration of a well-known song performed on the electric guitar is U2's blazing, bone-rattling song "Vertigo."

5　　　(30) A fourth type of guitar is the Dobro. (31) Though not many people know about the Dobro or think of it as a guitar, it is one of the hardest forms of guitar to learn. (32) The Dobro is an instrument that is very small and is placed on a table so the strings are parallel to the ground. (33) The player then takes a guitar pick and plucks the strings as if finger picking but with a pick. (34) In addition, instead of using fingers to produce certain pitches from the guitar, the player uses a slide. (35) A slide is usually either a small piece of wood with metal, or a glass tube into which a finger is inserted. (36) The Dobro uses an electric guitar pick-up, which gives it a country guitar sound. (37) A prime example of the Dobro twang can be heard in the classic country song "An Old Cowboy's Dream" by Don Edwards.

6　　　(38) Although guitars come in various shapes and styles and produce a wide range of sounds, each one has the same basic idea: a set of strings pulled to a certain tension to combine different pitches and create something that everyone enjoys—music.

*Practice 6*

## READING AND EVALUATING THE ESSAY

Complete the activities below after you have read the essay a second time.

**1.** What kind of title does the writer use? ........................................................................

**2.** What type of introduction does the writer use? ........................................................

**3.** Underline the thesis statement.

**4.** For each of the body paragraphs, underline the topic sentence. Circle the classification transition words. List two major details for each paragraph below.

Major Details (Paragraph 2): ........................................................................................

........................................................................................................................................

........................................................................................................................................

........................................................................................................................................

For more on types of titles, introductions, and conclusions, see Chapter 14.

For more on thesis statements, see Chapter 13.

For more on topic sentences, see Chapter 3 and Chapter 13.

Major Details (Paragraph 3): _____

_____

_____

_____

Major Details (Paragraph 4): _____

_____

_____

_____

Major Details (Paragraph 5): _____

_____

_____

_____

**5.** What type of conclusion does the writer use? _____

**6.** What is the purpose of the essay? Explain your answer. _____

> For more on purpose and audience, see Chapter 2.

_____

**7.** Who is the audience for the essay? Explain your answer. _____

_____

**8.** What did you like best about the essay? Why? _____

_____

_____

**9.** What about the essay could be improved? _____

_____

_____

*Practice 6*

# Writing Assignments for a Classification Essay

Plan and illustrate your essay with one or more photographs of your own choosing. Write caption(s) for the photograph(s) that reflect your point(s).

## Considering Audience and Purpose

Assume you are a member of Students Against Destructive Decisions (SADD). The original mission of this group focused on preventing drunk driving. However, SADD has expanded its role to include several types of destructive decisions such as underage drinking, other drug use, violence, depression, and suicide. Many people do not know about this expanded focus. To get the word out about SADD, your local chairperson has asked you to write an essay to accompany short video clips (acted out by other local members) that will be posted on YouTube.com. Your purpose is to describe the different types of destructive decisions for which SADD offers help.

## Writing for Everyday Life

Many of us have an ideal in mind when we think about a person who fulfills a particular role in our lives: a mate, a job, a teacher, a friend, and so on. What are the traits of any one of these ideals? Write a tribute to a boss, company, friend, teacher, or family member in which you describe the ideal traits of a boss, job, friend, mate, or child.

## Writing for College Life

Assume that you are a student in a college music appreciation course, and your class is discussing how types of music reveal cultural values. What types of music best reflect American culture? Write an essay for this class that identifies three or four types of American music. (Feel free to change the term "American" to reflect any culture of your choice.)

## Writing for Working Life

Assume you are an employee at a grocery store that has been receiving a record number of complaints such as the following examples: empty shelves, rude or slow cashiers, sticky floors, no one to answer questions, and so on. Write a letter for the employee suggestion box in which you classify typical customer complaints and discuss types of employee attitudes that could reduce complaints.

## Additional Classification Topics

Kinds of vacations people take

Types of technology that record or play music

The basic food groups in a balanced diet

The market for a particular product, celebrity, or experience: *Harry Potter* novels, Halle Berry, or white water rafting

Styles of personal expression: fashion, clothing, or interior design

Categories of movies, television shows, or books

# Developing Your Point in a Comparison and Contrast Essay

Many ideas become clearer when you evaluate them in relation to one another.

- In your personal life, comparing and contrasting products before a purchase makes you a wise shopper.

- In your college life, you will be asked to compare and contrast leaders, governments, cultures, literature, writers, and philosophies in a wide range of courses such as history, humanities, English, science, and economics classes.

- In your working life, you may compare and contrast bids on a job, phone or Internet services for your office, or prospective employees during an interview process.

> For information on writing a comparison and contrast paragraph, see Chapter 9.

The **comparison and contrast essay** shows the similarities and differences between or among topics based on comparable points. The following transition words signal comparison and contrast.

## Transition Words That Signal Comparison

| | | | | |
|---|---|---|---|---|
| alike | in a similar fashion | just as | resemble | similarly |
| as | in a similar way | just like | same | |
| as well as | in like manner | like | similar | |
| equally | in the same way | likewise | similarity | |

## Transition Words That Signal Contrast

| | | | |
|---|---|---|---|
| although | conversely | differently | nevertheless |
| as opposed to | despite | even though | on the contrary |
| at the same time | difference | in contrast | on the one hand |
| but | different | in spite of | on the other hand |
| by contrast | different from | instead | still |

# A Comparison and Contrast Essay: One Student Writer's Response

Read the following student comparison and contrast essay written by student J. R. Hill for an English class. Then, complete the activities and answer the questions that follow.

### Reading the Waves

1      (1) Along the edges of Florida's East coast lie miles and miles of inviting blue-green ocean water and alluring sun-bleached beaches to which thousands of bronzed surfers flock on any given day. (2) Each of these beaches varies in its sand composition, reef formations, and surfing conditions. (3) Although the East coast of Florida is made mainly of soft, sandy beaches and a hard ocean

bottom, for every mile traveled from Miami to Jacksonville, no beach along the Atlantic coast remains the same as the specific conditions change that cause waves to form and break. (4) Two main surf spots, the Ponce Inlet Jetty and the Sun Glow Pier, only a few miles apart, represent the distinctly different surfing experiences available on Florida's East coast.

2      (5) The first difference between the Ponce Inlet Jetty and the Sun Glow Pier is the shape of the beaches. (6) Many expert surfers looking for a challenge choose the Ponce Inlet Jetty because of its rocky beach formation off which waves form. (7) The Inlet has a long stretch of rocks jutting up from the beach and reaching hundreds of feet out into the ocean, creating a cove. (8) In contrast, the Sun Glow Pier does not have a rock formation hemming in an inlet off which the waves can form. (9) Instead this coast stretches out as an unbroken, barrier-free contour of beach, ideal for beginner surfers.

3      (10) The floor of the ocean and thus the depth of the water just off the coast of the Ponce Inlet Jetty and the Sun Glow Pier also differ significantly. (11) On the one hand, because of the protective jetty at Ponce Inlet, the sand on the ocean floor there does not dramatically shift so the depth of the ocean floor near the jetty remains fairly consistent and uniform. (12) On the other hand, since Sun Glow Pier does not have a rock jetty, the sand there constantly shifts and redistributes the depth of the ocean floor near the coast. (13) The few Pier pilings add to the unevenness of the water's depth. (14) Sand gathers around the pilings and leaves holes where sand is swept away between pilings.

4      (15) Not only do the beaches, ocean floor, and water depth differ, but also the formation of waves at the two locations varies greatly. (16) At the Ponce Inlet Jetty, the waves form off the rock jetty and shape into a solid, organized wave. (17) When a wave comes to shore, the jetty pushes it into an A shape, also called an A-frame wave or peak. (18) The A-frame gains size in a matter of seconds to form a clean, structured, and powerful wave. (19) The wave then breaks on

*Sun Glow Pier* beach

the fairly flat or uniform ocean bottom on top of two or three feet of water. (20) Unlike the well-formed, powerful waves of Ponce Inlet, the waves at Sun Glow have no solid objects (such as the rock jetty and the even ocean floor) off which to push. (21) Without solid objects and consistent water depth to help form it, the wave remains in its natural form. (22) In its natural form, the wave breaks in unorganized sections because the uneven depth of the ocean floor does not push the wave to break evenly. (23) The wave may look as if it is crumbling from the top to the bottom.

5       (24) The variations in the waves at these two beaches offer two very different surfing experiences. (25) The duration and flexibility of the surfer's ride differ at each location. (26) The consistent depth of water at the Ponce Inlet Jetty makes the wave break harder and faster, which enables the surfer to gain fast speeds. (27) At these fast speeds, the surfer is able to execute a great number of technical maneuvers. (28) After completing one maneuver, the surfer still has enough wave power to push through into the next maneuver. (29) Many surfers enjoy this long ride with clean conditions, making the Ponce Inlet Jetty a popular surf spot for expert surfers, as well as those who are learning to master more intricate moves. (30) In contrast, due to the uneven bottom and the unorganized, quickly crumbling waves, the waves at the Sun Glow Pier lose a great amount of power. (31) Unlike the longer ride at the Ponce Inlet Jetty, this weaker wave at the Sun Glow Pier leaves the surfer a short amount of time to complete maneuvers. (32) Generally, a surfer can only complete one or two maneuvers, and once a maneuver is completed, the surfer is left to fight for speed to continue on the wave to shore. (33) The wave at the Sun Glow Pier is great for the beginner surfer who needs to learn the basics and understand waves.

▼ *Ponce Inlet Jetty*

6       (34) The Ponce Inlet Jetty and the Sun Glow Pier, though only a few short miles apart, are two entirely different beaches. (35) These two spots are prime examples of the different surfing experiences available to surfers along Florida's East coast. (36) So before surfers grab their boards, they should carefully read their wave!

Practice 7

## READING AND EVALUATING THE ESSAY

Complete the activities below after you have read the essay a second time.

**1.** What kind of title does the writer use? ...........................................................................

**2.** What type of introduction does the writer use? ...........................................................

**3.** Underline the thesis statement.

**4.** For each of the body paragraphs, underline the topic sentence. Circle the comparison and contrast transition words. List two major details for each paragraph below.

Major Details (Paragraph 2): ...........................................................................................

.....................................................................................................................................

Major Details (Paragraph 3): ...........................................................................................

.....................................................................................................................................

Major Details (Paragraph 4): ...........................................................................................

.....................................................................................................................................

Major Details (Paragraph 5): ...........................................................................................

.....................................................................................................................................

**5.** What type of conclusion does the writer use? ...........................................................

**6.** What is the purpose of the essay? Explain your answer. ............................................

.....................................................................................................................................

**7.** Who is the audience for the essay? Explain your answer. ...........................................

.....................................................................................................................................

**8.** What did you like best about the essay? Why? ..........................................................

.....................................................................................................................................

**9.** What about the essay could be improved? ................................................................

.....................................................................................................................................

For more on types of titles, introductions, and conclusions, see Chapter 14.

For more on thesis statements, see Chapter 13.

For more on topic sentences, see Chapter 3 and Chapter 13.

For more on purpose and audience, see Chapter 2.

# Writing Assignments for a Comparison and Contrast Essay

Plan and illustrate your essay with one or more photographs of your own choosing. Write caption(s) for the photograph(s) that reflect your point(s).

## Considering Audience and Purpose

Assume you have just moved from a large city to a small town, and other members of your family or friends are considering making the same move. Write a letter that discusses the differences (or similarities) between living in a particular large city (such as Chicago, New York, or Atlanta) and living in a small town of your choice.

## Writing for Everyday Life

Assume you have an account on a social networking Web site, such as Facebook or MySpace, and you compose and post your thoughts on a regular basis. Recently, you have noticed that many of us see a tremendous change in our circumstances, attitudes, or beliefs. This week you are writing about the specific ways that you or someone you know has changed over time or due to a specific event. Contrast what someone you know or you were like earlier in life to what that person or you are like currently.

## Writing for College Life

Assume you have been working with two of your peers on a required group project and the two students differed greatly in their performance. What were the differences in their attitudes, work habits, and products? Use the goals stated on a course syllabus as the context your evaluation of their performances. Write the required report to your teacher in which you contrast your peers' performance.

## Writing for Working Life

Assume you are a realtor, and a client of yours is moving into the area from across the country. Your client has asked you to identify a couple of homes in a specific price range. You have found two homes in which your client may be interested. How do the two homes compare in terms of location, price, square footage, and special features? Write a letter to your client that compares and contrasts the two homes.

## Additional Comparison and Contrast Topics

Two pieces of music, art, or books

A scene before and after a terrible storm

Comparable products: Palm Pilots and other personal digital assistants

Communication habits of men and women

Dating customs of different cultures or generations

Disciplining children as opposed to punishing them

An original and a remade movie, or a book and a movie based on it

# Developing Your Point in a Definition Essay

You may encounter definitions most often in academic settings. However, the definition pattern of organization is also helpful in all areas of life.

- In your personal life, knowing the definition of "whole grains" and being able to identify examples that fit the definition will protect you against false advertising and enable you to make healthful choices.

- In your college life, you will be expected to know the specialized meanings and examples of many terms in each content area.

For information on writing a definition paragraph, see Chapter 10.

- In your working life, you need to understand the terms of your company's insurance policy and examples of what is covered so you can make a claim when needed or offer reasonable coverage to your employees.

In the **definition essay,** the writer explains the meaning of a new, difficult, or special term. A definition may include traits, comparisons, causes, or effects. In addition, a writer may include an explanation of what the term or concept is *not*. Examples are used to illustrate the various components or elements of the term being defined. The following key words and transition words signal the definition pattern of organization.

## Key Words and Transition Words That Signal Definition

| **Key Words:** | are | denotes | is | means |
|---|---|---|---|---|
| | connotes | indicates | is not | suggests |
| **Transition Words:** | also | in addition | one trait | |
| | another trait | in particular | specifically | |
| | for example | like | such as | |

## A Definition Essay: One Writer's Response

Read the following definition essay. Read the essay a second time, then, complete the activities and answer the questions that follow.

### Just What Is a Blog?

1      (1) What exactly is a blog?  (2) Is it a movie creature from outer space that eats clueless teenagers?  (3) Is it a Scandinavian Desert?  (4) Is it some special type of lumber?  (5) Actually, the term *blog* is a shortening of the phrase "web log."  (6) It is essentially an online journal, diary, or collection of articles, which is arranged in reverse chronological order, with the latest articles or "postings" appearing first.  (7) "Bloggers" are those individuals or groups who create blogs, and the blogs they write cover a wide range of topics, including personal observations, politics, hobbies, and even official corporate news.  (8) In the past few years, the "blogosphere," as the blog community is sometimes known, has exploded in popularity.

(9) A form of online communication, a blog serves as an important alternative source for news, opinion, and information outside the mainstream media.

2    (10) It is important to note that a blog is not a forum of hard news full of carefully verified facts. (11) Thus, a blog is not necessarily a reliable source of information, and any information gained from a blog should be checked against a known to be reliable source. (12) A blog is not private; information posted on a blog is communicated to the World Wide Web. (13) Nor does a blog necessarily offer a true portrait of a blogger. (14) Information on a blog could be erroneous, or even fictitious. (15) Understanding what a blog is not enables full and safe enjoyment of what a blog offers.

3    (16) Blogs appeal to people because of their spontaneity, informality, and passion; they reflect the fact that most of us gather and absorb information in an unstructured way. (17) First, blogs resemble informal conversations with friends, as opposed to the sanitized and filtered content of most types of media. (18) Most blogs are personal, as the following blog excerpt demonstrates: "It's funny how nothing changes between friends. (19) When Matt and Anson arrived, it was as if we had never missed a day. (20) Things just fell into place." (21) Second, blog postings are often spontaneous expressions, like views shared around the water coolers at work; some bloggers have even been fired for their off-the-cuff postings. (22) For example, Amy Nora Burch was fired for posting unflattering comments about her job at Harvard University in 2004. (23) "Most of it is total heat of the moment stuff," Burch said, according to an article published in *The Harvard Crimson*. (24) Of course not all spontaneous postings lead to such serious outcomes. (25) Third, blog postings are often fueled by controversies. (26) As blogs have grown in popularity and influence, political consultants, news services, and corporations have begun using them as tools to communicate and in some instances, manipulate. (27) When a controversial issue hits the blogs, it sometimes causes what is called a "blogstorm" or "blog swarm." (28) Such a blogstorm occurred the moment CBS national news anchor Dan Rather claimed proof that President George W. Bush received preferential treatment during his National Guard duty.

4    (29) Blogs are easy to set up and offer a rich array of options. (30) Many easy to use software packages, such as Moveable Type and Blogjet, are available for creating blogs, and the many hosting sites available for blogs such as Blogger and LiveJournal are also simple to use and free. (31) For example, the instructions to set up a blog at Blogger, (www.blogger.com), read "Create a blog in three easy steps: create an account; name your blog; choose a template." (32) In addition to being easy to set up, blogs offer a rich communication environment. (33) Because blogs are web-based, many of them take advantage of the power of hyperlinking, which allows them to link their content to other sites or other blogs dealing with similar themes or more in-depth information. (34) "Blogrolls" are lists of other blogs linked to a particular article. (35) Feedback comment systems allow blog readers to respond to postings in a blog and create a discussion thread similar to those found on online discussion boards. (36) Some blogs also incorporate audio and video content into their postings. (37) Automation tools have even been developed that allow blogs to talk to each other and keep their content updated!

5    (38) Blogs are a good example of the unexpected effects of new technologies. (39) Because of blogs, friends and family members can enjoy instant and ongoing communication. (40) Pictures of a new baby can be instantly and simultaneously shared with family members who live in various parts of the country or world. (41) Because of blogs, people who would never meet in person are able to connect online. (42) Star Wars junkies, skateboarders, vegans, dog lovers—anyone with any special interest can develop a blog and instantly connect with others who share their passion. (43) Because of blogs, information is easier to access. (44) For example, blogs provided evacuees from hurricane Katrina with coveted information about the neighborhoods and homes they had to leave behind and to which they longed to return. (45) One such blogger, Brian Oberkirch (http://slidell.weblogswork.com), offered information about and photographs of Slidell, Louisiana. (46) Blogs like this one respond to the need of the moment and offer a surprising depth of vital information, as in this case, to homeowners, employers, and employees so they could make reasonable, informed decisions about their futures.

6    (47) If you've never seen a blog before, a good place to start is Google's Blog Search. (48) There you can search blogs by keywords such as "pets" or "movies." (49) And if you have some thoughts you would like to share with the world, you might want to give blogging a try!

**READING AND EVALUATING THE ESSAY**

Complete the activities below after you have read the essay a second time.

**1.** What kind of title does the writer use? ........................................................................

**2.** What type of introduction does the writer use? ........................................................

**3.** Underline the thesis statement.

**4.** For each of the body paragraphs, underline the topic sentence. Circle the definition signal words. List two major details for each paragraph below.

Major Details (Paragraph 2): ..........................................................................................

........................................................................................................................................

Major Details (Paragraph 3): ..........................................................................................

........................................................................................................................................

Major Details (Paragraph 4): ..........................................................................................

........................................................................................................................................

Major Details (Paragraph 5): ..........................................................................................

........................................................................................................................................

**5.** What type of conclusion does the writer use? ..........................................................

**6.** What is the purpose of the essay? Explain your answer. ...........................................

........................................................................................................................................

**7.** Who is the audience for the essay? Explain your answer. ..........................................

........................................................................................................................................

**8.** What did you like best about the essay? Why? .........................................................

........................................................................................................................................

**9.** What about the essay could be improved? ...............................................................

........................................................................................................................................

For more on types of titles, introductions, and conclusions, see Chapter 14.

For more on thesis statements, see in Chapter 13.

For more on topic sentences, see Chapter 3 and Chapter 13.

For more on purpose and audience, see Chapter 2.

# Writing Assignments for a Definition Essay

Plan and illustrate your essay with one or more photographs of your own choosing. Write caption(s) for the photograph(s) that reflect your point(s).

## Considering Audience and Purpose

Assume you are in need of financial aid to continue your education, and you have found several available scholarships from a particular organization such as the following: The Hispanic Scholarship Fund, The United Negro Scholarship Fund, The Organization of Chinese Americans, or the Truman Scholarship. All of these scholarships require essays. Most of these essays ask candidates to define some aspect of themselves. Adapt one of the following topics to the organization of your choice, and write an essay to compete for a scholarship:

**1.** Define your heritage based on its significance.

**2.** Define yourself as a leader.

**3.** Define the kind of contribution you hope to make.

## Writing for Everyday Life

Assume a couple in your family or the family of someone you know is going to celebrate their 50th anniversary and their union has served as a model of a strong and loving relationship. What would you say has made their partnership so successful? Write the text for a speech you will deliver at their anniversary celebration in which you define *partnership* and honor their life together.

## Writing for College Life

Assume that in a college health class you have been studying about the connection between the mind and body and how important self-understanding is to a healthful lifestyle. How well do you know yourself? What brings you joy? What is your idea of a fulfilling, purposeful life? What is your mission? How do you want to be remembered? Write an essay that expresses a mission statement for your life in which you define your ideals and goals.

## Writing for Working Life

Assume you are starting a small business, such as a restaurant, a fitness club, a toy store, or some kind of specialty shop. To receive financial backing from investors, you have been asked to write a mission statement for your business. Write an essay that defines your small business. What service or commodity are you selling? Who are your potential customers? Why is this service or commodity needed? Where is the best location for your business? How will your product or service be superior to other similar products or services?

## Additional Definition Topics

A computer term such as a computer virus, spam, or search engine

A disorder such as insomnia, anorexia, Type 2 Diabetes, or Seasonal Affective Disorder

A natural phenomenon such as a sinkhole, tropical depression, fault line, or coral reef

# Developing Your Point in a Cause and Effect Essay

Understanding the relationship between cause and effect is a vital critical thinking skill that enhances all areas of life.

- In your personal life, understanding the cause of a misunderstanding, or recognizing the effect of an over-the-counter or prescription drug can protect your relationships and your health.

- In your college life, you will be asked to analyze the causes and effects of wars, inventions, discoveries, natural disasters, economic recessions, or mental and physical diseases. An analysis of causes and effects deepens your understanding of information in every content area.

- In your working life, to ensure success you need to understand why a product sells, reasons for poor performance, or the effects of decisions on employee morale or the company's budget.

> For information on writing a cause and effect paragraph, see Chapter 11.

A writer uses the **cause and effect essay** to explore why something happened or what results came from an event. A cause explores the reason something happens, and an effect examines the result or outcome. The following transition words signal cause and effect.

## Transitions That Signal Cause and Effect

| | | | | | |
|---|---|---|---|---|---|
| accordingly | because of | due to | leads to | since | therefore |
| as a result | consequently | if…then | results in | so | thus |

## A Cause and Effect Essay: One Writer's Response

Read the following cause and effect essay from the National Institute on Alcohol Abuse and Alcoholism. Read the essay a second time, then, complete the activities and answer the questions that follow.

### Alcoholism: Getting the Facts

1    (1) For most people who drink, alcohol is a pleasant accompaniment to social activities. (2) Moderate alcohol use—up to two drinks per day for men and one drink per day for women and older people—is not harmful for most adults. (3) (A standard drink is one 12-ounce bottle or can of either beer or wine cooler, one 5-ounce glass of wine, or 1.5 ounces of 80-proof distilled spirits.) (4) Nonetheless, a large number of people get into serious trouble because of their drinking. (5) Currently, nearly 17.6 million adult Americans abuse alcohol or are alcoholic. (6) Several million more adults engage in risky drinking that could lead to alcohol problems. (7) These patterns include binge drinking and heavy drinking on a regular basis. (8) In addition, 53 percent of men and women in the United States report that one or more of their close relatives has a drinking problem. (9) Due to the scope of this problem, it

is important to understand the effects of alcoholism and alcohol abuse, as well as identify their causes.

**2**     (10) Alcoholism, also known as "alcohol dependence," is a disease with at least four recognizable effects or symptoms. (11) One impact of alcoholic dependence is a strong craving for alcohol. (12) An alcoholic feels a strong need, or compulsion, to drink. (13) Another impact is a loss of control: alcoholics cannot limit their drinking on any given occasion. (14) People who are not alcoholic sometimes do not understand why an alcoholic can't just "use a little willpower" to stop drinking. (15) However, alcoholism has little to do with willpower. (16) Alcoholics are in the grip of a powerful craving that can be as strong as the need for food or water. (17) Third, alcohol dependence eventually results in physical dependence: withdrawal symptoms, such as nausea, sweating, shakiness, and anxiety, occur when an alcoholic stops drinking. (18) Finally, a tolerance for alcohol develops. (19) Thus the need to drink greater amounts of alcohol in order to "get high" occurs.

**3**     (20) Alcohol abuse differs from alcoholism in that it does not result in an extremely strong craving for alcohol, loss of control over drinking, or physical dependence. (21) Alcohol abuse, a pattern of drinking, leads to one or more of the following four situations within a 12-month period. (22) Alcohol abuse often leads to failure to fulfill major work, school, or home responsibilities. (23) Drinking occurs in situations that are physically dangerous, such as while driving a car or operating machinery. (24) Alcohol-related legal problems are recurring, such as being arrested for driving under the influence of alcohol or for physically hurting someone while drunk. (25) Finally, drinking continues despite ongoing relationship problems that are caused or worsened by the drinking. (26) Although alcohol abuse is basically different from alcoholism, many effects of alcohol abuse are also experienced by alcoholics.

**4**     (27) The long-term consequences of alcohol misuse are serious —in many cases, life threatening. (28) Heavy drinking can increase the risk for certain cancers, especially those of the liver, esophagus, throat, and larynx (voice box). (29) Heavy drinking can also cause liver cirrhosis, immune system problems, brain damage, and harm to the fetus during pregnancy. (30) In addition, drinking increases the risk of death from automobile crashes as well as recreational and on-the-job injuries. (31) Furthermore, both homicides and suicides are more likely to be committed by persons who have been drinking. (32) In purely economic terms, alcohol-related problems cost society approximately $185 billion per year. (33) In human terms, the costs cannot be calculated.

**5**      (34) Many people wonder why some individuals can use alcohol without problems but others cannot. (35) Alcohol misuse occurs for several reasons. (36) One important reason has to do with genetics. (37) Scientists have found that having an alcoholic family member makes it more likely that if a person chooses to drink he or she too may develop alcoholism. (38) Genes, however, are not the whole story. (39) In fact, scientists now believe that certain factors in a person's environment influence whether a person with a genetic risk for alcoholism ever develops the disease. (40) A person's risk for developing alcoholism can increase based on the person's environment, including where and how he or she lives; family, friends, and culture; peer pressure; and even how easy it is to get alcohol.

**6**      (41) Those who choose to ignore these facts about alcoholism and alcohol abuse may be the very ones who will suffer the devastating effects associated with drinking-related problems.

—Adapted from "Getting the Facts," National Institute on Alcohol Abuse and Alcoholism (2001)

*Practice 9*

## READING AND EVALUATING THE ESSAY

Complete the activities below after you have read the essay a second time.

**1.** What kind of title does the writer use? _____

**2.** What type of introduction does the writer use? _____

_____

**3.** Underline the thesis statement.

**4.** For each of the body paragraphs, underline the topic sentence. Circle the cause and effect transition words. List two major details for each paragraph below.

Major Details (Paragraph 2): _____

_____

Major Details (Paragraph 3): _____

_____

Major Details (Paragraph 4): _____

_____

Major Details (Paragraph 5): _____

**5.** What type of conclusion does the writer use? _____

**6.** What is the purpose of the essay? Explain your answer. _____

_____

**7.** Who is the audience for the essay? Explain your answer. _____

_____

**8.** What did you like best about the essay? Why? _____

_____

**9.** What about the essay could be improved? _____

_____

For more on types of titles, introductions, and conclusions, see Chapter 14.

For more on thesis statements, see Chapter 13.

For more on topic sentences, see Chapter 3 and Chapter 13.

For more on purpose and audience, see Chapter 2.

# Writing Assignments for a Cause and Effect Essay

Plan and illustrate your essay with one or more photographs of your own choosing. Write caption(s) for the photograph(s) that reflect your point(s).

## Considering Audience and Purpose

Assume you are a volunteer with an organization such as Meals on Wheels, Habitat for Humanity, or Scouts, or that you volunteer at a particular place such as a school, hospital, or animal shelter. You have been asked to give a speech to an audience of college students to raise awareness about volunteering. Write a speech that discusses the need for and benefits of volunteering.

## Writing for Everyday Life

Many of us have rebelled against our parents (or another authority figure) or know someone who has. What are some of the things against which youth rebel? Why? Is most youthful rebellion harmless or are serious long-term effects more likely? Why? Write an encouraging letter to a young person who is in conflict with authority that explains some of the causes and possible effects of youthful rebellion.

## Writing for College Life

Assume you are enrolled in a sociology class discussing the ways in which technology has changed society during your lifetime or over the lifetime of your grandparents. What are some of the intended benefits or unexpected outcomes of having televisions, automobiles, dishwashers, digital recorders, cell phones, iPods, or other pieces of technology? Write an essay for this class explaining the effects of a specific piece of technology on modern culture.

## Writing for Working Life

Assume your company has asked you to speak about the "elements of success" during an employee training day.  Think of highly successful people such as Oprah Winfrey, Bill Gates, Rita Rossi Colwell, Michael Jordan, Hillary Rodham Clinton, Reverend Billy Graham, or Soraya.  What motivates or drives people to such high levels of success? Write a speech to motivate a group of work colleagues by explaining the reasons for success.

## Additional Cause and Effect Topics

Excessive mood swings or compulsive behavior

Low or high self-esteem

Benefits of a particular exercise: walking, jogging, so on

Benefits of humor

A natural disaster such as a hurricane, tornado, or tsunami

Benefits of team sports

Addiction to or withdrawal from a drug such as nicotine or caffeine

# Developing Your Point in a Persuasive Essay

Persuasion is used in every aspect of life.

For information on writing a persuasive paragraph, see Chapter 12.

- In your personal life, you come across attempts to persuade you in magazine, radio, and television advertisements. As a parent, you may persuade your children to eat healthful foods and get lots of exercise. Or you may persuade your partner to go on a much needed vacation.

- In your college life, you will be asked to take stands on issues in all the areas you study. For example, in a social science class, you may want to argue for or against gun control or in a science class, you may take a stand for or against cloning.

- In your working life, you use persuasion when you try to convince a prospective employer that you are the best candidate for the job. Or you may need to write your own advertisement to get people to come to your store or restaurant.

In a **persuasive essay,** a writer takes a strong stand on a debatable issue and offers thoughtful, convincing reasons in its support. To create a credible argument, a writer uses facts and examples, offers expert and informed opinions, considers consequences, and answers the opposition. The following transitions signal persuasion.

## Transition Words Used to Signal Persuasion

| | | | | |
|---|---|---|---|---|
| accordingly | even so | in conclusion | nonetheless | therefore |
| admittedly | finally | indeed | obviously | thus |
| although | first (second, third, etc.) | of course | to be sure |
| because | for | in fact | on the one hand | truly |
| but | furthermore | in summary | on the other hand | undoubtedly |
| certainly | granted | last | since | |
| consequently | hence | meanwhile | some believe | |
| despite | however | nevertheless | some may say | |

## A Persuasion Essay: One Writer's Response

Read the following persuasion essay. Read the essay a second time, then, complete the activities and answer the questions that follow.

### Ban Cell Phones: Save Lives

1       (1) No one understands the dangers of using a cell phone while driving better than Rob and Patti Pena. (2) On November 3, 1999, their 2-year-old daughter Morgan Lee died as a result of injuries sustained in a car crash the previous day. (3) As she sat securely strapped into her car seat in the back seat of her mother's car, a driver who ran a stop sign while using his cellular phone broadsided their car. (4) The only legal penalty the driver faced was a $50 fine and two traffic tickets.

(5) Regrettably, the tragic loss of Morgan Lee is not an isolated case. (6) According to a study by the Harvard Center for Risk Analysis, researchers estimated that the use of cell phones by drivers caused approximately 2,600 deaths. (7) Cell phone use while driving should be banned.

2       (8) Of course, not everyone agrees that talking on a cell phone while driving should be outlawed. (9) In fact, many believe that this behavior is no more dangerous than the many other tasks drivers perform while driving. (10) Obviously, drivers constantly multitask as they eat, fiddle with the radio or air conditioner, light a cigarette, apply makeup, read a map, and converse with their passengers. (11) Obviously, common sense dictates that these tasks should be kept to a minimum. (12) Certainly, any activity that absorbs a driver's attention has the potential to adversely affect the driver's control of the vehicle and reaction to hazards and traffic signals. (13) However, to suggest that one set of careless behaviors excuses another reckless behavior defies common sense. (14) Common sense also suggests that the dangers posed by these distractions do not compare to the dangers posed by using a cell phone while driving.

3       (15) Human Factors experts study the relationship between human limitations and the design of technology. (16) These experts note that drivers face visual, auditory, mechanical, and cognitive distractions. (17) Using a cell phone while driving incorporates every one of these distractions. (18) Darla Burton offers an excellent example of how using a cell phone while driving combines all four.

4       (19) The cell phone in Darla's purse rings as she speeds down the Interstate. (20) Immediately, she becomes visually distracted as she takes her eyes off the road and leans across the front seat to grab her purse. (21) The insistent ringing serves as an auditory alarm that urges her to hurry her movements. (22) As she rummages for the phone in her purse and fumbles with the mechanics of opening and answering the flip phone, she swerves out of her lane. (23) A passing motorist blares his car's horn in warning; Darla jerks her car back into her own lane. (24) The caller is her boyfriend, and with an angry voice, he continues an argument that began days ago. (25) Darla, distracted cognitively as she argues with her boyfriend, becomes lost in the conversation and unaware of her bearings. (26) Suddenly, she notices that her exit is looming quickly. (27) Without thinking or looking in her rear view and side mirrors, she veers across three lanes to make the exit. (28) Luckily, she narrowly avoids sideswiping another vehicle.

(29) Darla's behavior is typical of many people who use a cell phone while driving.

5       (30) Those who oppose banning cell phone use while driving argue that hands-free cell phones reduce these risks, and they do, but not enough. (31) Hands-free cell phones may limit visual and mechanical distractions, but auditory and cognitive distractions are still issues of concern. (32) Some believe that these distractions are no different than the distraction of talking with a passenger in the car. (33) However, talking on a cell phone is significantly different than talking with a passenger in a car. (34) First, a passenger in a vehicle often contributes to the safety of the driving situation by providing an additional set of eyes and ears to warn against road hazards. (35) When a driving situation demands the focused attention of the driver, a passenger in the car helps control the flow of conversation so that the driver can safely attend to the task of driving. (36) In addition, most people are conditioned to immediately respond to a ringing phone. (37) This need to answer often overrides convenience or safety issues and drags attention away from the challenges of the road.

6       (38) The sheer number of cell phone users also adds to the seriousness of the problem. (39) There are currently 190 million cell phone users in this country alone. (40) A record 24 million new cell phone subscribers signed up between June 2004 and June 2005. (41) According to a 1995 *Prevention Magazine* survey, 85% of cell phone owners drive while using their cell phones. (42) If that trend has continued, then about 162 million drivers currently talk on their phones while driving, at least some of time. (43) In addition, current in-car communication services allow users to check e-mail and calendars, surf the web, and even send faxes while driving. (44) The wireless industry plans to offer an even wider range of mobile options such as digital streaming, which have the potential to further distract drivers.

7       (45) Remember Morgan Lee Pena and the thousands of other possible victims of someone's need to stay plugged in. (46) Join the fight to ban cell phone use while driving. (47) Write to your politicians, and tell them to support cellular phone legislation. (48) Urge them to ban cell phone use while driving and to enact strong penalties against violators. (49) Write to your cellular provider and ask the company to support laws that restrict cellular phone use while driving. (50) Finally, if you take a cell phone with you in your car, set a good example; pull over and stop before you make or take a call. (51) Tell your friends and family to do the same for their safety and the safety of others. (52) Stay safe! (53) Save lives! (54) Don't talk; just drive!

**READING AND EVALUATING THE ESSAY**

Complete the activities below after you have read the essay a second time.

**1.** What kind of title does the writer use? ........................................................................................

**2.** What type of introduction does the writer use? ........................................................................

**3.** Underline the thesis statement.

**4.** For each of the body paragraphs, underline the topic sentence. Circle the persuasion signal words. List two major details for each paragraph below.

Major Details (Paragraph 2): ........................................................................................................................

........................................................................................................................................................................

Major Details (Paragraph 3): ........................................................................................................................

Major Details (Paragraph 4): ........................................................................................................................

Major Details (Paragraph 5): ........................................................................................................................

........................................................................................................................................................................

Major Details (Paragraph 6): ........................................................................................................................

........................................................................................................................................................................

........................................................................................................................................................................

**5.** What type of conclusion does the writer use? ..........................................................................

**6.** What is the purpose of the essay? Explain your answer. ........................................................

........................................................................................................................................................................

........................................................................................................................................................................

**7.** Who is the audience for the essay? Explain your answer. ......................................................

........................................................................................................................................................................

**8.** What did you like best about the essay? Why? ........................................................................

**9.** What about the essay could be improved? ..............................................................................

> For more on types of titles, introductions, and conclusions, see Chapter 14.

> For more on thesis statements, see Chapter 13.

> For more on topic sentences, see Chapter 3 and Chapter 13.

> For more on purpose and audience, see Chapter 2.

# Writing Assignments for a Persuasive Essay

Plan and illustrate your essay with one or more photographs of your own choosing. Write caption(s) for the photograph(s) that reflect your point(s).

## Considering Audience and Purpose

Assume you are a reporter for your college's newspaper. Identify a problem that affects many people on your campus, such as poor lighting in the parking lot, inadequate parking, or poor food service. Write a column calling for administrative action to correct the problem. Your purpose is to offer compelling evidence that action must be taken.

## Writing for Everyday Life

Think about the amount of graphic violence and sexual content on television shows and the numbers of hours people spend watching these images. Should sponsors such as Kellogg, Nike, McDonald's, and Wal-Mart support shows that contain graphic violent and sexual content? Write a letter to a company that sponsors a particularly graphic television show to persuade the company to withdraw its sponsorship.

## Writing for College Life

Assume you are taking a sociology course, and you have been studying about the impact of clothes (or fashion) on human behavior. Your professor directs your attention to Northwest High School, where school uniforms will soon be required. What are some of the reasons administrators and parents might have for supporting school uniforms, and what are some of the reasons students may oppose them? Write a letter to the principal of the school taking a strong stand for or against school uniforms for students attending Northwest High School.

## Writing for Working Life

Assume you are the manager of a retail store in a local mall, and one of your employees has consistently performed at a high level. Write a letter to your supervisor in which you recommend a promotion and raise for your employee.

## Additional Persuasive Topics

Animal testing for cosmetic or medical research

Manned space flights

Abstinence-only sex education courses

Stricter gun laws

Surveillance cameras installed in all public places

Decriminalization of marijuana

# Developing Your Point in a Layered-Plan Essay

Often, writers find that the most effective way to express their view about a particular topic is to layer several patterns of organization into one essay.

- In your personal life, you may find it necessary to write an apology for a misunderstanding with a family member or friend. In your letter, you may find it helpful to discuss the *types* of stresses you have been facing, the *effects* such stresses have had upon you, and the *reasons* you value your friend or family member.

- In your college life, you will combine patterns of organization as you study topics in greater depth. For example, in humanities you may choose to write about the *origin*, *types*, and *impact* of art or artifacts produced by a particular culture.

- In your working life, you may need to write a report that *defines* a problem, *compares* several solutions, and *recommends* a course of action.

In an **essay that layers patterns of organization**, a writer divides the topic into subsections based on a series of patterns of organization best suited for each paragraph that develops the main point. For example, "alcoholism," discussed in an earlier essay by using causes and effects, could also be discussed by layering several patterns of organization. As a disease, alcoholism has recognizable stages or cycles that could be discussed using process. In addition, several types of treatment are available and could be discussed using classification. Or perhaps sharing personal testimonies or case histories of recovering alcoholics in the form of narratives could convince someone to seek help. Many other topics also can be developed in greater depth by layering plans.

Transition words used within each paragraph signal the type of pattern of organization used to develop that particular paragraph. Therefore, draw from the lists of transitions given throughout this chapter for each of the specific patterns of organization as needed.

# A Layered-Plan Essay: One Student Writer's Response

Study the following layered-plan essay written by student Doug Frazier. Read the essay a second time, then, complete the activities and answer the questions that follow.

### The Games People Play

1    (1) Games have always been a part of human culture. (2) Archeologists have uncovered the use of board games as far back as 4000 B.C. in ancient Babylonia. (3) While board games apparently appeared as the first type of game, other forms such as card games and tiled games evolved as people began to understand, enjoy, and develop the concept of games. (4) The variety and enjoyment of games expanded as technology advanced through the millennia.

(5) Most recently, over the past 30 years, the newest and perhaps most radical change to games has occurred with the invention of the computer video game. (6) The advent of computer video games enabled a significant jump in gaming evolution. (7) While video games share many of the same traits as traditional games, the distinct qualities of computer games intensify both the dangers and the pleasures of gaming.

2    (8) To appreciate the impact of video games on the gaming experience, a general understanding of a few types and features of traditional games is necessary. (9) Overall, traditional games often reflect three types of intense, real-life experiences: physical combat or skill, intellectual strategy, and chance. (10) The group of games based on physical skills is made up of a wide range of activities such as races, archery, and darts; the outcome of these games relies upon the physical abilities of the players. (11) Another group of games are based on strategy, such as chess, and rely upon the player's ability to make rational decisions. (12) Many games combine the first two types of games so that players need both physical skill and strategy to win such as in organized sports like soccer, baseball, and football. (13) The third type of game utilizes chance and often uses dice or some kind of random number selection that dictates the outcome; examples of these games include bingo and lotteries. (14) Often games of chance also combine with strategy, so that knowledge or skill helps determine the outcome. (15) For example, through a series of plays, Monopoly and poker combine chance and strategy to determine a winner.

3    (16) All of these traditional games share a few basic traits. (17) First, games usually offer an avatar or icon that represents the player; in Monopoly the original avatars were metal tokens based on objects found in households across America (the flat iron, purse, lantern, car, thimble, shoe, top hat, and the rocking horse); in sports the avatars are the team's name and mascot like the Eagle for the Philadelphia Eagles in the National Football League. (18) Traditional games, also, present an environment that challenges the players or allows the players to challenge each other, and traditional games keep track of the player's success or scores. (19) In addition, traditional games foster social interaction; part of the fun of playing is experiencing the game with someone else.

**4**      (20) A comparison of traditional games to video games finds many similarities. (21) Just like traditional games, video games offer avatars. (22) For example, in the video game *King Kong* based on director Peter Jackson's version of the classic story, players can choose the adventurer Jack Driscoll as the avatar, or choose Kong, thus playing the game through the eyes of the ape. (23) Both traditional and video games present environments in which challenges are posed by the game player and opponent; in addition, both traditional and video games keep track of a player's success or score and reward the players when they overcome challenges or challengers. (24) Moreover, video games actually combine physical skill, strategy, and chance. (25) Physical skill is needed to rapidly figure out and adapt to the immense amount of visual information provided on the video screen. (26) In addition, the player must make rational decisions based on this information and make moves in a logical sequence. (27) Thus video games, like many traditional games, require strategy. (28) Finally, many video games are programmed to allow apparently random events to occur, so they are similar to games of chance as well.

**5**      (29) Although traditional and video games are similar, they do indeed differ in drastic ways. (30) Traditional games are much more unpredictable than video games. (31) Traditional board and card games require other players to enrich the environment and to create the uncertainty which generates the fun. (32) Video games, on the other hand, are a form of artificial intelligence (A.I.) programmed into the computer. (33) While A.I. is impressive, it is ultimately limited and lacks the unpredictable flexibility of human thought; therefore, the outcomes of the challenges are ultimately much more predictable. (34) Traditional games and video games differ in the social experiences they offer. (35) A.I. fosters an antisocial experience. (36) Often, video players do not need other players. (37) Traditionally, games have been seen as such an enjoyable activity partly because of the time spent making and enjoying friends. (38) During this time, players learn how to win and lose with dignity and to respect the integrity of others. (39) In contrast, many video games absorb individual players in countless hours of isolated play. (40) The great majority of these games also demand that players engage in simulated antisocial acts of murder and mayhem. (41) For example, "Carmageddon" is described on the package as "The racing game for the chemically imbalanced." (42) The goal of this gory video game is to "waste contestants, pedestrians, and farmyard animals for points and credit."

(43) Some critics of video games consider these differences from traditional games alarming and dangerous.

**6** (44) Experts warn that violent video games can have a negative impact. (45) These types of video games may increase aggressive thoughts, feelings, and behaviors; arouse hostility; and decrease helping behaviors. (46) Because video game players must make active decisions to choose violent strategies to win, players may learn that violence is fun and rewarding. (47) Another negative effect may be that players become numbed or blunted emotionally to violence and come to accept violence as a normal part of life. (48) Because players view violence as inevitable, they may not develop the skills needed to make nonviolent choices when they are faced with real life challenges.

**7** (49) The ways in which video games differ from traditional games may present some reasons for caution; still the distinctive nature of video games offers some positive pleasures. (50) A video game player often learns how to play the game through trial and error by playing. (51) So video games are fun to explore. (52) As the player explores the world of the video game, he or she must rethink choices and come up with strategies based on new information. (53) In addition, to achieve ultimate victory, a player must think about the short-term and long-term effects of each decision or move in the game. (54) Finally, many players enjoy figuring out the limits of the game. (55) The fun lies in figuring how the game's program works and if there are any flaws in the program. (56) Thus, video games make critical thinking enjoyable.

**8** (57) Traditional and computer games share many traits. (58) Both require physical skill, chance, and strategy to win. (59) However, video games offer a different kind of gaming experience. (60) Video games are often violent and antisocial by nature, yet they make problem solving a fun activity. (61) Some critics consider video games far more dangerous than traditional games.

*Practice 11*

**READING AND EVALUATING THE ESSAY**

Complete the activities below after you have read the essay a second time.

**1.** What kind of title does the writer use? ......................................................................

**2.** What type of introduction does the writer use? ...................................................

**3.** Underline the thesis statement.

**4.** For each of the body paragraphs, underline the topic sentence. Circle the layered-plan signal words. List two major details for each paragraph below.

Major Details (Paragraph 2): ..............................................................................................

......................................................................................................................................................

Major Details (Paragraph 3): ..............................................................................................

......................................................................................................................................................

Major Details (Paragraph 4): ..............................................................................................

......................................................................................................................................................

Major Details (Paragraph 5): ..............................................................................................

......................................................................................................................................................

Major Details (Paragraph 6): ..............................................................................................

Major Details (Paragraph 7): ..............................................................................................

......................................................................................................................................................

**5.** What type of conclusion does the writer use? .....................................................

**6.** What is the purpose of the essay? Explain your answer. ..................................

......................................................................................................................................................

**7.** Who is the audience for the essay? Explain your answer. ...............................

......................................................................................................................................................

**8.** What did you like best about the essay? Why? ..................................................

**9.** What about the essay could be improved? .............................................................

> For more on types of titles, introductions, and conclusions, see Chapter 14.

> For more on thesis statements, see Chapter 13.

> For more on topic sentences, see Chapter 3 and Chapter 13.

> For more on purpose and audience, see Chapter 2.

# Writing Assignments for a Layered-Plan Essay

Plan and illustrate your essay with one or more photographs of your own choosing. Write caption(s) for the photograph(s) that reflect your point(s).

## Considering Audience and Purpose

Assume you are a dissatisfied customer with several complaint issues, and you are writing a formal complaint to the manager. Identify the types of complaints you have; discuss the causes of your dissatisfaction, and list the steps you expect the manager to take to rectify the situation.

## Writing for Everyday Life

Technological advances are rapidly accelerating. How important is it to stay abreast of the new technologies? Why? What are the types of new technologies, such as podcasting or multimedia cell phones? Which ones are most accessible, easy to use, affordable, or important? Why? Write a consumer report for an online posting in which you analyze the importance of keeping up with technology.

## Writing for College Life

Assume you are taking a college humanities course, and you have been studying the concept of cultural traditions. Many of us have favorite traditions or rituals that have been handed down to us by our families or cultures. How does a tradition or ritual reflect a particular family, culture, heritage, or value? Write an essay in which you analyze the significance of a particular ritual or tradition.

## Writing for Working Life

Assume you work in an environment full of conflict, and you have learned effective conflict resolution skills. Identify some typical conflicts that occur on a particular job: Between a team supervisor and a team member at a car dealership? Between a waiter and a diner? Between colleagues at a walk-in health clinic? What causes these conflicts? What are the steps to effective conflict resolution? Write a report for a supervisor that documents a conflict, evaluates the causes of the conflict, and recommends steps to resolve the conflict.

## Additional Layered-Plan Topics

| | |
|---|---|
| Minimum wage | Inspiring or effective teachers |
| National identity cards | A popular public figure |
| A living will | Internet fraud |

*Review*

**REVIEW:** MAKING YOUR POINT USING PATTERNS OF ORGANIZATION

Complete the chart by filling in the blanks with information from the chapter:

**A descriptive essay** describes a person, place, or object based on its location or the way it is arranged in ..................... ; relies upon ..................... details such as sight, sound, smell, taste, and touch to create vivid mental images so that the reader can see what is being described.

**A narrative essay** shows a series of ..................... or actions that occur during a specific period of .....................

**A process essay** shows actions in time order (also called chronological order) that can be repeated at any time, with similar results for three reasons:

    **1.** To give steps, ....................., or procedures for completing a task.

    **2.** To analyze or study the steps, ....................., or phases of a process.

    **3.** To explain how to complete a task and to analyze the process.

**An illustration essay** offers a focused main idea about a particular topic and then offers a series of ..................... or ..................... to clarify or support the main idea.

**A classification essay** sorts or divides ideas into smaller groups and then describes the common ..................... of each subgroup. The writer lists each ....................., describes its characteristics, and offers examples that represent the group. Because groups and subgroups are listed, transitions that suggest additional categories are often used to ensure coherence.

**A comparison and contrast essay** shows the ..................... and ..................... between or among two topics based on comparable points.

**A definition essay** explains the meaning of a new, difficult, or special ......................
A definition may include traits, comparisons, causes, or effects. In addition, a writer may include an explanation of what the term or concept is ...................... Examples are used to illustrate the various components or elements of the term being defined.

**A cause and effect essay** discusses why something happened or what results came from an event. A cause explores the ..................... something happens, and an effect examines the ..................... or outcome.

**A persuasive essay** takes a strong stand on a debatable issue and offers thoughtful, convincing reasons in its support. To create a credible argument, a writer uses ..................... and ....................., offers expert and informed ....................., considers consequences, and answers the ......................

**A layered-plan essay** divides the topic into subsections based on a ..................... of ..................... of organization best suited for each paragraph that develops the main point.

REVISING

# PART 4

# Mastering Grammar, Punctuation, and Mechanics with MyWritingLab

# 16

### Preview

- Subjects
- Verbs
- The Simple Sentence

# Subjects, Verbs, and Simple Sentences

A simple sentence, also called an *independent clause*, includes a subject and verb and expresses a complete thought.

## Subjects

A **subject** is the person, place, object, or topic about which a writer expresses a focused thought or makes an assertion. To identify a subject, ask: Who or what did this? Alternatively, ask: Who or what is this?

### Simple Subjects

- **Simple Subject, Type 1:** A single person, place, object, or topic is the focus of thought.

SUBJECT→ Wilma Mankiller served as the first female

chief of the Cherokee Nation from 1985–1995.

Make a difference by voting.

← *"YOU" IS UNDERSTOOD, BUT NOT STATED, AS THE SUBJECT OF THE SENTENCE, WHICH IS A COMMAND.*

### Compound Subject

Two or more people, places, objects, or topics are the subjects of a focused thought.

*COMPOUND SUBJECTS*

Florida, Texas, and California lead the national

growth of online banking.

*COMPOUND SUBJECTS ARE OFTEN JOINED BY THE COORDINATING CONJUNCTION "AND."*

## Verbs

A **verb** makes an assertion about a subject. Three basic types of verbs include **linking verbs, action verbs,** and **helping verbs.** (See Chapters 25–26 for more information about verbs.)

### Linking Verbs

A **linking verb** connects the subject to a word that renames, describes, or defines the subject. Linking verbs often describe a state of being.

### Some Common Linking Verbs Are

*am, is, are, was, were, am being, has been…*

SUBJECT          LINKING VERB

The ice cream is cold and sweet.

## Action Verbs

An **action verb** shows the behavior of the subject.

*SUBJECT*          *ACTION VERB*

Justin and Mia prepared their house for the

upcoming storm.

## Helping Verbs

A **helping verb** is used with a main verb to create a verb phrase. Helping verbs are also used to form questions. The verbs *be, do,* and *have* can be used alone or as helping verbs.

┌──── *VERB PHRASE* ────┐

*HELPING VERB*      *MAIN VERB*

Jermaine has prepared a supply kit in case of an emergency.

# The Simple Sentence

A **simple sentence** is a group of related words that includes a subject and verb and expresses a complete thought. A simple sentence is also known as an **independent clause**. An idea that is missing a subject or verb is a fragment or incomplete thought.

## Distinguishing between a Fragment and the Simple Sentence

> For more information on correcting fragments, see Chapter 22.

**Fragment with missing subject:**

*VERB*

Uses her status as a superstar to bring media

attention to refugees around the world.

**Fragment with missing verb:**

*SUBJECT*

Angelina Jolie using her status as a superstar to bring

media attention to refugees around the world.

**Simple Sentence:**

*SUBJECT*          *VERB*

Angelina Jolie uses her status as a superstar to bring

media attention to refugees around the world.

For more practice with subjects, verbs, and simple sentences, go to www.mywritinglab.com>The Basic Sentence>Subjects, Verbs, and Simple Sentences I.

# OVERVIEW

# 17

## Preview

- A Compound Sentence
- A Complex Sentence
- A Compound/ Complex Sentence

# Compound and Complex Sentences

A compound sentence joins together two or more independent clauses. A complex sentence combines one independent or main clause and one or more dependent clauses.

## A Compound Sentence

A compound sentence is made up of two or more independent clauses. A **compound sentence** links two or more independent clauses together as **equally important** ideas.

### Two Ways to Combine Independent Clauses into a Compound Sentence

1. **A comma and a coordinating conjunction**: The coordinating conjunction serves as a transition that shows the relationship of ideas within the sentence. Use the acronym FANBOYS to help you remember the seven coordinating conjunctions—*for, and, nor, but, or, yet,* or *so.*

2. **A semicolon, conjunctive adverb, and a comma:** The conjunction shows the relationship of ideas within the sentence. In addition, the conjunctive adverb introduces the next clause. A comma follows the conjunctive adverb since it is an introductory element of the next clause:

*[Independent clause;] therefore, [independent clause.]*

# A Complex Sentence

A **complex sentence** contains one independent or main clause and one or more dependent clauses. A **dependent clause** expresses a **subordinate** or minor detail about an idea in the independent clause. A complex sentence joins independent and dependent clauses by placing a subordinating conjunction at the beginning of the dependent clause. **Subordinating conjunctions** state the relationship between the main clause and the subordinate clause.

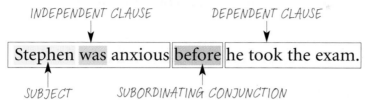

A special kind of subordinating conjunction is the relative pronoun. A **relative pronoun** connects the dependent clause to a noun in the main clause.

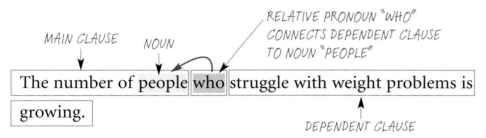

# A Compound-Complex Sentence

A **compound-complex sentence** is two or more independent clauses and one or more dependent clauses. A compound-complex sentence joins coordinate and subordinate ideas into a single sentence. All the punctuation rules for both compound and complex sentences apply to the compound-complex sentence.

For more practice with compound and complex sentences, go to www.mywritinglab.com>The Basic Sentence>Combining Sentences.

# Sentence Variety

Sentence variety is the use of sentences of different purposes, types, and lengths. **Sentence variety** adds interest and power to your writing. You can achieve sentence variety by varying the purposes, types, and openings of your sentences.

## Vary Sentence Purpose

### Four Purposes for Sentences

1. **Declarative sentences** make a statement to share information and are punctuated with a period. Declarative sentences are often used to state a main idea and supporting details.

> Carjacking has become one of the most prevalent crimes in many parts of the world.

2. **Interrogative sentences** ask a question and are punctuated with a question mark. Usually, the writer also provides an answer to the question. An interrogative sentence may be used to introduce a topic and lead into a topic sentence.

> How can you protect yourself from becoming a victim of a carjacking?

3. **Imperative sentences** give a command that demands an action and are punctuated with a period. Imperative sentences are often used to give directions to complete a process or persuade a reader to take action.

> Avoid becoming a victim of a carjacking. Follow these three steps.

4. **Exclamatory sentences** express a strong emotion and are punctuated with an exclamation point. Exclamatory sentences emphasize a significant point.

> Your life is more important than your car!

## Vary Sentence Types

You learned in Chapters 16 and 17 about the four types of sentences: simple, compound, complex, and compound-complex. When we rely on one type of sentence more than the others, our writing becomes dull and flat, like a speaker delivering a speech in a monotone. Vary your use of sentence types to show that ideas are equal in importance, or that one idea is more important than another.

**Coordinating ideas** makes each idea equal in importance. To combine coordinate ideas, use a comma and a coordinating conjunction (FANBOYS: *for, and, nor, but, or, yet,* or *so*).

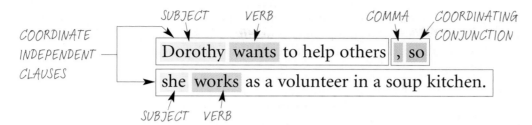

**Subordinating ideas** makes one idea dependent on (and less important than) another idea. To make an idea subordinate, use a subordinating conjunction (*although, after, as, because, before, since, unless,* etc.). If the new subordinate clause begins the sentence as an introductory element, include a comma at the end of the subordinate clause to set it off from the main independent clause.

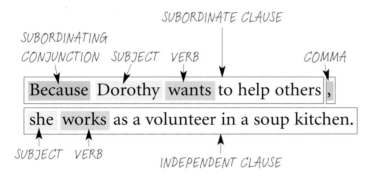

# Vary Sentence Openings

Most often, we begin our sentences with the subject followed by the verb. To add interest and to shift the emphasis of an idea, you can vary the ways in which you begin a sentence. You have already worked with several types of sentence openings: participle phrases, appositives, and dependent clauses. Two additional ways to begin a sentence include using adverbs and prepositional phrases. As introductory elements in a sentence, both an adverb and a prepositional phrase are set off with a comma.

**An adverb** Describes or modifies another adverb, a verb, or an adjective, and usually ends in *-ly: angrily, beautifully, frequently.*

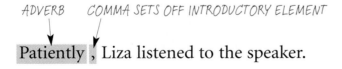

**A prepositional phrase** begins with a preposition and ends with a noun or pronoun, the object of the preposition.

# Vary Sentence Length

To add interest to your writing, vary the length of your sentences. When a writer relies too heavily on one length of sentence, the writing seems dull, flat, or uninteresting. Too many long sentences make a piece boring or confusing. Too many short sentences can seem choppy and immature. The sentence-combining techniques you have learned throughout this chapter will also help you create sentences of varying lengths.

For more practice with sentence variety, go to www.mywritinglab.com > Writing Clear Sentences > Sentence Variety.

# Sentence Clarity: Point of View, Number, and Tense

Sentence clarity creates a logical flow of ideas through consistency in person, point of view, number, and tense.

## Use Consistent Person and Point of View

The term **person** refers to the use of pronouns to identify the difference between the writer or speaker, the one being written or spoken to, and the one being written about or spoken of. **Point of view** is the position from which something is considered, evaluated, or discussed; point of view is identified as first person, second person, or third person. Person and point of view also communicate tone.

### Three Points of View

| Person | Traits | Pronouns |
|---|---|---|
| **First Person** | The writer or speaker; informal, conversational tone | singular: *I, me* <br> plural: *we, our* |
| **Second Person** | The one being written or spoken to; can remain unstated; informal, conversational tone | singular: *you* <br> plural: *you* |
| **Third Person** | The one being written about or spoken of; formal, academic tone | singular: *he, she, it, one* <br> plural: *they* |

### Illogical Shift in Person

An abrupt or **unnecessary shift in person or point of view** causes a break in the logical flow of ideas. When you revise for consistency, remember that the number of the verb may need to change as well.

**Illogical Shift in Person:**

*THIRD PERSON*

Everyone wants to improve gas mileage no matter what type of vehicle you drive.

*SECOND PERSON*

**Revision:**

*THIRD PERSON*

Everyone wants to improve gas mileage no matter what type of vehicle he or she drives.

*PRONOUN AND VERB AGREE IN NUMBER*

# Use Consistent Number

The term *number* refers to the difference between a singular noun or pronoun and plural nouns and pronouns. Once you choose a point of view, carefully edit your writing to ensure **consistent use of number**.

## Illogical Shift in Number

When pronouns act as the subject of a verb, they, too, must agree in number. An abrupt or **unnecessary shift in number** causes a break in the logical flow of ideas.

**Illogical Shift in Person:**

*PLURAL NOUN*

Children use a wide range of electronic gadgets,

yet it is most likely a health hazard.

*SINGULAR VERB*

*SINGULAR, THIRD-PERSON PRONOUN*

**Revision:**

*PLURAL NOUN*

Children use a wide range of electronic gadgets,

and they are most likely a health hazard.

*PLURAL VERB*

*PLURAL, THIRD-PERSON PRONOUN*

# Use Consistent Tense

**Consistent tense** expresses the logical sequence of events or existence. Verb *tense* expresses the time or duration of an action or state of being. Primary tenses include three timeframes: The **past** *was*; the **present** *is*; the **future** *will be*.

# Illogical Shift in Tense

Abruptly changing from one verb tense to another without a logical reason, also called an **illogical shift in tense**, breaks the logical flow of ideas and causes confusion.

**Illogical Shift
in Tense:**

*PRESENT TENSE*

Monica **does** not **rely** solely on the classifieds to

find a job; she **followed** other leads.

*PAST TENSE*

**Revision:**

*PRESENT TENSE*

Monica **does** not **rely** solely on the classifieds to

find a job; she **follows** other leads.

*PRESENT TENSE*

For more practice with sentence clarity, go to
www.mywritinglab.com > Writing Clear Sentences >
Sentence Clarity: Point of View, Number, and Tense
(I, II, and III).

# 20

## Preview

- Parallel Words
- Parallel Phrases
- Parallel Clauses
- Punctuation for Parallelism

# Parallelism

**Parallelism** is the expression of equal ideas—similar words, phrases, or clauses—in a sentence in the same, matching grammatical form. Parallel expressions bring clarity, interest, and power to a piece of writing.

## Parallel Words

Parallel structure uses a pair or series of closely related compound words to emphasize a point. Parallel words often, but not always, use similar **suffixes** (word endings).

- **Parallel Words**

   **Nonparallel:**

   *NOUN*   *ADJECTIVE*

   Prehistoric Paleo-Indians were predators and wandering.

   **Revised for Parallelism:**

   *PARALLEL NOUNS*

   Prehistoric Paleo-Indians were predators and wanderers.

   **Nonparallel:**

   *ADVERB*   *PREPOSITIONAL PHRASE*

   Paleo-Indians skillfully hunted game and with diligence gathered berries.

   **Revised for Parallelism:**

   *PARALLEL ADVERBS*

   Paleo-Indians skillfully hunted game and diligently gathered berries.

   **Nonparallel:**

   *NONPARALLEL VERBS*

   They flaked and crafting flint into spears.

   **Revised for Parallelism:**

   *PARALLEL VERBS*

   They flaked and crafted flint into spears.

# Parallel Phrases

Parallel structure uses a pair or series of closely related compound phrases to emphasize a point. Parallel phrases repeat similar word patterns or groups.

- Parallel Phrases

**Nonparallel:**

INFINITIVE PHRASE    GERUND PHRASE

The Mayas learned to build cities, jewelry crafting, and to develop trade, around A.D. 300.

INFINITIVE PHRASE

**Revised for Parallelism:**

PARALLEL INFINITIVE PHRASES

The Mayas learned to build cities, to craft jewelry, and to develop trade, around A.D. 300.

# Parallel Clauses

Parallel structure uses a set of closely related clauses to emphasize a point. Parallel structure begins with a clause and continues with clauses to create a balanced, logical statement. Use parallel words and phrases within clauses.

For more information on sentence types and sentence elements, see Chapter 16, "Subjects, Verbs, and Simple Sentences," and Chapter 17, "Compound and Complex Sentences."

- Parallel Clauses

**Nonparallel:**

INDEPENDENT CLAUSE

Only a few million people inhabited the Americas by 1490, yet roughly 75 million people who were living in Europe.

DEPENDENT CLAUSE (ILLOGICAL MIXED STRUCTURE)

**Revised for Parallelism:**

PARALLEL INDEPENDENT CLAUSES

Only a few million people inhabited the Americas by 1490, yet roughly 75 million people inhabited Europe.

# Punctuation for Parallelism

The comma and the semicolon (sometimes along with coordinating conjunctions), and numbered, lettered, or bulleted items in a list signal ideas of equal importance. Ideas marked by these pieces of punctuation are best expressed with parallelism.

**Coordinating conjunctions** always signal an equal relationship among words, phrases, and clauses. Use commas between parallel items in a series. Use a comma with a coordinating conjunction to join independent clauses.

**Examples**

To build a relationship, do not criticize, condemn, or complain.

COMMAS

PARALLEL WORDS (VERBS)

COORDINATING CONJUNCTION

PARALLEL GERUND PHRASES (NOUNS: SUBJECTS)

Reacting calmly, listening carefully, and speaking thoughtfully can defuse disagreements.

COMMAS     COORDINATING CONJUNCTION

PARALLEL INDEPENDENT CLAUSES

Criticism makes others resentful, yet praise makes others joyful.

COMMA     COORDINATING CONJUNCTION

**Semicolons** signal two or more closely related independent clauses.

SEMICOLON

Immediacy is the union between people; it is the creation of oneness; it is the communication of interest.

PARALLEL INDEPENDENT CLAUSES     SEMICOLON

For more practice with parallelism, go to www.mywritinglab.com > Writing Clear Sentences >Parallelism.

# Comma Splices and Fused Sentences

A comma splice is an error that occurs when a comma is used by itself to join two sentences. A fused sentence is an error that occurs when two sentences are joined without any punctuation.

## Comma Splice

A **comma splice** occurs when a comma is used by itself (without a coordinating conjunction) to join two independent clauses.

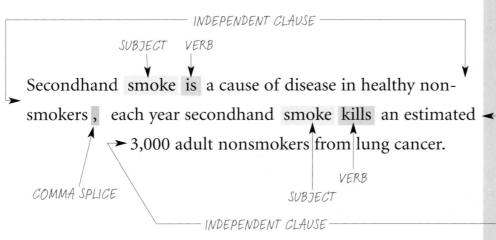

## Fused Sentence

A **fused sentence** sentence occurs when two independent clauses are joined without any punctuation.

## Four Ways to Correct Comma Splices and Fused Sentences

As a writer, you have the choice of several ways to correct or avoid comma splices and fused sentences. Each method creates a specific effect. Most experts recommend using a variety of these methods, rather than always relying on the same one.

## 1. Separate sentences using a period and capital letter.

**Incorrect:**

────────── INDEPENDENT CLAUSE ────────── ┌── INDEPENDENT CLAUSE ──┐

Secondhand smoke causes respiratory problems. It also irritates the eyes.

*ADDED PERIOD* *CAPITALIZED LETTER STARTS 2ND SENTENCE*

## 2. Join sentences with a comma followed by a coordinating conjunction.

**Incorrect:**

────────── INDEPENDENT CLAUSE ──────────

Secondhand smoke causes respiratory problems, and it also irritates the eyes.

*ADDED COMMA AND COORDINATING CONJUNCTION*

────────── INDEPENDENT CLAUSE ──────────

## 3. Join sentences with a semicolon, or join sentences with a semicolon followed by a conjunctive adverb such as *also, for example, however, then, therefore,* and *thus.*

────────── INDEPENDENT CLAUSE ────────── ┌── INDEPENDENT CLAUSE ──┐

Secondhand smoke causes respiratory problems; it also irritates the eyes.

*ADDED SEMICOLON*

────────── INDEPENDENT CLAUSE ──────────

Secondhand smoke causes respiratory problems; in addition, it irritates the eyes.

*ADDED SEMICOLON AND CONJUNCTIVE ADVERB*

────────── INDEPENDENT CLAUSE ──────────

## 4. Join sentences using subordinate ideas.

─────────────── DEPENDENT CLAUSE ─────────────── ┌── INDEPENDENT CLAUSE ──┐

**While** secondhand smoke **causes** respiratory problems, it also **irritates** the eyes.

*ADDED SUBORDINATING CONJUNCTION*          *ADDED COMMA TO SET OFF DEPENDENT CLAUSE*

> For more information on complex sentences, see Chapter 17, "Compound and Complex Sentences."

For more practice with comma splices and run-ons, go to www.mywritinglab.com > Recognizing and Correcting Errors > Comma Splices and Run-ons.

**OVERVIEW**

# 22

**Preview**

- Sentences and Fragments
- Types of Fragments

# Fragments

A fragment is an incomplete thought.

## Sentences and Fragments

A **sentence** contains a subject, a verb, and all the information needed to clearly express a complete thought.

**SENTENCE:** Complete Thought-Complete Information

**FRAGMENT:** Incomplete Thought-Missing Information

A **fragment** is missing one of the following: a subject, a verb, or both subject and verb.

**Fragment (Missing an Independent Clause):**

## Types of Fragments

This section discusses two common types of fragments: the phrase fragment and the clause fragment. A writer may use two techniques to revise fragments into sentences:

- Combine existing ideas.
- Add missing ideas

### Phrase Fragments

A **phrase** is a group of words that acts as a single unit. A phrase is a fragment because it does not contain both a subject and a verb.

**PHRASE**

**Revised to Combine Ideas:**

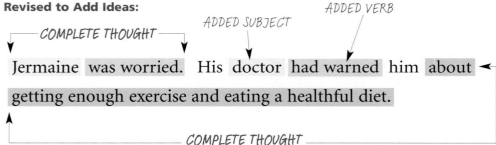

**Revised to Add Ideas:**

## Clause Fragments

A **clause** is a set of words that contains a subject and a verb. A **dependent clause** expresses an incomplete thought or fragment.

For more on dependent and subordinate clauses, see Chapter 17.

**DEPENDENT CLAUSE**

A **dependent clause**, also known as a **subordinate clause**, does not make sense on its own.

A **subordinating conjunction** states the relationship between two clauses:

### RELATIVE CLAUSE

One type of dependent clause is the relative clause, such as *who scored the winning home run*. A **relative clause** describes a noun or pronoun in an independent clause. A **relative pronoun** (such as *who, whom, whose, which,* and *that*) introduces the relative clause and relates it to the noun or pronoun it describes.

Join the relative clause to the independent clause that contains the word it describes.

**Revised to Combine Ideas:**

For more practice with comma splices and run-ons, go to www.mywritinglab.com > Recognizing and Correcting Errors > Comma Splices and Run-ons.

# Misplaced and Dangling Modifiers

A modifier is a word or phrase that describes, clarifies, or gives more information about another word in a sentence.

## Misplaced Modifiers

A **misplaced modifier** is a word or phrase illogically separated from the word it describes. The following examples and revisions illustrate the most common types of misplaced modifiers.

### Types of Misplaced Modifiers

**MISPLACED WORDS** A misplaced word is separated from the word it limits or restricts.

**Example**

*WORD "ONLY" DESCRIBES ?*

*?*　　　　　　　　　　　　　　　　*?*

Belle Glade, Florida only has been flooded twice by hurricanes.

**Revision #1**

*WORD "ONLY" DESCRIBES "TWICE"*

Belle Glade, Florida has been flooded only **twice** by hurricanes.

**Revision #2**

Only Belle Glade, Florida has been flooded twice by hurricanes.

*WORD "ONLY" DESCRIBES "BELLE GLADE"*

**MISPLACED PHRASE** A phrase that describes a noun is placed next to the wrong noun and separated from the noun it describes.

**Example**

*PHRASE "WITHOUT HER GLASSES" DESCRIBES ?*

*?*　　　　　　　　　　*?*

She couldn't tell what kind of animal it was without her glasses.

**Revision**

*PHRASE "WITHOUT HER GLASSES" DESCRIBES "SHE"*

Without her glasses, she couldn't tell what kind of animal it was.

*ADDED COMMA SETS OFF INTRODUCTORY PHRASE*

**Example**

Jammed into his backpack, Sean hunted through the papers.

↑ PHRASE "JAMMED INTO HIS BACKPACK" DESCRIBES ?

↑ ADDED COMMA SETS OFF INTRODUCTORY PHRASE

**Revision**

Sean hunted through the papers jammed into his backpack.

PHRASE "JAMMED INTO HIS BACKPACK" DESCRIBES PAPERS

**MISPLACED CLAUSE** A dependent clause that describes a particular word is placed next to the wrong word and is separated from the word the clause describes.

**Example**

CLAUSE "WHO GAVE BIRTH TO TWINS" DESCRIBES ?

The 60-year-old woman was hounded by the reporter who gave birth to twins.

**Revision**

CLAUSE "WHO GAVE BIRTH TO TWINS" DESCRIBES "WOMAN"

The 60-year-old woman who gave birth to twins was hounded by the reporter.

# Dangling Modifiers

A **dangling modifier** is a phrase that describes a word not stated in the sentence.

**EXAMPLES** What or whom do these phrases describe in each sentence below?

**Sentence #1**

While cleaning the house, a fifty dollar bill turned up.

**Sentence #2**

Observing the wildlife, the canoe glided through the waters.

**Sentence #3**

Running in second place, the finish line came into view.

## Dangling Modifiers: Two Revision Tips

**REVISION TIP #1** Change the dangling modifier into a logical clause with a subject and a verb.

**Revised Sentence #1**

ADDED SUBJECT AND VERB TO CREATE DEPENDENT CLAUSE

While I was cleaning the house, a fifty dollar bill turned up.

**Revised Sentence #2**

*ADDED SUBORDINATING CONJUNCTION, SUBJECT, AND VERB TO CREATE DEPENDENT CLAUSE*

As we were observing the wildlife, the canoe glided through the waters.

**Revised Sentence #3**

*ADDED SUBJECT AND VERB TO CREATE INDEPENDENT CLAUSE*

I was running in second place; the finish line came into view.

*ADDED SEMICOLON JOINS TWO INDEPENDENT CLAUSES*

**REVISION TIP #2** Revise the main clause to include the word being modified.

**Revised Sentence #1**

*PHRASE "WHILE CLEANING THE HOUSE" DESCRIBES ADDED SUBJECT*

While cleaning the house, I found a fifty dollar bill.

*ADDED SUBJECT AND VERB*

**Revised Sentence #2**

*PHRASE "OBSERVING THE WILDLIFE" DESCRIBES ADDED SUBJECT*

Observing the wildlife, we glided the canoe through the waters.

*ADDED SUBJECT*

**Revised Sentence #3**

*PHRASE "RUNNING IN SECOND PLACE" DESCRIBES ADDED SUBJECT*

Running in second place, I saw the finish line come into view.

*ADDED SUBJECT AND VERB*

For more practice with misplaced and dangling modifiers, go to www.mywritinglab.com > Recognizing and Avoiding Errors > Misplaced and Dangling Modifiers.

# 24

**Preview**

- Subject-Verb Agreement
- Key Verbs in the Present Tense: *To Have, To Do, To Be*
- Subject-Verb Agreement Tips

# Subject-Verb Agreement: Present Tense

In the present tense, subjects and verbs must agree in number. Singular subjects must take singular verbs; plural subjects must take plural verbs.

## Subject-Verb Agreement

The following chart uses the sample verb "think" to illustrate present tense agreement in number.

| Present Tense Agreement | | |
|---|---|---|
| | Singular **Subject** and **Verb** | Plural **Subject** and **Verb** |
| First Person | I think | We think |
| Second Person | You think | You think |
| Third Person | He She It ⎤—thinks | They think |

For standard verbs, only the third person singular verb is formed by adding *-s* or *-es*.

| Third person singular subject | → | present tense verb ends with *-s* or *-es* |
|---|---|---|
| He She It | → → → | apologizes accepts catches |

## Key Verbs in the Present Tense: *To Have, To Do, To Be*

Three key verbs are used both as main verbs and as helping verbs to express a wide variety of meanings: *to have, to do,* and *to be*. Memorize their present tense singular and plural forms to ensure subject-verb agreement.

| *To Have:* Present Tense | | |
|---|---|---|
| | Singular **Subject** and **Verb** | Plural **Subject** and **Verb** |
| First Person | I have | We have |
| Second Person | You have | You have |
| Third Person | He She It — has | They have |

| *To Do:* Present Tense | | |
|---|---|---|
| | Singular **Subject** and **Verb** | Plural **Subject** and **Verb** |
| **First Person** | I do | We do |
| **Second Person** | You do | You do |
| **Third Person** | He / She / It does | They do |

The verb *to do* is often used with the adverb "not" to express a negative thought. Frequently this negative is stated in the form of the contractions *doesn't* and *don't* that combine the verb and the adverb into shorter words. The verb part of the contraction must still agree with its subject.

| *To Do* and *Not:* Contraction Form | | |
|---|---|---|
| | Singular **Subject** and **Verb** | Plural **Subject** and **Verb** |
| **First Person** | I don't agree | We don't agree |
| **Second Person** | You don't seem well | You don't seem well |
| **Third Person** | He / She / It doesn't care | They don't care |

The *to be* verb is unusual because it uses three forms in the present tense: *am*, *is*, and *are*.

| *To Be:* Present Tense | | |
|---|---|---|
| | Singular **Subject** and **Verb** | Plural **Subject** and **Verb** |
| **First Person** | I am | We are |
| **Second Person** | You are | You are |
| **Third Person** | He / She / It is | They are |

# Subject-Verb Agreement Tips

## Subjects Separated from Verbs

The standard order of ideas in a sentence places the subject first, immediately followed by the verb. However, subjects are often separated from their verbs by **prepositional phrases**. The object of the preposition can never be the subject of a sentence. The verb of a sentence agrees with the subject, not the object of the preposition.

**Example**

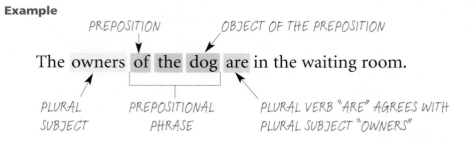

PREPOSITION    OBJECT OF THE PREPOSITION

The owners of the dog are in the waiting room.

PLURAL          PREPOSITIONAL    PLURAL VERB "ARE" AGREES WITH
SUBJECT         PHRASE           PLURAL SUBJECT "OWNERS"

## Subjects after Verbs

In some instances, a writer may choose to place the subject after the verb.

*There* and *Here* are never the subject of a sentence. Both of these words signal that the subject comes after the verb.

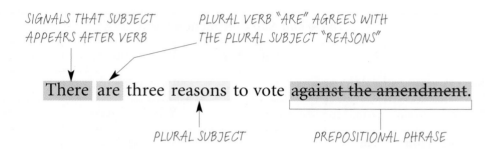

SIGNALS THAT SUBJECT          PLURAL VERB "ARE" AGREES WITH
APPEARS AFTER VERB            THE PLURAL SUBJECT "REASONS"

There are three reasons to vote ~~against the amendment.~~

PLURAL SUBJECT               PREPOSITIONAL PHRASE

**Agreement in Questions** relies on understanding that the subject comes after the verb or between parts of the verb.

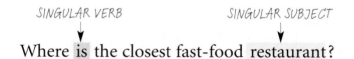

SINGULAR VERB               SINGULAR SUBJECT

Where is the closest fast-food restaurant?

For more practice with subject-verb agreement, go to www.mywritinglab.com > Recognizing and Avoiding Errors > Subject-Verb Agreement: Present Tense.

# The Past Tense of Verbs

The past tense of verbs describes actions or events that have already occurred.

## Regular Verbs in the Past Tense

Preview
- Regular Verbs in the Past Tense
- Irregular Verbs in the Past Tense

The following chart states the general rule for forming the past tense of regular verbs, the spelling rules for exceptions, and examples of each rule.

| Rules for Forming Past Tense of Regular Verbs | | |
|---|---|---|
| | **Base Form** | **Past Tense** |
| **General Rule:** Regular verbs form the past tense by adding **-ed** to the base form of the verb. | walk → | walk**ed** |
| **Spelling Exceptions:** There are several exceptions to the way in which regular verbs form the past tense: | | |
| 1. When the base form of the verb ends in **-e**, only add **-d**. | live save → | live**d** save**d** |
| 2. When the base form of the verb ends with a consonant and **-y**, delete the **-y** and add **-ied** in its place. | cry try → | cr**ied** tr**ied** |
| 3. When the base form of the verb ends with **-p** or **-it**, double the last letter before adding the **-ed**. | stop permit → | sto**pped** permi**tted** |

## Irregular Verbs in the Past Tense

The past tense of irregular verbs does not use **-ed** or conform to uniform spelling rules with clear exceptions. The chart below lists the base form and past tense form of five of the most commonly used irregular verbs.

| Five of the Most Common Irregular Verbs in the Past Tense | | | |
|---|---|---|---|
| **Base Form** | **Past Tense** | **Base Form** | **Past Tense** |
| get | got | see | saw |
| go | went | take | took |
| say | saw | | |

# Key Verbs in the Past Tense:
## *To Have, To Do, To Be*

Three key irregular verbs are used both as main verbs and as helping verbs to express a wide variety of meanings: *to have, to do,* and *to be.*

| To Have | To Do | To Be |
|---------|-------|-------|
| had | did | was (singular) |
| | | were (plural) |

## Three often confused helping verbs: *Can, Could, Would*

- *Can* expresses an ability in the present tense.

  *"CAN" EXPRESSES A MENTAL ABILITY*

  I can solve mathematical equations.

- *Could* expresses an ability, opportunity, possibility, or permission in the past tense.

  *"COULD" EXPRESSES A PHYSICAL ABILITY*

  She could run a marathon.

  *"COULD" EXPRESSES A LOST OPPORTUNITY*

  You could have tried harder than you did.

  *"COULD" EXPRESSES POSSIBILITY*

  He could have been the culprit.

  *"COULD" EXPRESSES PERMISSION*

  He said that we could begin the driving test.

- *Would* expresses past routine or intention in the past tense.

  *"WOULD" EXPRESSES PAST ROUTINE*

  He would win every race.

  *"WOULD" EXPRESSES PAST INTENTION*

  She said she would do the dishes.

For more practice with the past tense of verbs, go to www.mywritinglab.com > Recognizing and Avoiding Errors > The Past Tense of Verbs.

# The Past Participle

A participle is a verb form that can be used to establish tenses or voices, or it can be used as a modifier, which describes, restricts, or limits other words in a sentence.

## Past Participles of Regular Verbs

In general, regular verbs form the past participle by adding -ed to the base form of the verb. Just as with the simple past tense, there are several spelling exceptions for the past participle of regular verbs.

| Base Form | Past Tense | Past Participle |
|-----------|------------|-----------------|
| live | liv**ed** | liv**ed** |
| cry | cr**ied** | cr**ied** |
| permit | permi**tted** | permi**tted** |

> For more about the simple past tense, see Chapter 25.

## Past Participles of Irregular Verbs

As with the simple past tense, irregular verbs do not use -ed to form the past participle. Nor does the past participle of irregular verbs conform to uniform spelling rules with clear exceptions. In addition, the past participle forms of many irregular verbs vary from their past tense forms. The following chart lists the base form, past tense form, and past participle of eight of the most commonly used irregular verbs.

| Eight of the Most Common Irregular Past Participles | | |
|-----------|------------|-----------------|
| **Base Form** | **Past Tense** | **Past Participle** |
| be | was, were | been |
| get | got | gotten |
| give | gave | given |
| go | went | gone |
| have | had | had |
| say | said | said |
| see | saw | seen |
| take | took | taken |

## Using the Present Perfect Tense

The **present perfect tense** connects the past to the present. The present perfect tense states the relationship of a past action or situation to a current, ongoing action or situation. The present perfect tense is formed by joining the helping verbs **has** or **have** with the past participle.

### Preview
- Past Participles of Regular Verbs
- Past Participles of Irregular Verbs
- Using the Present Perfect Tense
- Using the Past Perfect Tense
- Using the Passive Voice (*To Be* and the Past Participle)
- Using the Past Participle as an Adjective

**The purposes of the present perfect tense are:**

- **to express change from the past to the present.**

PRESENT PERFECT "HAS IMPROVED" EXPRESSES
CHANGE FROM THE PAST ACTION TO A PRESENT ONE

PAST ACTION

Jamel was sick for three weeks, but he has improved.

- **to express a situation or action that started in the past and continues to the present.**

PRESENT PERFECT "HAVE RACED" EXPRESSES AN ONGOING
ACTION, WHICH STARTED IN THE PAST AND IS CONTINUING NOW

Carmen and Michelle have raced stock cars for several years.

PRESENT PERFECT

Past
action/event

Present
action/event

Future
action/event

# Using the Past Perfect Tense

The **past perfect** connects two past actions or situations. The past perfect is formed by joining the helping verb **had** with a past participle.

**The purposes of the past perfect tense are:**

- **to connect a previous action or event with a later action or event.**

PAST ACTION #1: THE PAST PERFECT "HAD LEFT" SHOWS THAT THIS ACTION
OCCURRED EVEN BEFORE THE OTHER PAST ACTION "SAMUEL WENT..."

PAST ACTION #2

Samuel went to Starbucks, but everyone had left.

- **to express an action or event that happened before a certain past time.**

PAST ACTION #1: THE PAST PERFECT "HAD STUDIED" SHOWS THAT THIS
ACTION OCCURRED EVEN BEFORE THE OTHER PAST ACTION "SHE TOOK..."

PAST ACTION #2

Before she took the test, Suzanne had studied for three weeks.

PAST PERFECT

Past
action/event #1

Past
action/event #2

Present

Future

# Using the Passive Voice
## (*To Be* and the Past Participle)

Action verbs establish the **active voice** by expressing what the subject of a sentence does. When the subject of a sentence receives the action (or is acted upon), the sentence is in the **passive voice.** The combination of *to be* with a past participle establishes the passive voice. In addition, the passive voice can be expressed in every tense.

**The purpose of the passive voice is to tell the reader what is done to a subject.**

**Active Voice**

*SUBJECT "CONSTANCE" PERFORMS THE ACTION*

Constance took herself to the hospital.

**Passive Voice**

*SUBJECT "CONSTANCE" RECEIVES THE ACTION*

Constance was taken to the hospital.

# Using the Past Participle as an Adjective

The past participle is often used as an adjective that modifies a noun or pronoun. Both regular and irregular forms of the past participle are used as adjectives.

**The purposes of the past participle as an adjective are:**

- **to describe a noun or pronoun with a word or phrase.**

*PARTICIPLE PHRASE*

Destroyed by the wind, these houses will be raised again by hope.

*PARTICIPLE "DESTROYED" DESCRIBES NOUN "HOUSES"*

- **to describe the subject by completing a linking verb in the sentence.**

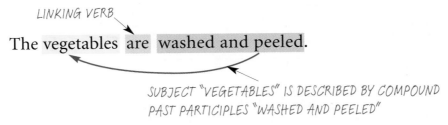

*LINKING VERB*

The vegetables are washed and peeled.

*SUBJECT "VEGETABLES" IS DESCRIBED BY COMPOUND
PAST PARTICIPLES "WASHED AND PEELED"*

For more practice with the past participle, go to
www.mywritinglab.com > Recognizing and Avoiding
Errors > The Past Participle.

# 27

**Preview**
- Nouns
- Pronouns

# Nouns and Pronouns

A noun names a person, animal, place, or thing. A pronoun stands in the place of a noun that has been clearly identified earlier in the text.

## Nouns

Often, nouns are the first words we learn to speak as we hear the names of people and things that we want or need. The word "noun" comes from the Latin word *nomen* which means "name." A **noun** names a person, animal, place, object, element, action, or concept.

One type of noun is the proper noun. A **proper noun** names an individual person, place, or thing. A proper noun is always capitalized. The second type of noun is the common noun. A **common noun** is a general name for any member of a group or class. A common noun is not capitalized.

| Two Types of Nouns | |
|---|---|
| **Proper Noun** | **Common Noun** |
| Barnes & Noble | bookstore |
| Olive Garden | restaurant |

## Count and Noncount Nouns

**Count nouns** name distinct individual units of a group or category. Most singular count nouns are formed by adding *-s* or *-es*. However, many singular count nouns use irregular spellings in their plural form.

| Examples of Count Nouns | | |
|---|---|---|
| | **Singular** | **Plural** |
| **Regular** | age<br>baby | ages<br>babies |
| **Irregular** | calf<br>deer | calves<br>deer |

Noncount nouns name a nonspecific member of a group or category. Noncount nouns, which are typically common nouns, do not have plural forms. Noncount nouns name things that cannot be divided into smaller parts. Often, noncount nouns represent a group of count nouns.

| Examples of Noncount Nouns and Corresponding Count Nouns | |
|---|---|
| **Noncount Noun**<br>air, oxygen, steam<br>anger, happiness, grief | **Count Noun**<br>gases<br>emotions |

# Articles and Nouns

An **article** is a type of adjective that describes a noun as being general or specific.

**Indefinite articles:** *A* and *an* are used before a singular noun that refers to any member of a larger group: *a cat, an umbrella*. These articles are often used to introduce a noun for the first time in the discussion. Use *a* before a noun that begins with a consonant: *a cat*. Use *an* before a noun that begins with a vowel: *an umbrella*.

**Definite article:** *The* is used before a singular or plural noun that refers to a specific member of the larger group: *the cat, the hat*. The article *the* is often used to indicate a noun that has already been introduced into the discussion. "A cat is at the front door; the cat looks hungry."

**Zero article:** No article is used before the noun. An example: *Time is money*. Use zero article to refer to general ideas.

# Pronouns

**Pronouns and antecedents** work closely together to communicate an idea. A **pronoun** refers to or stands in the place of a noun that has been clearly identified earlier in the discussion. An **antecedent** is the noun to which a pronoun refers. Every pronoun should refer clearly and specifically to one particular antecedent.

ANTECEDENT OF PRONOUN "IT"     PRONOUN "IT" REFERS TO ANTECEDENT "PACKAGE"

When the FedEx package arrived, the receptionist put it on the front counter.

In the preceding example, the pronoun "it" clearly refers to the antecedent "package." To make sure your writing is clear, avoid faulty pronoun references.

## Avoid Pronoun Reference to More Than One Antecedent

PROBLEM:

The pronoun does not clearly and unmistakably refer to one specific antecedent.

PRONOUN "IT" REFERS TO ?

Jared threw the remote control at the television because it was broken.

ANTECEDENT OF "IT"?

**CORRECTION:**

Correct by replacing the pronoun with a noun.

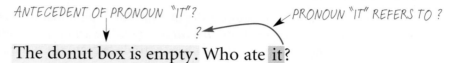

Jared threw the remote control at the television because the remote control was broken.

*ADDED NOUN REPLACES PRONOUN WITH NO CLEAR ANTECEDENT*

# Avoid Pronoun Reference to Implied or Missing Antecedent

**PROBLEM:**

The antecedent is not stated or is missing.

*ANTECEDENT OF PRONOUN "IT"?*           *PRONOUN "IT" REFERS TO ?*

The donut box is empty. Who ate it?

**CORRECTION #1:**

Correct by replacing the pronoun with a noun.

*ADDED NOUN REPLACES PRONOUN WITH NO CLEAR ANTECEDENT*

The donut box is empty. Who ate the last donut?

*SUBJECT AND VERB IMPLY THAT "IT" IN THE ABOVE SENTENCE REFERS TO A DONUT*

**CORRECTION #2:**

Correct by rewording to include a clear antecedent for the pronoun.

*ANTECEDENT OF PRONOUN "IT"*           *PRONOUN "IT" REFERS TO ANTECEDENT "DONUT"*

The last donut is gone. Who ate it?

For more practice with nouns and pronouns, go to www.mywritinglab.com > Recognizing and Avoiding Errors > Nouns and Pronouns (I, II, and III).

# Adjectives and Adverbs

An adjective describes a noun or a pronoun. An adverb describes a verb, an adjective, or another adverb.

## Adjectives

An **adjective** modifies—in other words, it describes—a noun or a pronoun. It answers one or more of the following questions:

- What kind?
- Which one?
- How many?

*ADJECTIVE "LOUD" DESCRIBES NOUN "VOICE"*

Maya has a loud voice.

An **adverb** modifies, or describes, a verb, an adjective, or another adverb. It answers one or more of the following questions:

- How?
- Why?
- When?
- Where?
- To what extent?

*VERB "TALKS" DESCRIBED BY ADVERB "LOUDLY"*

Maya talks loudly.

## Participles as Adjectives

Many adjectives are formed by adding *-ed* or *-ing* to verbs. These **participle adjectives** serve two purposes: The *-ed* form describes a person's reaction or feeling; the *-ing* form describes the person or thing that causes the reaction.

The amazed crowd watched the fireworks display.

The amazing fireworks display lit up the entire sky.

# Nouns and Verbs Formed as Adjectives

In addition to the *-ed* and *-ing* word endings, many adjectives are formed by other types of word endings.

| | | | | | | | | |
|---|---|---|---|---|---|---|---|---|
| **Common Adjectives** | | | | | | | | |
| **Word Endings** | *-able* *-ible* | *-ful* | *-ic* | *-ish* | *-ive* | *-less* | *-ly* *-y* | *-ous* |
| **Examples** | acceptable | bashful | alcoholic | boorish | abusive | cheerless | actually | ambiguous |

## Placement of Adjectives

A careful writer not only chooses the precise word for impact, but also arranges words in the most effective order for the greatest impact on the reader.

Adjectives can appear before a noun.

The nervous suspect offered an alibi.

Adjectives can appear after **linking verbs** such as *is, are, were, seems,* and *appears.*

The alibi seemed plausible.

Adjectives can appear after **sensory verbs**—those that describe physical senses—such as *look, smell, feel, taste,* and *sound.*

The suspect looked frightened.

# Adverbs

The most common use of adverbs is to describe verbs. In addition, adverbs modify other types of words such as adjectives and other adverbs. In purpose, adverbs answer the reporter's questions *When? Where?* and *How?*

Many adverbs are derived from adjectives, many adverbs end in *-ly*, and many adverbs are gradeable based on degree or quantity. The following chart lists some of the most frequently used adverbs based on the type of information they provide.

| | | | | |
|---|---|---|---|---|
| **Common Adverbs** | | | | |
| **Time, Frequency, or Sequence** | **Place** | **Manner** | **Certainty or Negation** | **Degree or Quantity** |
| **When?** | **Where?** | **How?** | **How?** | **How much?** |
| already | everywhere | badly | certainly | almost |
| finally | here | fast | clearly | completely |
| regularly | somewhere | quickly | not | entirely |
| usually | there | well | never | not |
| | | | | very |

# How to Use the Comparative and Superlative

Adjectives and adverbs take the form of three degrees: **absolute, comparative,** and **superlative.** The degrees of adverbs are formed by adding the suffixes *-er* or *-est* or by using *more* or *most*. For example, *more* or *most* establishes a degree of comparison with adverbs that end in *-ly*.

## Absolute

The absolute degree makes no comparison, or makes a one-to-one comparison (in which the adjective or adverb describes both things equally).

Raisins and prunes are sweet.

Raisins are as sweet as prunes.

## Comparative

The comparative degree compares and makes distinctions between two people or things, usually by using the adverb *more* or *less* or adding the suffix *-er*.

Raisins are sweeter than prunes.

Riana acted more generously than her sister [acted].

## Superlative

The superlative degree makes distinctions among three or more people or things, usually by using the adverb *most* or *least* or adding the suffix *-est*.

This is the sweetest prune I have ever eaten.

For more practice with adjectives and adverbs, go to www.mywritinglab.com > Recognizing and Avoiding Errors > Adjectives and Adverbs (I and II).

# 29

**Preview**

- Commas

# The Comma

A comma is a valuable, useful punctuation device because it separates the structural elements of a sentence into manageable segments.

# Commas

The primary purpose of the **comma** is to make a sentence easy to read by indicating a brief pause between parts of the sentence that need to be separated.

## Commas with Items in a Series

Use commas to separate a **series of items** in a list. A series of items in a list can be **three** or more words, phrases, or clauses. In addition, a series of items can be made up of subjects, verbs, adjectives, participles, and so on. Items in a series are parallel and equal in importance.

**Series of Words**

COMMAS SET OFF SERIES OF WORDS        COMMAS SET OFF SECOND SERIES OF WORDS

Marissa, Evan, and Kanisha   skate, swim, and ski.

**Series of Phrases**

COMMAS SET OFF SERIES OF PHRASES

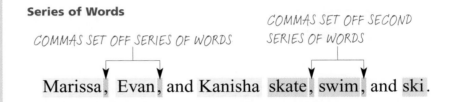

Marissa enjoys skating on ice, swimming in the ocean, and skiing down a snowy slope.

> For more information about parallel structure, see Chapter 20, "Parallelism."

**Series of Clauses**

Marissa is an athlete who trains consistently, who eats sensibly, and who competes well.

COMMAS SET OFF SERIES OF CLAUSES

# Commas with Introductory Elements

Use commas to set off the introductory element of a sentence. **Introductory elements** are ideas that appear at the beginning of a sentence. Introductory elements come before a main clause. Introductory elements can be a word, phrase, or clause.

**Introductory Word**

*COMMA SETS OFF INTRODUCTORY WORD*

Overall, good health is achieved through wise choices.

**Introductory Phrase**

*COMMA SETS OFF INTRODUCTORY PHRASE*

To achieve good health, one should exercise on a regular basis.

**Introductory Dependent Clause**

*COMMA SETS OFF INTRODUCTORY DEPENDENT PHRASE*

As Maria increased her physical activity, her sense of well-being improved.

# Commas to Join Independent Clauses

Use a comma with a coordinating conjunction to join two or more equally important and logically related independent clauses. To join sentences with a coordinating conjunction, place the comma before the conjunction. The acronym **FANBOYS** identifies the seven coordinating conjunctions: *for, and, nor, but, or, yet,* and *so.*

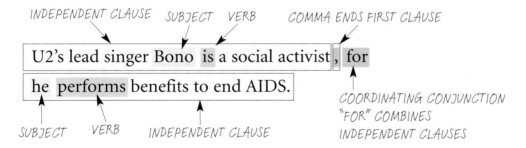

# Commas with Parenthetical Ideas

Use commas to set off a parenthetical idea. A **parenthetical idea** is an idea that interrupts a sentence with information that is **nonessential** to the meaning of the sentence. Such an idea could be enclosed in parentheses. However, more often, a comma comes before and after such an idea. These interruptions can be words, phrases, or clauses.

**Parenthetical Word**

*COMMAS SET OFF PARENTHETICAL WORD*

The demanding customer was, however, a generous tipper.

**Parenthetical Phrase**

*COMMAS SET OFF PARENTHETICAL PHRASE*

The polite customer, surprisingly heartless, left no tip.

**Parenthetical Clause**

*COMMAS SET OFF PARENTHETICAL CLAUSE*

Jennifer, who had been working a 12-hour shift, smiled at the sight of the generous tip.

## Commas with Quotations

For more information about proper use of quotation marks, see Chapter 31, "Quotation Marks."

Use commas after a verb that introduces a quotation. The comma is used to set off the "said" clause, called the **speech tag**, and the comma is placed before the quoted information.

*COMMA SEPARATES SPEECH TAG FROM THE QUOTATION*

Mr. Newell said, "Let's begin the meeting promptly, please."

For more practice with the comma, go to www.mywritinglab.com > Punctuation and Mechanics > The Comma.

# The Apostrophe

The apostrophe is used to show ownership and to form contractions by replacing omitted letters or numbers.

## The Apostrophe

The apostrophe is used for two general purposes: to show ownership and to form contractions.

### The Apostrophe for Ownership

The **possessive form** of a noun and some pronouns is created by using an apostrophe followed, at times, by an *-s*. The possessive tells the reader that someone or something owns or possesses the next stated thing.

The following chart lists and illustrates the rules for using an apostrophe to show possession.

| Using the Apostrophe for Ownership | | |
|---|---|---|
| **To Show Possession for** | **Correct Use of Apostrophe** | **Example** |
| A singular noun | add ' | my husband's job |
| A singular noun ending with *-s* | add ' or add 's | the boss' memo<br><br>James's home |
| A regular plural noun ending with *-s* | add ' | the writers' colony |
| An irregular plural noun | add 's | women's clothing |

| Using the Apostrophe for Ownership (*continued*) | | |
|---|---|---|
| **To Show Possession for** | **Correct Use of Apostrophe** | **Example** |
| Compound words | add 's | vice president's speech <br><br> sister-in-law's business <br><br> (Note: Do not confuse the possessive form with the plural form, as in *sisters-in-law*) |
| Joint ownership of an item | add 's to the last noun | Abbott and Costello's comedy |
| Individual ownership | add 's to the end of both nouns | Clinton's and Bush's approaches to public speaking <br><br> (Each president has his own approach.) |
| Indefinite pronouns ending with "*one*" or "*body*" | add 's | someone's computer |

# The Apostrophe for Contractions

An apostrophe is used to indicate the omission of letters to form a *contraction*. Most often, a **contraction** is formed to join two words to make one shorter word such as *don't* for *do not*. An apostrophe ( ' ) takes the place of the letter or letters that are dropped to form the contraction.

The following chart illustrates how contracted verbs are formed.

| **Apostrophe Use in Common Contractions** <br> The apostrophe replaces omitted letters. | | |
|---|---|---|
| 'm <br><br> *APOSTROPHE REPLACES "A" IN "I AM"* <br><br> I am = I'm | | 's <br><br> *APOSTROPHE REPLACES "I" IN "IT IS"* <br><br> it is = it's |
| 're <br><br> *APOSTROPHE REPLACES "A" IN "YOU ARE"* <br><br> you are = you're | | 've <br><br> *APOSTROPHE REPLACES "HA" IN "I HAVE"* <br><br> I have = I've |
| n't <br><br> *APOSTROPHE REPLACES "O" IN "IS NOT"* <br><br> is not = isn't | | 'll <br><br> *APOSTROPHE REPLACES "WI" IN "I WILL"* <br><br> I will = I'll |

# Common Misuses of the Apostrophe

Quite often, the apostrophe is misused in several specific ways. The following chart lists and illustrates these common misuses of the apostrophe. Always base your use of an apostrophe on a specific rule. Proofread your writing for these common mistakes.

- **Do not use an apostrophe to form a plural noun.**

| Correct Plural | Incorrect Plural |
|---|---|
| homes | home's |
| books | book's |

- **Do not use an apostrophe to form a possessive pronoun.**

| Correct | Incorrect |
|---|---|
| ours | our's |
| hers | her's |
| theirs | their's |

- **Do not omit the apostrophe to form the possessive indefinite pronoun.**

| Correct | Incorrect |
|---|---|
| one's | ones |
| everybody's | everybodys |

- **Do not confuse contractions with similar sounding words.**

| Contraction | Possessive Pronoun |
|---|---|
| it's (it is) | its |
| who's (who is) | whose |
| they're (they are) | their |

For more practice with the apostrophe, go to www.mywritinglab.com > Punctuation and Mechanics > The Apostrophe.

# 31

**Preview**

- Quotation Marks

# Quotation Marks

Quotation marks are used to set off exact words either written or spoken by other people or to set off titles of short works.

## Quotation Marks

### General Guidelines for Using Quotation Marks

**1.** Place commas ( , ) and periods ( . ) inside the quotation marks ( " " ).

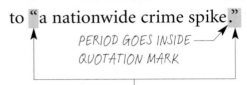

The article said gangs and guns contributed

to "a nationwide crime spike."

*PERIOD GOES INSIDE QUOTATION MARK*

*QUOTATION MARKS ENCLOSE EXACT WORDS FROM THE ARTICLE*

**2.** Place semicolons ( ; ) and colons ( : ) outside the quotation marks.

*QUOTATION MARKS ENCLOSE EXACT WORDS OF THE SPEAKER "WE"*

We must say "no more violence"; we must strengthen

gun control laws.

*SEMICOLON GOES OUTSIDE QUOTATION MARK*

**3.** Place a question mark ( ? ) inside quotation marks when it is part of the quotation. Place a question mark outside quotation marks when the larger sentence is a question, but the quotation included in it is not.

*QUOTATION MARKS ENCLOSE EXACT WORDS OF THE SPEAKER "WE"*

We should ask, "How does violence in movies and

music affect youth?"

*QUESTION MARK GOES INSIDE QUOTATION MARK BECAUSE IT IS PART OF THE QUOTATION. (THE QUOTATION IS A QUESTION.)*

QUOTATION MARKS ENCLOSE EXACT
WORDS OF THE SPEAKER "WE"

Did she really say "no more violence"?

QUESTION MARK GOES OUTSIDE QUOTATION MARK BECAUSE THE SENTENCE
ITSELF IS A QUESTION, BUT THE QUOTATION INCLUDED IN IT IS NOT.

**4.** Use single quotation marks for quoted information—or titles of short works—
that appear within direct quotation.

DOUBLE QUOTATION MARK INDICATES START
OF QUOTED MATERIAL FROM NEWSPAPER

The *USA Today* article reports, "The Justice Department
promises '$50 million this year to combat gangs and guns.' "

SINGLE QUOTATION MARK INDICATES
START OF QUOTED MATERIAL FROM
JUSTICE DEPARTMENT

SINGLE QUOTATION MARK INDICATES END OF
QUOTED MATERIAL FROM JUSTICE DEPARTMENT.
DOUBLE QUOTATION MARK INDICATES END OF
QUOTED MATERIAL FROM NEWSPAPER.

## Punctuating Direct Quotations

One part of a direct quotation is the **speech tag** or the credit given to the source, the
person who spoke or wrote an idea. A speech tag is formed by a subject (the speaker)
and a verb that indicates the subject is speaking. The following examples highlight
the correct use of commas, periods, capitalization, and quotation marks based on the
placement of the speech tag.

- **Speech tag at the beginning of quote**

COMMA SETS OFF
SPEECH TAG

QUOTATION MARKS ENCLOSE EXACT
WORDS OF THE SPEAKER "MOTHER"

Mother said, "Your brother is depressed."

SPEECH TAG

CAPITAL LETTER BEGINS
QUOTED MATERIAL

PERIOD INSIDE QUOTATION MARK

- **Speech tag in the middle of quote**

QUOTATION MARKS ENCLOSE
FIRST HALF OF THE SENTENCE
OF THE SPEAKER "I"

QUOTATION MARKS ENCLOSE SECOND HALF
OF THE SENTENCE OF THE SPEAKER "I"

LOWERCASE LETTER BEGINS SECOND
PART OF INTERRUPTED QUOTE

"I think you're right," I replied, "because he isn't eating or sleeping."

COMMA INSIDE
QUOTATION MARK

SPEECH TAG

COMMA SETS OFF
SPEECH TAG

PERIOD INSIDE
QUOTATION MARK

- **Speech tag at the end of quote**

QUOTATION MARKS ENCLOSE EXACT
WORDS OF THE SPEAKER "MOTHER"

"Do you think he would agree to get some professional help?"
Mother asked.

SPEECH TAG

QUESTION MARK INSIDE QUOTATION MARK

# Titles

Quotation marks are also used to set off the titles of short works such as essays, short stories, short poems, songs, articles in magazines, TV episodes, and chapter titles in books.

- Follow the general rules for using quotation marks.
- Do not use quotation marks to set off titles of larger publications such as magazines, newspapers, and books. These larger publications are set off with italics or underlining.

QUOTATION MARKS SET OFF SONG TITLE

Enrique Iglesias scored a big hit with the release of his single "Dimelo."

For more practice with quotation marks, go to www.mywritinglab.com > Punctuation and Mechanics > Quotation Marks.

# End Punctuation

End punctuation marks the end of a complete thought. The **punctuation marks** that indicate the end of a sentence (called **end punctuation**) are **the period**, **the question mark**, and **the exclamation point**. Each of these end punctuation marks indicates the purpose or type of a sentence.

For more information on types and purposes of sentences, see Chapter 18, "Sentence Variety."

## The Period

| End Punctuation | Type of Sentence | Purpose of Sentence |
|---|---|---|
| The Period ( . ) | Ends a declarative statement<br><br>Ends an imperative statement | To inform<br><br>To command without urgency |

SUBJECT   VERB   PERIOD ENDS DECLARATIVE STATEMENT

Incandescent light bulbs waste energy.

DECLARATIVE STATEMENT

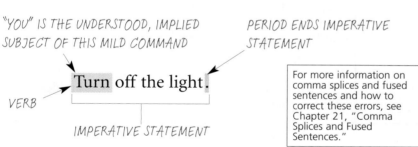

"YOU" IS THE UNDERSTOOD, IMPLIED SUBJECT OF THIS MILD COMMAND   PERIOD ENDS IMPERATIVE STATEMENT

Turn off the light.

VERB

IMPERATIVE STATEMENT

For more information on comma splices and fused sentences and how to correct these errors, see Chapter 21, "Comma Splices and Fused Sentences."

## The Question Mark

| End Punctuation | Type of Sentence | Purpose of Sentence |
|---|---|---|
| The Question Mark ( ? ) | Ends an interrogative statement | To question |
| | May invert order of subject and helping verb | To question |
| | May begin with *what*, *who*, or *how* | To ask a direct question |
| | Often uses a helping verb such as *do, can, will*, or *would* | To make a request |

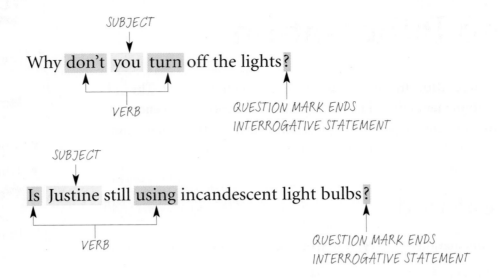

# The Exclamation Point

| End Punctuation | Type of Sentence | Purpose of Sentence |
|---|---|---|
| The Exclamation Point( ! ) | Ends an exclamatory statement | To express strong emotion |
| | Ends a strong imperative (command) | To express urgency, warning, or a forceful command |
| | Ends an interjection, a single word or phrase used as an exclamation that stands apart from the rest of a sentence | To cry out, to utter an emotion |
| | Used with interjections beginning with *how* or *what* | To emphasize an idea |

**Example**

For more practice with end punctuation, go to www.mywritinglab.com > Punctuation and Mechanics > End Punctuation: Period, Question Mark, and Exclamation Point.

# Capitalization

Capitalization clearly identifies the beginning of a new idea or the names of specific people, places, and things.

## Capitalization

**Capitalization** refers to writing letters (and sometimes words) in uppercase letters. The most frequent usage of capitalization, however, is writing a word with its first letter in uppercase (and the rest of its letters in lowercase) to indicate the beginning of a sentence.

Following seven basic rules will ensure proper use of capitalization in your writing.

**RULE 1: Capitalize the first word of every sentence.**

*INITIAL CAPITAL LETTERS IN THE FIRST WORD OF EVERY SENTENCE INDICATE THE START OF A NEW SENTENCE AND A NEW THOUGHT*

Extreme horror films provide thrill rides for loyal fans.

**RULE 2: Capitalize the pronoun *I*.**

*ALWAYS CAPITALIZE THE FIRST-PERSON SINGULAR PRONOUN "I"*

Because I keep my eyes closed through most of a horror movie, I think they are a waste of my money.

**RULE 3: Capitalize the first letter of the first words in written greetings and salutations (for example, *Dear friends,* or *Best regards*).**

*ALWAYS CAPITALIZE THE FIRST LETTER OF THE FIRST WORDS IN WRITTEN GREETINGS OR CLOSINGS (IN LETTERS, MEMOS, EMAILS, ETC.)*

Dear Mr. Sanchez:

I am writing to protest your support of horror films. As a sponsor of this type of film, you foster fear and violence in our culture. Until you stop sponsoring horror films, I will no longer buy items from your company.

Sincerely,

Dorothea Simmons

**RULE 4: In titles of publications, such as books, magazines, newspapers, songs, poems, plays, and articles, capitalize the first letter of the first and last words, the principal words, and the first word that comes after a semicolon or a colon.**

Do not capitalize the first letters of the following in titles, unless they are the first or last word or come after a semicolon or colon: articles (*a, an, the*), prepositions (such as *in, of,* and *with*), and conjunctions (such as *and, but,* and *for*).

ALWAYS CAPITALIZE THE FIRST LETTER OF
THE FIRST WORD IN A PUBLICATION TITLE

"Eight Top Jobs for Parents"

ALWAYS CAPITALIZE THE FIRST LETTER OF THE
PRINCIPAL WORDS IN A PUBLICATION TITLE

## RULE 5: Capitalize the first letters in all essential words in proper nouns.

**Proper nouns** name specific people, places, things, and events. Proper nouns include people's names; certain titles of people (see Rule 6 for details), places, and regions; organizations and associations; and publications. Each of the examples in the chart below illustrates various rules for capitalizing proper nouns.

**Note** the capitalization of initials and abbreviations. Do not capitalize common nouns.

|  | **Common Nouns** | **Proper Nouns** |
|---|---|---|
| **People** | a professor<br>an officer | Professor Walker<br>Captain Rivera or Capt. Rivera |
| **Places and Regions** | a country<br>a street | Mexico<br>Main Street |
| **Things** | a language<br>a company | English<br>Apple, Inc. |
| **Events, Time Periods** | a day<br>an era | Friday<br>the Middle Ages |

## RULE 6: Capitalize the first letter of the title of a person when the title precedes the person's name.

Some writers capitalize the first letter of a title of very high rank even when it follows a proper name. Capitalization of the first letter of a title is also common if it appears at the end of a letter, email, or other correspondence, following the person's name. Do not capitalize those titles when they appear on their own as common nouns (without modifying a particular person's name).

*ALWAYS CAPITALIZE THE FIRST LETTER OF A PERSON'S TITLE WHEN IT APPEARS BEFORE THE PERSON'S NAME*

*WHEN A PERSON'S TITLE APPEARS AFTER THE PERSON'S NAME, THE INITIAL LETTER OF THE TITLE REMAINS LOWERCASE*

Doctor Kit Doughney          Kit Doughney, a medical doctor

**RULE 7:** Capitalize proper adjectives. Proper adjectives are formed from proper nouns.

| Proper Noun | Proper Adjective |
| --- | --- |
| Africa | Africans |
| Shakespeare | Shakespearean |

Use and capitalize brand-name trademarks as proper adjectives such as Kleenex tissue or Scotch tape.

For more practice with capitalization, go to www.mywritinglab.com > Punctuation and Mechanics > Capitalization.

# 34

**Preview**

- Rules for Improving Your Spelling

# Improving Your Spelling

To spell correctly is to understand the rules for properly arranging letters in a word.

## Rules for Improving Your Spelling

Improving your spelling involves understanding rules about the use of suffixes and prefixes.

### Understand How Suffixes Are Used

A **suffix** is added to the end of a **base word** (a word's original meaning) to change the use or meaning of the word. Suffixes begin with either a vowel or a consonant, which affects the spelling rules for adding them to base words. The following chart lists a few common vowel and consonant suffixes, along with their meanings and examples.

| Vowel Suffix | Meaning | Example |
|---|---|---|
| -able -ible | able to | touch able, vis ible |
| -ed | past tense of a verb | talk ed, walk ed |
| -en | present or past participle | bitt en, writt en |
| -er | one who is or does | play er, adopt er |
| -er | comparison | bigg er, small er |
| -es | plural of a noun | dress es, box es |
| -es | singular present tense of a verb | wash es, finish es |
| -ous | full of | danger ous, luxuri ous |

| Consonant Suffix | Meaning | Example |
|---|---|---|
| -ful | full of | wonder ful, care ful |
| -ly or -y | like | gent ly, week ly |
| -ness | state of being | happi ness, faithful ness |
| -ment | state of | govern ment, state ment |
| -s | plural of a noun | doctor s, worker s |
| -s | singular present tense of a verb | run s, quit s |

The rules of spelling words with suffixes vary. The next several sections explain and illustrate the various spelling rules for adding suffixes.

## Add -*s* or -*es* to Nouns and Verbs to Form the Plural

- **Add -*s* to form the plural of most regular nouns, including those that end with *o*.**

video + s ⟶ videos

- **Add -*es* to nouns that end with a consonant immediately before a final *o*.**

hero + es ⟶ heroes

- **Add -*s* to most regular verbs to form the singular present tense in the third person.**

ask + s ⟶ asks

- **Add -*es* to form the plural of nouns and to third person present tense verbs that end in *ch*, *sh*, *s*, *x*, or *z*.**

| **Nouns** | | **Verbs** | |
|---|---|---|---|
| watch + es | watches | buzz + es | buzzes |

## Double the Final Consonant in Words with One Syllable

Many **one syllable** words end in a **consonant** with a **vowel** immediately **before** it. (*Hint*: Remember **CVC**.) For a word with one syllable, one consonant, and one vowel, double the final consonant when adding a vowel suffix. The final consonant is *not* doubled when adding a consonant suffix.

s i t   +   sits   *OR*   sitter

*Exception:* Do not double the final consonant of words that end in *w*, *x*, or *y* as in the following examples: **snowing, boxer, obeys.**

## Double the Final Consonant in Words with More Than One Syllable

Words with more than one syllable often end with a vowel immediately before a **consonant**. (*Hint*: Remember **VC**.) If the final syllable is stressed or emphasized in its pronunciation, **double the final consonant**.

control      controlled      controlling

# Drop or Keep the Final *E*

- **Drop the *e* when the base *word ends* with a *silent e* and the *suffix begins* with a *vowel*.**

$$\text{advance} + \text{-ing} \longrightarrow \text{advancing}$$

- **Drop the *e* when a *vowel comes immediately before* the silent *e*.**

$$\text{true} + \text{-ly} \longrightarrow \text{truly}$$

- **Keep the *e* when the base *word ends* with a silent *e* and the *suffix begins* with a *consonant*.**

$$\text{advance} + \text{-ment} \longrightarrow \text{advancement}$$

# Change or Keep the Final *Y*

- **When a *consonant* appears before the final *y*, change the *y* to *i*.**

$$\text{supply} + \text{-ies} \longrightarrow \text{supplies}$$

- **When a *vowel* appears before the final *y*, keep the *y*.**

$$\text{obey} + \text{-ed} \longrightarrow \text{obeyed}$$

- **Keep the *y* when adding the suffix *-ing*.**

$$\text{cry} + \text{-ing} \longrightarrow \text{crying}$$

# Choose *ie* or *ei*

A helpful way to remember how to use *ie* and *ei* in spelling is to think of the following rhyme:

"***i*** before ***e*** except after ***c*** or when sounds like *ay* as in *neighbor*

or *weigh*"

There are, however, some exceptions to the *ie*, *ei* rule that should be memorized:

*ie*: species, science, conscience

*ei*: height, either, neither, leisure, seize, counterfeit, foreign

For more practice with spelling, go to
www.mywritinglab.com > Punctuation and Mechanics >
Improving Your Spelling.

# Reading Selections

**What's the Connection Between Reading and Writing?**

**Understanding the Connection Between Reading and Writing**

**Applying the Point: The Connection Between Reading and Writing**

**Ten Reading Selections**

**DESCRIPTION**
*Maya Lin's Design Submission to the Vietnam Memorial Competition*
**Maya Lin**

**NARRATION**
*New Directions*
**Maya Angelou**

**PROCESS**
*How to Write a Personal Letter*
**Garrison Keillor**

**ILLUSTRATION**
*Don't Call Me a Hot Tamale*
**Judith Ortiz Cofer**

**CLASSIFICATION**
*The Ways of Meeting Oppression*
**Martin Luther King, Jr.**

**COMPARISON—CONTRAST**
*A Fable for Tomorrow*
**Rachel Carson**

**DEFINITION**
*What Is Poverty?*
**Jo Goodwin-Parker**

**CAUSE—EFFECT**
*Why We Crave Horror Movies*
**Stephen King**

**PERSUASION**
*Statement of Senator Joe Lieberman on Rating the Ratings System*
**Joe Lieberman**

*The Hip-Hop Summit Action Network Statement for the Senate Committee on Government Affairs Hearing on Entertainment Ratings July 25, 2001*
**Russell Simmons**

# Reading Selections

## Reading and writing are mirror reflections of the thinking process.

The connection between reading and writing is a natural one. Effective writers are often avid readers. They know that reading and studying well-written pieces by other writers is one way to become a better writer. To begin your thinking about the connection between reading and writing, complete the following activity.

# What's the Connection Between Reading and Writing?

*Practice 1*

> **YOUR COLLEGE EXPERIENCE REQUIRES THAT YOU READ AND WRITE.**
>
> Many students agree that reading and writing are related, but often, they do not actively make use of the connection. To gauge your own understanding and use of the connection between reading and writing, answer the following questions in your notebook. Brainstorm or share your answers in a small group discussion.
>
> - Do you enjoy reading? Why or why not?
>
> - Do you think reading is an important activity? Why or why not?
>
> - Do you enjoy writing? Why or why not?
>
> - Do you think writing is an important activity? Why or why not?
>
> - What do you read for school? For work? For personal enjoyment? For general information?
>
> - If you don't read much, what could or should you read for school, work, personal enjoyment, or general information?
>
> - How often do you write? Why? What kind of writing do you do: journal writing, creative writing, academic assignments, business reports and letters, electronic emailing or blogging?
>
> - What are some specific ways you think reading can help a writer?

# Understanding the Connection Between Reading and Writing

Reading benefits a writer in many ways. For example, by reading, a writer gains the following:

- New vocabulary
- Different opinions on a topic
- Additional facts about a topic
- Details that support an opinion
- Varying ways to apply writing techniques
    - Ways to use punctuation
    - Ways to use fresh or creative expressions
    - Ways to write sentences
    - Ways to organize ideas
    - Ways to open and close an essay

The more you read, the more you know and the more you have to write about.

   A major similarity between reading and writing is that each is a thinking process best accomplished in specific stages; careful thought before, during, and after reading a selection or writing a piece improves your ability to do both. The following chart correlates the stages of the reading and the writing processes by listing the similarities between each of their phases.

# The Connection Between Reading and Writing

| | Reading | Writing |
|---|---|---|
| **Phase 1:** | Preread: Ask questions and skim details to discover the writer's purpose and point | Prewrite: Ask questions to generate details to discover your purpose and point for writing; read for information to use in your writing |
| **Phase 2:** | Read: Comprehend the writer's purpose and point; take note of key words, main ideas, major supports | Draft: Communicate your purpose and point with the use of key words, main ideas, and supporting details |
| **Phase 3:** | Review and Reflect: Achieve and reinforce clear understanding of the writer's purpose and point; adjust your views based on new information gained through reading | Revise: Rephrase or reorganize ideas to clearly support your point; ensure reader's understanding of your purpose and point |
| **Phase 4:** | Record: Discuss changes in your thinking based on new information learned through reading; respond to the writer's ideas with your new insights based on new understandings; use all the phases of the writing process | Edit: Create an error-free draft that reflects your new insights and skills as a writer |

As you can see, reading and writing mirror each other. Becoming strong in one makes you strong in the other.

Practice 2

Working together with a small group of your peers, use the reporter's questions (*Who? What? When? Where? How? Why?*) to generate prereading and prewriting questions. Create general questions about the writer's purpose, main idea, supporting details, logical order, or word choice. Use your own paper.

# Applying the Point: The Connection Between Reading and Writing

The fundamental connection between reading and writing is thinking: thinking about the meaning of what you read and what you say, and thinking about the connection between what you read and what you write. To fully realize the connection between reading and writing, you need to be an active and focused thinker. Two active thinking-reading-writing tasks are annotating a text and writing a summary. The following discussions take you through several steps that show you how to think, read, think again, reread, and then write—as a strategy to improve your writing.

## How to Annotate a Text

Use your writing skills throughout the reading process to ensure that you are an active thinker. Annotate the text, take notes, and write journal entries, summaries, and critical responses to what you read. Annotating the text before and during reading is an active thinking-reading-writing strategy. You have been taught to ask questions as a prereading thinking task. When you read, annotate your text as you find the answers to your questions.

The word *annotate* suggests that you "take notes" on the page of the text. Writing notes in the margin of the page as you read focuses your attention and improves your concentration. Annotating also will improve your understanding of the writer's purpose and point. You can note questions or answers quickly where they occur, move on in your reading, and later return to those details for clarification. In addition to writing notes, you can underline, circle, or highlight important terms, definitions, examples, or other key ideas. After reading, a review of your annotations will make responding to the material easier and more efficient. The following techniques are often used to annotate a text. Use these as guidelines to develop your own system for annotating a text.

| Annotation Techniques |
|---|
| • Underline the main idea once. |
| • Underline major supporting details twice. |
| • Circle or highlight key words or special terms. |
| • Place small question marks above unknown words. |
| • Signal steps in a process or list by using numbers. |
| • Point out important concepts with symbols such as a star or a check. |
| • Write recall questions in the margin where the answer is found. |
| • Write a statement for an implied idea. |
| • Write a summary. |

Use your annotations to guide your written response to a piece of writing. The following selection has been annotated for you as an illustration.

### The Death of President Lincoln

*By Walt Whitman*

*April 16, '65.*—I find in my notes of the time, this passage on the death of Abraham Lincoln: He leaves for America's history and biography, so far, not only its most dramatic reminiscence—he leaves, in my opinion, the *greatest*, best, most *memories*

characteristic, artistic, <u>moral personality</u>. Not but that he had faults, and show'd them in the Presidency; but honesty, goodness, shrewdness, conscience, and (a new virtue, unknown to other lands, and hardly yet really known here, but the founda-

*Keeping the United States undivided!*

tion and tie of all, as the future will grandly develop,) UNIONISM, in its truest and amplest sense, form'd the hard-pan of his character. These he <u>seal'd with his life</u>. The tragic splendor of his death, purging, illuminating all, throws round his form, *?crown?*

his head, an aureole, that will remain and will grow brighter through time, while history lives, and love of country lasts. By many has this Union been help'd; but if one *legal guardian or keeper*

name, one man, must be pick'd out, he, most of all, is the <u>conservator</u> of it, to the *?French expression for "it will be fine"*

future. He was assassinated—but the Union is not assassinated—*ça ira!* One falls, and another falls. The soldier drops, sinks like a wave—but the ranks of the ocean *?           ?*

eternally press on. Death does its work, obliterates, literates, a hundred, a thousand—President, general, captain, private—but <u>the Nation is immortal</u>.

—Whitman, Walt. *Prose Works*. Philadelphia: David McKay, 1892; Bartleby.com, 2000. www.bartleby.com/229/. 12 August 2007.

*Implied Main Idea: Lincoln preserved the UNION of the states; both he and the United States are immortal.*

Choose a selection from the 10 reading selections. Annotate the text. After you have annotated the text, recall and record in your notebook what you remember about the selection.

*Practice 3*

# How to Write a Summary

A summary includes only the most important points of a text. A summary is a restatement of the main idea and the major supporting details. The length of the summary should reflect the length of the passage you are trying to understand. For example, a paragraph might be summarized in a sentence or two; an article might be summarized in a paragraph, and a much longer document may be summarized in several paragraphs.

Writing a summary by relying on the annotations you make during reading is an excellent way to check your understanding of what you read. Always use the writer's name and the title of the text in your summary. The following summary is based on the annotations of the Walt Whitman piece about Abraham Lincoln's death.

> In his short note "The Death of President Lincoln," dated April 16, 1865, Walt Whitman honors the memory of the fallen president for his devotion to "Unionism," for being a faithful keeper of the future, for ensuring that it will be fine and that the "Nation is immortal."

Write a summary based on the annotations you made for the reading selection you used in Practice 3. Use your own paper.

## A Reading Strategy for a Writer

As you read the 10 selections included in this section, use the following reading strategy to make the connection between reading and writing. Read each selection three times. Read it once just to enjoy the writing. Then, reread the piece to annotate it for understanding. Then, read a third time to study the piece more closely to prepare for a written response. The following steps are a guide to how to get the most out of your reading.

# Reading Like a Writer

**Before Reading** Write a journal entry about the topic, title, and vocabulary. What do you already know, believe, or feel about the topic? Skim the text to identify and look up new or difficult words.

**During Reading** Annotate the text. Underline or highlight key terms, definitions, and main ideas. Generate questions to guide your thinking as you read; these questions will help you recall information after you read. Look for the answers to these questions and annotate the text when you come across the answers. Many college textbooks provide comprehension questions after a section of information. Feel free to use these after reading questions to focus your attention as you read.

**After Reading** Think, discuss, and write about what you read. Each of the 10 reading selections has four discussion questions about the writer's main idea, relevant details, logical order, and effective expression. These directed thinking activities are called "After Reading Discussion Questions: Meaning, Structure, and Expression." Your writing will improve as you learn how other writers handle these elements.

**Discuss it** Use your annotations to compare your views about a text with those of your classmates. Be open to ideas you had not considered. Add information to your notes. Discuss possible written responses.

**Write about it** Respond in writing to the text. Each of the 19 reading selections has three activities called "Thinking Prompts to Move from Reading to Writing."

# Ten Reading Selections

## Description

## Maya Lin's Design Submission to the Vietnam Memorial Competition

MAYA LIN

Born in 1959 in Athens, Ohio, Maya Lin, as a senior at Yale University, submitted the winning design in a national competition for the Vietnam Veterans Memorial that now stands in Washington, D.C.

Lin, a Chinese American, designs spaces that make room for individuals within the landscape.

**Before Reading** Write a journal entry about the Vietnam Memorial. What do you know about it? Have you seen it? What was its impact on you? If you have not seen it, do you want to? Why or why not? Why are monuments and memorials important?

Walking through this park-like area, the memorial appears as a rift in the earth—a long, polished black stone wall, emerging from and receding into the earth. Approaching the memorial, the ground slopes gently downward, and the low walls emerging on either side, growing out of the earth, extend and converge at a point below and ahead. Walking into the grassy site contained by the walls of the memorial we can barely make out the carved names upon the memorial's walls. These names, seemingly infinite in number, convey the sense of overwhelming numbers, while unifying those individuals into a whole. For this memorial is meant not as a monument to the individual but rather, as a memorial to the men and women who died during this war, as a whole. 1

The memorial is composed not as an unchanging monument, but as a moving composition, to be understood as we move into and out of it; the passage itself is gradual, the descent to the origin slow, but it is at the origin that the meaning of the memorial is to be fully understood. At the intersection of these walls, on the right side, at the wall's top, is carved the date of the first death. It is followed by 2 the names of those who have died in the war, in chronological order. These names continue on this wall, appearing to recede into the earth at the wall's end. The names resume on the left wall, as the wall emerges from the earth, continuing back to the origin, where the date of the last death is carved, at the bottom of this wall. Thus the war's beginning and end meet; the war is "complete," coming full circle, yet broken by the earth that bounds the angle's open side, and contained within the earth itself. As we turn to leave, we see these walls stretching into the distance, directing us to the Washington Monument, to the left, and the Lincoln Memorial, to the right, thus bringing the Vietnam Memorial into an historical context. We the living are brought to a concrete realization of these deaths.

3

Brought to a sharp awareness of such a loss, it is up to each individual to resolve or come to terms with this loss. For death, is in the end a personal and private matter, and the area contained with this memorial is a quiet place, meant for personal reflection and private reckoning. The black granite walls, each two hundred feet long, and ten feet below ground at their lowest point (gradually ascending toward ground level) effectively act as a sound barrier, yet are of such a height and length so as not to appear threatening or enclosing. The actual area is wide and shallow, allowing for a sense of privacy, and the sunlight from the memorial's southern exposure along with the grassy park surrounding and within its walls, contribute to the serenity of the area. Thus this memorial is for those who have died, and for us to remember them.

4

The memorial's origin is located approximately at the center of the site; its legs each extending two hundred feet towards the Washington Monument and the Lincoln Memorial. The walls, contained on one side by the earth, are ten feet below ground at their point of origin, gradually lessening in height, until they finally recede totally into the earth, at their ends. The walls are to be made of hard, polished black granite, with the names to be carved in simple Trajan letter. The memorial's construction involves recontouring the area within the wall's boundaries, so as to provide for an easily accessible descent, but as much of the site as possible should be left untouched. The area should remain as a park, for all to enjoy.

**Vocabulary** Before, during, and after reading the selection, annotate the text and write in your journal. Create a list of vocabulary words, along with their definitions, and give examples of their use from the selection you just read.

## After Reading Discussion Questions: Meaning, Structure, and Expression

1. **Main Idea:** Work as a group to write a summary that answers the following questions: What purpose did Maya Lin have for writing this essay? Who is her intended audience? What is the main idea of the essay?
2. **Relevant Details:** Lin writes, "For death, is in the end a personal and private matter, and the area contained with this memorial is a quiet place, meant for personal reflection and private reckoning." Based on the details in her description, how does the memorial represent this belief?
3. **Logical Order:** As Lin gives her physical description of the memorial, she explains the significance of each detail. Do her explanations help create a mental image of the memorial? Would it have been just as effective to give an uninterrupted physical description and then explain the purpose of each detail in a separate section? Why or why not?

**4. Effective Expression:** Of the 1,421 essays submitted in the design competition for the Vietnam Memorial, this essay won. In what ways did Lin use effective expression to communicate her vision? Identify three effective expressions in the essay. Discuss the reasons for your selections.

## Thinking Prompts to Move from Reading to Writing

**1.** Just as the memorials erected in Washington, D.C. represent people and events of historical significance, many communities build memorials to honor local individuals, groups of people, or events. Describe such a memorial in your community. Use your description to convey the significance of the memorial.

**2.** Identify a person, place, or event that is worthy of a memorial. Design a memorial and write an essay that describes your design and the significance of the honor.

# Narration

## New Directions

### MAYA ANGELOU

An acclaimed poet, award-winning writer, activist, performer, director, and teacher, Maya Angelou was born on April 4, 1928, in St. Louis and raised in Stamps, Arkansas. Dr. Angelou has authored twelve bestselling books including *I Know Why the Caged Bird Sings* and her current bestseller *A Song Flung Up to Heaven.* In January 1993, she became only the second poet in U.S. history to have the honor of writing and reciting her original work at a Presidential Inauguration. Angelou is hailed as one of the great voices of contemporary literature. The following essay is an excerpt from her book *Wouldn't Take Nothing for My Journey Now* (1993).

**Before Reading** Write a journal entry about making a life change. Have you ever made a significant change in your life? What were the advantages or disadvantages of making the change? Was it easy? If life has not changed for you, what would you change about your life if you could?

In 1903 the late Mrs. Annie Johnson of Arkansas found herself with two toddling sons, very little money, a slight ability to read and add simple numbers. To this picture add a disastrous marriage and the burdensome fact that Mrs. Johnson was a Negro. 1

When she told her husband, Mr. William Johnson, of her dissatisfaction with their marriage, he conceded that he too found it to be less than he expected and had been secretly hoping to leave and study religion. He added that he thought God was calling him not only to preach but to do so in Enid, Oklahoma. He did not tell her that he knew a minister in Enid with whom he could study and who had a friendly, unmarried daughter. They parted amicably, Annie keeping the one-room house and William taking most of the cash to carry himself to Oklahoma. 2

Annie, over six feet tall, big-boned, decided that she would not go to work as a domestic and leave her "precious babes" to anyone else's care. There was no possibility of being hired at the town's cotton gin or lumber mill, but maybe there was a way to make the two factories work for her. In her words, "I looked up the road I was going and back the way I come, and since I wasn't satisfied, I decided to step off the road and cut me a new path." She told herself that she wasn't a fancy cook but that she could "mix groceries well enough to scare hunger away from a starving man." 3

She made her plans meticulously and in secret. One early evening to see if she was ready, she placed stones in two five gallon pails and carried them three miles to the cotton gin. She rested a little, and then, discarding some rocks, she walked in the darkness to the saw mill five miles farther along the 4 dirt road. On her way back to her little house and her babies, she dumped the remaining rocks along the path.

That same night she worked into the early hours boiling chicken and frying ham. She made dough and filled the rolled-out pastry with meat. At last she went to sleep.     5

The next morning she left her house carrying the meat pies, lard, an iron brazier, and coals for a fire. Just before lunch she appeared in an empty lot behind the cotton gin. As the dinner noon bell rang, she dropped the savors into boiling fat, and the aroma rose and floated over to the workers who spilled out of the gin, covered with white lint, looking like specters.     6

Most workers had brought their lunches of pinto beans and biscuits or crackers, onions and cans of sardines, but they were tempted by the hot meat pies which Annie ladled out of the fat. She wrapped them in newspapers, which soaked up the grease, and offered them for sale at a nickel each. Although business was slow, those first days Annie was determined. She balanced her appearances between the two hours of activity.     7

So, on Monday if she offered hot fresh pies at the cotton gin and sold the remaining cooled-down pies at the lumber mill for three cents, then on Tuesday she went first to the lumber mill presenting fresh, just-cooked pies as the lumbermen covered in sawdust emerged from the mill.     8

For the next few years, on balmy spring days, blistering summer noons, and cold, wet, and wintry middays, Annie never disappointed her customers, who could count on seeing the tall, brown-skin woman bent over her brazier, carefully turning the meat pies. When she felt certain that the workers had become dependent on her, she built a stall between the two hives of industry and let the men run to her for their lunchtime provisions.     9

She had indeed stepped from the road which seemed to have been chosen for her and cut herself a brand-new path. In years that stall became a store where customers could buy cheese, meal, syrup, cookies, candy, writing tablets, pickles, canned goods, fresh fruit, soft drinks, coal, oil, and leather soles for worn-out shoes.     10

Each of us has the right and the responsibility to assess the roads which lie ahead, and those over which we have traveled, and if the future road looms ominous or unpromising, and the roads back uninviting, then we need to gather our resolve and, carrying only the necessary baggage, step off that road into another direction. If the new choice is also unpalatable, without embarrassment, we must be ready to change that as well.     11

**Vocabulary**   Before, during, and after reading the selection, annotate the text and write in your journal. Create a list of vocabulary words, along with their definitions, and give examples of their use from the selection you just read.

**After Reading Discussion Questions:**  Meaning, Structure, and Expression

1. **Main Idea:** Work as a group to write a summary that answers the following questions: What purpose did Maya Angelou have for writing this piece? Who is her intended audience? What is the main idea of the essay? What is the significance of the title of the book from which the selection was taken? How does this piece reflect that title?

2. **Relevant Details:** Angelou captures the reality of daily life in 1903 for Annie Johnson and her community. List the details that paint this realistic picture; consider organizing your list based on sensory details. Describe the society or type of community in which Johnson lived. Are any of the details of this story similar to or different from today's society or parts of your community? In what ways?

3. **Logical Order:** Angelou ends her essay with a paragraph that explains the lesson she wants her reader to learn from Johnson's life. What is the impact of this paragraph on you as a reader? Is the concluding paragraph necessary? Why or why not? Why do you think Angelou waits to the end of the essay to explain her point? Would the essay be as effective if she began by stating this point? Why or why not?

4. **Effective Expression:** A key statement in the essay is made by Annie Johnson, "I looked up the road I was going and back the way I come, and since I wasn't satisfied, I decided to step off the road and cut me a new path." Explain the meaning of the metaphors "road" and "path." What "road" was Johnson on? What "path" did she cut for herself? Are these metaphors effective? Why or why not?

## Thinking Prompts to Move from Reading to Writing

1. Think of an important lesson you have learned, or a truth about life that you think everyone needs to know. Write a narrative essay that illustrates this lesson or important truth about life.

2. Have you or someone you know made a decision to make a major life change? Was the change positive or negative? Was the change difficult to make? In the end, was the change worth the effort? Write a narrative that illustrates the significance of making a decision to change.

# Process

---

# How to Write a Personal Letter

## GARRISON KEILLOR

Born in Anoka, Minnesota, in 1942, Garrison Keillor is the host and writer of *A Prairie Home Companion* and *The Writer's Almanac* heard on public radio stations across the country and the author of more than a dozen books, including *Lake Wobegon Days, The Book of Guys, Love Me, Homegrown Democrat,* and *Pontoon: A Novel of Lake Wobegon.*

**Before Reading**  Write a journal entry about letter writing. Do you or does anyone you know write letters? Why do you think letter writing is declining? How is writing a personal letter different from other kinds of writing?

We shy people need to write a letter now and then, or else we'll <u>dry up</u> and <u>blow away</u>. It's true. And I speak as one who loves to reach for the phone, dial the number, and talk. The telephone is to shyness what Hawaii is to February; it's a way out of the woods. *And yet* a letter is better. 1

Such a sweet gift—a piece of handmade writing, in an envelope that is not a bill, sitting in our friend's path when she trudges home from a long day spent among savages and wahoos, a day our words will help repair. They don't need to be immortal, just sincere. She can read them twice and again tomorrow: "You're someone I care about, Corinne, and think of often, and every time I do, you make me smile." 2

We need to write; otherwise, nobody will know who we are. They will have only a vague impression of us as "A Nice Person" because, frankly, we don't shine at conversation, we lack the confidence to thrust our faces forward and say, "Hi, I'm Heather Hooten; let me tell you about my week." Mostly we say "Uh-huh" and "Oh really." People smile and look over our shoulder, looking for someone else to meet. 3

So a shy person sits down and writes a letter. To be known by another person—to meet and talk freely on the page—to be close despite distance. To escape from anonymity and be our own sweet selves and express the music of our souls. The same thing that moves a giant rock star to sing his heart out in front of 123,000 people moves us to take ballpoint in hand and write a few lines to our dear Aunt Eleanor. *We want to be known.* We want her to know that we have fallen in love, that we have quit our job, that we're moving to New York, and we want to say a few things that might not get said in casual conversation: "Thank you for what you've meant to me. I am very happy right now." 4

The first step in writing letters is to get over the guilt of *not* writing. You don't "owe" anybody a letter. Letters are a gift. The burning shame you feel when you see unanswered mail makes it harder to pick up a pen and makes for a cheerless letter when you finally do. "I feel bad about not writing, but I've been so busy," etc. Skip this. Few letters are obligatory and they are "Thanks for the wonderful gift" and "I am terribly sorry to hear about George's death" and "Yes, you're welcome to stay with us next month." Write these promptly if you 5 want to keep your friends. Don't worry about other letters, except love letters, of course. When your true love writes, "Dear Light of My Life, Joy of My Heart, O Lovely Pulsating Core of My Sensate Life," some response is called for.

Some of the best letters are tossed off in a burst of inspiration, so keep your writing stuff in one place where you can sit down for a few minutes, and—"Dear Roy, I am in the middle of an essay but thought I'd drop you a line. Hi to your sweetie too"—dash off a note to a pal. Envelopes, stamps, address book, everything in a drawer so you can write fast when the pen is hot. A blank white 8" × 11" sheet can look as big as Montana if the pen's not so hot; try a smaller page and write boldly. Get a pen that makes a sensuous line, get a comfortable typewriter, a friendly word processor—whichever feels easy to the hand.

Sit for a few minutes with the blank sheet of paper in front of you, and meditate on the person you will write to; let your friend come to mind until you can almost see him or her in the room with you. Remember the last time you saw each other and how your friend looked and what you said and what perhaps was unsaid between you, and when your friend becomes real to you, start to write. Write the salutation, "Dear You," and take a deep breath and plunge in. A simple declarative sentence will do, followed by another and another. Talk about what you're doing and tell it like you were talking to us. Don't think about grammar, don't think about style, don't try to write dramatically, just give us your news. Where did you go, who did you see, what did they say, what do you think?

If you don't know where to begin, start with the present: "I'm sitting at the kitchen table on a rainy Saturday morning. Everyone is gone, and the house is quiet." Let your description of the present moment lead to something else; let the letter drift gently along. The toughest letter to crank out is one that is meant to impress, as we all know from writing job applications; if it's hard work to write a letter to a friend, maybe you're trying too hard to be terrific. A letter is only a report to someone who already likes you for reasons other than your brilliance. Take it easy.

Don't worry about form. It's not a term paper. When you come to the end of one episode, just start a new paragraph. You can go from a few lines about the sad state of pro football to the fight with your mother to your cat's urinary tract infection to a few thoughts on personal indebtedness and on to the kitchen sink and what's in it. The more you write, the easier it gets, and when you have a true friend to write to, a *compadre,* a soul sibling, then it's like driving a car; you just press on the gas.

Don't tear up the page and start over when you write a bad line; try to write your way out of it. Make mistakes and plunge on. Let the letter cook along and let yourself be bold. Outrage, confusion, love—whatever is in your mind, let it find a way to the page. Writing is a means of discovery, always, and when you come to the end and write "Yours ever" or "Hugs and Kisses," you'll know something that you didn't when you wrote "Dear Pal."

Probably your friend will put your letter away, and it'll be read again a few years from now, and it will improve with age. And forty years from now, your friend's grandkids will dig it out of the attic and read it, a sweet and precious relic that gives them a sudden clear glimpse of you and her and the world we old-timers knew. Your simple lines about where you went, who you saw, what they said, will speak to those children, and they will feel in their hearts the humanity of our times.

You can't pick up a phone and call the future and tell them about our times. You have to pick up a piece of paper.

6

7

8

9

10

11

12

Vocabulary  Before, during, and after reading the selection, annotate the text and write in your journal. Create a list of vocabulary words, along with their definitions, and give examples of their use from the selection you just read.

## After Reading Discussion Questions:  Meaning, Structure, and Expression

1. **Main Idea:** Work as a group to write a summary that answers the following questions: What purpose did Garrison Keillor have for writing this essay? Who is his intended audience? What is the main idea of the essay?
2. **Relevant Details:** Keillor's advice about how to write a personal letter does not begin until the fifth paragraph. How are the details in the first four paragraphs related to his main point? Would the essay be as effective without these paragraphs? Why or why not?
3. **Logical Order:** Keillor describes a step-by-step process for writing a personal letter. Map out the steps in the order he suggests them. Do you agree with his advice? Would you change the order of any of the steps? Would you add or delete any steps? Why or why not?
4. **Effective Expression:** Keillor is often praised for his light-hearted, easy-to-read style. Find three expressions that are amusing in tone. Explain the reasons for your selections.

## Thinking Prompts to Move from Reading to Writing

1. This essay offers clear instructions about how to write a letter based on Keillor's expertise in and understanding of the writing process. Think of a task or process that you understand or have mastered through experience. Write an essay that explains the significance of the task or process and the steps necessary to successfully accomplish it.
2. Keillor advises in paragraph 9, "Don't worry about form. It's not a term paper." His statement indicates differences among writing a personal letter for everyday life, writing a term paper for college life, and writing letters and reports for working life. How might the writing process change for each of these situations? Write an essay that describes how to write a term paper or a letter of application for a job. Use Keillor's essay as a model.

# Illustration

## Don't Call Me a Hot Tamale

### JUDITH ORTIZ COFER

Born in 1952 in Puerto Rico and raised in Paterson, New Jersey, Judith Ortiz Cofer is an acclaimed poet, novelist, and essayist. Her writings explore the experiences of being a minority as a Hispanic woman. She is currently the Regents' and Franklin Professor of English and Creative Writing at the University of Georgia.

**Before Reading** Write a journal entry about your experiences with stereotypes. Have you ever been stereotyped? Describe the incident. What are some common stereotypes in our culture? How are these stereotypes harmful?

1. On a bus to London from Oxford University, where I was earning some graduate credits one summer, a young man, obviously fresh from a pub, approached my seat. With both hands over his heart, he went down on his knees in the aisle and broke into an Irish tenor's rendition of "Maria" from *West Side Story*. I was not amused. "Maria" had followed me to London, reminding me of a prime fact of my life: You can leave the island of Puerto Rico, master the English language, and travel as far as you can, but if you're a Latina, especially one who so clearly belongs to Rita Moreno's gene pool, the island travels with you.

2. Growing up in New Jersey and wanting most of all to belong, I lived in two completely different worlds. My parents designed our life as a microcosm of their *casas* on the island—we spoke in Spanish, ate Puerto Rican food bought at the *bodega,* and practiced strict Catholicism complete with Sunday mass in Spanish.

3. I was kept under tight surveillance by my parents, since my virtue and modesty were, by their cultural equation, the same as their honor. As teenagers, my friends and I were lectured constantly on how to behave as proper *señoritas.* But it was a conflicting message we received, since our Puerto Rican mothers also encouraged us to look and act like women by dressing us in clothes our Anglo schoolmates and their mothers found too "mature" and flashy. I often felt humiliated when I appeared at an American friend's birthday party wearing a dress more suitable for a semiformal. At Puerto Rican festivities, neither the music nor the colors we wore could be too loud.

4. I remember Career Day in high school, when our teachers told us to come dressed as if for a job interview. That morning, I agonized in front of my closet, trying to figure out what a "career girl" would wear, because the only model I had was Marlo Thomas on TV. To me and my Puerto Rican girlfriends, dressing up meant wearing our mother's ornate jewelry and clothing.

5. At school that day, the teachers assailed us for wearing "everything at once"—meaning too much jewelry and too many accessories. And it was painfully obvious that the other students in their tailored skirts and silk blouses thought we were hopeless and vulgar. The way they looked at us was a taste of the cultural clash that awaited us in the real world, where prospective employers

and men on the street would often misinterpret our tight skirts and bright colors as a come-on.

It is custom, not chromosomes, that leads us to choose scarlet over pale pink. Our mothers had grown up on a tropical island where the natural environment was a riot of primary colors, where showing your skin was one way to keep cool as well as to look sexy. On the island, women felt freer to dress and move provocatively since they were protected by the traditions and laws of a Spanish/Catholic system of morality and machismo, the main rule of which was: *You may look at my sister, but if you touch her I will kill you.* The extended family and church structure provided them with a circle of safety on the island; if a man "wronged" a girl, everyone would close in to save her family honor. 6

Off-island, signals often get mixed. When a Puerto Rican girl who is dressed in her idea of what is attractive meets a man from the mainstream culture who has been trained to react to certain types of clothing as a sexual signal, a clash is likely to take place. She is seen as a Hot Tamale, a sexual firebrand. I learned this lesson at my first formal dance when my date leaned over and painfully planted a sloppy, overeager kiss on my mouth. When I didn't respond with sufficient passion, he said in a resentful tone: "I thought you Latin girls were supposed to mature early." It was only the first time I would feel like a fruit or vegetable—I was supposed to *ripen,* not just grow into womanhood like other girls. 7

These stereotypes, though rarer, still surface in my life. I recently stayed at a classy metropolitan hotel. After having dinner with a friend, I was returning to my room when a middle-aged man in a tuxedo stepped directly into my path. With his champagne glass extended toward me, he exclaimed, "Evita!" 8

Blocking my way, he bellowed the song "Don't Cry for Me, Argentina." Playing to the gathering crowd, he began to sing loudly a ditty to the tune of "La Bamba"—except the lyrics were about a girl named Maria whose exploits all rhymed with her name and gonorrhea. 9

I knew that this same man—probably a corporate executive, even worldly by most standards—would never have regaled a white woman with a dirty song in public. But to him, I was just a character in his universe of "others," all cartoons. 10

Still, I am one of the lucky ones. There are thousands of Latinas without the privilege of the education that my parents gave me. For them every day is a struggle against the misconceptions perpetuated by the myth of the Latina as whore, domestic worker or criminal. 11

Rather than fight these pervasive stereotypes, I try to replace them with a more interesting set of realities. I travel around the U.S. reading from my books of poetry and my novel. With the stories I tell, the dreams and fears I examine in my work, I try to get my audience past the particulars of my skin color, my accent or my clothes. 12

I once wrote a poem in which I called Latinas "God's brown daughters." It is really a prayer, of sorts, for communication and respect. In it, Latin women pray "in Spanish to an Anglo God/with a Jewish heritage," and they are "fervently hoping / that if not omnipotent, / at least He be bilingual." 13

**Vocabulary**  Before, during, and after reading the selection, annotate the text and write in your journal. Create a list of vocabulary words, along with their definitions, and give examples of their use from the selection you just read.

# After Reading Discussion Questions: Meaning, Structure, and Expression

1. **Main Idea:** Work as a group to write a summary that answers the following questions: What purpose did Judith Ortiz Cofer have for writing this essay? Who is her intended audience? What is the main idea of the essay? What is the significance of the title?

2. **Relevant Details:** Cofer relies mostly on personal experience to make her point about stereotypes based on race or gender. Does she provide enough details to make her point convincingly? Would the use of facts or expert opinions strengthen her point? Why or why not?

3. **Logical Order:** Cofer opens her essay with an example from her personal life. Is this an effective opening for the essay? Why or why not? Compare the introduction of the essay to the conclusion of the essay. How does the conclusion relate to the introduction? Is this an effective conclusion? Why or why not? What other ways could Cofer have opened or closed her essay?

4. **Effective Expression:** Based on Judith Ortiz Cofer's choice of words, how would you describe the tone of this essay? Is it angry, embarrassed, disappointed, confrontational, or candid, or does it communicate some other attitude about stereotypes? Identify three expressions that illustrate the tone of the piece. Explain the reasons for your selections.

## Thinking Prompts to Move from Reading to Writing

1. Cofer makes a connection between culture and fashion. According to her description, Hispanic fashion for women is "flashy," "mature," and "sexy" with "ornate jewelry" and "tight skirts and bright colors." Write an essay in which you illustrate how fashion represents a particular culture. For example, illustrate fashion in the Hip-Hop culture.

2. Cofer's essay illustrates the stereotypes she faces as a Hispanic woman. Identify and exemplify a stereotype that you or someone you know has encountered. For example, what are some stereotypes that elderly people face?

# Classification

## The Ways of Meeting Oppression

MARTIN LUTHER KING, JR.

During the Civil Rights Movement, Martin Luther King, Jr. preached and lived out the philosophy of nonviolent resistance to overcome oppression and create a just society. Through his leadership, he proved the power of this method to combat racial segregation. King defines his philosophy of nonviolent resistance in this essay.

**Before Reading**  Write a journal entry about your experiences with oppression. Have you or someone you know ever been treated unfairly? How does unfair treatment make you feel? What is the natural reaction to unfair treatment?

Oppressed people deal with their oppression in three characteristic ways. One way is acquiescence: the oppressed resign themselves to their doom. They tacitly adjust themselves to oppression, and thereby become conditioned to it. In every movement toward freedom some of the oppressed prefer to remain oppressed. Almost 2800 years ago Moses set out to lead the children of Israel from the slavery of Egypt to the freedom of the promised land. He soon discovered that slaves do not always welcome their deliverers. They become accustomed to being slaves. They would rather bear those ills they have, as Shakespeare pointed out, than flee to others that they know not of. They prefer the "fleshpots of Egypt" to the ordeals of emancipation. 1

There is such a thing as the freedom of exhaustion. Some people are so worn down by the yoke of oppression that they give up. A few years ago in the slum areas of Atlanta, a Negro guitarist used to sing almost daily: "Been down so long that down don't bother me." This is the type of negative freedom and resignation that often engulfs the life of the oppressed. 2

But this is not the way out. To accept passively an unjust system is to cooperate with that system; thereby the oppressed become as evil as the oppressor. Noncooperation with evil is as much a moral obligation as is cooperation with good. The oppressed must never allow the conscience of the oppressor to slumber. Religion reminds every man that he is his brother's keeper. To accept injustice or segregation passively is to say to the oppressor that his actions are morally right. It is a way of allowing his conscience to fall asleep. At this moment the oppressed fails to be his brother's keeper. So acquiescence— while often the easier way—is not the moral way. It is the way of the coward. The Negro cannot win the respect of his oppressor by acquiescing; he merely increases the oppressor's arrogance and contempt. Acquiescence is interpreted as proof of the Negro's inferiority. The Negro cannot win the respect of the white people of the South or the peoples of the world if he is willing to sell the future of his children or his personal and immediate comfort and safety. 3

A second way that oppressed people sometimes deal with oppression is to resort to physical violence and corroding hatred. Violence often brings about momentary results. Nations have frequently won their independence in battle. But in spite of temporary victories, violence never brings permanent peace. It solves no social problem; it merely creates new and more complicated ones. 4

Violence as a way of achieving racial justice is both impractical and immoral. 5
It is impractical because it is a descending spiral ending in destruction for all.
The old law of an eye for an eye leaves everybody blind. It is immoral because it
seeks to humiliate the opponent rather than win his understanding; it seeks to
annihilate rather than to convert. Violence is immoral because it thrives on
hatred rather than love. It destroys community and makes brotherhood
impossible. It leaves society in monologue rather than dialogue. Violence ends
by defeating itself. It creates bitterness in the survivors and brutality in the
destroyers. A voice echoes through time saying to every potential Peter, "Put up
your sword." History is cluttered with the wreckage of nations that failed to
follow this command.

If the American Negro and other victims of oppression succumb to the 6
temptation of using violence in the struggle for freedom, future generations
will be the recipients of a desolate night of bitterness, and our chief legacy to
them will be an endless reign of meaningless chaos. Violence is not the way.

The third way open to oppressed people in their quest for freedom is the way 7
of nonviolent resistance. Like the synthesis in Hegelian philosophy, the
principle of nonviolent resistance seeks to reconcile the truths of two
opposites—the acquiescence and violence—while avoiding the extremes and
immoralities of both. The nonviolent resister agrees with the person who
acquiesces that one should not be physically aggressive toward his opponent;
but he balances the equation by agreeing with the person of violence that evil
must be resisted. He avoids the nonresistance of the former and the violent
resistance of the latter. With nonviolent resistance, no individual or group need
submit to any wrong, nor need anyone resort to violence in order to right a
wrong.

It seems to me that this is the method that must guide the actions of the 8
Negro in the present crisis in race relations. Through nonviolent resistance the
Negro will be able to rise to the noble height of opposing the unjust system
while loving the perpetrators of the system. The Negro must work passionately
and unrelentingly for full stature as a citizen, but he must not use inferior
methods to gain it. He must never come to terms with falsehood, malice, hate,
or destruction.

Nonviolent resistance makes it possible for the Negro to remain in the South 9
and struggle for his rights. The Negro's problem will not be solved by running
away. He cannot listen to the glib suggestion of those who would urge him to
migrate en masse to other sections of the country. By grasping his great
opportunity in the South he can make a lasting contribution to the moral
strength of the nation and set a sublime example of courage for generations yet
unborn.

By nonviolent resistance, the Negro can also enlist all men of good will in his 10
struggle for equality. The problem is not a purely racial one, with Negroes set
against whites. In the end, it is not a struggle between people at all, but a
tension between justice and injustice. Nonviolent resistance is not aimed against
oppressors but against oppression. Under its banner consciences, not racial
groups, are enlisted.

**Vocabulary** Before, during, and after reading the selection, annotate the text
and write in your journal. Create a list of vocabulary words, along with their
definitions, and give examples of their use from the selection you just read.

## After Reading Discussion Questions: Meaning, Structure, and Expression

1. **Main Idea:** Work as a group to write a summary that answers the following questions: What purpose did Martin Luther King, Jr. have for writing this essay? Who is his intended audience? What is the main idea of the essay? What is the significance of the title?

2. **Relevant Details:** What are the three ways that people deal with oppression, according to King? Which way does King recommend people deal with oppression? Do you agree with his opinion? Why or why not?

3. **Logical Order:** King presents these three ways of dealing with oppression in a specific order. Why did he choose this order? Would the essay be as effective if he changed the order of these three major details? Why or why not?

4. **Effective Expression:** Throughout the essay, King refers to African Americans as Negroes. Why do you think he used this term? What is the tone of this essay, based on King's use of language? Is the tone angry, disillusioned, hopeful, spiritual, or some other tone? Identify three expressions that illustrate the tone of the piece. Explain the reasons for your selections.

## Thinking Prompts to Move from Reading to Writing

1. In his essay, King discusses a particular social problem: oppression of the African American before and during the Civil Rights Movement. Identify and discuss three types of current social problems of great importance.

2. King opens his essay with the statement, "Oppressed people deal with their oppression in three characteristic ways." Identify a specific group of people who face particular challenges, and discuss the characteristic ways in which they deal with the situation. Consider the following suggestions: the ways students typically deal with the demands of pursuing an education; the ways one deals with a disability or handicap; the ways people react to death or loss.

# Comparison–Contrast

## A Fable for Tomorrow

### RACHEL CARSON

Born in Springfield, Pennsylvania, in 1902, Rachel Carson lived the rugged life of a farmer's daughter. A biologist, environmentalist, and nature writer, Carson became a foreleader in the environmental movement. Her book *Silent Spring* raised the alarm and instigated change in national attitudes and policies about pesticides. She was awarded the Presidential Medal of Freedom.

**Before Reading**  Write a journal entry about your views about the environment. Are you concerned about the environment? Why or why not? What do you think is the greatest threat to our environment? Why? What should be done?

1  There was once a town in the heart of America where all life seemed to live in harmony with its surroundings. The town lay in the midst of a checkerboard of prosperous farms, with fields of grain and hillsides of orchards where, in spring, white clouds of bloom drifted above the green fields. In autumn, oak and maple and birch set up a blaze of color that flamed and flickered across a backdrop of pines. Then foxes barked in the hills and deer silently crossed the fields, half hidden in the mists of the fall mornings.

2  Along the roads, laurel, viburnum and alder, great ferns and wildflowers delighted the traveler's eye through much of the year. Even in winter the roadsides were places of beauty, where countless birds came to feed on the berries and on the seed heads of the dried weeds rising above the snow. The countryside was, in fact, famous for the abundance and variety of its bird life, and when the flood of migrants was pouring through in spring and fall people traveled from great distances to observe them. Others came to fish the streams, which flowed clear and cold out of the hills and contained shady pools where trout lay. So it had been from the days many years ago when the first settlers raised their houses, sank their wells, and built their barns.

3  Then a strange blight crept over the area and everything began to change. Some evil spell had settled on the community: mysterious maladies swept the flocks of chickens; the cattle and sheep sickened and died. Everywhere was a shadow of death. The farmers spoke of much illness among their families. In the town the doctors had become more and more puzzled by new kinds of sickness appearing among their patients. There had been several sudden and unexplained deaths, not only among adults but even among children, who would be stricken suddenly while at play and die within a few hours.

4  There was a strange stillness. The birds, for example—where had they gone? Many people spoke of them, puzzled and disturbed. The feeding stations in the backyards were deserted. The few birds seen anywhere were moribund; they trembled violently and could not fly. It was a spring without voices. On the mornings that had once throbbed with the dawn chorus of robins, catbirds, doves, jays, wrens, and scores of other bird voices there was now no sound; only silence lay over the fields and woods and marsh.

On the farms the hens brooded, but no chicks hatched. The farmers complained that they were unable to raise any pigs—the litters were small and the young survived only a few days. The apple trees were coming into bloom but no bees droned among the blossoms, so there was no pollination and there would be no fruit.

5

The roadsides, once so attractive, were now lined with browned and withered vegetation as though swept by fire. These, too, were silent, deserted by all living things. Even the streams were now lifeless. Anglers no longer visited them, for all the fish had died.

6

In the gutters under the eaves and between the shingles of the roofs, a white granular powder still showed a few patches; some weeks before it had fallen like snow upon the roofs and the lawns, the fields and streams.

7

No witchcraft, no enemy action had silenced the rebirth of new life in this stricken world. The people had done it themselves.

8

This town does not actually exist, but it might easily have a thousand counterparts in America or elsewhere in the world. I know of no community that has experienced all the misfortunes I describe. Yet every one of these disasters has actually happened somewhere, and many real communities have already suffered a substantial number of them. A grim specter has crept upon us almost unnoticed, and this imagined tragedy may easily become a stark reality we all shall know.

9

**Vocabulary** Before, during, and after reading the selection, annotate the text and write in your journal. Create a list of vocabulary words, along with their definitions, and give examples of their use from the selection you just read.

## After Reading Discussion Questions: Meaning, Structure, and Expression

1. **Main Idea:** Work as a group to write a summary that answers the following questions: What purpose did Rachel Carson have for writing this essay? Who is her intended audience? What is the main idea of the essay? What is the significance of the title?

2. **Relevant Details:** When Carson begins her concluding paragraph by stating, "This town does not actually exist," she admits that she has used a fictitious example to make her point. Does she provide enough details to make her point convincingly? Would the use of facts or expert opinions strengthen her point? Why or why not? What is the effect of her sudden admission of using a fictitious example?

3. **Logical Order:** Carson contrasts two descriptions of a fictional place: what the place was like before it was damaged by pesticides and what the place looked like after the damage occurred. Does she organize these contrasting views point by point or by presenting one block of ideas (description of the place before it was damaged) and then another (description of the place after it was damaged)? Do you think she chose the more effective method for ordering her details? Why or why not?

4. **Effective Expression:** To make her point, Carson describes sensory details of sights and sounds to create vivid mental images in the reader's mind. Identify four sensory details: two that depict the town before it changed and two that depict the town after it changed. What impact do these details have on the reader?

# Thinking Prompts to Move from Reading to Writing

1. Carson uses sensory details to describe the change of seasons in this fictitious town, such as "in spring, white clouds of bloom drifted above the green fields." Write an essay that contrasts the seasons as they occur in a particular place. Use sensory details to depict the contrast of sights, sounds, aromas, or textures among the seasons.

2. "A Fable for Tomorrow" is a story that warns the reader about the negative effects of pesticide by contrasting before and after images. Identify a specific problem such as gangs, graffiti, drug abuse, alcoholism, an eating disorder, or obesity. Write a fable that warns against this problem by contrasting before and after situations.

# Definition

---

## What is Poverty?

### JO GOODWIN-PARKER

The following selection was published in *America's Other Children: Public Schools Outside Suburbs*, by George Henderson in 1971 by the University of Oklahoma Press. The author specifically requests the right to her privacy and offers no additional information about herself for public use. In her essay, a personal testimony about living in poverty, she speaks directly to the reader.

**Before Reading**  Write a journal entry about your response to poverty. How would you define poverty? Why are people poor? How does society react to the poor? Do you think our government does enough to help poor people? What can be done to fight poverty?

You ask me what is poverty? Listen to me. Here I am, dirty, smelly, and with no "proper" underwear on and with the stench of my rotting teeth near you. I will tell you. Listen to me. Listen without pity. I cannot use your pity. Listen with understanding. Put yourself in my dirty, worn out, ill-fitting shoes, and hear me. 1

Poverty is getting up every morning from a dirt- and illness-stained mattress. The sheets have long since been used for diapers. Poverty is living in a smell that never leaves. This is a smell of urine, sour milk, and spoiling food sometimes joined with the strong smell of long-cooked onions. Onions are cheap. If you have smelled this smell, you did not know how it came. It is the smell of the outdoor privy. It is the smell of young children who cannot walk the long dark way in the night. It is the smell of the mattresses where years of "accidents" have happened. It is the smell of the milk which has gone sour because the refrigerator long has not worked, and it costs money to get it fixed. It is the smell of rotting garbage. I could bury it, but where is the shovel? Shovels cost money. 2

Poverty is being tired. I have always been tired. They told me at the hospital when the last baby came that I had chronic anemia caused from poor diet, a bad case of worms, and that I needed a corrective operation. I listened politely—the poor are always polite. The poor always listen. They don't say that there is no money for iron pills, or better food, or worm medicine. The idea of an operation is frightening and costs so much that, if I had dared, I would have laughed. Who takes care of my children? Recovery from an operation takes a long time. I have three children. When I left them with "Granny" the last time I had a job, I came home to find the baby covered with fly specks, and a diaper that had not been changed since I left. When the dried diaper came off, bits of my baby's flesh came with it. My other child was playing with a sharp bit of broken glass, and my oldest was playing alone at the edge of a lake. I made twenty-two dollars a week, and a good nursery school costs twenty dollars a week for three children. I quit my job. 3

Poverty is dirt. You can say in your clean clothes coming from your clean house, "Anybody can be clean." Let me explain about housekeeping with no money. For breakfast I give my children grits with no oleo or cornbread without eggs and oleo. This does not use up many dishes. What dishes there are, I wash in cold water and with no soap. Even the cheapest soap has to be saved for the baby's diapers. Look at my hands, so cracked and red. Once I saved for two months to buy a jar of Vaseline for my hands and the baby's diaper rash. When I had saved enough, I went to buy it and the price had gone up two cents. The baby and I suffered on. I have to decide every day if I can bear to put my cracked sore hands into the cold water and strong soap. But you ask, why not hot water? Fuel costs money. If you have a wood fire it costs money. If you burn electricity, it costs money. Hot water is a luxury. I do not have luxuries. I know you will be surprised when I tell you how young I am. I look so much older. My back has been bent over the wash tubs every day for so long, I cannot remember when I ever did anything else. Every night I wash every stitch my school age child has on and just hope her clothes will be dry by morning.

Poverty is staying up all night on' cold nights to watch the fire knowing one spark on the newspaper covering the walls means your sleeping child dies in flames. In summer poverty is watching gnats and flies devour your baby's tears when he cries. The screens are torn and you pay so little rent you know they will never be fixed. Poverty means insects in your food, in your nose, in your eyes, and crawling over you when you sleep. Poverty is hoping it never rains because diapers won't dry when it rains and soon you are using newspapers. Poverty is seeing your children forever with runny noses. Paper handkerchiefs cost money and all your rags you need for other things. Even more costly are antihistamines. Poverty is cooking without food and cleaning without soap.

Poverty is asking for help. Have you ever had to ask for help, knowing your children will suffer unless you get it? Think about asking for a loan from a relative, if this is the only way you can imagine asking for help. I will tell you how it feels. You find out where the office is that you are supposed to visit. You circle that block four or five times. Thinking of your children, you go in. Everyone is very busy. Finally, someone comes out and you tell her that you need help. That never is the person you need to see. You go see another person, and after spilling the whole shame of your poverty all over the desk between you, you find that this isn't the right office after all—you must repeat the whole process, and it never is any easier at the next place.

You have asked for help, and after all it has a cost. You are again told to wait. You are told why, but you don't really hear because of the red cloud of shame and the rising cloud of despair.

Poverty is remembering. It is remembering quitting school in junior high because "nice" children had been so cruel about my clothes and my smell. The attendance officer came. My mother told him I was pregnant. I wasn't, but she thought that I could get a job and help out. I had jobs off and on, but never long enough to learn anything. Mostly I remember being married. I was so young then. I am still young. For a time, we had all the things you have. There was a little house in another town, with hot water and everything. Then my husband lost his job. There was unemployment insurance for a while and what few jobs I could get. Soon, all our nice things were repossessed and we moved back here. I was pregnant then. This house didn't look so bad when we first moved in. Every week it gets worse. Nothing is ever fixed. We now had no money. There were a few odd jobs for my husband, but everything went for food then, as it does now. I don't know how we lived through three years and three babies, but we did. I'll tell you something, after the last baby I destroyed

4

5

6

7

8

my marriage. It had been a good one, but could you keep on bringing children in this dirt? Did you ever think how much it costs for any kind of birth control? I knew my husband was leaving the day he left, but there were no goodbye between us. I hope he has been able to climb out of this mess somewhere. He never could hope with us to drag him down.

That's when I asked for help. When I got it, you know how much it was? It was, and is, seventy-eight dollars a month for the four of us; that is all I ever can get. Now you know why there is no soap, no needles and thread, no hot water, no aspirin, no worm medicine, no hand cream, no shampoo. None of these things forever and ever and ever. So that you can see clearly, I pay twenty dollars a month rent, and most of the rest goes for food. For grits and cornmeal, and rice and milk and beans. I try my best to use only the minimum electricity. If I use more, there is that much less for food. 9

Poverty is looking into a black future. Your children won't play with my boys. They will turn to other boys who steal to get what they want. I can already see them behind the bars of their prison instead of behind the bars of my poverty. Or they will turn to the freedom of alcohol or drugs, and find themselves enslaved. And my daughter? At best, there is for her a life like mine. 10

But you say to me, there are schools. Yes, there are schools. My children have no extra books, no magazines, no extra pencils, or crayons, or paper and most important of all, they do not have health. They have worms, they have infections, they have pink-eye all summer. They do not sleep well on the floor, or with me in my one bed. They do not suffer from hunger, my seventy-eight dollars keeps us alive, but they do suffer from malnutrition. Oh yes, I do remember what I was taught about health in school. It doesn't do much good. 11

In some places there is a surplus commodities program. Not here. The country said it cost too much. There is a school lunch program. But I have two children who will already be damaged by the time they get to school. 12

But, you say to me, there are health clinics. Yes, there are health clinics and they are in the towns. I live out here eight miles from town. I can walk that far (even if it is sixteen miles both ways), but can my little children? My neighbor will take me when he goes; but he expects to get paid, one way or another. I bet you know my neighbor. He is that large man who spends his time at the gas station, the barbershop, and the corner store complaining about the government spending money on the immoral mothers of illegitimate children. 13

Poverty is an acid that drips on pride until all pride is worn away. Poverty is a chisel that chips on honor until honor is worn away. Some of you say that you would do something in my situation, and maybe you would, for the first week or the first month, but for year after year after year? 14

Even the poor can dream. A dream of a time when there is money. Money for the right kinds of food, for worm medicine, for iron pills, for toothbrushes, for hand cream, for a hammer and nails and a bit of screening, for a shovel, for a bit of paint, for some sheeting, for needles and thread. Money to pay in money for a trip to town. And, oh, money for hot water and money for soap. A dream of when asking for help does not eat away the last bit of pride. When the office you visit is as nice as the offices of other governmental agencies, when there are enough workers to help you quickly, when workers do not quit in defeat and despair. When you have to tell your story to only one person, and that person can send you for other help and you don't have to prove your poverty over and over and over again. 15

I have come out of my despair to tell you this. Remember I did not come from another place or another time. Others like me are all around you. Look at us with an angry heart, anger that will help. 16

Source: From "What is Poverty?" by Jo Goodwin-Parker in *America's Other Children: Public Schools Outside Suburbia,* by George Henderson. Copyright © 1971 by University of Oklahoma Press, Norman. Reprinted by permission of the publisher. All rights reserved.

**Vocabulary**  Before, during, and after reading the selection, annotate the text and write in your journal. Create a list of vocabulary words, along with their definitions, and give examples of their use from the selection you just read.

## After Reading Discussion Questions:  Meaning, Structure, and Expression

1. **Main Idea:** Work as a group to write a summary that answers the following questions: What purpose did Jo Goodwin-Parker have for writing this essay? Who is her intended audience? What is the main idea of the essay?
2. **Relevant Details:** Parker offers her own life experiences to define poverty. Does she provide enough details to make her point convincingly? Would the use of facts or expert opinions strengthen her point? Why or why not?
3. **Logical Order:** Parker defines poverty with a series of seven statements that begin with "Poverty is." Summarize her definition of poverty using these seven statements. Do you agree with the order in which she presents these statements? Why or why not?
4. **Effective Expression:** Based on Parker's choice of words, how would you describe the tone of this essay? Is it angry, embarrassed, disappointed, reflective, sad, or optimistic, or does it communicate some other attitude about poverty? Identify three expressions that illustrate the tone of the piece. Explain the reasons for your selections.

## Thinking Prompts to Move from Reading to Writing

1. Often, people do not understand what they have not experienced. Parker defines poverty for people who have never experienced it. In the last sentence in the first paragraph, she commands her readers to step into her shoes so they can learn from her experiences. Assume the view of one who understands an issue such as depression, addiction, or prejudice based on experience. Write an essay that defines the issue so that someone who has not experienced it can better understand the problem.
2. In her essay, Parker defines the problem of poverty, but she does not offer a solution, other than to say "look at us with an angry heart, anger that will help." What kind of anger will help this situation? Respond to Parker by writing an essay that defines this kind of anger. Consider using a phrase like "Anger that will help is" to reply to specific points she raises in her essay.

# Cause–Effect

## Why We Crave Horror Movies

STEPHEN KING

Stephen King, born in Portland, Maine in 1947, has been writing full-time since the 1973 publication of his novel *Carrie*. He has since published over 40 books and has become one of the world's most successful writers.

**Before Reading**  Write a journal entry about your reaction to horror movies. Do you enjoy horror movies? Why or why not? Why do you think horror movies are so popular? Do graphically violent horror movies have a harmful effect on society? Explain your reasons.

1   I think that we're all mentally ill: those of us outside the asylums only hide it a little better—and maybe not all that much better, after all. We've all known people who talk to themselves, people who sometimes squinch their faces into horrible grimaces when they believe no one is watching, people who have some hysterical fear—of snakes, the dark, the tight place, the long drop . . . and, of course, those final worms and grubs that are waiting so patiently underground.

2   When we pay our four or five bucks and seat ourselves at tenth-row center in a theater showing a horror movie, we are daring the nightmare.

3   Why? Some of the reasons are simple and obvious. To show that we can, that we are not afraid, that we can ride this roller coaster. Which is not to say that a really good horror movie may not surprise a scream out of us at some point, the way we may scream when the roller coaster twists through a complete 360 or plows through a lake at the bottom of the drop. And horror movies, like roller coasters, have always been the special province of the young; by the time one turns 40 or 50, one's appetite for double twists or 360-degree loops may be considerably depleted.

4   We also go to re-establish our feelings of essential normality; the horror movie is innately conservative, even reactionary. Freda Jackson as the horrible melting woman in *Die, Monster, Die!* confirms for us that no matter how far we may be removed from the beauty of a Robert Redford or a Diana Ross, we are still light-years from true ugliness.

5   And we go to have fun.

6   Ah, but this is where the ground starts to slope away, isn't it? Because this is a very peculiar sort of fun indeed. The fun comes from seeing others menaced—sometimes killed. One critic has suggested that if pro football has become the voyeur's version of combat, then the horror film has become the modern version of the public lynching.

7   It is true that the mythic, "fairytale" horror film intends to take away the shades of gray. . . . It urges us to put away our more civilized and adult penchant for analysis and to become children again, seeing things in pure blacks and whites. It may be that horror movies provide psychic relief on this level because this invitation to lapse into simplicity, irrationality and even outright madness is extended so rarely. We are told we may allow our emotions a free rein . . . or no rein at all.

8   If we are all insane, then sanity becomes a matter of degree. If your insanity leads you to carve up women like Jack the Ripper or the Cleveland Torso

Murderer, we clap you away in the funny farm (but neither of those two amateur-night surgeons was ever caught, heh-heh-heh); if, on the other hand your insanity leads you only to talk to yourself when you're under stress or to pick your nose on the morning bus, then you are left alone to go about your business . . . though it is doubtful that you will ever be invited to the best parties.

The potential lyncher is in almost all of us (excluding saints, past and present; but then, most saints have been crazy in their own ways), and every now and then, he has to be let loose to scream and roll around in the grass. Our emotions and our fears form their own body, and we recognize that it demands its own exercise to maintain proper muscle tone. Certain of these emotional muscles are accepted—even exalted—in civilized society; they are, of course, the emotions that tend to maintain the status quo of civilization itself. Love, friendship, loyalty, kindness—these are all the emotions that we applaud, emotions that have been immortalized in the couplets of Hallmark cards. . . .    9

When we exhibit these emotions, society showers us with positive reinforcement; we learn this even before we get out of diapers. When, as children, we hug our rotten little puke of a sister and give her a kiss, all the aunts and uncles smile and twit and cry, "Isn't he the sweetest little thing?" Such coveted treats as chocolate-covered graham crackers often follow. But if we deliberately slam the rotten little puke of a sister's fingers in the door, sanctions follow—angry remonstrance from parents, aunts and uncles; instead of a chocolate-covered graham cracker, a spanking.    10

But anticivilization emotions don't go away, and they demand periodic exercise. We have such "sick" jokes as, "What's the difference between a truckload of bowling balls and a truckload of dead babies?" (You can't unload a truckload of bowling balls with a pitchfork . . . a joke, by the way, that I heard originally from a ten-year-old.) Such a joke may surprise a laugh or a grin out of us even as we recoil, a possibility that confirms the thesis: If we share a brotherhood of man, then we also share an insanity of man. None of which is intended as a defense of either the sick joke or insanity but merely as an explanation of why the best horror films, like the best fairy tales, manage to be reactionary, anarchistic, and revolutionary all at the same time.    11

The mythic horror movie, like the sick joke, has a dirty job to do. It deliberately appeals to all that is worst in us. It is morbidity unchained, our most base instincts let free, our nastiest fantasies realized . . . and it all happens, fittingly enough, in the dark. For those reasons, good liberals often shy away from horror films. For myself, I like to see the most aggressive of them—*Dawn of the Dead,* for instance—as lifting a trap door in the civilized forebrain and throwing a basket of raw meat to the hungry alligators swimming around in that subterranean river beneath.    12

Why bother? Because it keeps them from getting out, man. It keeps them down there and me up here. It was Lennon and McCartney who said that all you need is love, and I would agree with that.    13

As long as you keep the gators fed.    14

**Vocabulary** Before, during, and after reading the selection, annotate the text and write in your journal. Create a list of vocabulary words, along with their definitions, and give examples of their use from the selection you just read.

## After Reading Discussion Questions: Meaning, Structure, and Expression

1. **Main Idea:** Work as a group to write a summary that answers the following questions: What purpose did Stephen King have for writing this essay? Who is his intended audience? What is the essay's main idea?

2. **Relevant Details:** In paragraphs 10 and 11, King uses children as examples to support his point. Why do you think he uses these examples? Do you think these examples are typical of most children? Do you agree that these examples effectively support his point? Why or why not?

3. **Logical Order:** King declares his thesis in paragraph 11. Locate his thesis statement. Why do you think King waited until this late in the essay to state his thesis? Reread his introduction. What is his opening point? Why do you think he opened his essay with this idea? How would the impact of the essay change if King had stated his thesis in the opening paragraph?

4. **Effective Expression:** To make his point, King appeals to our senses and prior experiences with references to roller coasters, Jack the Ripper, lynching, and alligators. Discuss how each of these images supports his point.

## Thinking Prompts to Move from Reading to Writing

1. King offers reasons that explain the positive effects of horror movies. However, many disagree with this view and see the violence in horror movies as a negative factor in our society. Write an essay that explains the negative impact of horror movies.

2. King claims that we are "all mentally ill" and that horror movies appeal to the "worst in us." However, many believe that humans are basically good. The famous American essayist Emerson once encouraged us "to look into yourselves and do good because you are good." Write an essay that illustrates the goodness and positive impact of human nature. Consider, for example, the reasons and effects of Habitat for Humanity or other charities or volunteer organizations.

# Persuasion

## Statement of Senator Joe Lieberman on Rating the Ratings System

### JOE LIEBERMAN

Born on February 24, 1942 in Stamford, Connecticut, Joe Lieberman is now serving his fourth term representing Connecticut in the United States Senate. According to his official website, Joe Lieberman is "dedicated to strengthening America's families and renewing our common values by working with parents to improve the culture in which they raise their children." This essay was submitted to the United States Committee on Government Affairs in 2001.

**Before Reading** Write a journal entry about graphic material and the government's role in censorship. Are some movies, music, and video games are too sexually or violently explicit? Why is graphic material so popular? Do you pay attention to the various media rating systems? Are the current rating systems effective? Should government be more involved in controlling graphic material? Explain your thinking.

Good morning. We are here today to revisit an issue that parents repeatedly raise with just about anyone who will listen—the challenge they face in raising healthy children in today's 500-channel, multiplexed, videogamed, discmanned universe. 1

That is a reflection of the quantity of time children spend consuming and using media—an average of 6-1/2 hours a day, according to the Annenberg Public Policy Center. But it is even more a reflection of the quality of the messages about sex and violence kids are being exposed to by the entertainment media—messages which too often reject rather than reflect the basic values parents are trying to instill—and the growing sense that the totality of these messages is having a harmful influence on the attitudes and behaviors of our children, and therefore on the safety and moral condition of our country. 2

There are limits to what we in government can do to respond to these concerns—because of our devotion to the First Amendment, and because governments don't raise children, parents do. At the same time, though, there are some things that we can do—hopefully with the movie, music, video game, and television industries—to empower parents and make the hard job of raising healthy children a little easier. 3

One way to empower is to inform. Over the years, the major entertainment media have developed rating and labeling systems, largely at the urging of public advocates, to offer parents and consumers information about the content of their products and help parents exercise more informed control over their children's media diets. And over that time, these ratings, particularly those of the movie industry, have become cultural icons. 4

But as the content and marketing practices of the entertainment media have become worse, we have been hearing more and more concerns about how these ratings systems work. There have been specific criticisms about their reliability, visibility, and understandability. And there have been general complaints that 5 the ratings do not provide parents with enough information about content—about the levels of sex, violence, and vulgarity in each product—to make the right choice for their children. Last year, for example, a Gallup survey found that 74 percent of parents said the movie, music and television ratings were inadequate on that count.

Those concerns culminated in a letter sent to policymakers last month by a distinguished coalition of researchers, medical groups, and child development experts, which recommended a complete overhaul of media ratings. That letter, initiated by the National Institute on Media and the Family, argued that the different ratings are often applied inconsistently, that many parents find the multiplicity of rating icons confusing, and, as a result, that the ratings are not adequately serving their purpose—helping parents or protecting kids. To fix this problem, the signers of the letter called for replacing the existing formats with a new uniform rating system, monitored by an independent oversight committee and grounded in sound research.

6

I thought this was an important statement with a provocative proposal that deserved more public discussion. I believe that is one critical way in which we in government can help parents, to provide a platform, facilitate a dialogue, and ideally build common ground. That is the aim of our hearing today—to flesh out the concerns raised in the NIMF's letter and explore the merits of their recommendations, to hear the response of industry keepers of these rating systems, and see if there is any agreement on ways to improve the ratings to better inform parents.

7

I have expressed interest in the idea of uniform ratings before—as have others in Congress, including Senators McCain and Clinton, and in the entertainment industry, notably Disney President Robert Iger—and I remain interested in it. Many parents appear interested as well—a survey by the Kaiser Family Foundation being released today found that 40 percent of parents believe that a uniform rating system would be more useful than the current approach, and only 17 percent think it would be less useful. So today we will hear the arguments in favor of switching to a single system, as well as the industry's objections to it.

8

I hope the entertainment industry witnesses come with an equally open mind, particularly on the question of providing more and better information. For some time now many of us have voiced dissatisfaction with the recording industry's one size-fits-all parental advisory program, which provides a solitary stickered warning to parents of "explicit content." We have urged the major record companies to expand and clarify their system and tell parents what kinds of explicit content are in the lyrics. Those same criticisms and calls for change were repeated vociferously at a hearing before the House Telecommunications Subcommittee last week, as I understand it, and Ms. Rosen ruled out adding any content descriptions to the recording industry's labeling system. I hope in our discussion today that Ms. Rosen will reconsider that position.

9

I also hope that Mr. Valenti will alter the outrageous suggestion he makes in his response to the aforementioned letter from the NIMF that there is serious doubt about whether violence in the media poses a risk of harm to our children.

10

If we are looking for an industry model, I would point to the video game rating system, which is administered by the independent Electronic Software Ratings Board (ESRB). The ESRB system, which was a response to Congressional hearings, pairs age-based icons with detailed content descriptors in a clear, concise, and informative format. I believe it is the best media rating system in existence.

11

Ultimately any potential reforms in the ratings will be meaningless if parents don't use them. We need to remind parents of their responsibilities as we renew our call for more and better information in the ratings. 12

One last word about the First Amendment, which is one thing all of us seem to support. We are not talking about any legislation or government regulation today. But I want to warn the industry again that the best way to invite censorship is to disengage from this discussion and tune out the larger concerns of millions of American parents about media influence on our kids and our country. Indeed, the most striking finding of the Kaiser survey to me was that 48 percent of parents would support government regulations to limit the amount of violent and sexual content in early evening TV shows. That is an outcry that begins to express just how frustrated and angry America's parents are about the state of our culture and its impact on our children. 13

## Vocabulary
Before, during, and after reading the selection, annotate the text and write in your journal. Create a list of vocabulary words, along with their definitions, and give examples of their use from the selection you just read.

## After Reading Discussion Questions:
Meaning, Structure, and Expression

1. **Main Idea:** Work as a group to write a summary that answers the following questions: What purpose did Joe Lieberman have for writing this essay? Who is his intended audience? What is the essay's main idea?
2. **Relevant Details:** Lieberman relies on several outside sources for details to support his point, such as the Annenberg Public Policy Center, a Gallup survey, the National Institute on Media and the Family, a Kaiser Family Foundation survey, and the Electronic Software Ratings Board. Identify the details provided by each of these sources. Is the information from each source objective or biased? Are these details convincing enough to persuade his audience to agree with him? Why or why not?
3. **Logical Order:** Lieberman addresses opposing views in paragraphs 3, 10, and 13. What are these opposing views? Why do you think he spaced them in separate parts of his essay instead of addressing them all in one paragraph? Would his point be more effective if he had discussed those points in one paragraph? Why or why not?
4. **Effective Expression:** Lieberman uses the first person pronoun "I" around a dozen times in this essay. Find these first person statements. Why does he use the first person pronoun? Is his use of first person effective in his effort to convince the audience to agree with him? Why or why not?

## Thinking Prompts to Move from Reading to Writing

1. Locate a copy of a rating system such as the ones provided by the Motion Picture Association of America (mpaa.org) or the Electronic Software Ratings Board (www.esrb.org). Write an essay that supports or opposes a particular rating system. Use examples from the media and address opposing views to convince your reader to agree with you.
2. Write a letter about the ratings system to an elected representative from your area. Ask your representative or senator to support or oppose a government-sponsored rating system for the entertainment industry. To find your elected representative, go to the government website *Thomas: Legislative Information on the Internet* at thomas.loc.gov.

# The Hip-Hop Summit Action Network Statement for the Senate Committee on Governmental Affairs Hearing on Entertainment Ratings, July 25, 2001

## RUSSELL SIMMONS

Born in 1957 and raised in Hollis, Queens, New York City, Russell Simmons, rap record producer and artist manager, is credited with the explosive entry of rap music onto the national music scene in the late 1980s. He is the co-owner and founder of the rap label Def Jam Records and head of Rush Artist Management, the largest black-owned music business in the United States. This essay was submitted as testimony to the United States Committee on Government Affairs in 2001.

**Before Reading**  Write a journal entry about the values and role models provided by the music industry. For example, does Hip Hop provide positive or negative content and role models for youth? Explain your opinion. Should graphic material be banned or censored? Why or why not?

My name is Russell Simmons and I am submitting this statement on behalf of the Hip Hop Summit Action Network and its Executive Director, Minister Benjamin Muhammad. I am Chairman of the Hip Hop Summit Action Network and I have worked in the music and entertainment industry for more than twenty-five years. Minister Benjamin is the former Executive Director and CEO of the NAACP and has over thirty-five years of experience in civil and human rights.

The Hip Hop Summit Action Network is the broadest national coalition of Hip Hop artists, entertainment industry executives, civil rights and community leaders. Established this year, the mission of the Hip Hop Summit Action Network is to support Hip Hop and freedom, justice, equality and empowerment for all based on the principles of freedom of speech, music and art creativity, and the universality of humanity.

I regret that despite our request to the Committee there is neither space nor time for me to testify today. Not simply because I, both individually and on behalf of the Hip Hop generation have some important things to say about these issues, but also because many of us feel that these hearings are really about us, and it would be better in our view to hear from us and speak to us directly before you pass judgment and deny our fundamental rights.

But let me start with something positive. The Hip Hop community has decided to take a leadership position toward the evolution of our artistic destiny and responsibility. We convened an historic summit last month in New York and we are planning others In Los Angeles and Miami in August to explore questions related to violence in our own communities, racial profiling, police brutality, representation of women, and the profanity of poverty . . . and how we can work from within our industry to expand and elevate the artistic presentation of our culture and experience.

Although we know that the harsh underlying social realities that some of our music exposes have not changed much in our communities, we are committed to speaking the truth. We believe that we must continue to tell the truth about the street if that is what we know and we must continue to tell the truth about God if that is who we have found. Part of telling the truth is making sure that you know, and talk more about what you know than to speak or do music to appease those who are in power. Hip Hop represents truth telling, speaking the truth to ourselves and speaking the truth to power out of the context and condition of our community.

The Congress of the United States should not censor free speech nor artistic expression. It is unconstitutional for government intrusion or dictation concerning "labeling of music" or "rating of music" that has the effect of denying free speech. 6

What is offensive is any attempt by the government to deny the expression of words and lyrics that emerge out of a culture that has become the soul of America. In fact Hip Hop has now grown to become a global cultural and artistic phenomena. 7

Congress should not attempt to legislate preferences in music, art and culture. 8

My final point is that this is often largely about race. And it makes some of us very concerned that few will publicly admit that this effort to censure Hip Hop has deep seated racial overtones. Hip Hop emerged out of the African American experience. Eminem is a successful white Hip Hop artist who, power to him, has excelled and profited from the genre of black music. He stands on the shoulders of other originators of Hip Hop. The Federal Trade Commission's report on explicit content disproportionately focused on black Hip Hop artists. This report is flawed scientifically as well as morally and culturally and should not, therefore, be used as a basis for constructing a system of "ratings" in regard to music and other forms of entertainment. 9

Simply put, we conclude by appealing to the Senate Committee on Government Affairs to refrain from censoring, labeling, or rating our music and culture in the absence of understanding and appreciation of our artistic work which represents the genius of our culture and talent of our youth, in fact all youth of today . . . black, white, Latino, Asian and all others. 10

Thank you.

**Vocabulary**  Before, during, and after reading the selection, annotate the text and write in your journal. Create a list of vocabulary words, along with their definitions, and give examples of their use from the selection you just read.

## After Reading Discussion Questions: Meaning, Structure, and Expression

1. **Main Idea:** Work as a group to write a summary that answers the following questions: What purpose did Russell Simmons have for writing this essay? Who is his intended audience? What is the essay's main idea?
2. **Relevant Details:** Who does Simmons rely on as an expert opinion? What factual details does he provide to support his point? In paragraph 9, Simmons claims the Federal Trade Commission's report on explicit content is "flawed scientifically as well as morally and culturally and should not, therefore, be used." What evidence does he offer to support this claim? Overall, does Simmons offer enough details to convince his audience to agree with him? Why or why not?
3. **Logical Order:** Simmons says, "My final point is that this is often largely about race." What does he mean by this statement? Why did he wait to introduce race as his final point? Would his overall message be stronger if he addressed the issue of race earlier in his essay? Why or why not?

4. **Effective Expression:** Simmons uses a number of emotionally laden expressions such as "racial profiling," "police brutality," and "genius." Identify other instances of his use of emotional language. What effect does Simmons hope to have on his audience? Explain your reasons. Do you think he achieved the effect he wanted? Why or why not?

## Thinking Prompts to Move from Reading to Writing

1. Create a ratings system that gives parents enough information about the content of a movie, song, video game, or television show. Write an essay that convinces Russell Simmons and the entertainment industry to accept your ratings system.

2. Simmons describes Hip Hop as exposing and "speaking the truth" about "harsh underlying social realities." He goes on to say that the music "must continue to tell the truth about the street." Do you agree or disagree with this view? What are the "harsh realities" and the "truth of the street" to which he refers? Does the music encourage change or reinforce these "truths"? Write a letter to Simmons in which you offer support for or opposition to his view. Use examples from his essay and Hip Hop music to support your stand.

# Text Credits

Angelou, Maya, "New Directions," from *Wouldn't Take Nothing for My Journey Now* by Maya Angelou, copyright © 1993 by Maya Angelou. Used by permission of Random House, Inc.

Carson, Rachel. "A Fable for Tomorrow" from SILENT SPRING by Rachel Carson. Copyright © 1962 by Rachel L. Carson, renewed 1990 by Roger Christie. Reprinted by permission of Houghton Mifflin Company and the Frances Collin Literary Agency. All rights reserved.

Cofer, Judith Ortiz "Don't Call me a Hot Tamale" or "The Myth of the Latin Woman: I Just Met a Girl Named Maria," from *The Latin Deli: Prose and Poetry*. Copyright © 2003.

Crosby, Olivia. "Associate Degree: Two Years to a Career or a Jump Start to a Bachelor's Degree." Washington, D.C.: U.S. Department of Labor.

De Vito, Joseph A. *The Interpersonal Communication Book,* 10th ed. Published by Allyn and Bacon, Boston, MA. Copyright © 2004 by Pearson Education. Adapted by permission of the publisher.

De Vito, Joseph A. *Messages: Building Interpersonal Communication Skills,* 4th ed. Boston: Allyn and Bacon, 1999.

Goodwin-Parker, Jo. "What is Poverty?" in *America's Other Children: Public Schools Outside Suburbia*, by George Henderson. Copyright © 1971 by University of Oklahoma Press, Norman. Reprinted by permission of the publisher. All rights reserved.

Haines, John. Excerpt from "Snow," copyright © 1989 by John Haines. Reprinted from *The Owl in the Mask of the Dreamer* with the permission of Graywolf Press, St. Paul, Minnesota.

Hasselstrom, Linda M. "Why One Peaceful Woman Carries a Pistol," in Land Circle, Fulcrum, Inc., 1991. Used by permission.

"Hawaii's Fun-Fueled Activity Book: Clean Fuels." Honolulu Clean Cities Website. www.hawaii.gov/dbedt/ert/cc/index.html

Jaffe, Michael L. *Understanding Parenting,* 2nd ed., p. 241 Figure "Self-Esteem and Self Confidence," © 1997 Pearson Education, Inc. Reproduced by permission of Pearson Education, Inc. All rights reserved.

Keillor, Garrison. "How to Write a Personal Letter," from *We Are Still Married*. Copyright 1987 by International Paper Company. Reprinted by permission of Garrison Keillor.

King, Martin Luther Jr. "Ways of Meeting Oppression," from *Stride Towards Freedom*. Copyright © 1963 Dr. Martin Luther King Jr.; copyright renewed by Coretta Scott King. Reprinted by arrangement with the Heirs to the Estate of Martin Luther King Jr., c/o Writers House as agent for the proprietor, New York, NY.

King, Stephen. "Why We Crave Horror Movies." Reprinted with permission. © Stephen King. All rights reserved. Originally appeared in *Playboy* (1982).

Lieberman, Joe. "Statement on Rating the Ratings System."

O'Connor, Karen, Sabato, Larry J., and Haag, Keith. *American Government: Continuity and Change, 2004*. Texas Edition. Pearson 2004. Used by permission of Longman Publishers.

O'Hanlon, Larry. "Honey Bee Die-off Alarms Beekeepers," *Discovery News*, February 5, 2007.

Simmons, Russell. "The Hip-Hop Summit Action Network Statement for the Senate Committee on Governmental Affairs Hearing on Entertainment Ratings," July 25, 2001.

Swetlow, Karen. "Children at Clandestine Methamphetamine Labs: Helping Meth's Youngest Victims." *OVC Bulletin*, U.S. Department of Justice, June 2003.

United States Department of Agriculture. "Balance the Food You Eat with Physical Activity—Maintain or Improve Your Weight." *Nutrition and Your Health: Dietary Guidelines for Americans*, December 1995.

United States Department of Health and Human Services. "Stroke," Women's Health.gov. The National Women's Health Information Center, March 26, 2006.

United States Equal Employment Opportunity Commission. "Facts about Sexual Harassment," March 13, 2006.

United States Park Service. "Maya Lin's Design Submission to the Vietnam Memorial Competition."

# Photo Credits

**Contents:** iii (top) David Buffington/Corbis; iii (bottom) ©David Pollack/Corbis; iv (top) Hans Neleman/ Corbis; iv (bottom) Wesley Hitt/ Alamy; v (top) © Bojan Brecelj/Corbis.

**Chapter 1:** 2 David Buffington/Corbis; 3 (top) Helene Rogers/Alamy; 3 (top center) ©fotofresh/Alamy; 3 (bottom center) ©Myrleen Ferguson Cate/PhotoEdit, Inc; 3 (bottom) ©Gary Conner/PhotoEdit, Inc; 5 (all) Dorling Kindersley Media Library; 7 (all) Dorling Kindersley Media Library;

**Chapter 2:** 14 RF Comstock/Corbis; 15 (top left) Chuck Savage/Corbis; 15 (top right) Image Source/Getty Images RF; 15 (bottom left) AP/Wide World Photos; 15 (bottom right) Royalty-Free/Corbis; 16 Michigan Board of Education 1994; 18 (bottom left) Merry Alpern/Corbis; 18 (bottom right) Royalty-free/Corbis; 18 (top left) Myrleen Ferguson/PhotoEdit, Inc; 18 (top right) Jessica Rinaldi/Reuters/Corbis; 20 (left)Aristide Economopoulos/Star Ledger/Corbis; 20 (right) Royalty-Free/Corbis; 21 (left) Royalty-Free/Corbis; 21 (right) Bettmann/Corbis; 22 (left) Aristide Economopoulos/Star Ledger/Corbis; 22 (center left) Royalty-Free/Corbis; 22 (center right) Royalty-Free/Corbis; 22 (right) Bettmann/Corbis; 24 Michigan State Board of Education 1994; 26 ©2004 David Farley; 28 Courtesy TRIMSPA; 30 Buddy Mays/Corbis; 32 Jose Luis Pelaez, Inc./Corbis; 38 Kevin Cooley/Stone/Getty Images.

**Chapter 3:** 50 ©Trains and Planes/Alamy; 52 (top) ©Bob Krist/Corbis; 52 (center) RF ©Image Source/Corbis; 52 (bottom left) ©Steve Chenn/Corbis; 52 (bottom right) ©Jerome Sessini/Corbis; 54 (top) ©David Muench/Corbis; 54 (bottom) ©Gene Blevins/LA Daily News/Corbis; 57 (left) ©Jeff Greenberg/PhotoEdit, Inc.; 57 (center) ©Michael Newman/PhotoEdit, Inc.; 57 (right) ©Bill Varie/Corbis; 63 ©David Wells/Corbis; 64 ©John Miller/Robert Harding World Imagery/Corbis.

**Chapter 4:** 68 ©David Pollack/Corbis; 69 Corbis/Bettmann; 70 (all) Corbis/Bettmann 71 (both) Corbis/Bettmann; 73 Corbis/Bettmann; 78 Tom & Dee Ann McCarthy/Corbis 80 Joseph Sohm/Corbis

**Chapter 5:** 88 (all) Douglas Kirkland/Corbis; 89 (top) Frank Micelotta/Getty Images; 89 (center) Dreamworks/David James/The Kobal Collection; 89 (bottom) Mike Blake/Corbis; 98 Dorling Kindersley Media Library.

**Chapter 6:** 106 © Rebecca Emery/Corbis; 107 (all) Dorling Kindersley Media Library; 109 (all) Dorling Kindersley Media Library; 112 Richard Hutchings/PhotoEdit, Inc.; 114 (far left) David Young-Wolff/PhotoEdit, Inc.; 114 (center left) Michael Newman/PhotoEdit, Inc.; 114 (center) Elizabeth Lippman/Corbis Sygma; 114 (center right) Jeff Greenberg/Alamy; 114 (far right) Tom Grill/Corbis; 115 (top) Gregor Schuster/zefa/Corbis; 115 (bottom) Ray Coleman/Photo Researchers, Inc; 116 (top) Larry Lilac/Alamy RF; 116 (bottom) Superstock.

**Chapter 7:** 124 Richard Drury/The Image Bank/Getty Images; 125 (left) Henry Diltz/Corbis; 125 (center) Eric Gaillard/Reuters/Corbis; 125 (right) Frank Trapper/Corbis; 127 (top) Henry Diltz/Corbis; 127 (center) Eric Gaillard/Reuters/Corbis; 127 (bottom) Frank Trapper/Corbis; 132 (left) David Young-Wolff/PhotoEdit, Inc.; 132 (center) George Shelley/Corbis; 132 (right) Blend Images/Alamy; 135 Radius Images/Alamy; 136 (top) © Envision/Corbis; 136 (top center) Dynamic Graphics Group/Creatas/Alamy; 136 (bottom center) Edward Kinsman/Photo Researchers, Inc.; 136 (bottom) Jose Luis Pelaez, Inc./Corbis.

**Chapter 8:** 144 Hans Neleman/Corbis; 145 (left) John Gress/Reuters/Corbis; 145 (center) Carlos Barria/Reuters/Corbis; 145 (right) Zack Seckler/Corbis; 148 (top) John Gress/Reuters/Corbis; 148 (center) Carlos Barria/Reuters/Corbis; 148 (bottom) Zack Seckler/Corbis; 152 Mauro Fermariello/Photo Researchers, Inc.; 154 ©David Turnley/Corbis.

**Chapter 9:** 166 (left) AP/Wide World; 166 (right) RF/Mick Roessler/Corbis; 167 (top left) NASA/Corbis; 167 (top right) NOAA/Corbis; 167 (center left) Robert Galbraith/Reuters/ Corbis; 167 (center right) Smiley N. Pool/Dallas Morning News/Corbis; 167 (bottom left) AP/Wide World Photos; 167 (bottom right) Smiley N. Pool/Dallas Morning News/Corbis; 169 (top to bottom)NASA/Corbis, NOAA/Corbis, Robert Galbraith/Reuters/Corbis, Smiley N. Pool/Dallas Morning News/Corbis, Smiley N. Pool/Dallas Morning News/Corbis, AP/Wide World Photos; 173 (left) ©Disney Enterprises; 173 (right) Private Collection/Scala/ Art Resource, NY ©2007 Estate of Marc Chagall/Artists Rights Society (ARS), NY; 175 ©Tony Freeman/PhotoEdit, Inc.; 176 (top) ©Robert W; Ginn/PhotoEdit, Inc.; 176 (bottom) ©Richard M; Abarno/Corbis.

**Chapter 10:** 184 Chloe Johnson/Alamy; 185 (left) Mike Powell/Corbis; 185 (top right) Kapoor Baldev/Sygma/Corbis; 185 (right center) Reuters/Corbis; 185 (bottom right) Jehad Nga/Corbis; 187 (top) Mike Powell/Corbis; 187 (center top) Kapoor Baldev/Corbis Sygma;187 (bottom center) Reuters/Corbis; 187 (bottom) Jehad Nga/Corbis; 193 (left) Chloe Johnson/Alamy; 193 (center) Art Kowalsky/Alamy; 193 (right) ©Thunderdog Studios, Inc;/Thunderdog Collective/Corbis; 195 Gene Blevins/ La Daly News/Corbis; 202 Dorling Kindersley Media Library.

**Chapter 11:** 204 George Diebold/Corbis; 205 (top left) Joseph Sohm/ChromoSohm Inc;/Corbis; 205 (all other photos) Courtesy Habitat for Humanity; 207 (top) Joseph Sohm/ChromoSohm Inc./Corbis; 211 (left) Patrik Giardino/Corbis; 211 (top right)©Hill Street Studios/Blend Images/Corbis RF; 211 (bottom right) RF ©LWA-Dann Tardif/Corbis; 212 Michael Newman/PhotoEdit, Inc.; 213 (top) Michael Newman/PhotoEdit, Inc.; 213 (bottom ) Tony Freeman/PhotoEdit, Inc.

# Index